AF227603

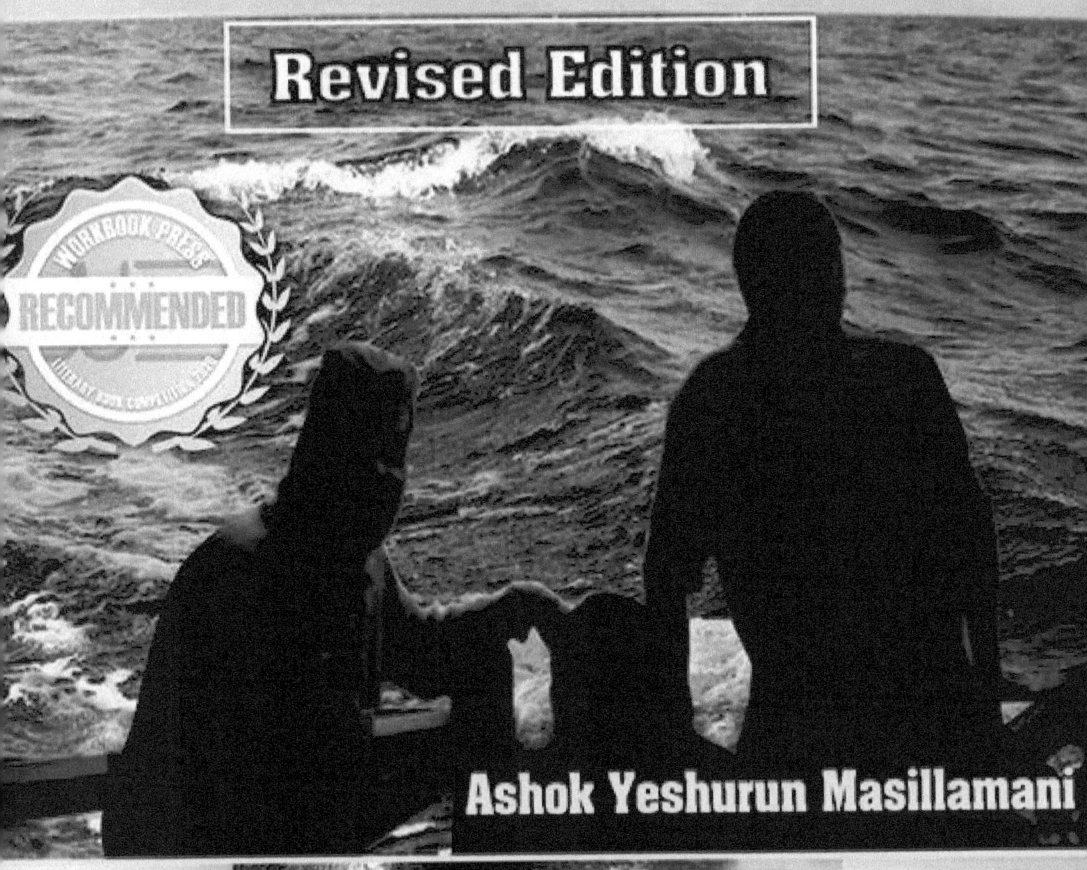

Three Men in SEA
Three Men in Southeast Asia
Wonders of Human Endeavour, Historical Mysteries and Nature's Bounty
Revised Edition
WORKBOOK PRESS
RECOMMENDED
Ashok Yeshurun Masillamani

WORKBOOK PRESS LLC
187 E Warm Springs Rd,
Suite B285, Las Vegas, NV 89119, USA

Website: https://workbookpress.com/
Hotline: 1-888-818-4856
Email: admin@workbookpress.com

Ordering Information:
Quantity sales. Special discounts are available on quantity purchases by corporations, associations, and others.
For details, contact the publisher at the address above.

ISBN-13:   978-1-958176-11-5 (Paperback Version)
                978-1-958176-12-2 (Digital Version)

REV. DATE: 09/03/2022

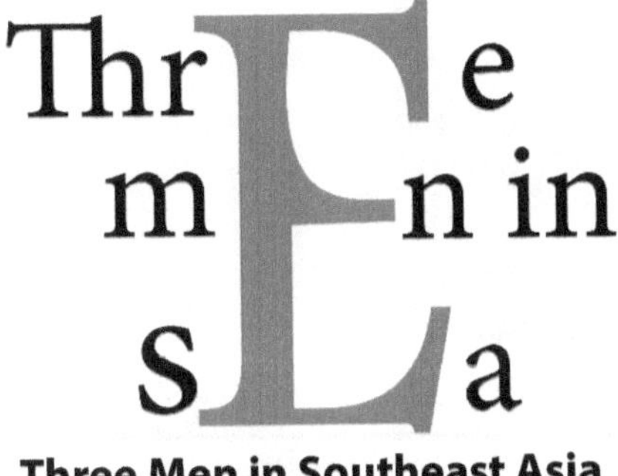

Three Men in Southeast Asia

Wonders of Human Endeavour, Historical Mysteries and Nature's Bounty

Ashok Yeshurun Masillamani

DEDICATION

To the cherished memory of my beloved father, Edward Rolandson Masilamani, a man loved and respected for his intellect, achievements, and contribution to society.

I feel privileged to have been loved, guided and inspired by his ability to make the best of life's highs and lows, which were lessons of experience. He believed in the potential of each person to activate himself, to break new ground and to set benchmarks of excellence and achievement.

Above all, I am grateful to him for instilling in me moral and spiritual values in his own solemn, unassuming way to make me a responsible human being and a citizen of the world.

I dedicate this to his memory by quoting the following words from my heart which genuinely reflects his personality:

> *Sometimes the most energetic people are*
> *the ones who love beyond all faults,*
> *cry behind closed doors and*
> *fight battles that nobody knows about.*

CONTENTS

FOREWORD

'Three Men in SeA' presents the enthralling travel tale of three friends through Thailand, Cambodia, Vietnam, Laos and Sri Lanka. The author also delves into his nativity with the Tamilian root, culture and meticulously documents some important details.

The narration reveals the scholarly bent of mind of the author and avidly leads the reader with facts and history of the vast Indian civilization from various resources. It will whet the appetite of the reader to discover the treasure-trove of the different cultures and unfold their implied meaning. Enjoy the reading and broaden your horizon.

The book is very informative and eminently readable. I have no doubt that this book with its overall contribution will induce the readers to visit many places, particularly the Southeast Asian countries.

I thank the author, Mr. Ashok Masillamani for giving me the privilege of writing these few lines and wish him every success in all his endeavors.

Fr. Bellarmine Fernando SDB
Former Salesian Provincial,
Rector and Parish Priest,
St. Mary's Co-Cathedral,
Chennai 600 001.

ACKNOWLEDGMENT

Kudos, to my pals Terry, Tony and Vela for their forbearance in putting up with an eccentric guy like me, right from our childhood days. Their tenacity to climb the ladder of success served as a 'wake-up' call to me to set my own house in order.

Got to love you, guys! God gives us our relatives, but thank God, we can choose our own friends and be accepted in all fullness with one's fault.

I thank God for the blessing of my dear mother Selvam Masilamani, and father E. R. Masilamani. The smashing fun I had with my sisters as kids are still etched in my mind. Those were carefree days of sheer joy and happiness. My father was a pillar of strength, worthy of emulation; he was also an unassuming and meritorious achiever in his own way. Thanks to you, *my dear father* for shaping my life.

I also recognize the love, the care, and the extensive support lavished on me continuously by my beloved wife, Christabel Geetha.

I am grateful to Terrence Davidson (Terry) for sowing in me the seed of his wanderlust to visit Southeast Asian countries. In fact, I feel blessed, and without you, Terry, this book would not have been written. We, Gerald and I—hail you as our Pole Star. We *THANK YOU* in capital letters from the bottom of our hearts.

The biggest thanks, I have reserved for Gerald for helping me prepare the manuscript, contributing his meticulous notes and thoughts, trying to make the paper worthy of acceptance. I appreciate his tireless efforts and long hours of reading and rereading the computed outputs. Gerald also contributed the episode of Cu Chi Tunnels in Vietnam and the narration on the Sri Lanka visit. He has given a fascinating account of his in-depth knowledge of the island.

On the personal side, I owe much to Gerald for the help I got from him during my career allied to engineering construction. It has been him, who opened my eyes to the splendor of architecture and the I value his friendship the most appreciated.

The list of my pals, especially Purvez Tehrani, who shared my joy and the carefree times, does not end, but I cannot name them all! It was Purvez who gave me the title or nickname 'Fapa' in a crazy party that I had with my old friends.

I cannot overlook the contribution of my ancestors who have helped me develop as a child of God. Not only did they nurture the fundamentals of faith in me, but they have also made me a responsible representative of the community and a dutiful citizen to the country and the world at large. I salute these men and women of yesteryears and acknowledge their influence in my life in kindling their spirit of achievement in me.

It would be apt to remember the words of Henry W. Longfellow:

> *Lives of great men, all remind us,*
> *we can make our lives sublime*
> *and departing, leave behind us,*

footprints on the sands of time.

The light of one noble life can kindle the flame in another and make the world a better place to live in— with peace on earth and goodwill towards all men. **Lead, kindly light...**

DECLARATION

Here is the compilation of thoughts from a confused and scattered mind that intended to break free of all bondage to absolute freedom, further prepared to jump into any adventure both known and unknown without any fear of consequences, except being mindful of safety mechanism built within one'own subconsciousness. The outcome may be a concoction of cocktail with no barrier or boundary and without any specific structure. Hence it cannot fit into any particular genre. This is only a superficial understanding of what I gathered or was made to understand. Though I start this on a pedestrian platform, I absolutely believe that the faith to which I am born, and embedded with, would uphold and enlighten me to a beautiful finish.

I have so many thoughts inside me that I want to say,
but I'm not sure how to tell them
so I just keep them bottled inside,
but one day they're all going to spill out
and I am scared of how that's going to turn out.

And we, buddies, the triumvirate 'Gerald, Terry and I' who share a universal love for traveling have made this journey to Southeast Asia the most joyous event of our lives. The quick wit and remarkable sense of humor shared by us kept us tension-free throughout our days of togetherness.

INTRODUCTION

This is a semi-biographical adventure, peppered with observations and facts collected by us, the 'Trio' (Terry, Gerald and me), and spiced and decorated with cherry-picked anecdotes during our recent trip to *Thailand, Cambodia, Laos, and Vietnam. These countries are best visited as a traveler, not as a tourist. Yep! There is a whale of a difference between the two!*

Though this narration is a monologue, it echoes the inner voices and experiences of all three of us. In my view, a successful writer should not only be knowledgeable about the subject matter but also, be good at a little bit of gossip, while pleasantly relating events and stories with harmony but with humor. I hope the outcome justifies this endeavor.

We owe a 'big thanks' to our tour agent, who made our travel both enjoyable and memorable by arranging comfortable staying and, above all, for assigning the 'know-all type' of charming ladies who surprised us with their fund of information and knowledge about each and every place we visited.

The 'Triumvirate'

We are not like the Great Triumvirates.

1. *Julius Caesar, Marcus Crassus and Gnaeus Magnus*
2. *Augustus, Marcus Aemilius Lepidus and Mark Antony*

3. Socrates, Plato, and Aristotle
4. The Chera, Chola and Pandya kings of the great South Indian Kingdoms

but three ordinary men on a voyage with a lust for wandering at odd ages.

Terrence Davidson comes from a reputed family whose father hailed from Kailasapuram in Tirunelveli District, South India. His father served as an officer in the Customs Department, Government of India. His mother was much ahead of her time in a cultural sense and was cosmopolitan in her outlook. Terry is now an Indian American. His present profession is allied to certain legal aspects aiding the poor and needy in New York State. He has recently created a state-of-the-art software that performs accurate sentence calculations.

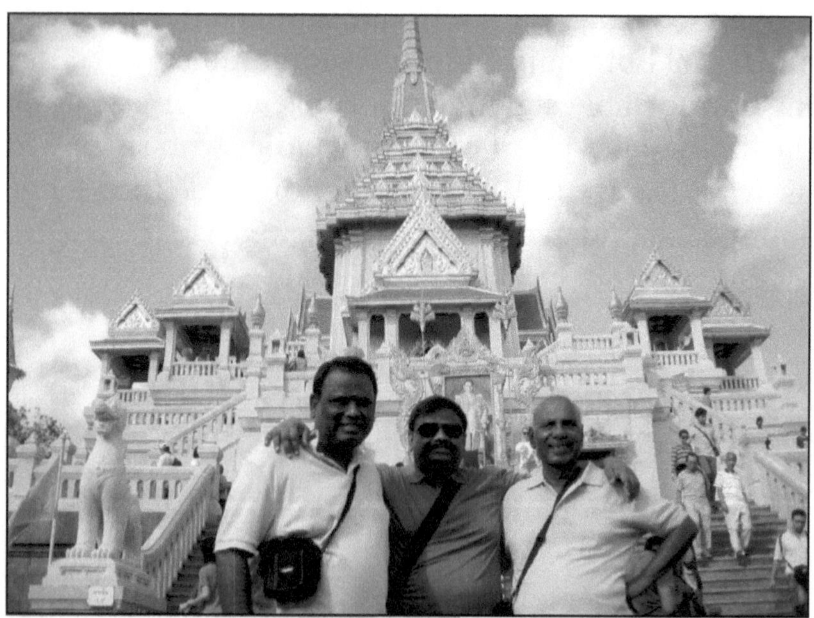

Ashok, Terry and Gerald

He is the president and CEO of Sentence Calculator Inc., a New York-based company. He is a lovable person with a large heart and compassion in its most real sense. Whenever we found ourselves like damsels in distress financially, he would rush to our rescue like the proverbial knight in shining armor! A man with a 'deeeep' pocket! My boyhood friend. It is no gainsaying that Terrence Davidson, a.k.a. Terry is a humdinger amongst a connoisseur of the beautiful things of life and us!

Gerald Ravel is a man of profound wisdom, who rose to great heights from humble beginnings. He had the unique privilege of serving as an architect at the highest level in a leading architectural firm in Chennai. Through his expertise, he was able to steer the firm to its zenith. His mentor rewarded him and helped him to establish a fortune. A great friend of Ashok for the past two decades, he, in turn, became a mentor for him.

Ashok Yeshurun Masillamani is the author and fellow-traveler with Terry and Gerald. More about him would be presented at the tail end of this book or followed by an additional one. By profession, he is a civil engineer who is in the consulting and construction industry with a rich experience for forty years. He also excelled in the field of architecture, interior design, and decoration. Masi Minerals and Exports is one more concern he started, dealing with trade of natural stones and other mineral products.

Spark That Kindled

Be it a great discovery, achievement, or adventure, it occurs when people catch sight of the tiniest spark that flashes across their minds. The outcome depends upon how they take these sparks forward and develop them into a flame for action.

Our friends Tony and Ruku were celebrating their twenty-fifth wedding anniversary in October 1999 at Rockland County, New York. The couple had arranged for a very grand party in Nyack Grande, Nyack, NY 10960. Our friends from all over the world converged to attend the function. It was celebrated in a dignified manner. Some of us remained in New York to travel around the city. Terry, my dearest friend, had rented an apartment for his friends in uptown New York City overlooking Hudson River and George Washington Bridge. At night, I used to gaze through the bay window to view the majestic George Washington Bridge, illuminated with neon lights, and there were the lights of moving automobiles and decorated steamers and pleasure cruises passing through the Hudson Bay. Terry used to enjoy being with me, and we used to walk at night on Broadway, stepping into different pubs and bars. We would go at night for Broadway shows. Most of our friends began to leave as per their schedule. I continued to be there for some more time, shunting between the rented apartment and Tony's house, occasionally visiting Washington and Maryland. Hence, Terry used to spend most of the time with me. One of the significant events was Thanksgiving Day in 1999. We also visited the Niagara Falls and many malls, Palisades, Nanuet, including Woodbury Common. We were dining at all sorts of restaurants. During that time, I visited the Twin Towers a couple of times from where I looked with wonder at the grandeur of the Big Apple, now realizing the shocking reality that I would never be able to visit those monumental and magnificent buildings since they would never be there. The consequence of that happening and the events that followed that shook the world had touched my heart. I will bring out my thoughts on this later.

It was during this time that Terry said, "Let us plan a trip, Ashok, and let it be the one we would really enjoy spending our time together." I was only too happy to consider that, and as we were discussing different places, we hit upon Southeast Asian countries, of which we do not read much in newspapers except for their estranged relationship with the USA every now and then. During that time, the Statue of Liberty was closed for renovation. I left in early December 1999.

Terry's suggestion to travel to Southeast Asia, which began as a spark, lingered in me; thus, our travel plan was initiated. It was followed up on a day in the middle of June 2011, when my dearest and long-standing friend Terrence Suresh Joshua Davidson, with whom I have had a close association for the past five decades, called me to convey the good news that he was planning an extended furlough to spend in peace to be relieved of all tensions and to recoup from the stress that he had undergone in creating a state-of-the-art software for Sentence Calculation. He expressed his desire to meet all his old friends to share his happiness with them.

Terry, as we call him, was born a free bird. He always wanted to be so. He exercised his freedom to the fullest, beaming with joy at all times. Sometimes he used to go overboard. His father was a generous, lovable, and good-hearted person; he was flamboyant in his thoughts. This broader sense of polished interactive skill got embedded in Terry and both his sisters,

Shanthi and Angela. They were very great personalities too. Shanthi was an ICS officer with a colorful career attached to military estates. Angela was more responsible, and she held a position as a great doctor of neurology. She was also a great soloist with an alto voice. She was always a straightforward, down-to-earth person with practical ideas. Due to family reasons, the elder sisters decided to settle their only brother Terry in marriage at an early age. Terry, by himself, was knowledgeable, and could always compete and perform better in adversity. This potential had him placed with a topnotch data processing company in the early years of his career. He still proved his best. Terry moved with his family to New York, where he had the privilege of completing two masters from Columbia University. Since then, he has been well placed and reaching higher goals. However, Terry could not be contained in one place in America because of his commitments in India. He was so attached to his sisters that he agonized over them—Angela and Shanthi. When they were ill and needed him by their side, who would be always there. At the fag end of their lives, he spent a lot of time showering his absolute love and care for them. As a brother, he did all that he could always do; he would call them often to share his joy and miseries!

A special note on Angela who was also very close to me as an elder sister. She narrated these words to me that still lingers in my memory: *Ashok! When you are young and youthful, West is always best. But when you are old and frail, home is always best..*

One more incident that I came across during Terry's recent visit to Chennai. We happened to meet one of Angela Davidson's seniors in the Doveton Corrie High School of Vepery, Chennai. When she was 14 years old, she had written these words in his autograph book on 8 December 1962:

The future belongs still more to the heart
than to the mind...
To love is the only thing which can occupy
and fill up eternity...
The infinite requires the inexhaustible.

To me, Terry is my dearest friend. I was close to his family. He calls me 'Fapa' endearingly. Whenever he was in a celebratory mood, he would like to meet me or invite me to parties; when disappointed or depressed, I was the first one he would call to share his grief

When Terry called me in June 2011, he expressed his desire to visit places like Bangalore, Cochin, Coimbatore, as well as Kailasapuram in Tirunelveli District, Tamil Nadu, his native place. He wanted to renew his kinship with his uncles, aunts, and cousins.

For a get-together with his friends, Terry wanted me to look for a short-term stay-in resort, preferably overlooking the sea. Gerald, Pervez and I started hunting for a suitable cottage (ranch house) near the sea. Gaius, my second son, drove us all over near the beachfront area up to Mahabalipuram to find a suitable place using his contacts. After a great deal of scouting around, we zeroed upon a luxuriously furnished dream house, nestling in a well-manicured lawn with a swimming pool and a gazebo on the beach. There was a janitor, a housemaid and also a cook available on 24×7 service.

Finding the resort well suited to Terry's specification, I went ahead reserving the villa. But Terry took a month-long sabbatical from chatting with me. Realizing the initial enthusiasm and the plan petering out and with the prospect of holidaying in the merry company of our friends in limbo, I conveyed my apprehension to Terry, and then he came out with a new plan.

"Ashok! Why don't we come out of the mold and stick to our original travel plan? Let us plan for a trip to Southeast Asia viz. Vietnam and its neighboring countries, including Cambodia, which are significant for their cultural heritage. Let us be clear about the trip. Our plan of travel should be off the beaten track, away from the much-trumpeted *Europe in 10 Days, Spectacular Singapore,* or Go Goa pattern of holidaying. Let us rework our plan for an 'unchartered' journey in Southeast Asian regions, steeped in archaeology and history—Laos, Cambodia, Vietnam, and Sri Lanka."

> *Come, Fairies, take me out of this dull world, for I would ride with you upon the wind and dance upon the mountains like a flame!*

This revised plan of Terry struck and rekindled the spark into flame in my thoughts, and I found it exciting, even though I was not sure if the 'off-beaten track' was a proper phrase to describe the countries he had planned for. I soon started preparing and giving the final shape to our travel plan. Gerald's physical and moral support was requested to building this travel plan. He lent his shoulders willingly. We established contacts with various reputed travel agents with IATA memberships and global representatives. Terry too supported this idea of ours.

Meanwhile, the travel program to Southeast Asia went viral on the net, among the inner circle of our friends who became enthusiastic and eager to cast their lot to join us for the tour. Overwhelmed with such the spontaneous response, I was in a state of exhilaration, a vacation overseas with my friends. Heartened by the happy turn of events, I soon settled down to the task of e-mailing the itinerary and the budget required for this tour to the participants. We had extensive discussions and finally fixed 20 January 2012 as the day of reckoning for the take-off!

But as the day of our departure was nearing, the circle of 'would-be participants' began to shrink. One after the other, citing various personal reasons, they opted out, leaving Terry and me alone in the shrunken circle. Finding the team and our original plan crumbling little by little and fearing that Terry too might throw in the towel, I felt uneasy. Whenever any reference was made to the expedition, I had to paraphrase the expression coined by a famous French king, "The team ... it is I." In fact, I was crestfallen, being caught between the Scylla of not wrecking the fond plan of Terry and the Charybdis of my friends excusing themselves from participation.

Feeling sorry for me, Gerald told me what Pete Hamill, a noted music journalist, had said about not giving up an endeavor: "Men often saw the world in sports terms. For example, take the prizefighters. You would never know what a fighter was made of until he had been knocked down. Second-raters stayed down and took the count, whereas the great ones always got up." Yes, I did get up, taking a firm decision not to abandon our pet dream at any cost. I sat to devise the task of finding a 'breakthrough' for this impasse.

In Sanskrit, there is an idiomatic expression 'Bhageeratha Prayatnam,' meaning 'an impossible task, but which one could achieve with persistence.' It is derived from a mythological tale, how King Bhageeratha did endless penance to the gods, and finally, Lord Shiva came to his rescue of bringing to the earth, the holy river Ganga, a great source of religious significance to the Hindus. I was inspired by this famous expression and was determined to resuscitate the plan of our travel from going awry.

Hence, I went into high gear to revive the tour arrangement, though I felt earlier that it was almost getting defunct. I broached the idea to Gerald, to join the trip, saying, "Come what may let the three of us give shape to the original program of setting sail, as planned." Terry too liked the idea. Yes! We three were all geared up to launch our travel plan to the Southeast Asian regions to touch and savor the rich tapestry of each country's unique culture, cuisine, landscape, and people!

But *(this is a big But)* there was a question uppermost in Gerald's mind. He hardly had any acquaintance with Terry, whereas Terry and I have been boyhood friends, and so would he not feel like an odd man out in our company? Though the budget was of little concern to him, would he be *en-rapport* and comfortable with us both? WHo then decided to ask this pertinent Q to me. Brushing aside and dispelling his skepticism, I assured him that he would find Terry to be a personification of friendliness, with 'noooo' pretentions about himself, a wholesome outstanding character he would like. *(I introduced him to Terry, who rose from his lounge chair to fetch him a glass of fruit juice instead of asking the room attendant who was standing beside him. Though it sounds trivial, it mattered a lot to Gerald. Later, he confided in me that he was convinced by the simple, informal trait of Terry with whom he developed a good rapport during our trip to Southeast Asia.)*

After Gerald gave his formal consent for his participation, he told me that he had always wanted to visit Southeast Asian countries and it mattered little which part of the region we would visit.

After concluding with Gerald's total acceptance, Terry and I took off to visit Kailasapuram, the place of his birth, to seek blessings from his grand old uncles and aunts. After that, we visited Tirunelveli and Tuticorin. From there, we also took a trip to Panchalamkurichi. There, the then ruler Veera Pandiya Kattabomman had fought many battles with the British Lord Jackson. Unfortunately, he was betrayed by the Yattayapuram King. Thus, he lost his final battle. Veera Pandiya Kattabomman was taken to the gallows by Jackson, but no sooner did he stand before the scaffold than he jumped into the noose and hanged himself before his captor could execute him. This happened at Kayathar in 1799. Such was the determination and courage of native Tamilians, later sprouted to be Dravidians in deep South India, who would never forego their self-esteem at any cost.

We also visited the palace in Yattayapuram, which is the birthplace of Subramania Bharathi, a great Tamil patriot, a poet and freedom fighter from 1882 to 1921. We visited his ancestral home where he was born and grew up to become a great poet. We have taken photographs of his own handwritten lyrics and poems, many of his letters and many more documents.

While we were away, Gerald had collected information on a lantern lecture by an archaeologist and epigraphist in a college auditorium in Chennai. The presentation was 'Angkor Wat: A Blend of Spirituality and Epitomising Man's Devotion to God'. It was a piece of godsend information that coincided with our travel plan. The three of us attended the lecture. The speaker said, "Angkor Wat represents the universe-space in miniature form, and the central tower is Mount Meru, the seat of the gods. It was built by King Suryavaraman II in the year AD 1152, contemporary with the great Cathedrals of Chartres and Canterbury. The monuments of Angkor are acclaimed as the largest and best-preserved religious structures in the world." The lecture, as well as browsing of some more books related to this subject, inspired us to emerge from vicarious travelers to real ones. After the affirmative conclusion of our tour plan with a lot of material information of the proposed places of our visit and acceptance of the budget, we three struck the deal wholeheartedly. Thus, the original idea was vitalized.

> *The beautiful thing about any travel plan is*
> *that you always know what cannot happen.*

Thus the ***Three Men in SeA*** was born.

TRAILBLAZER

I must confess, by reading a few travel-guide books, I soon found myself as an armchair traveler, and the desire of visiting these countries physically slowly gathered momentum in me with intensity.

Here is a brief summary of the Southeast Asian countries of which we were to set about, introduced to you with a bouquet of snippets from travelogues.

THAILAND

A perfect gateway to Southeast Asia epitomizing all the fascination of that region in one country; a vivid kaleidoscope of glittering temples, spectacular palm-fringed beaches and graceful, smiling faces everywhere

Bangkok: Bustling capital with its pride of the glittering grand palace, Temple of the Emerald Buddha and the solid gold one weighing 5½ tons at Wat Traimit, floating market rice barge and Rose Garden depicting rural lifestyles

Pattaya: One of the best known palm-fringed beaches in Asia offering water sports and throbbing nightlife. It is a Mecca for Sun, fun, sand, and sea

Phuket Island: Aptly categorized as a 'flawless pearl of the Andaman Sea,' with superb white sandy beaches and sparkling turquoise sea

CAMBODIA

Historical mysteries, cultural inputs of excellence due to the advent of South Indian trade and influence

Phnom Phen: Present capital of Cambodia, National Museum, providing a fascinating insight into the rich history of Khmer race

Siem Reap: A gateway to the temples of Angkor

Angkor Wat: One of the seven wonders of the ancient world; architectural excellence and human endeavor influenced by Tamil

LAOS

An offshoot of Khmer excellence with peace and harmony within itself

Vientiane: A sleepy nostalgic capital beside Mekong River

Bolaven Plateau: A natural citadel high above the Mekong River with a lot of waterfalls and lush forest

Luong Phabang: UNESCO World Heritage Site where rule was administered in the early days

Phonsavan: A world-famous tourist spot—Historical Plain of Jars and Silk Route

VIETNAM

A charming country with rich beauty landscapes

Hanoi: Capital city where motivation of a tiny man induced and enchanted people to fight for their own land

Halong Bay: One of Vietnam's most spectacular natural wonders

Ho Chi Minh City: Lively bustling city (formerly the French colonial city of Saigon)

Cu Chi Tunnels: A peasant's nest for safety from dangerous mammals

The Mekong Delta: The awesome expressed in all geography school books

Da Nang and Hoi An: Economic heartland with a lot of waterfalls, forests and ancient trading port

SRI LANKA

A mixed cultural race shared between Singhalese and Tamils; a divided nation from the beginning

Colombo: Commercial capital of Sri Lanka lives on the main international maritime route

Mount Lavinia: Golden sandy beaches

Kandy: Central Plateau and seat of Pandiyan Emperor

Negombo: Beach resort with good accommodation

Nuwara Eliya: Countryside with tea plantation

Trincomalee: A natural harbour, mainly Tamilian area

Galle Fort: A UNESCO World Heritage Site

One for All and All for One Mantra

Now back to ourselves: We had a brainstorming session, dealing with *Do's and Don'ts.*

It is imperative that we should agree to disagree.

a. We should enjoy our drink by relishing it, not gulping à la Devadas.
b. Never drink on the road. You would never know what you're getting into, and it is better to keep your head clear and eyes focused always. Besides, with so many things to see and experience, why would anyone want to get drunk while journeying?
c. We were to adhere strictly to healthy food avoiding fatty food and doing warm-up exercise daily.
d. *'Zip your lips and shake your hips' would be our day-to-day mantra.*
e. Never be out of range of each other's radar.

Three Blind Mice

As the day of departure was fast approaching, we got down to the task of packing—first-aid kits, medicines, etc., and of course, a dozen passport-sized photos of ours. It will not be out of place to acknowledge our wisdom of selecting the tour operators who meticulously planned our itinerary, choosing very comfortable staying, healthy food and arranging the 'know-all type' of charming guides to boot. Yes, a 'big thanks' to the management of our tour agent, who made our travel relaxed and travail free!

The day of our departure had dawned. From our hallucination-visions and dreams of the places, we would visit, from the imaginations of the beautiful beaches crowded bazaars, and the mirage of happiness, fun, and frolic, we were on the threshold of emerging into reality. We were the three musketeers with the motto. You would prefer to walk and your All for one and one for all', launching on tour to the unknown countries, unknown cultures, unknown languages, etc., ready to run like the *Three Blind Mice, hoping no farmer's wife is waiting there to cut our tails (no pun intended) with a carving knife.*

Spending as much time with your companions as possible is wise.

Learn about their quirks and find out whether a true comradeship can be nurtured or not (if companion wants to take a coach ride, it is better to kiss him good-bye). Honestly, we had no idea what we were getting ourselves into!

We were ready to set sail to Southeast Asia, and that's when Tolkien's 'The Road Goes Ever On' keeps haunting us.

> *Still 'round the corner, there may wait for*
> *A new road or secret gate;*
> *And though I oft have passed them by,*
> *A day will come at last when I*
> *Shall take the hidden paths, that run*
> *west of the Moon, East of the Sun..*

Take-Off

After dusk, we headed to the Anna International Airport, Chennai, to board Thai Airways. We encountered heavy traffic en route. Gaius (my younger son) was at the wheel, weaving in and out dexterously.

As always it was a 'break-neck' dash to the airport, generally by a frequent flyer! A last-minute rush, never a leisurely drive, we had one eye on our wristwatch and the other on the passing landmarks, to orient ourselves to assess how far we had traversed and how close it was to the airport. Finally, we could see the green hills appearing on to our left, and we knew we had made it just in time. The airport stood right across. We reached the departure hall; our bags were x-rayed, and collecting the boarding pass, we lined up in the queue to board the aircraft.

I recalled the famous quotation of George Winters: *"If God had really intended men to fly, he'd make it easier to get to the airport."*

We boarded the Thai Airways around midnight. The air hostesses, clad in their traditional dress, bowed gracefully and welcomed us on board (they were as shy as receptionists in big luxury hotels). Our air hostess said "Kap un cap" shyly, her tongue stumbling over the unfamiliar syllables. This gesture of welcoming made us realize how a simple *Hello, Vanakkam, Bon Voyage,* or *Bonsoir,* with an endearing smile and a cheer could go a long way in propelling us to feel the flight a pleasant one! Long-distance trips are tiring, and it was in the middle of the night when we took off and bade farewell to our sleep. It was annoying when your co-passengers seated in your row insisted on being served the complimentary bar and soft drinks quite often, a source of irritation.

But on the flight, Gerald was relieved to find many tourists in their twilight years. I told him that it is more important to stay young at heart. After all, aging is inevitable. Age is only a number, so why sit down and bother yourself? One should move on and not give too much importance to this factor of our life. *(I, also, have attained an age when I cannot fit in the candles on my birthday cake.*

CHAPTER 1

THAILAND

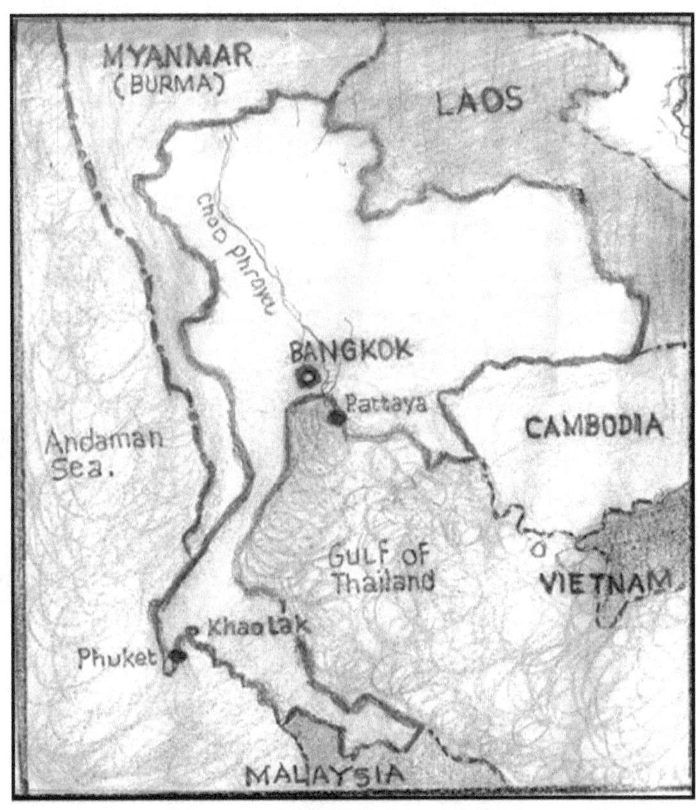

Bangkok:	A perfect gateway to Southeast Asia
Wat Phro Keo:	Temple in the complex of Royal Palace
Wat Traimit:	Solid gold Buddha weighing 5½ tons
Pattaya:	Windsurfing, water skiing, and scuba diving
Phuket:	National Museum, Buddha statues in terracotta and stone sculptures

Bangkok: A Perfect Gateway to Southeast Asia

We arrived in Bangkok in the early hours of the morning on 21 January 2012. Gerald and I had our passports stamped with entry visa against payment, whereas Terry, being an Indian American, was exempted. As we looked around, we were awestruck with the architectural marvel of the airports: columns-free triangulated web designed steel trusses spanning a mind-boggling 55 meters roofed with tension fabric cover, intermixed with monitor-type roofing to admit natural light and cross ventilation. It took minutes for us to decipher the technological innovation of the structure. A mile-long corridor interspaced with walk-a-later! In short, the design of the airport is an excellent example of how aesthetics and functionality could work in a large structure. Your heart and your mind get fixated on it. A piece of advice to the travelers: always carry at least a bunch of your photographs. If you can download an entry check-in Form 1, you could do the immigration process very fast without any delay. Otherwise, to shorten your suspension, one ought to pay one thousand Thai Baht bucks.

Our appointed travel guide greeted us on our arrival. Soon we left the airport for a long drive towards our hotel, a luxurious and commendable one. The balcony, overlooking magnificent surroundings with greeneries and a vast swimming pool, was a sight to be savored.

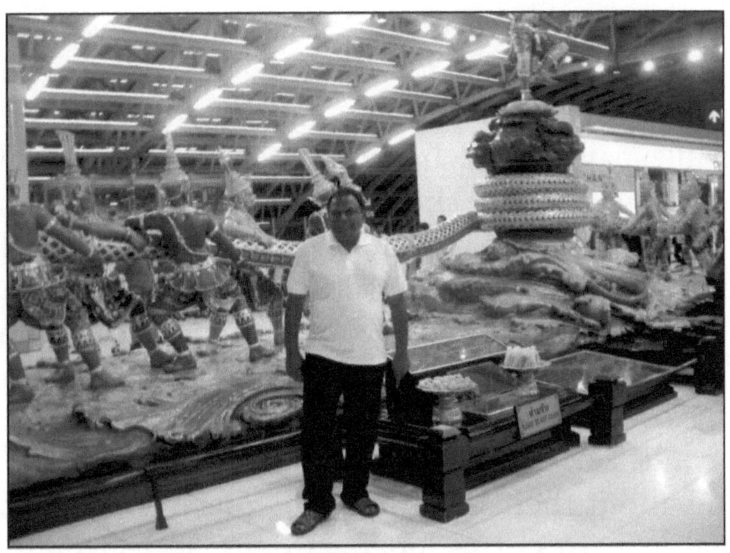

Suvarnabhumi Airport at Bangkok

We were happy to land at Bangkok, a world of charm, with its foam-kissed beaches, the smiling sylph-like beauties, and the masseurs. Being an all-embracing microcosm of Southeast Asia, Thailand is a perfect gateway to our onward journey to Southeast Asian countries. Hailed as a land of one thousand smiles, Bangkok enchants travelers like Maugham and Conrod.

The kingdom of Thailand is about the size of France. It is constitutionally a monarchy. 'Siam,' the former name of Thailand, means 'gold.' It is a fascinating country bordered by Laos in the northeast, Myanmar in the northwest, the Gulf of Thailand in the south, and Malaysia in the far south. To my surprise, I found that Thailand was never ruled by any European country; hence it does not have any disturbing history or a chequered past.

Bangkok is a veritable paradise for shoppers—much sought after for silks, lacquerware, wood carvings, precious stones, embroidery, substantial foldable paper fans, hand-painted motifs. You will do well using your skills for bargaining. You come across a colorful and noisy mixture of temples, shopping malls, chaotic traffic, excellent hotels and smiling, courteous people. Yet amidst the cacophony of the traffic jams and aroma of the spicy food being cooked in the market stalls and street walks, we could see the tranquility of saffron-clad monks going about their daily life. The place is filled with visual surprises of secluded gardens, appearing from nowhere, trimmed with ponds and water lilies all over. The physical layout of Bangkok is well planned. The bylines are called *Soi*, with number sequence corresponding to the location; so if you identify the site with Soi number, getting to any place would not be very difficult. One could use the metro for travel; the transport system is very user-friendly.

"Massage?" our guide asked us. "Yes," we said in chorus, our bodies aching for rejuvenation. The masseurs in their efficiency were indistinguishable from the massage therapists in swanky but expensive spas and massage parlors. The oil massage rejuvenated our aching muscles and gave us a new lease on life. If you yearn for an invigoration of your senses and your bodies, try one of the many wellness oases in Bangkok, leave your cares behind and let yourself be pampered. After a lunch of fresh seafood curry, sticky rice, noodle soup, etc., we took a well-earned afternoon nap to get ready for an evening visit to the shopping malls. We noticed that Bangkok is an

Aladdin's cave for shoppers where bargains abound in everything.

Indira Market is an upmarket shopping complex, dotted with innumerable shops, selling pins to anchors. We bought helicopter toys, a lot of goodies, souvenirs, take-home knick-knacks for a good value of the money. We then walked around to get the feel of the city, window shopping. For dinner, we had French onion soup and chicken fried rice in a hygienically maintained wayside restaurant. We soon hit the hay after a tiring day.

Getting up late in the morning, Gerald and I walked toward a missionary church prayer hall. We prayed for a while before walking back to the hotel. As he could not keep pace with me, I lost track of him midway. I had no idea where on earth he could have been. I was even toying with a view of putting an 'ad' in the 'Missing Column' of the local dailies. After an hour-long search, I spotted him. Terry was getting impatient and upset while waiting for us. Though it was nothing to make a song about, it ended in a minor scuffle between Gerald and me.

We went on a tour beyond Bangkok for a day. The old-world charm still prevails among its historical temples—a heritage style that is unique to Thai tradition. In short, we found the city of Bangkok, a sort of an appetizer or entrée to Thailand's main menu—what with its ancient pagodas, palaces, colorful patterns of lush green paddy fields, picturesque walking areas and thriving cottage industries by skilled craftsmen.

We visited various traditional Buddhist pagodas with their golden spires rising to the skies. They were surrounded by curving pebbled pathways, adding a touch of Zen with moss-covered boulders. We spent hours walking around the place with a sense of equilibrium in our minds and far from the mad rush of tourists.

Later, we drove to the most visited temple, Wat *Traimit*, where the world's largest Buddha made of solid gold, with a weight of 5½ tons and a height of 3 meters, was enshrined. It was said to be cast in the thirteenth century. The temple was a solemn place with the background of a 'sing-song,' monotone-chanting of the monks. We then visited Bangkok's oldest synagogue, the most famous *Wat Pho*. It is the most extensive temple in Bangkok, with its colossal *Reclining Buddha*, 150 feet long, depicting Lord Buddha entering Nirvana. The face of the gilded statue, sporting a beaming smile (five feet wide), and the large black feet are beautifully inlaid with mother of pearls. Another outstanding feature next to the Reclining Buddha is a group of four royal chedis dedicated to the first four Kings of the Chakri dynasty.

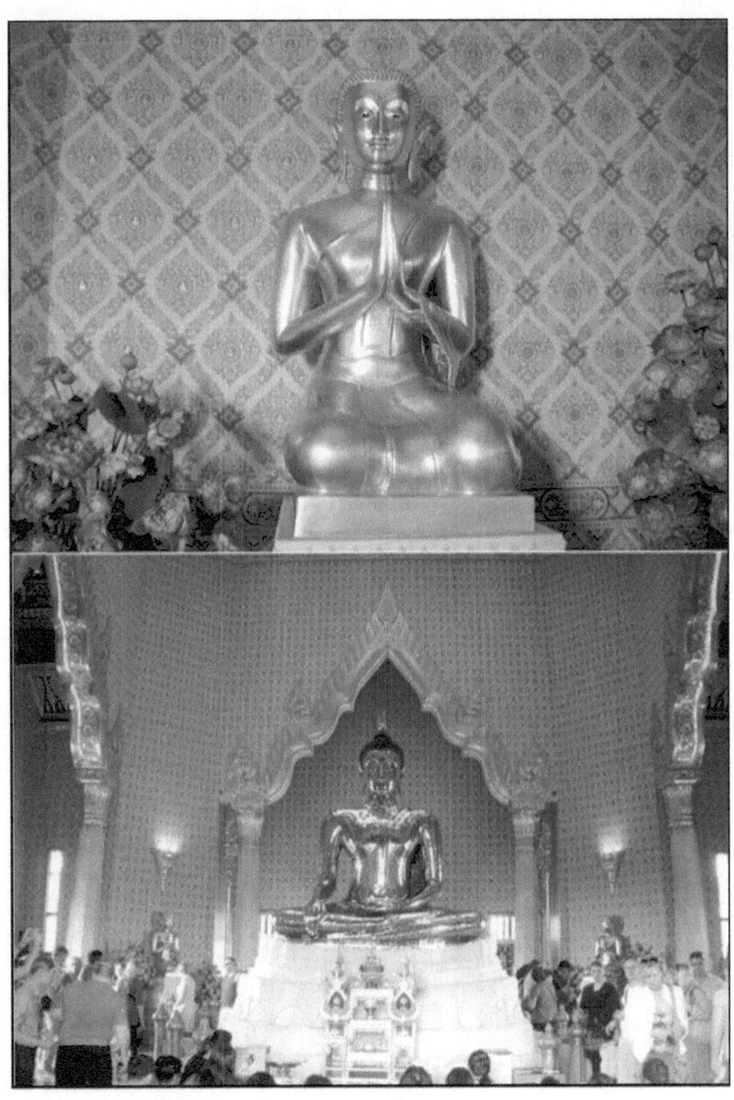

Solid Gold Buddha and Emerald Buddha Statue at Wat Traimit Temple

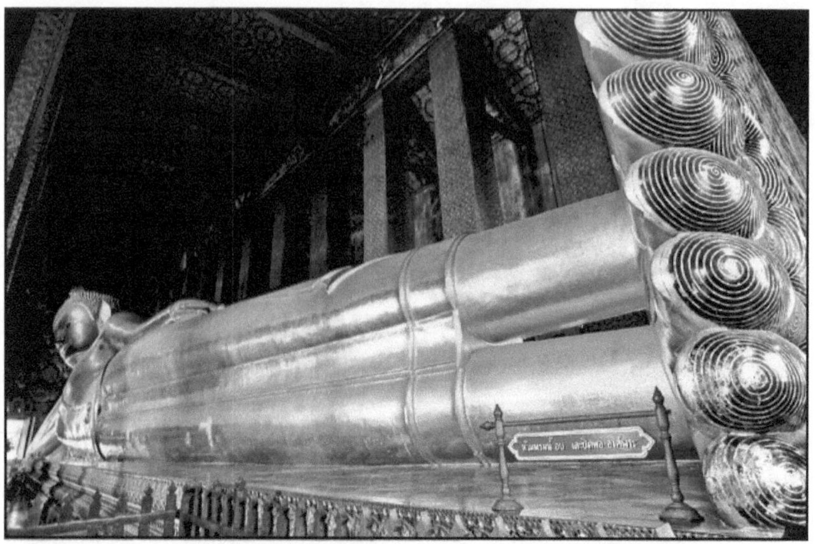

Reclining Buddha Statue at Wat Pho

The walls inside were decorated with diagrams from history, literature and animal husbandry, turning the whole complex into Thailand's first university in the eighteenth century. As I was enjoying the fresco paintings, I sensed the need for a storyteller beside me so that I would have appreciated even better.

The clinking metallic noise distracted me while I was lost in admiring the painting. The guide explained that the tinny sound was caused by the dropping of coins in *hundies* kept in rows against the wall. Perceiving my interest to drop coins, she helped me exchange a currency note into a handful of coins, instructing me to cut one by one in the rows of metallic containers and whatever my intentions were (*if they were honorable*) would be answered by the gods!

Then off to the *Royal Palace*, the largest teak wooden building in the world that is skillfully constructed without using a single nail. We enjoyed spending our time at the museum where they had a *collection* of antique jewelry, artifacts gathered from a bygone era, bejeweled betel-nut sets, gatherings of the old European furniture and exquisite Thai handicrafts. The visitors were also entertained with classical dances.

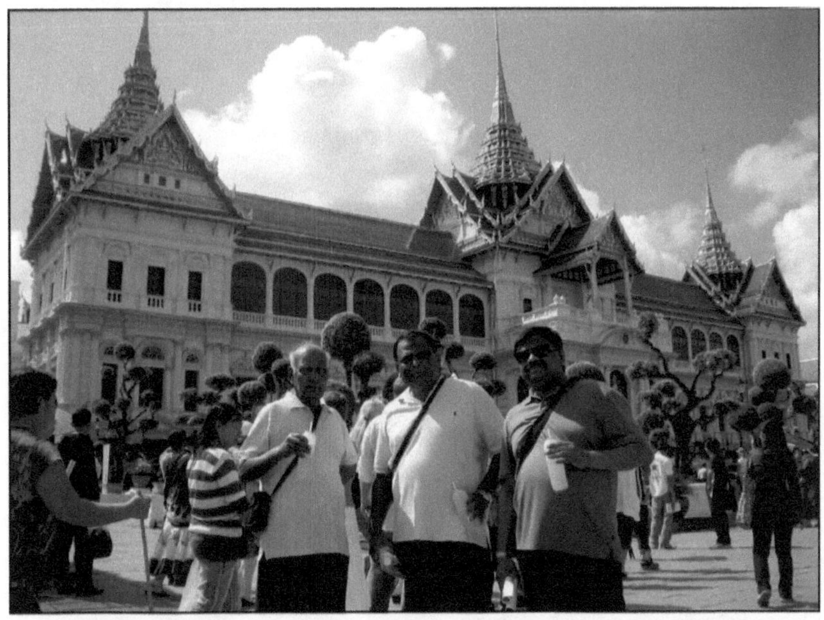

Three Men at Wat Phra Kaeo (Royal Grand Palace)

The one that fascinated me, and still lingers in my mind, was the oldest and most famous temple in the Royal Palace complex, Wat Phra Kaeo, glittering with gold leaf, porcelain and figured glass. The temple houses Thailand's most revered image, the Emerald Buddha. A 'must' for all visitors!

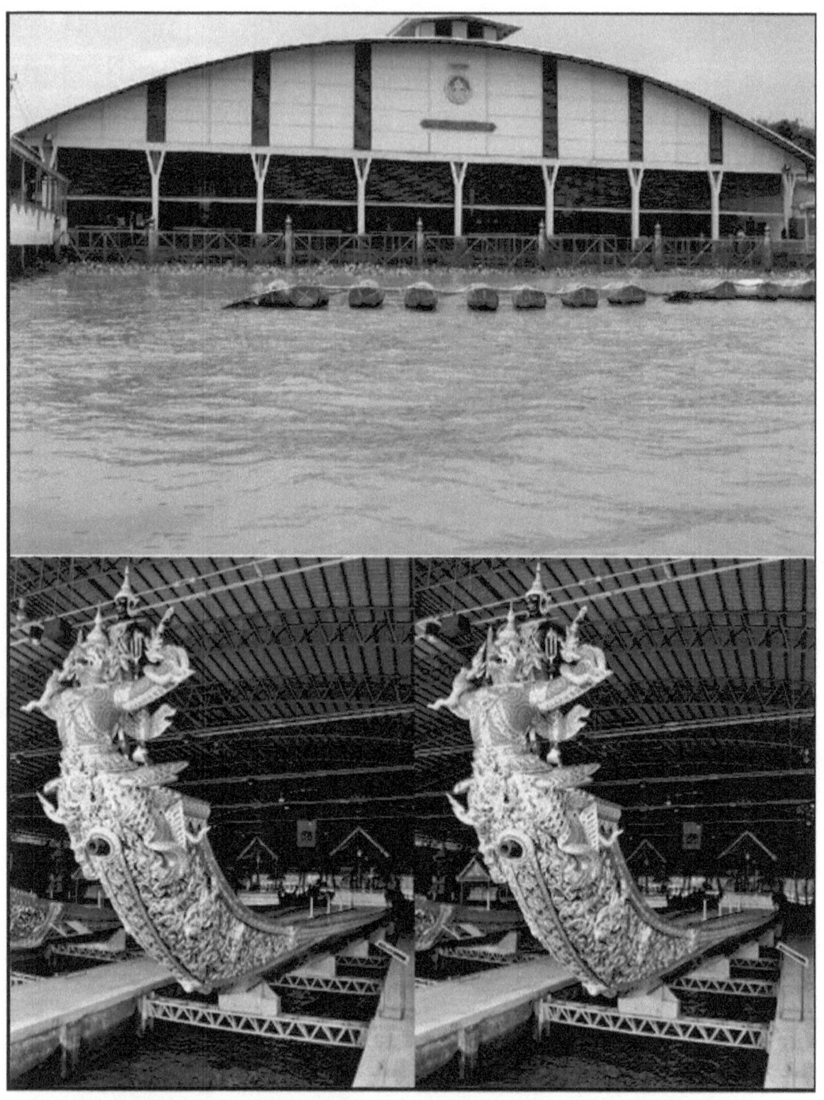

National Museum of Royal Barge at Bangkok

After lunch at a riverside restaurant, we sailed in a speedboat along Thonburi Klongs. Thonburi is the western part of Bangkok situated on the right side of the Chao Phaya River. We came across islets, floating markets selling fish and vegetables, etc., and rows and rows of quaint villas. We saw how ramshackle houses, built on stilts, lie alongside modern bungalows on either side of the river (aptly referred to as *'the Venice of the East'*). Sailing by boat along the canals gives you a firsthand impression of the beautiful life along Bangkok's waterways. The Royal Barge Museum and the Temple of Dawn (*Wat Arun*) were unique in their splendor. While sailing, we saw yellow flags along with the national flags fluttering atop the markets, in all public buildings and most of the residential quarters. When we enquired about the flags, our guide said, "Yellow is the favorite color of our king. We express our love and respect to our beloved ruler by hoisting yellow

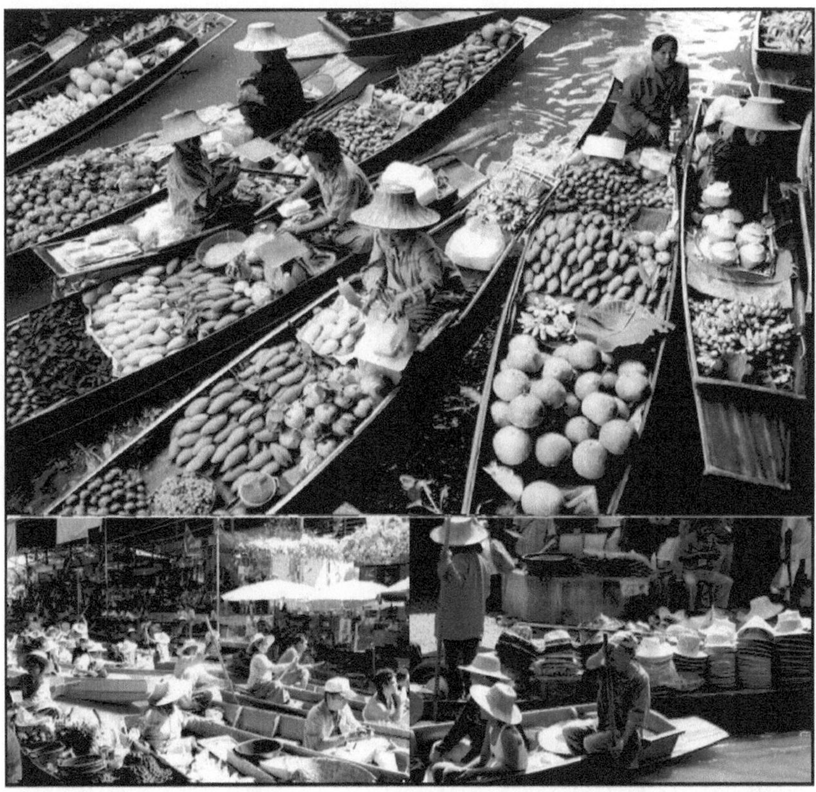

Floating Market at Bangkok

flags. We also want to identify with him through color. Most of us wear yellow colors during this month-long celebration of his birthday! Long live the king! Yes! *"Long live the gracious king!"* we repeated in unison.

On our drive back to the city, we saw the resplendent yellow flags, proudly fluttering by the side of national flags. We reckoned that it was an entirely spontaneous, untutored gesture of the people, and what a sweet and simple way of demonstrating their love, reverence and solidarity with him by sporting his favourite colour!

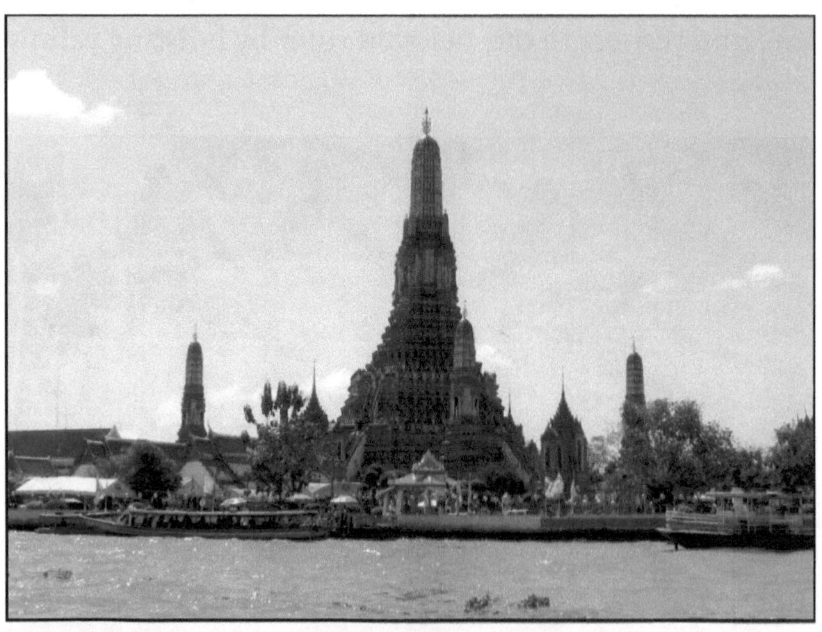

Wat Arun at Chao Praya River, Bangkok

In the evening, we drove towards the Industrial Road Ring bridges, crossing over *Chao Phraya River,* downstream from Bangkok. The main road in the industrial zone is connected by two 600 feet high cable-stayed bridges and four entrances. Along the sides of each tower, LED lights were installed, which changed colors in various intensities and effects, enthralling us with spectacular visuals against the background of the star-studded sky. The shape and features of the pinnacles of the arches were inspired by the nearby Buddhist temples. Later, we went on a drive towards the *KMB* shopping mall. Most of the shops pulled down their shutters around 9.00 p.m. Late in the evening, we dined at an outdoor eating place, well-known for its spicy seafood.

It was evening; a sort of drowsiness descended on us and sensed our odd state of mind, our friendly cab driver drove us towards Bangkok Central Railway Station (Huo Lamphong), a heritage building built in 1910. Soon our feelings gave way to joy in seeing families and giggling children, hawkers and commuters trooping in and out of the station, which presented a vast space of cleanliness and orderliness. An enormous multi-colored portrait-painting of Rama and the much-beloved King Chulolongkom hung in the waiting room. This king had played a significant role in modernizing Thailand, introduced political reforms, founded the system of education to all his subjects, laid a network of roads and established communication and railways way back in 1891. He is still revered as the founding father of the country.

Walking along the streets with glittering lanterns during the season of the Chinese New Year was heavenly. We did not feel the ticking away of time, and it was around midnight when we sauntered into a wayside restaurant, run by the most beautiful waitress I will ever be held. No! Don't get me wrong, and I don't usually go about ogling women. This is only aesthetic. "A thing of beauty is a joy forever." If there were to be a beauty contest for waitresses, she surely would crown herself, hands down.

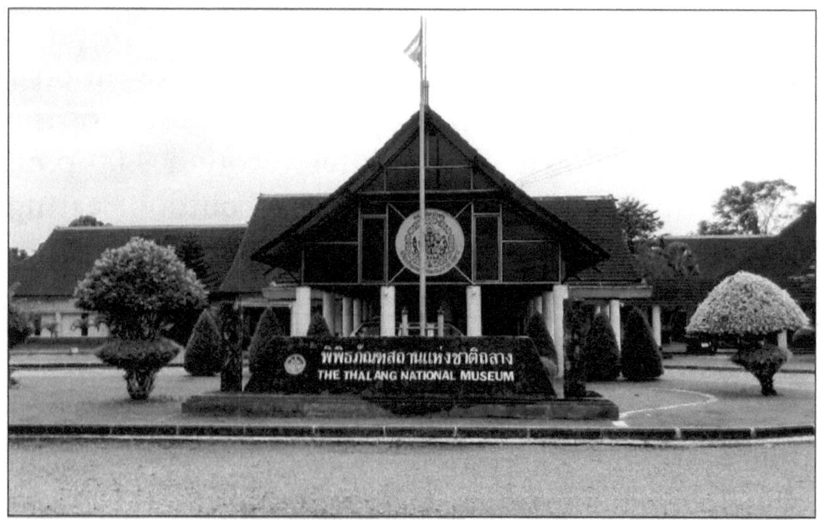

The Thailand National Museum

Rewinding our trip to Bangkok, we felt that although it is relatively a small city capital but with enough richness to fill an encyclopedia—its shopping, golden temples, beachside fun, friendly people and legendary nightlife are the ultimate in excellence. You can relax and meditate in the soothing sun and calm sea. The natural ambiance is bound to exhilarate your senses. Traveling down south, leaving the city behind, we saw several Buddhist temples in distinct Thai architecture with steeply peaked roofs surrounded by green paddy fields and softly swaying palms, pretty beaches, and abundant drinking holes. Snorkeling and the delicious Thai cuisine were added attractions.

In Thailand, an eye estimation will tell the visitors that women come out in equal numbers or even more than men on the street. Unlike in most parts in

India, primarily urban areas, where women are more concentrated in offices, educational institutions or similar places, Thai women are found in trades of all sorts. They walk freely in solitude, even in the dead of night.

Finding it was too late to drive back to our rooms, we decided to check in at a neighborhood hotel for the night. The hotel we had picked was distinctive in its seediness. We observed a steady flow of all sorts of people, and as we stepped on a staircase leading to our rooms, there was a young leering cat-faced girl, sitting on the base of the stairs, sporting thigh-high boots, and making kissing noises at me. Tucking the end of my jeans, she asked me, "You want *boom-boom?*"

"Yes! I do," said I, laughing at the suddenness of her query. I had to decline the offer. No! Not because I didn't want to, but being years older than her and happily married with two grown-ups, I was too physically exhausted to be driven through the portals of sensual indulgence. This was not an isolated incident. It happened to us many a time in Pattaya and Bangkok, where Thai beauties were offering fun and pleasure. But my preference was (I cannot vouch for others) to be happily and gently pummelled by the nimble fingers of nymphs in massage parlors, with gong music playing softly and scented incense with its fragrant odor wafting around me. But it still echoes in our ears, the numerous offerings of pleasant evenings, "You want *boom-boom?*" Later on, I realized *boom-boom* was a familiar rhyme you hear all over as you walk down the street of Bangkok, Pattaya, and Phuket; free-flowing love is in abundance, but with a price, of course.

It was almost midnight when we went for a leisure stroll to see 'Bangkok by night,' the nocturnal capital of Asia, with neon-lit skylines, men and women, mostly tourists, dancing in abandon to loud music, sexual hugging on the streets, etc. The cacophony was just deafening. The city was still busy and bright with grubby bars, and risqué floor shows and shopping centers selling Thai silks.

Bangkok, the destination for sex tourist joints, was sleazy, loud and noisy. But the salesgirls in many shops were as shy as hostesses at coffee shops in star hotels. They walked with their heads held high with stately grace. Neon-lit bars, cabarets, massage parlors, Thai boxing, and the classical fairy-like dancing were the highlights of Bangkok by night!

Though Thailand's tourism is driven by a flourishing sex industry, a movement emerging aims at ensuring equality of opportunity to all, removing the discrimination by gender and empowering the fair sex in the administration of the country, giving them a broader platform to voice their views. In this modern world, women's organizations and student movements are becoming aware of their rights and a need to establish an egalitarian society. However, the UN study has reported that 63 percent of the Thai population finds it acceptable for a man to hit his wife and this rash of beating incidents has pockmarked the nation.

Pattaya Beach

The following morning, Gerald and I attended a church service conducted in the Thai language. Then we went for a four-hour-long drive to *Pattaya Beach*. This is a lovely beach for a relaxed sit-down, sunbathing and watching the calm blue sea! Nightlife here is not for the 'holier-than-thou's'!

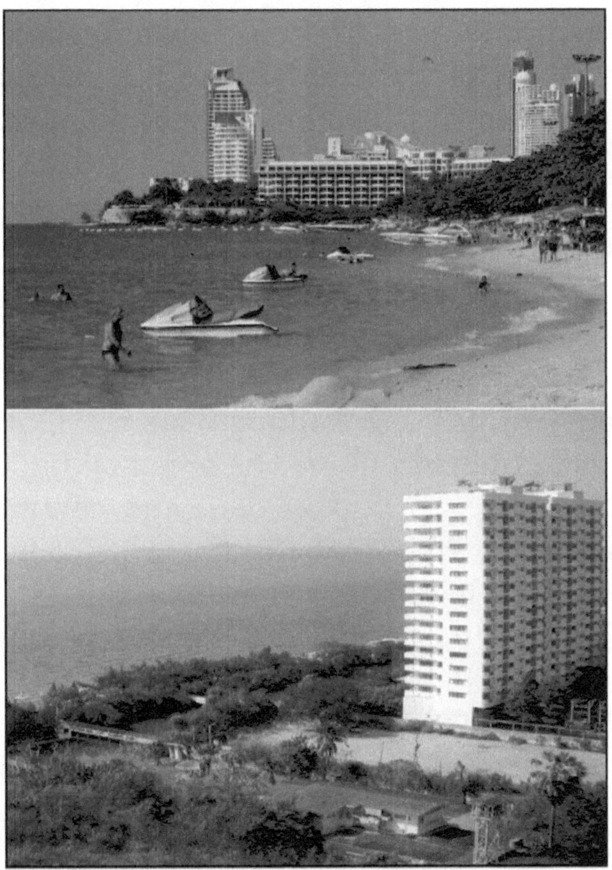

Pattaya Beach

'An imminent possibility of a terrorist attack in Bangkok had the US government circulating a warning on 13 January 2012 to their nationals cautioning them from visiting the country. This had prompted as many as twenty countries to issue similar warnings, resulting in a significant dip in tourist inflow. Bangkok contradicted this issue, stating that Thailand has friendly relationship

with all the countries, including the Middle East, and hence the threat did not exist, etc. Incidentally, there was a heavy surge of Russian tourists in Bangkok and Vietnam during our stay there.'

Truly, the talk was there of Muslim insurgency, looming large in the southern region of Thailand, bordering Malaysia. The majority of the population in the south are Muslims. The Thai government is taking steps to negotiate peace with these separatist groups.

Later we checked into our appointed hotel. It was a twenty-one-storied tower block located in an upscale sector of Pattaya, situated on a peninsula flanked by the beach within easy walking distance. Our suites were on the fifteenth floor. The breathtaking view of the immaculate tropical gardens and commanding superb view of the beach from the balcony at the fifteenth-floor level was a treat to our eyes. A beer festival late in the evening sponsored by our hotel was organized in an adjacent promenade. Multiple brands of beer were offered to us for sampling. Pumping ourselves with a tiny bit of spirit, we drove to Walker Street. Full of watering holes, thumping tunes, strip joints, girly bars—it could be intimidating and a hard sell for the uninitiated.

What Ernest Hemingway had said about the night life in Madrid, "There, the people do not go to bed until they killed the night", is true about Pattaya also. We also picked up an amusing anecdote about him from a fellow traveller, the veracity of which cannot be accounted for. (Hemingway, a confirmed votary of Bacchus, used to frequent a bar on Rue Cambon in Paris. One day, he went to the bartender to ask her to mix a drink devoid of odour so that 'Bloody Mary' couldn't smell on his breath. Mary was his third or fourth wife and that is the story behind that cocktail.)

Unaccompanied by Gerald and Terry, I went for a flower show which was artistically and aesthetically presented. Then to a fish pedicure. Immerse your feet in a fish tank, soon to be nibbled by hundreds of tiny fish, sending a very tickling sensation especially when bitten between the toes. It would help to remove the corns with a tingling sensation of the soles. We saw a road show of the Chinese New Year celebration, with half-a-mile-long mammoth-sized paper dragon with claws and wings symbolising the dragon year. The paper dragon with colourful glittering scales and ferocious-looking fangled mouth spewing fire and smoke was expertly manipulated by persons carrying poles hidden behind colourful silk cloths. It was deafening and the noise decibel increased higher and higher till it threatened to demolish the entire mechanism of our ears.

Beer guzzling, lascivious dancing with hair let down were the nightly occurrences on this street. Brash and highly commercialized nightlife favors the single male. Every night was party night for us either at the beach or at the neighborhood with loud music and the DJ, ensuring that she had the crowd on their feet, swinging or swaying to her music in excellent spirits. Yummy eats were served. Thus we had scrumptious night outs, which means we were stumbling back to our hotel rooms in the wee hours of the morning (*in our case, a respectable 3 a.m.!*).

We had American-style breakfast on the rooftop. I fortified myself with plenty of orange juice. Terry joined me later, he helped himself to a bucketful of fruit juice and plenty of vegetable salad. In the evening, we strolled towards the beach. It was crowded with Russian tourists who were busy clicking the setting sun while lounging on the beach. Terry and I walked towards the beach, leaving Gerald to relax in a lounge chair.

Later, we had arranged with the hotel management for an out-of-town Thai massage parlor. We were directed to a village looking for the sybarite. We soon found ourselves in a thatched room with the natural cool breeze wafting through bamboo screens. It was dimly lit, with scented candles, soothing music, clean fluffy towels, and a comforting silence, occasionally broken by the sound of our own contented snore, as the masseuses gently kneaded and straightened every knot in the body, kneeling on the back of my thighs, tugging the kinks out of my arms. Poking her elbows, tracking it down my spine, she used her toes to dig into my vertebrae. She then punched the upper regions of my back. She worked on my arms twisting one, then the other. With her knees, she massaged my kidneys, and she hammered the kinks out of my back. After kneading my calves with her heels, she turned me over, punched my legs, and gave an open-handed workout on my thighs. The whole exercise took about an hour. What bliss! Both physically and mentally, we got appeased. We were served with cakes and tender coconut water, leaving us to feast our eyes on Nature's bounty surrounding us.

On the way back to the hotel, via a long beach road, we got into a crowd full of tourists indifferent swampy attires. After witnessing a live Thai boxing and karate bout, we were back to our room physically battered.

We could hardly believe when we were told that *Pattaya* was a sleepy village, a sort of fishermen's hamlet just forty years back. Now it is figured in all tourist brochures as a Mecca for sunbathing, fun and sea! Boasting every imaginable water sport, from windsurfing and water skiing to parasailing and snorkeling, we found the usual trade practice of wanton commercialization at this potential tourists' paradise. All around were rows and rows of shops selling souvenirs, seashells and other cute things, restaurants specializing in seafood cooked to your preference, cool tender coconut water for quenching your thirst. Shacks were found in abundance along the beach. Nightlife was raucous and appealing to the 'more liberated.' It is absolutely no gainsaying that *Pattaya* is a magnet for tourists worldwide. All things catered to all types of people's demands.

The following morning, we walked barefoot on the powdery white sand of the beach, taking in the clear blue-green color of the sea. We felt hypnotized. We joined a special package for a sail into the wilderness, the group consisting of multinationals. They were all very friendly since we all had gone on vacation to enjoy nature and its bounty. There was a lot of sea and sunbathing sit-outs near the sea where I had the pleasure of water scootering deep into the sea with a guide behind me. For every particular sport, there is a fee. I chose to bargain with my linguistic power and body language. I succeeded in flattering him that

I like a supernatural, and he would be fortunate to guide me around the awesome sport of waters scootering. One small tip I want to share with any traveler or anyone for the matter, one ought to rip–open the person who is you dealing with while you are beginning yourself to him or her. This gives you the foundation for informality between person to person thus he or she becomes yours, they can take you to the ultimate in whatever connection you are engaged in. Therefore, my guide became a friend he sat at the back of me taught me the initial technicality of straight run and control of speed, left and right turn. The top of it all you can rotate circle in high-speed splashing water around you. I took off with this input on high-speed scootering where I rode over the waves. You take off to a great height and land on the scooter skies safely. You can snail through, you can rip off, and you could do whatever you like. But you have to be mindful of wearing your life jacket and know your extent. This is very important. My friend guide doubled my time because of the impact I made on him. We also took a sky-gliding trip; that experience also was excellent as the previous water scootering. After that, we took a special ferry for scuba diving and snorkeling. We were divided into groups of five, and I joined with four young men from Iran with whom I picked up a long conversation. They were very friendly and warm. They did not bother about the politics around their country, but only shared the brotherhood of humanness with other tourists. I mainly got along very well with them. As we were getting ready by wearing the requisite headgear, our guide, a jovial chap, instructed us how to interpret his sign language and the direction to follow, interspersed with comical gestures, he was always standing by our side as our guardian angel, encouraging us to dive into the sea deeper without any reservation or inhibition. The build-up of my tension soon took a backseat.

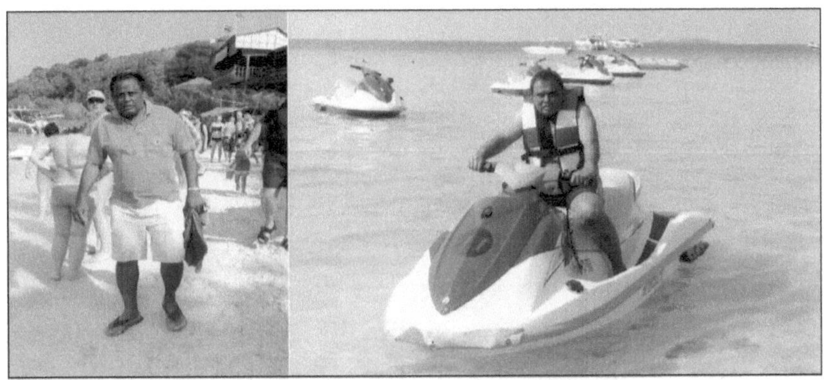

Water Scootering at Pattaya

For every group of five, a leader was chosen, and as we walked on the floor of the sea in the twilight, we were led to a place of coral reefs. I found my legs were wobbly when I set my feet on the sandy floor, and with a bit of balancing, I saw myself walking steadily. The guide of our group gave each a kind of 'bread cube' as fish food while we were standing around the coral reefs. Soon a school of fish boldly gathered around me, nibbling the bread right from my palms. In no time, the food was gone, and I felt sorry for another school of fish and fed all of them. I took another piece from the guide and kept close to my mouth visor. All the fish and other sea mammals charged near my mouth trying to nibble on the little food I had, I was transcended to another world. I felt I had become sea mammal being smooched intensely by many mermaids. There I was never to wake up from the feeling, in the bargain, I had loosened myself from the group chain. Then somebody tapped me on the back. It was my guide trying to lead me back. The little crumbs had been finished. Once it was completed, the fish were asking for more, but finding nothing in my hand to offer them, they left me. I was crestfallen. I could honestly say that it was the best day of my life. In the deep blue sea, there were hundreds of fish in different colors: yellow with black stripes, jet-black dotted ones, ornamental blue and green sea urchins, and more, swarming around me in circles. I was breathing through the snorkel, and a fantastic new world was rushing towards me across coral reef mountains. As I resurfaced, I felt humbled at the thought that the sea harboring such an abundant and buzzing marine life beneath was looking calm and tranquil on the surface. Climbing back on the upper deck of the boat, we felt heavenly, munching sliced pineapple and watermelon, and sipping some refreshing tender coconut water. The ferry brought us back to Pattaya, and we were driven to our hotel.

Walker Street: Pleasure Paradise

We felt exhausted having loafed from the morning and spending late hours at night. Constraints of age were justifiable. Hence, we rested the whole day preparing us for an all-night on Walker Street (a pleasure paradise) for fun and frolic.

We began to chat about the good old days. Terry recalled the early days of our friendship. Our conversation veered around our 'sepia-tinted' days, recalling our boyhood pranks, infused with turbulent, puppy love of those teeny days with dollops of mischief and fun, caring a *tuppence* for any lofty idealism. My full circle of friends was of the same age group, being born within two years of one another, all of us hailing from Purasawalkam, a zone in the heart of the city of Chennai. Parveez, Terry, Vela, Tony and of course, Rukmani, the *prima donna* of our consort who infused entertainment and laughter. A joyful person, just the sort that brightens up your souls!

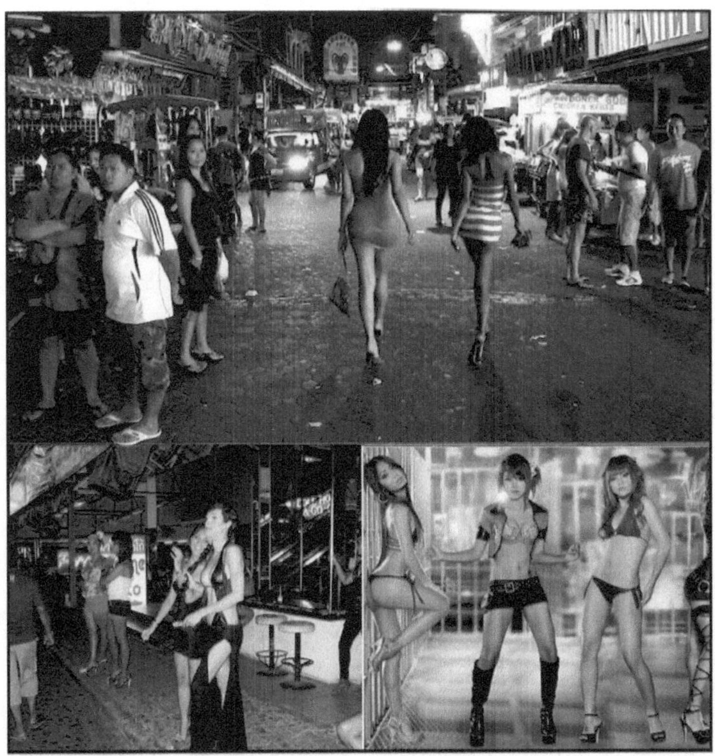

Walker Street at Pattaya

We were all-lovable friends, meeting in the usual spot at the appointed time, sitting on railings near the YMCA and Doveton Corrie School, coinciding with the closing hours of the girls' school, chasing a fast-moving electric train and triumphantly boarding it, chasing skirts, singing lewd lyrics, etc. However much we tried to pose as presentable young men, our efforts fell flat and bore no fruit. Those were the days of gay abandon, hopping from one place to another, like cats on a hot tin roof. The most frequented area of ours was the YWCA adjoining Ritherdon Road (*In 1843, Major General Augustus Williams Ritherdon, who served in the erstwhile Madras Army, was residing with his family and cousins in a palatial house in Purasawalkam-Vepery area which may have led to the naming of the road*).

As evening began to fall, in all excitement we hired a cab from our hotel and proceeded to Walkers Street. We were dropped at the top of a long, crowded road said to be reaching to the beach at the other end. The loud music that filled the air as we walked down the street flooded with water holes rejuvenated our spirits. The atmosphere makes you feel really youngish seeing women standing in every nook and corner with the dress code of STD (short tight dress). There is dancing all over even on the road and all the restaurants. The DJs are fabulous— they make you blend with the music. The young girls hang around calling you all the time to partner with you for drink and dance. The passage of time is never felt. Boom-Boom is spelled out everywhere. It was around 4 in the morning when we returned to our hotel. A night never to be forgotten on Walker Street.

The next day we visited the National Museum, housing a collection of Thailand's artistic riches. Buddha statues in terracotta and stone sculptures depict Buddhist rites. Walking across, we visited the ancient Royal Palace, exhibiting arrays of *Thai object d'arts* of the thirteenth-century black stone inscription (earliest record of Thai's alphabet), old masks intricately carved, ivory howdahs, old musical instruments and an ornate teak funeral chariot belonging to the royal family.

Later in the evening, we again participated in a beer festival similar to the one at Bangkok (courtesy of our hotel). We helped ourselves to mugs of beer of different variety. There was a lot of music, dancing, salsa and a brilliant display of pyrotechnics, etc. There were games too. Beer cups were arranged in a triangular formation on top of a long table. It was named 'ping-pong with beer pong.' The task was to aim and throw the ball to make it land on a cup. If it hits the target, you get to glug the booze. You are offered three 'tries,' meaning three more mugs! Later we went to the Gem Art Gallery. Thailand is very famous for that. We picked up some precious stone jewelry for our spouses.

We hired a share auto rick, found it quite roomy, and with legs stretched out, we went for a very long drive in the main thoroughfare. (I would say that the rick is an ideal mode of transport to gain a panoramic view and the feel of the neighborhood.) The fare was very minimal. We reached a shopping mall of a multi-storied structure with central sky-lit lobby and skywalks for buying some tit-bits. Then jazz concert, and on the top floor of the mall, Terry had a facial massage by Thai masseurs and Gerald for pedicure massage (he liked the tingling sensation of numerous fish nibbling the corns of his feet) followed by an aromatherapy massage. They found it to be so relaxing and a stress-buster after hectic days of traveling. I told them in detail about my endeavor with importers of the granite products and the positive sign of export orders in the pipeline. Terry and Gerald shared my joy and said that it calls for a grand celebration, a cocktail dinner in the posh restaurant at the basement level of our hotel.

We woke up in the wee hours of the following morning. We felt highly rejuvenated. We befriended an American naval officer, a fellow inmate of the hotel commissioned for maritime exercise in the South China Sea, a strapping youngster with tattoos all over his body. That guy was full of entertainment and laughter. In short, a friendly guy who regaled us with his personal jokes and other exciting episodes.

He said that traveling Thailand would not be complete without visiting *Phuket*. "It should have been at the top of your holiday itinerary, man!" The southernmost tip is Laen Prompthep. The main attraction would be the dramatic sunset, and we could enjoy the island coach tour along the jungle, countryside farmhouses, rice fields, mango orchards, etc. He said that we would feel divine and would remember him for the rest of our lives as we experience the charm of beachside frolic, unwind by the poolside, enjoy the luxury of a spa, etc. Given the *buzz* about sneaking a visit to the popular tourist destination, I sought the approval of Terry and Gerald. The answer was a strong yes from both!

Though it was not part of our itinerary, we were smitten by the description of the place by the sea, an ideal location for sunbathing, snorkeling, etc., and we were ready for the go! Driving back to Bangkok, saying adieu to Pattaya, we

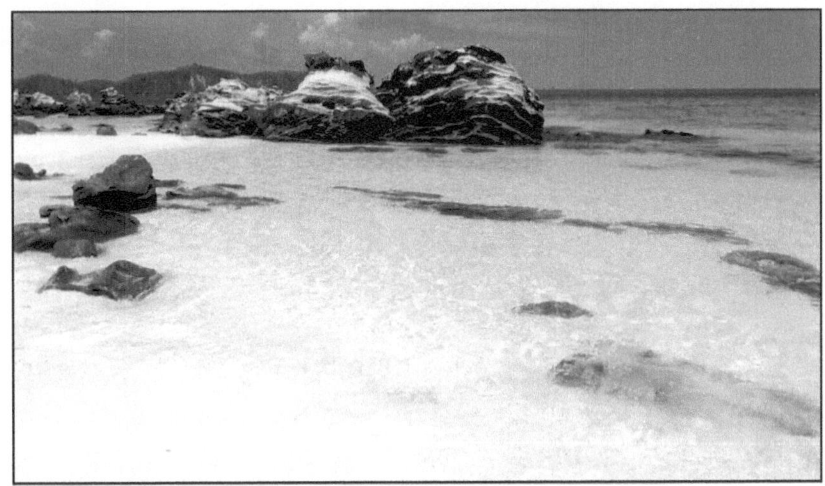

Phuket Beach

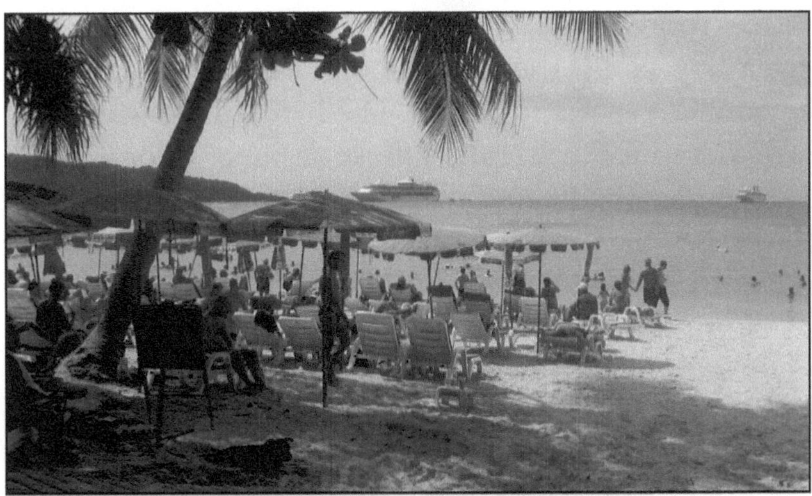

Patong Beach

soon found ourselves airborne in a Thai Domestic Airline to Phuket—a relatively large island south of the mainland (pronounced as 'pocket'). So popular is Pattaya that we found ourselves in the company of many tourists from Bangkok in the one hour 's flight.

Phuket

If you are a seafood lover, you could gorge into some delectable Thai delicacies at some lovely restaurants near the pristine white sandy beaches of Phuket. A perfect retreat to spend some quality of life!

An island of luxuriant green carpeted with rubber plantations, rainforests and paddy fields, it is thirty miles long and thirty miles wide, lying like a pearl in the Andaman Sea.

As we reached *Phuket*, we checked into a hotel in a tranquil, secluded setting amidst lush, tropical forest and the backdrop of the pearly white sandy beach, Here we enjoyed the luxury of a suite at the price of a regular deluxe room. It was a low-rise building of three blocks, extending along the beachfront. The island presented an aura of peace and charm. Life here was slow and the activities much slower than those of Bangkok or Pattaya. Surrounded by beautiful bays, coves, and a sparkling turquoise blue sea, with weird, unusual limestone outcrops, this is Phuket, an island sporting a string of palm-fringed sandy beaches and excellent seafood. Late in the evening, we drove to an accessible area frequented by revelers, *Patong Beach*, a complete contrast to the rest of the island, featuring an abundance of restaurants and gaudy bars of Pattaya fame.

Phuket is famous for its cuisine, fresh lobsters, king prawns, baked crabmeat and delicious fish. We had a gala dinner in an open-air restaurant, fringed by the beach, and the spread was delicious. Yes! Food for the gods! It was full moon night, and the Andaman Sea was sparkling with the reflection of the moon. We spent hours seated in comfortable chairs, watching the foamy crests of the waves, slapping the shore. It was peaceful, and nobody seemed to be in a hurry to go anywhere.

After a refreshing night's sleep, we got ready for sightseeing. There were many attractions for visitors. The pearl farm was one that engaged our attention. Preceded by a brief lecture in English on pearl farming, we were conducted into a vast shed where pearls were retrieved, and we could see the *modus operandi* of segregation, classification and finally dispatch to the sales center, from where we bought beautifully-strung pearl bangles and neck chains at an affordable cost. After a brief visit to the aquarium and waterfalls, followed by an hour-long drive to the north of Phuket, we visited *Khao Lak Beach*, which was practically empty, allowing us a panoramic view of the surroundings.

We had our hotel manager arrange for a safe spot in the Andaman Sea for water sports and snorkeling with selected groups of tourists. After a morning walk (we walked wherever our feet took us), we hired a pony-driven cart, arranged by our hotel manager, along with a dusty path leading through a casuarinas grove towards a timber-built restaurant on stilts, overlooking an exciting combination of beach, rocky headland and greeneries. The lunch served there was satisfying, the ambiance was out of the world with birds chirping, and butterflies flit-ing about, and we thoroughly appreciated our manager's thoughtful recommendation to this resort. It proved to be irresistible, an enticing place to unwind, with a mug of golden brown chilled frothies.

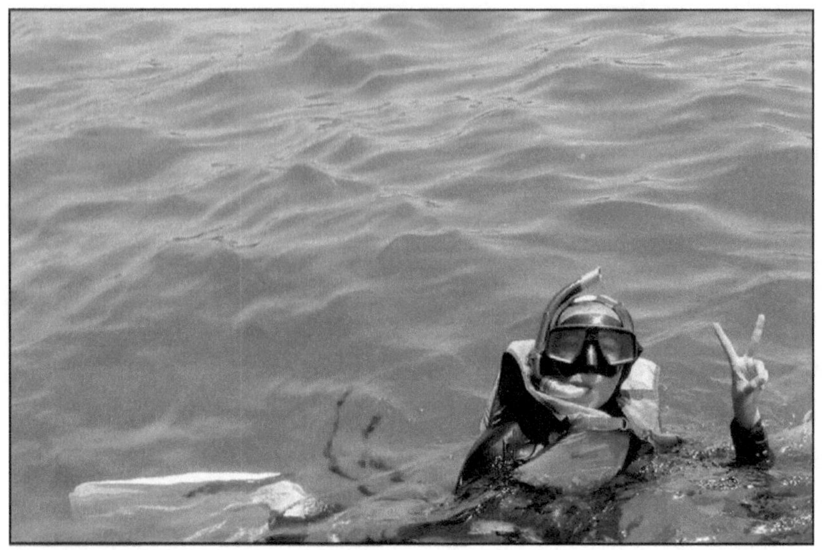

Snorkeling at Phuket

Snorkeling at Phuket

Joining a group of tourists, sail in a boat for snorkeling. In snorkeling, a leaded helmet is placed on your head. It is connected to the main ship that pumps in oxygen to enable you to stroll around the seabed. According to the leader of our group, Southeast Asia has the most prolific area of underwater life on planet Earth. It is ideal for exploration of the hidden world beneath the sea. Soon, we slid beneath the warm waters of the Andaman with our flippers kicking rhythmically. As narcosis enveloped our senses, what seemed to be a large, hard shadow slowly developed details. The colorful coral reefs and surroundings turned out to be an aquatic paradise, a marine life in extraordinary numbers. A magical moment of diving experience! The coral reef must be an underwater equivalent the beachside Club at Phuket of the Amazon forests, with

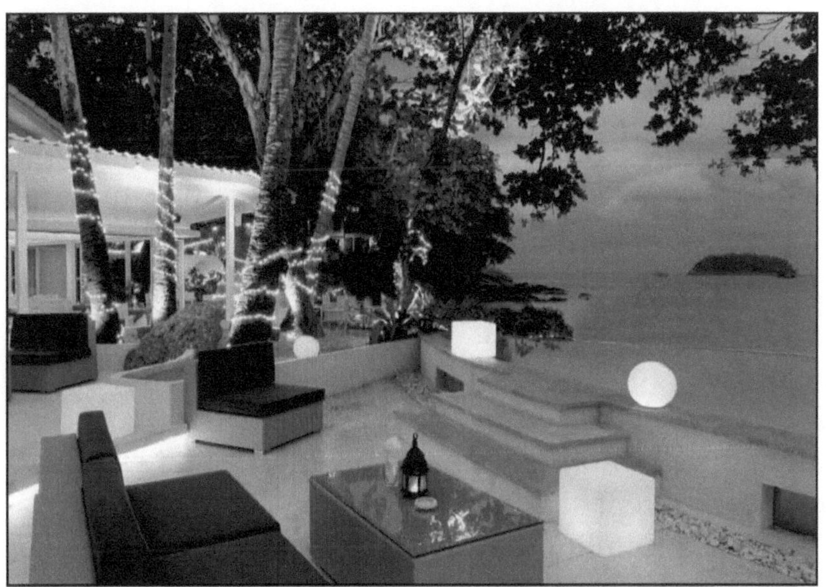

Beachside Club at Phuket

various species of fish, daringly brushing against you, face-to-face, with their unblinking round eyes. I was buzzed by the analytical school of fish and the dappled sunlight, filtering through the waters of the deep blue sea. We could see turtles, crabs, dolphins and whale sharks. We found an abundance of marine life like lionfish, scorpion fish, eagle rays and schools of fish are known as sea slugs, a name that does little justice to their entrancing colors and startling, beautiful forms. Suddenly a high-pitched squeal broke the silence. I asked our leader (in sign language) what it was, panicking. "Sharks! Babies! Harmless." My heart missed a beat. Meanwhile, a considerable fish 'Mantra Ray' gently glided by. "Also harmless," our guide gestured with her hands. With great relief, we surfaced on the sea. Reaching the shore after a tiresome, underwater feat, we stretched ourselves on the powdery white sands under the shade of a beach umbrella.

Another sign of Phuket's chic appeal was *Rekata Club* on the shores. We felt like royalty when we entered the club via a walk-through rain shower artificially created. The club garden had an 'infinity' swimming pool, gourmet restaurant, cocktail bars, sundecks, massage parlors and shopping boutiques—a picture-perfect spot for a romantic stroll around. The evening by the shore was dedicated to entertainment. The party continued well into the night. The wine was flowing, and our spirits kept soaring.

After a fulfilling day, we had to say 'bye' to Phuket to board the Bangkok Airlines for the return flight in the wee hours of the following morning and proceeded to the international airport for our onward journey to *Cambodia*.

CHAPTER 2

CAMBODIA

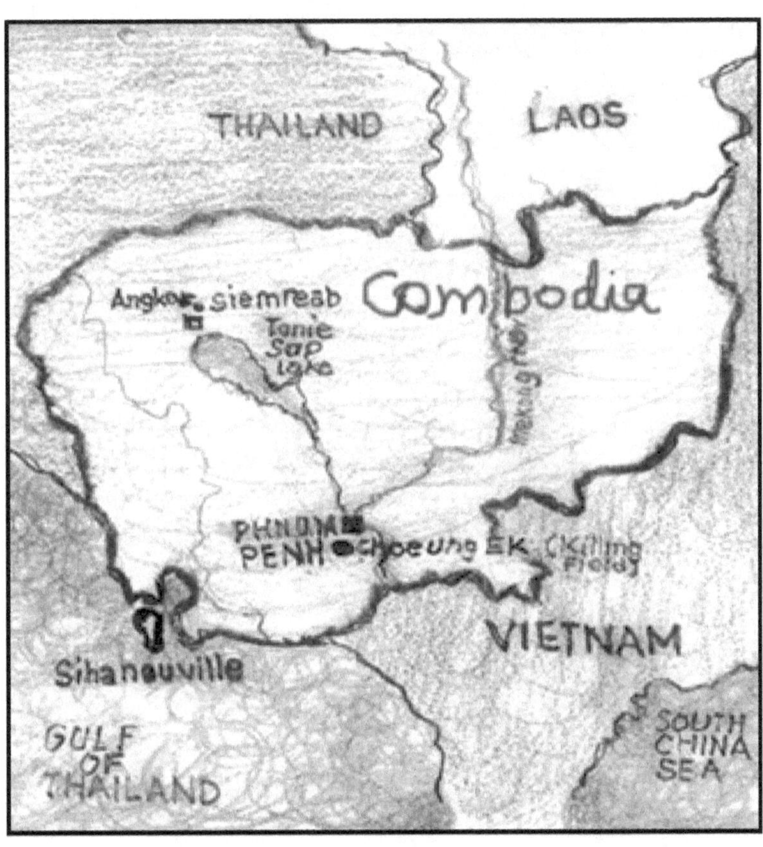

Phnom Penh:	Capital of Cambodia, for impressive tree-lined avenues and candy-colored French villas
National Museum:	Providing insight into the rich history of Khmer race
Central Market:	For shopping (good value for money)
Royal Palace and the Silver Pagoda:	Magnificent display of Cambodia's cultural riches

Angkor Region:	City of Angkor, a region of Siem Reap. Angkor region has around 50 to 80 temples (wats). Since tourism is the lifeblood of the town, there is a 'gold rush,' and Siem Reap is all set for a change to modernity
Angkor Thom:	The great city of power from where everything was Administered. It houses various functional buildings, including vast temple complex, Angkor Thom houses, Bayon Temple, Baphuan, Pimeneakas, Terrace of the Elephants and Leper King
Angkor Wat:	Has the world's largest temple of the Hindu god, Vishnu—one of the seven wonders of ancient world
Banteay Srei:	This temple is a 'Lady Temple', smaller than other temples in Angkor, built of red sandstone
Banteay Samre:	Banteay Samre is a Hindu temple, Angkor Wat style
Preah Khan:	It is a twelfth-century Buddhist temple in Angkor Thom
Ta Prom:	Once built as monastery and university, presently UNESCO's World Heritage place
Neak Pean:	Entwined serpents at Angkor with a Buddhist temple
Theam's House:	It is a training centre for Cambodian arts and crafts
Tonle Sap Lake:	Largest lake, important water resources for entire Cambodia, connecting with Phnom Penh, Siem Reap, and Angkor region
Pol Pot Demystified:	Choueng EK infamous killing field.
Khmer-Origin and History:	Ancient connections with South India and creating the greatest architectural wonders

From Bangkok, we took the direct flight to Phnom Penh, the capital of present Cambodia. This region was ruled by the Khmer empire from early times. We landed at the Pochentong International Airport. There was a little bit of communication gap with immigration authorities; most of it was sign language, which we had to understand slowly. We got over the initial formalities. While being photographed and stamped for a visa, I felt that there was a slight hint of a tip. We drove towards the riverfront area for our hotel that offered us an excellent value for the money. Our rooms had 'breeze balconies' at a stone's throw distance away from the river. This is a very stylish location near the National Bank of Cambodia.

Cambodia, for years, went behind a bamboo curtain due to multiple internal conflicts and battles among themselves. This formulated a chequered history of that nation. Cambodia has a hidden wealth of history and culture, a mosaic of stunning attractions and spectacular scenery from misty mountains to paddy fields. Pagodas and candy-colored villas of the French colonial past intertwined with the smiling faces of the people of the Khmer race! A living museum, history, and culture were galore. Camera-clicking tourists could be seen all over.

Cambodia, a war-torn country, returned to full democracy in 1998. The ruling party, *Cambodian People Party* (CPP), has been headed by Mr. Hun Sen as premier for a long time. The fast-growing economy of the Southeast Asian region is drawing investors' interest among the neighboring countries, especially South Korea. Cambodia has forged ahead with strong economic ties with China, Vietnam, Japan, and Korea.

Phnom Penh

Phnom Penh, the present capital city of *Cambodia,* may not have much to offer by way of the tourist attraction, but the impression, at first sight, was a contrast to The chaotic traffic snarls in Bangkok. A multitude of Buddhist monks in red robes was seen with bowls in their hands. We were told that even before Pol Pot, the government of Cambodia under French colonial rule or America's carpet bombing and their puppetry administration brought nothing but destruction, misery, torture, and death to the Cambodians. It was a pathetic tale of woe. *Phnom Penh* had a scruffy and a beaten-up look of suffering due to the extreme punishment it sustained at the cold hands of the savage mobs. There are some architectural splendors in the city. The Royal Palace is the residence of *Prince Ranarith,* the descendant of the Khmer empire. *The National Museum* provides a fascinating insight into the rich history of the Khmer people and its entire kingdom. A vast collection of the rich Khmer treasures and statuary French colonial-era villas is seen in the main post office and grand market. Many heritage buildings are being The Royal

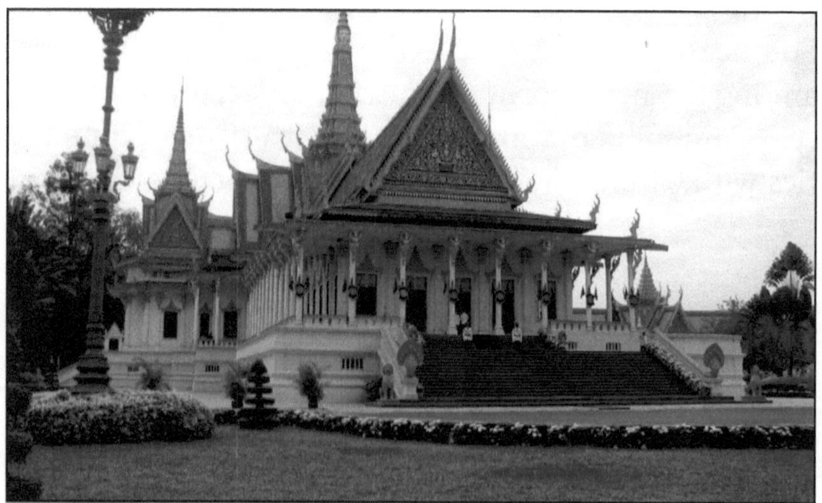

The Royal Palace at Phnom Penh

Palace at Phnom Penhrestored to their past glory. We were astounded to see a French chateau restored as a high-end luxury hotel, set in a walled compound with ornamental gates. Most of the modern architectural style of buildings pale into insignificance compared to these iconic medieval wonders.

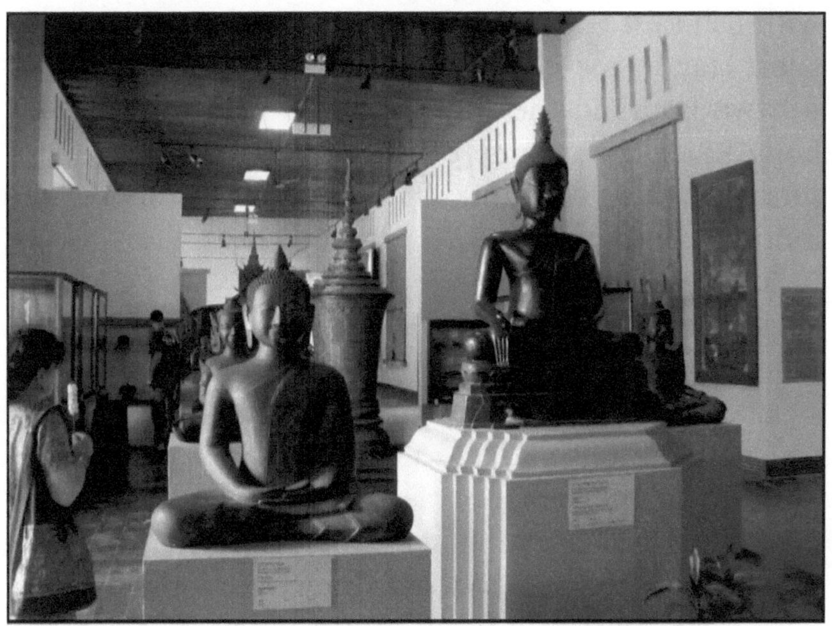

The National Museum – Phnom Penh

Like most Southeast Asians including Indians, there are divisions in cultural and behavioral pattern among different strata of society. The distinct division between the haves and have-nots prevails. The rich flaunting their wealth occupy beach areas like *Sihanoukville*, a beachfront surrounded by palm-fringed white sandy beaches. High-end residential complexes, beach resorts, weekend partying, etc., are springing all over these ideal settings.

The primary plus points related to Cambodia are beautiful weather, less density of people, good food, friendly companions and beautiful Khmer race women with graceful composure. On a side street of *Phnom Penh* was a beautiful garden with an open-air restaurant that captivated our view. Pretty Cambodian girls, flitting from table to table, served us piping-hot noodle soup with fish sauce. As we had a tight schedule during our short stay in the city, our guide suggested a boat ride for two hours in the afternoon in a yacht on the Mekong River for a group of fifteen people with a buffet lunch on the riverfront. After reaching the shore, our guide recommended us to prop up on a pillow for an hour's siesta on the bank of the river. It was a godsend suggestion, for the cool breeze wafting around us soon lulled us to snooze off!

Later in the evening, we drove around the city when we spotted an upmarket salon, *Seeing Hands* massage parlor. The interiors were aesthetically done with muted lighting and soothing instrumental music. The masseurs were blind and disabled. They were trained to feel with their hands the need of our bodies, to relax our muscles. It proved to be a sanctuary of soothing treatment that would revitalize our body and rejuvenate our mind. An hour-long massage, a sensual indulgence to relieve us of the body pain. Though the cost per hour was rather high, we did not mind the stiff price as the funds thus collected were funneled to the collective trust to empower the disabled Cambodians to 'stand' on their own legs. So we did not mind the cost.

The morning after, the weather was quite chilly but pleasant. The shopping bug got hold of us and soon. we sauntered towards a monumental building with a central dome, resembling a ziggurat of gigantic proportion. "This dome is the largest that we ever saw in our journey so far," said a few tourists. The building was suitably named as the Central Marketplace, consisting of four wings in a cruciform pattern. The gold jewelry, gems, precious stones, electronic items, apparels, and leather goods were displayed in a bun basket, which offered us an excellent opportunity for browsing and window shopping. We bought some tourist-oriented curios, and it required a real 'work-hard' bargaining (a far cry from Bangkok).

Phnom Penh was not dangerous to get around since was lighter. A 'must visit' attraction is the *Royal Palace* reflecting the most excellent example of the twentieth-century Khmer-inspired style of architecture. Though the palace is barred to tourist entry, several other buildings encompassing the palace complex were worth a visit, fulfilling our anticipation to relish the history, art, and culture of the place.

National Museum

At a short distance to the north of the Royal Palace is the museum in the traditional style of terracotta structure, consisting of four courtyards overlooking a well-tended garden dotted with a comprehensive display of sculpture, depicting mostly Hindu gods, and among them, we beheld a beautiful eight-armed statue of Lord Vishnu and Shiva dating back to the sixth century. The museum offers a full range display of bronze items. Silver Pagoda

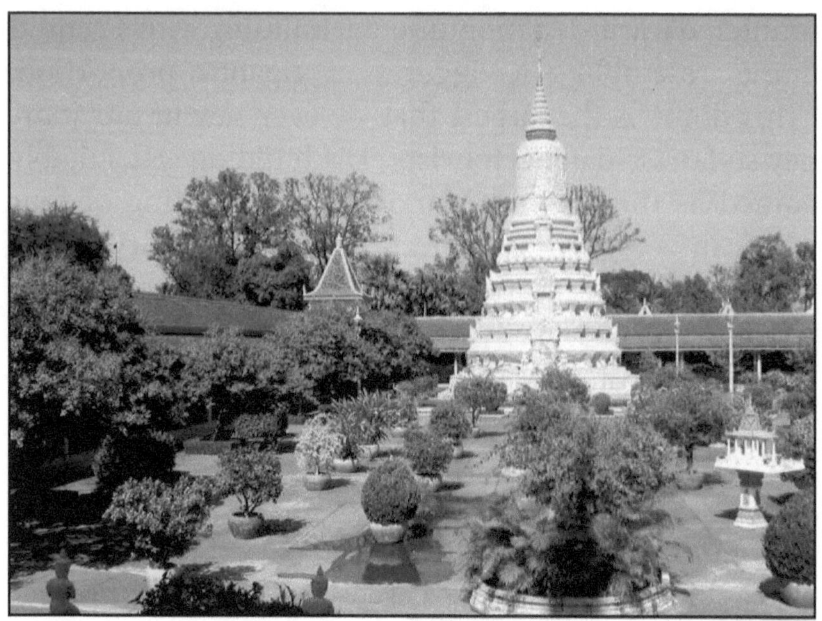

Silver Pagoda at Phnom Penh

at Phnom Penh and pottery, dating from the pre-Angkorian period to the classical Angkorian period, as well as the recent Khmer style. There is a strict prohibition on photography inside the museum. Among the exhibits, there was a good collection of post-Angkorian Buddhas, apart from statues of Apsaras, Nagas, etc., most of which were rescued from Angkor Wat during the civil war. Incidentally, one of the famous nine figures, forming a tableau displaying Bhima in a combat pose as portrayed in the Hindu epic *Mahabharata*, was looted from the tower of Angkor Wat during the genocidal internal conflict in 1970 and had found its way to *Northern Simon Museum* in the United States.

In the center of the courtyard is the Throne Hall, flanked by numerous images of Nagas (cobras) chiseled in stone, and an ornate ceiling painted with allegorical figures, depicting scenes from the Ramayana. On to our left, towards the main staircase, we saw the *Elephant Pavilion*, where the former kings mounted on caparisoned elephants would review the ceremonial procession. On our right was a similar building, housing the royal regalia and other exquisite jewelry, etc.

Across the complex, the much-coveted place of interest was the *Silver Pagoda*. The pagoda was constructed using timber in 1890. We were told by the guide that in 1975, the Khmer Rouge, a revolutionary organization while bulldozing the establishment to a brutal social restructuring with the ruthless massacre of multitudes of Cambodians had surprisingly spared the *Silver Pagoda* from vandalism. An ornamental, solid gold, portable bed for the king is displayed there. During his coronation ceremony, the king, wearing the diamond-studded crown, would be seated inside a palanquin carried by four bare-bodied muscular men.

We strolled into a library, but it was so dark and ill-lit that we had to strain our eyes at the display of sacred texts written on palm leaves. Within the compound area, there was a bell tower with intricately ornamented stonework.

After an exhausting day of sightseeing, followed by a shopping spree at the famous *Russian Market*, where we bought some tourist-oriented souvenirs, we returned to the hotel to be ready for our onward flight to Siem Reap. It was the original capital; later it was moved to Phnom Penh. We wonder for whatever reason!

Visitors arriving in Cambodia with packets of American bank notes are cautioned not to make even the slightest fold, even at the edges. The employees in money-changing bureaus at the airport carefully examine each and every currency, turning it one way or the other, also consulting their co-workers before exchanging. With Euros, the employee seems to be more lenient, but all the more discerning, with regards to U.S. dollar notes. Only new, undamaged, virginal bank notes are accepted. No more and no less! (We felt, it is nothing short of an international kerfuffle.)

Taking the domestic flight from Phnom Penh by the national 'Siem Reap Airways' we soon landed at the airport late at night.

Siem Reap

We landed at Siem Reap International Airport, which is located in the northwest of Cambodia. The airport itself speaks of the modesty of the people; it was not as flashy as other international airports. Instead, it had a homely and welcoming cottage kind of appearance. We had to get down from the plane and walk to the check-in counter. As we came out, we met our guide, a very young Cambodian girl with a broad Khmer smile. I was just floored by her simplicity and modesty. She, along with a driver, conveyed to us that they were waiting for our arrival from the afternoon. As she led us to the hotel, she was reciting the usual welcome address with flowery words about *Siem Reap*. From her presentation, we understood it is a sprawling town with expensive hotels. The boulevards were smooth with shrubs of uniform height in the middle of the road. The air was replete with the calm rural sort of honky-tonk plunked down in the middle of the jungle.

Siem Reap, Angkor:
An Extraterrestrial Handiwork

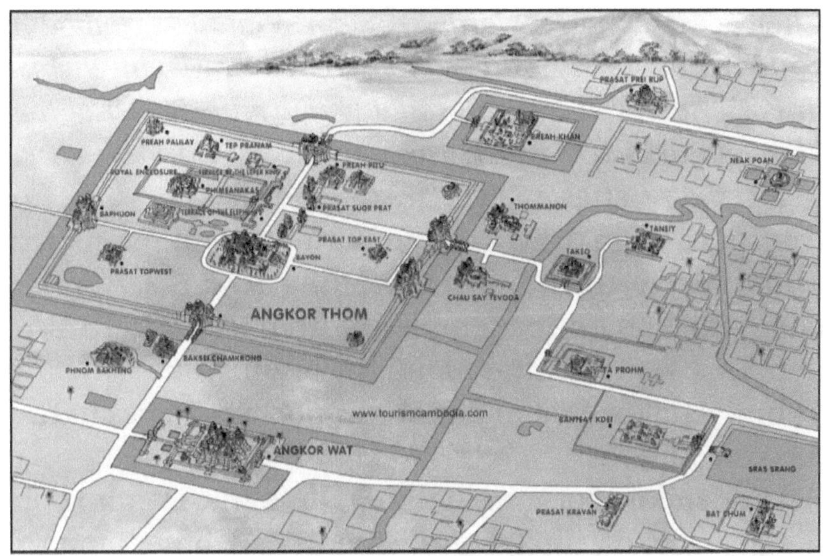

Map of Angkor City

Angkor Region

Little did we realize we were going to witness one of the most glorious civilizations that ever thrived in Southeast Asia. Today Cambodia is the fragment of a mighty Khmer empire of 800–1200 AD, which ruled much of the present Vietnam, Laos, and Thailand from the Angkor regions, the seat of their rule. Trade introduced the *Khmers* to Hinduism and Buddhism. This triggered the golden era of Indianised Khmer civilization that paved the way for the construction of over a thousand temples (wats), reflecting features and myths that directly emerged from India—the national pride of all the Khmers. This is a pilgrimage center for all tourists, a place of wild beauty, unparalleled in Southeast Asia.

Foremost in (ancient) architectural wonders of the world are the impressive remains of the great city of Angkor. *According to Trip Advisors 2013, Travellers' Choice Attraction Awards, Angkor Wat in Cambodia pulled rank at the second slot, preceded by Machu Pichu, in Peru, followed by Taj Mahal (India), in the list of top 25 landmarks of travelers from across the world.*

Next day after breakfast, our guide was there to transport us in a luxury cab with reclining seats for a long drive to the north heading towards Angkor city, well-known for temples of archaeological wonder. This visit was the highlight of our tour: Angkor Thom, Angkor Wat and other important places in the Angkor region.

Hidden for centuries in the depths of the Cambodian jungle, Angkor, capital of the medieval Khmer empire, is among the world's cultural treasures. In 1850, while hacking a path through the dense forest, a French missionary, Father Charles Emile, stumbled upon sprawling ruins of the ancient city. After his death, and almost a decade later, French naturalist Henn Mouhot, retracing his footsteps, cleared about a hundred wats (temples) dating from 900–1300 AD, with statues, bas-reliefs, and carvings, mostly depicting Hinduism and Hindu mythology (before the advent of Buddhism). This discovery made an international splash, triggering a great deal of interest in Cambodia.

The Angkor ruins revealed fabulously wealthy stone carvings, bas-reliefs, fresco painting, etc., decorating every wall and ceiling reclaiming from the stronghold of undergrowth and large roots. It was astounding to stand there, be humbled, and relatively feel insignificant. Like us, many tourists came to see the Angkor ruins. What was once a dense jungle which hid the secrets of Khmer civilization which consisted of magnificent monumental buildings, religious centers, trade center, hospitals, royal palaces, libraries, other auxiliary buildings, and the well-laid network of irrigation channels and water reservoirs finally could not hold on forever? The advent of archaeologists from many countries, taking great interest in unearthing the mysteries of this great civilization.

But the amazing part was how a civilization that had flourished once had declined and degenerated within a short period! How could the valiant, war-nurtured people disappear and vanish into thin air? Still, the historians have not found out how and where the complete evacuation could have occurred. Still, the mystery surrounds: why did they not, with such splendid civilization and culture, fight back? Archaeologists and historians are still searching to find the answer. Though the human civilization is 6,000 years old, the science of archaeology is only 200 years old. Maybe in the future, when the earth unfolds more of its secrets, the history of humanity will be rewritten.

Archaeologists after sieving through the historical and architectural parallel between countries were bewildered to find an exact resemblance in the form of corbelled arches in almost all the buildings and temples in the Angkor complex. Practically all stones s stepped slightly out from the one beneath) as in the Mayan primordial arches which were built centuries earlier in the jungles of Central America, half a planet away from the Angkor region.

The Europeans during the Renaissance period were skeptical about the reports of Angkor's magnificence related by the missionaries in the seventeenth century. In 1604, Reverend Father Quiroga De San Antonio, the Portuguese priest, came upon the city, and in 1672, a French missionary Pere Chevreui also reached it. One report by a Portuguese traveler described it as, "A forest of huge and terrifying ruins of palaces, halls, and temples the size of which would have been unbelievable if I had not seen them." The hydraulic network of basins, canals, and rice paddies being a source of subsistence for about millions of people were discovered too. I was overwhelmed by a subtle enchantment, going beyond aesthetic pleasure!

Angkor still remains and deserves to be called The Lost City—the fruit of centuries of craftsmanship abandoned to be covered by the dense Cambodian jungle. The ancient ruins in dense forests were mostly built out of sandstone, which tends to dissolve with prolonged dampness. Starting from the year 1930, the task of reclaiming, restoring and rebuilding with original materials was taken up, keeping in mind the original form of the structures.

Angkor Thom

While we were gazing all round at the marvelous structures and its ruins, we were encircled by numerous guides who spoke in different languages. We felt as though we had stepped into a time capsule humming with joie de vivre. We wandered among several fellow travelers. The entry fee was approximately $20 US for a single day. We opted for an elephant ride experience along the border of lush green meadows. An erected makeshift platform was there for us to step onto the back of the elephant. We felt like Maharajahs, riding on caparisoned elephants for a ceremonial procession. The elephants took almost an hour to go around the entire perimeter of the Angkor Thom complex, passing through the meadows. Gerald accompanied me while the guide went along with Terry. The guide was narrating and explaining the entire history of Angkor Thom and Angkor Wat and the various structures inside that. As we dismounted, we felt so humbled to see such massive animals bending their knees down meekly to enable us to dismount with ease. Being moved by this act, I turned around and looked at the licensed banana stalls from where I could purchase a lot of bananas. As I went near the elephants and fed them, a tiny, little one was charging and grabbing for more and more, while the big ones showed absolutely no sign of competition with the young one.

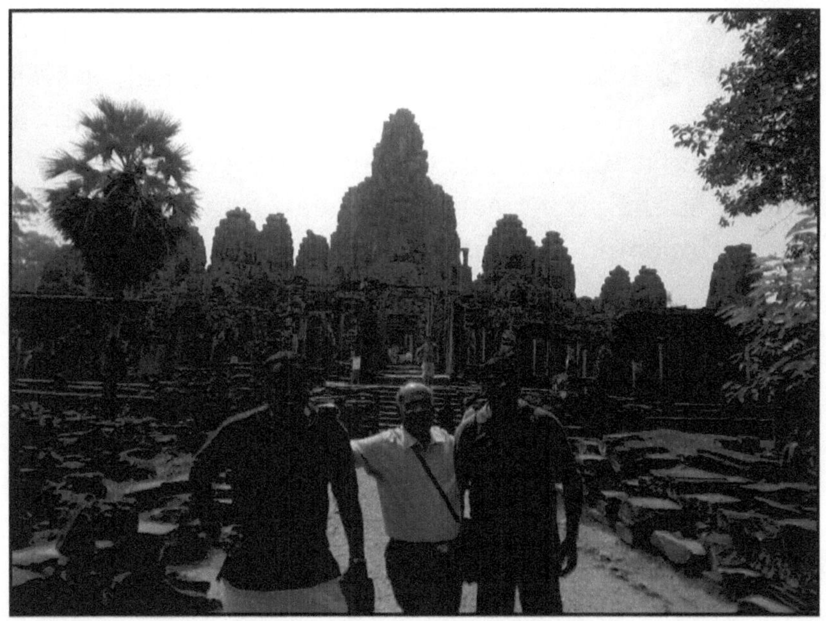

Angkor Thom at Siem Reap

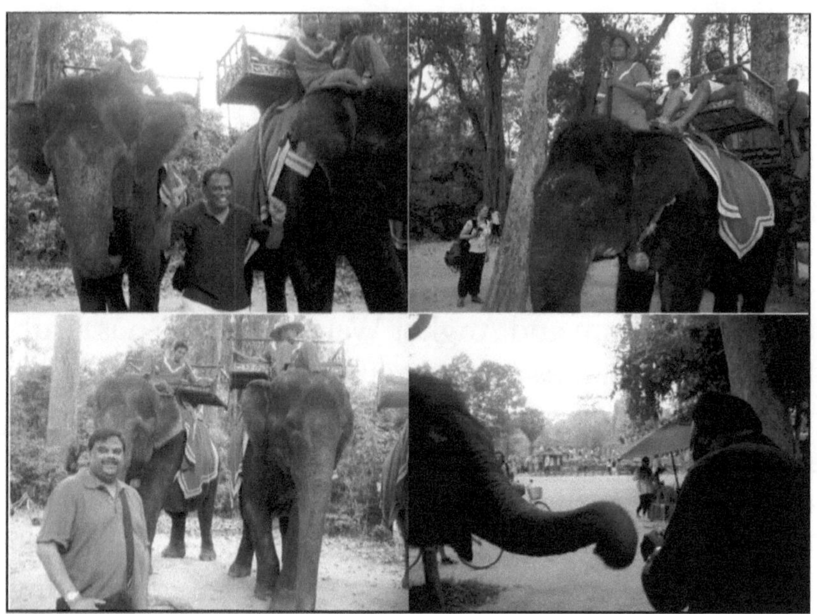

Elephant Riding and Feeding

After the elephant ride, we were getting into *Angkor Thom complex* at Angkor. It covers about 4 sq. Miles. Built by *Jayavarman VII* as his royal capital, it was abandoned in 1434. Angkor Thom is surrounded by a square moat which once teemed with crocodiles. We landed at the south gate entrance of Angkor Thom. The entire complex is surrounded by substantial water canals which are connected to the main artery of a perennial water source. I was informed that the intake and the outflow could be regulated to function within a certain range. These waterways were even found around Angkor Wat and other structures. I found the Khmers had excelled in irrigation and hydraulics techniques to ensure proper water supply and drainage. I noticed they could store water at different levels of the buildings to provide better stability and to maintain

The bearing capacity of the soil, thereby laying claim to their architectural excellence. This methodology of construction of massive structures helps the earth to maintain its bearing capacity of the soil within the required limits for the superstructures above. I noticed that this system had been implemented in all the ancient ruins of Angkor that I visited.

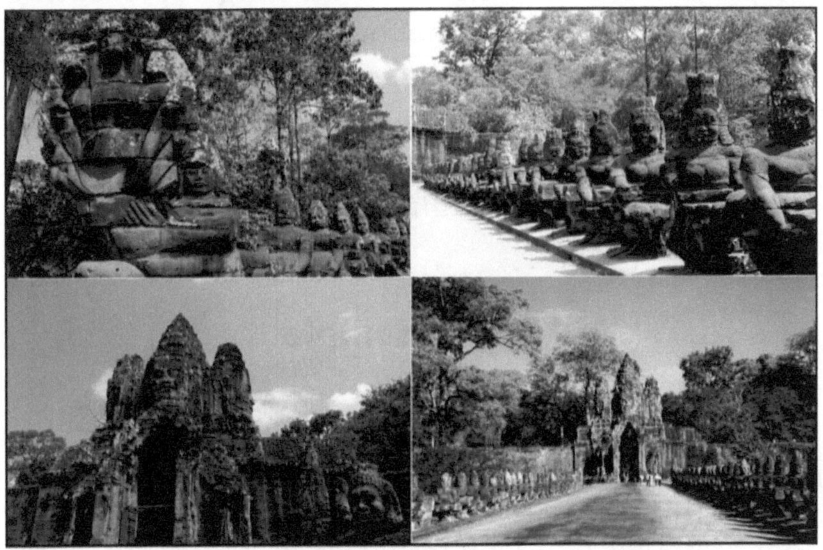

South Gate Entrance at Angkor Thom

As we approached the south gate, we saw to our astonishment that we were being greeted by huge Nagas (multi-headed serpents) with long tails, on either side of this sculptural monument. There were 54-balustrade sculptural statues of Apsaras on the left side representing the gods and figures of Asuras (demons) on the right side. Most of the sculptures were damaged. The canals all around were connected to the significant irrigation and hydraulic systems. As we were crossing over on the long laterite pathways, we looked at the statues and felt that the Apsaras were always at war with the Asuras and that the Asuras would win the final battle. On top of the entrance gate that was more than twenty meters, high were four faces opposite each other. These faces are perceived to present the merging of the human being *Jayavarman* VII who professed *Mahayana* Buddhism. He felt that he was god-king representing god himself, looking at the four corners of the world. This same character is reflected over the Temple of Bayon, which is located inside Angkor Thom. The rulers who followed *Jayavarman* VII either professed *Hinduism or Theravada Buddhism*.

Bayon Temple

As we entered the Angkor Thom complex, we had the feeling that it was not only a spectacular site but also one of the most spectacular ruins. (It was not just about temples like *Brihadishvara in Tanjore in Tamil Nadu or Halebid in Karnataka,* which we are familiar with) There were forts, libraries, a well-laid network of irrigation and hydraulic system, an excellent durbar hall, and storerooms. After the mystic evacuation and abandonment by the Khmer race, the complex was never altered or restored. The pristine glory of the building was neither tampered with nor replenished. But what I perceived at the site was that the ancient builders of the city had a maniac attraction for large sizes of behemoth proportions, both in horizontal and vertical scales, punctuated with a plethora of towers.

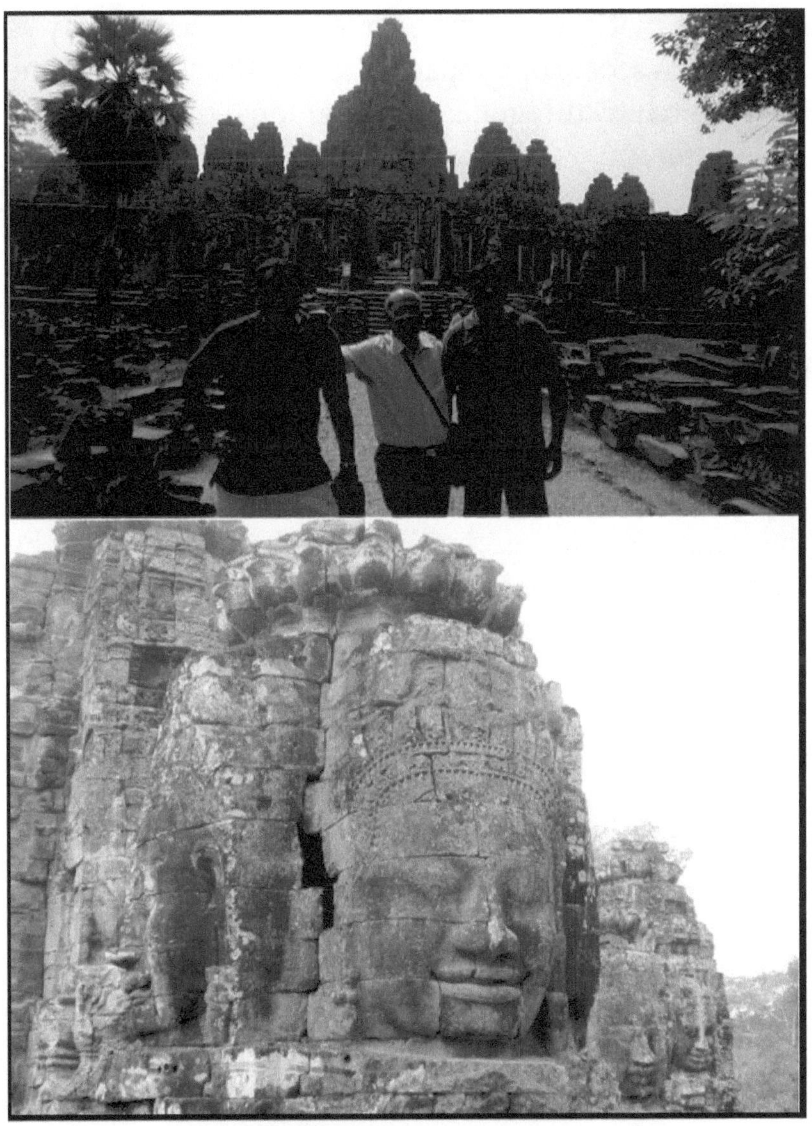

Bayon Temple at Angkor Thom Complex

The side walls of Angkor Thom are massive, nearly 7 meters in height and 7½ miles of total length, incorporating elaborate entrance gates and the pyramid temples of Baphuan and Pimeneakas. The area inside is so vast that it could have contained the entire city of Rome with a lot of open space to spare. The changes in the style of architecture reflected the gradual move from the *Hindu cult of Lord Vishnu* adopted by *King Suryavarman II* to that of *Buddhism*, professed by his successors (*Jayavarman VII*) at a later period. This could be seen in the massive *Bayon Temple*, which is centrally located in *Angkor Thom* city. It is an awe-inspiring 54-tower temple displaying about 216 slightly smiling stony faces that seemed to watch us with half-closed eyes. We felt our legs were weakening while gazing at these stony faces. Because of the massiveness of these towers, it appeared they were close to one another. They were connected by narrow corridors decorated with bas-relief and statues. I wonder how this could have been humanly possible to have been able to erect such massive and tall structures without machines. I am sure the laborers would have had to become cranes or elevators themselves. The carved decorative stone faces were executed to perfection. Every object seemed to converge to its vanishing point precisely. These three-dimensional figure creations with sharp curves and explicit expressions should undoubtedly have been performed by a master craftsman with a vivid imagination. We were chilled after seeing these large monumental structures.

Baphuon

Baphuon said to have been developed somewhere in the eleventh century by *Udayadityavarman II,* is dedicated to the *Hindu god, Shiva.* It adjoins the southern enclosure of the royal palace and its eastern gopuras lie on the same longitudinal axis as the *Terrace of Elephants*. This massive architectural structure is initially said to have covered approximately 10,000 to 12,000 sq meters with its height measuring 35 meters up to its terrace and 15 meters to its tower above. It is also said that the unfinished part of the *Baphuon* structure tower and other parts were completed by *Suryavarman II*. It had features like all other Khmer structures with its irrigation and hydraulic systems and also the three-tiered temple. Since it was built in the Hindu Tamilian style of architecture dedicated to Lord Shiva, it did not possess the faces of the apsaras as in *Bayon Temple*. It forms the north entry point to Angkor Thom. It became a no-go area for visitors because of its ruins.

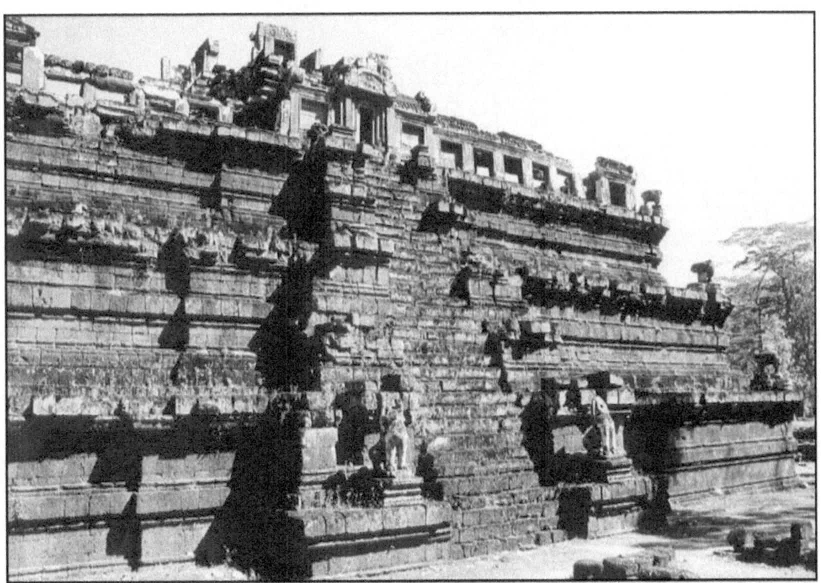

Baphuon Temple

Phimeanakas and Royal Enclosure

As you carry on further, you would come to cross Phimeanakas, the majestic structure of which belies the destruction inside. It is built in the form of a three-tiered pyramid temple. Maybe this idea had been borrowed from *Egyptian* architecture. While we found Baphuon built in Tamilian Gopuram style, the south gate entrance and Bayon temple had a combination of *Baroque* style. This *Phimeanakas* temple, which is five meters high, also has three tiers. It is situated inside the royal enclosure. There are two ponds inside, one for men and the other for women. There are carvings of mammals and marine animals all around the pond walls, giving an impression of Khmer art blending with nature. There is also a special washing place for rituals, maybe for use before worship. But these pools are presently used by locals for bathing purposes.

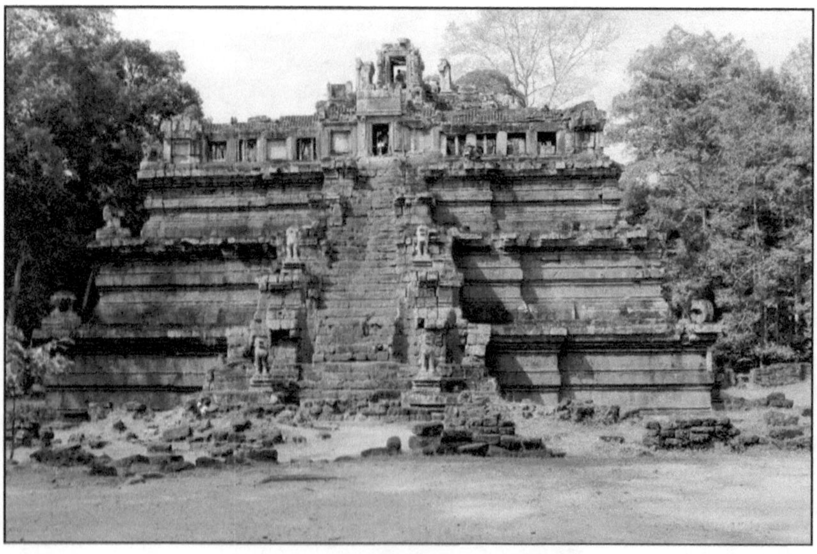

Phimeanakas Royal Enclosure

Terrace of Elephants

Three-headed elephants were guarding the stairs to this terrace, and ascending to the central platform, we saw a sculptured frieze of an elephant in combat-ready form adorning the facade. A 350-meter-long terrace garden served as the grandstand for the ruler to review the cavalry, horse-drawn chariots and elephant parade with mahouts in their colorful attires holding pennants and standards aloft.

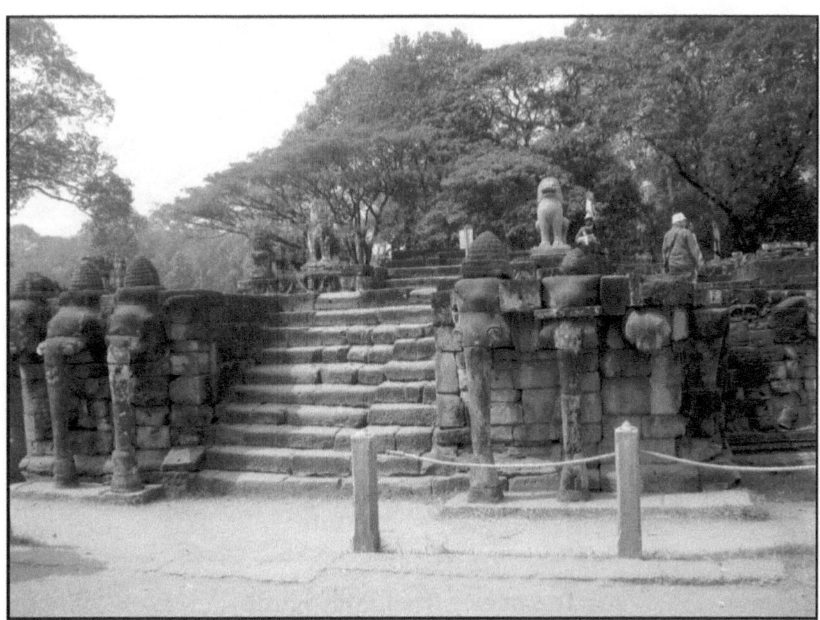

The Entrance of the Terrace of Elephants

Terrace of the Leper King

This is a platform 7 meters high on top, where stands a mammoth-sized nude asexual statue. Many theories have been advanced to explain the origin of its meaning. One was that a former Angkor king would have contracted leprosy; the other belief was that it was so named because of discoloration and moss growing on it, reminiscent of a person with the diocese. It was also used as a royal crematorium. The periphery of the retaining walls is decorated with meticulously crafted carvings and fresco paintings of seated apsaras. Besides, there were bas-reliefs of kings in royal splendor accompanied by the court princesses adorned with pearls.

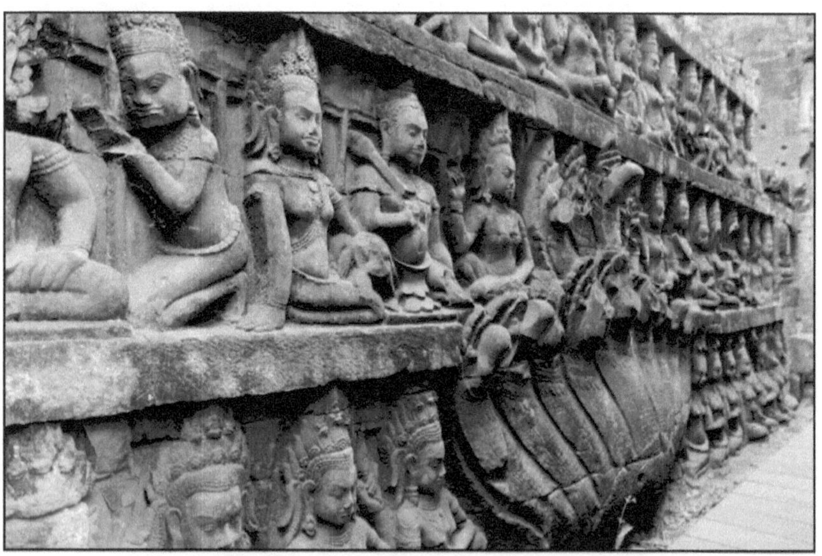

Terrace of the Leper King

The metamorphosis of temple architecture principles from Hinduism, identified with the pyramid-style temple (Mount Meru), to that of Buddhism (marked by the huge carved faces of the king terming himself as an earthly representation of God) is conspicuous on the great temple of Bayon. In the present days, one can only look in retrospect over the power of the Khmers, which had fallen into disrepute, and the forest has reclaimed the city, had left behind only creeper-infested ruins and the fading memory of a rich culture cut short in its prime! Most of the structures are in a dilapidated condition under renovation.

The visit had exhausted us entirely, and feeling sorry for us, the guide called for the driver who reached us within minutes and drove us to the restaurant. The multi-course Cambodian lunch was served to us in true Khmer style. We chilled ourselves with a couple of beers. After lunch, dessert and some rest, the guide drove us back to visit the Angkor Wat structure. It was awesome to see its reflection in the pond in front of it.

Angkor Wat

Angkor Wat is the finest, most extensive and best preserved of all the temples of Angkor. A masterpiece of human creativity and ingenuity! Its reflection on the waterfront overgrown with lotus leaves and flowers created an aura of melody and rhythm, reflecting the general philosophy of life with its highs and lows in succession. The lofty splendor and vast proportions of the temple are believed to be the most massive religious structure in the world ever constructed. A legendary expression denotes that a divine hand must have been involved in the building of Angkor Wat. Built from 900–1200 AD with 25,000 laborers, it is comparable in achievement to the Egyptian pyramids. The structure is 850

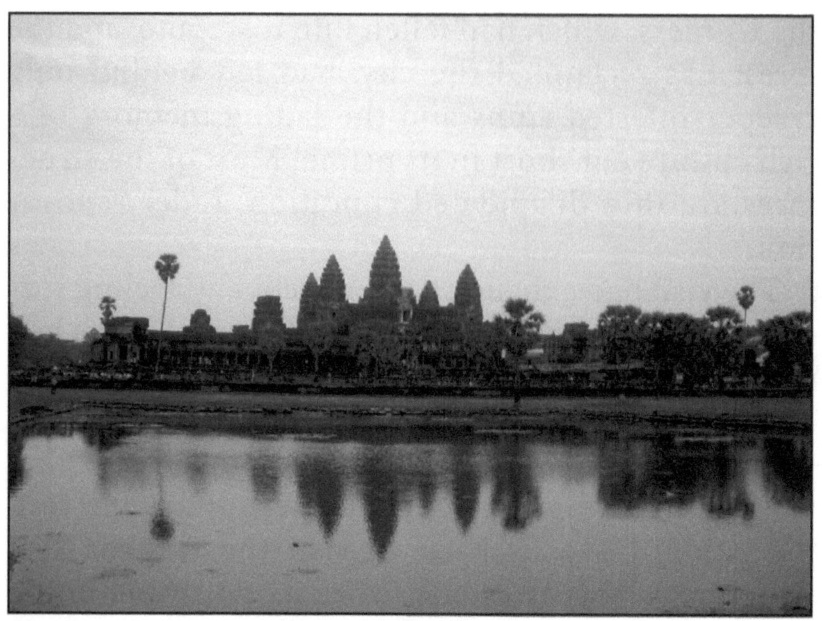

Angkor Wat Complex

meters wide. Angkor Wat Complex and 1,050 meters long, built with millions of tons of grey sandstone. Even more impressive is the intricate carving and sculpture of over 11,000 figurines, depicting life in Cambodia in the twelfth century in all its glory. Approached by a causeway, twice as long as the height of the tallest tower, the labyrinth of corridors is lined with elaborate sculptures and carvings, including a fifty-meter long wall frieze of legends about the churning of an 'ocean of milk,' a famous mythological episode in Hindu pantheism depicting the story of triumph of good over evil. It describes a tug of war between *Devas* (apsaras) representing naturally good and *asuras* (demons) symbolizing all that is evil. The ten-headed *Ravana* led the war using *Vasuki*, a long serpent that wound around a mountain.

The base of the hill was supported by a mammoth turtle (one of the *Lord Vishnu's* avatars), and the peak of the mountain, the Lord of *Goddess Indira*, balances the position to equilibrium to sustainment. At this juncture, the team of *Deva* and Asuras was in the process by jointly churning the Ocean of Milk to draw out the elixir of immortality to be possessed by each of their own group. The Asuras wanted the tail portion of the snake Vasuki. Thus, all the Devas were exposed to the proximity of the snake's head portion where the poison could exit. The snake Vasuki suffers to the ultimate, suddenly pumps out the deadly poison (Alakal). Fearing the consequences Lord Siva, seized it and swallowed the deadly poison and held the poison in his neck portion itself, that's how he becomes Nilakanta. The two teams of opponents were churning the ocean of milk, when physician of the Devas Dhanvantri, came with the elixir of immortality Lord Krishna in an attempt to prevent the potion from falling into the hands of the Asuras, incarnated to a beautiful damsel (Mohini) and enticed the Asuras and gave away the Amrita to the Devas.

Angkor Wat represents the pinnacle of Khmer art and culture, with the stunning blend of spirituality and symmetry, built by *King Suryavarman* II, compared to *King Louis XIV*, the builder of Versailles. *Suryavarman II* was one of the famous Khmer rulers, who elevated the worship of the Hindu god Vishnu to the state religion. Rectangular in the plan, the temple was once surrounded by a 400 feet wide moat with crocodiles, but it is slowly drying now. Angkor Wat reflects the supremacy of Khmer talent and creativity as observed in the fantastic art and architecture. Every inch of the iconic temple is covered with friezes, bas-relief ornate pillars with base and capitols, wall niches, with narratives from mythology, legends of *Puranas* and *Epics*. Different depictions of *Vishnu* and *Shiva's* avatars standing triumphantly after killing the demons could be seen. The bevy of apsaras, engraved with identical towering headdress and smiles in minute detail looked marvelous.

There was a sizeable surging crowd of tourists hurrying to and fro. But we took our own time walking around the temple. The stone blocks were kept in place by an interlocking system, and no binding material was employed. The rich tapestry, showcasing scenes from the *Ramayana, Mahabharata* and *Bhagavata Puranas* was exquisitely rendered.

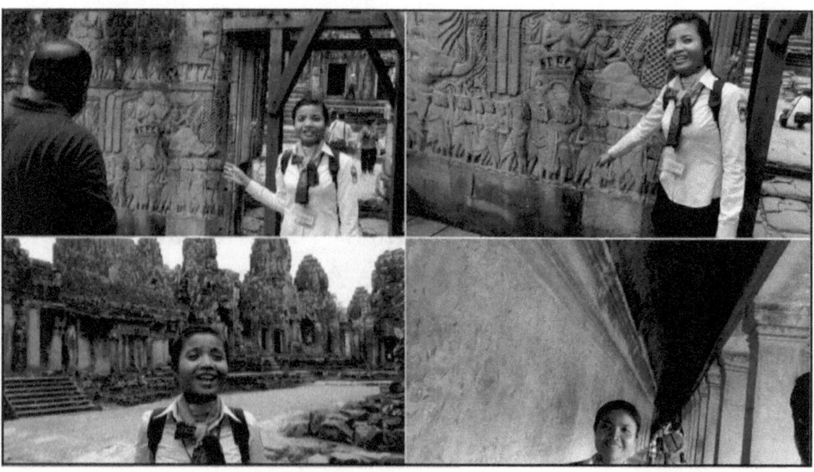

Bas-relief at Angkor Wat

At the entrance, on the right-hand side, there is the mandap, housing a giant statue of three-faced Vishnu, with his characteristic benign smile. The statue, hewn off a single block of sandstone, was initially placed precisely at the base of the central tower at the top, appropriate to his divinity and his glorified status in Hindu mythology, but later it was shifted to the present location when Buddhism was accepted as the state religion. Angkor Wat was believed to replicate the spatial universe in miniature form. The central tower, impressive in height, represents *Mount Meru*, providing ascension to the seat of the gods in heaven. The balustrades leading to the central temple are lined with sculptural heads of Nagas (cobras), representing the trials and tribulations that the human race is subjected to. The three-storeyed cultural temple complex is built of sandstone. The top storied bsists of five towers, the tallest one being sixty-five meters from ground level. It must have been the tower that had guided Henn Mouhot in his exploration and rediscovery of the vanished civilization of the Khmers.

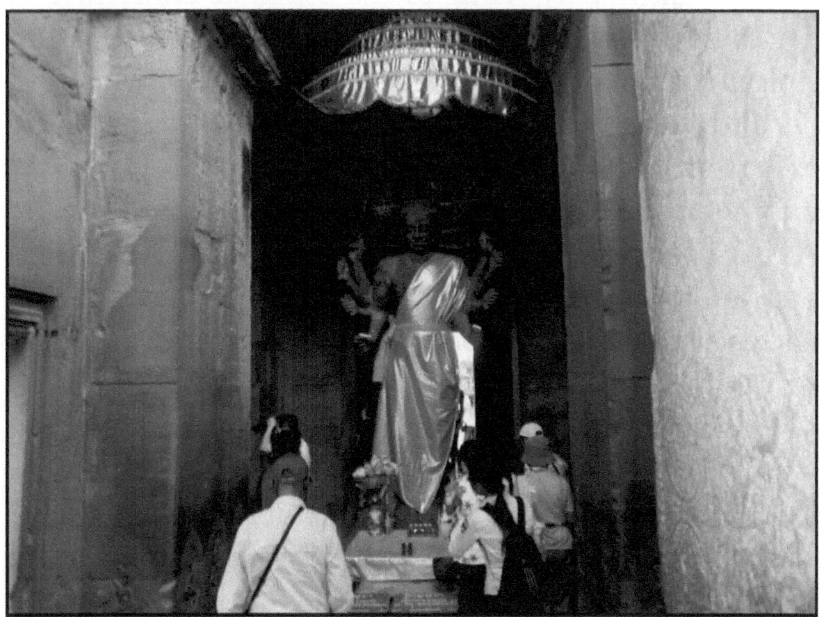

Three-faced Lord Vishnu at the Entrance

"It is greater than anything left to us by Greece or Rome," commented *Henn Mouhot* in 1860, when he beheld the beauty of the 1,000-year-old Angkor Wat temple that had remained veiled by Mother Nature for centuries. Mesmerized by the wonder that was revealed, *Mouhot* illustrated his discovery by writing in his diary, "A rival to that of Solomon, conceived and erected by some ancient Michelangelo." We readily agreed with the illustrious botanist's quotations. Angkor Wat appearing on the national flag is a point of deep pride to the Cambodians. This historic site was a *UNESCO-declared World Heritage Site* for its cultural and archaeological significance.

While entering the complex through the causeway, we noticed the monument being structured like a pyramid with three levels, each with rectangular galleries built around open courtyards in diminishing size, ultimately rising to the pinnacle consisting of five towers. It was distressing to see a once-great nation sink to such depths of depravity. People who had become victims losing their arms and legs in landmine explosions were seen singing in front of us. I should say it is the positive outcome of suffering, and thanks to the Angkor tourism, new business, more jobs, revitalized arts, and crafts, industrial explosions, etc., have started and contributed to a better tomorrow and a better-living standard!

Passing through a labyrinth of corridors and stepping up to reach a large terrace, we saw a raised podium with its large sculptural ornaments exhibiting impeccable craftsmanship. Was used as a dais for dancing. Dancing being part of the ancient Khmer religion, it was used as a form of paying homage to the gods. We spotted apsaras in glittering, colorful costumes. There were six damsels, rehearsing for a dance programme. Apsara dance dates back to a thousand years. It is an integral part of the culture of Cambodia. In this dance that we saw, the Apsara, a woodland spirit, is played by a woman wearing a tight-fitting traditional dress. Her graceful, sinuous gestures are codified to narrate the classical myths or religious stories.

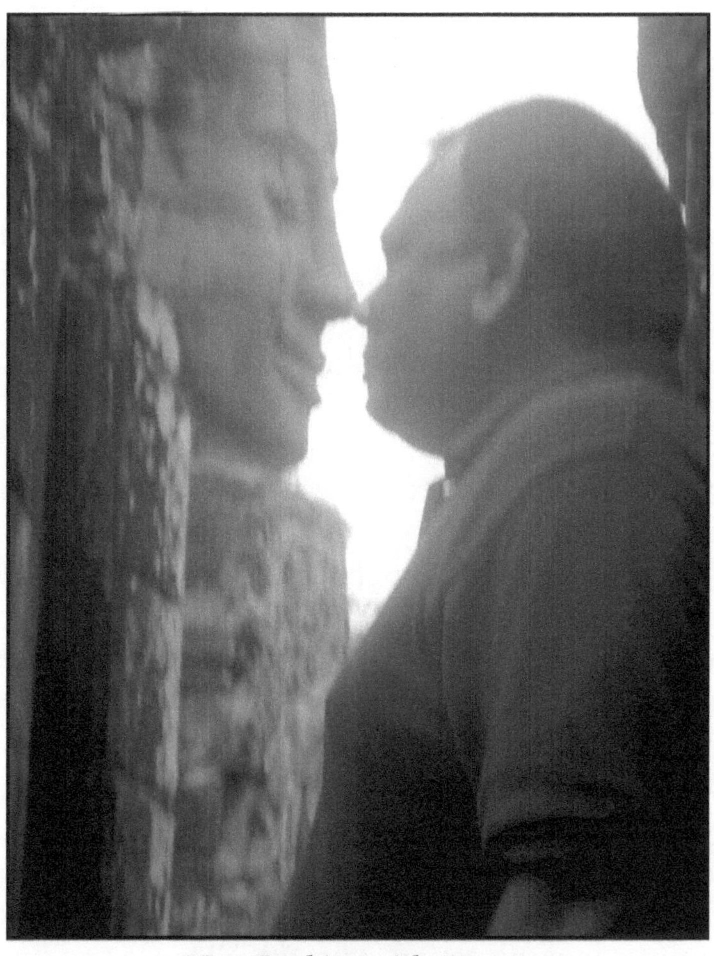

Nose Locking with Apsara

Nose locking with Apsara

In Hindu mythology, the Apsaras—similar to nymphs—are designated to inspire and enchant the gods, to spread peace and harmony for the welfare of humanity. The frescos on stone portray hundreds of apsaras sporting the same facial expressions. They are revered as one of the most famous contributions to the world of sculptural art during the era of Khmer civilization. The stone sculpture of apsaras wearing the veils did not cover their buxom bosoms. They were wearing tall headgears. We found that most of the visitors rest their hands on this bulbous carvings while entering the temple, leaving those parts of the stone little worn out.

With all curiosity, I stood spellbound looking at the apsaras, girls standing on the raised podium doing multiple steps with rhythm and grace. There was quite a bit of mixed crowd from all over the world watching the dance when suddenly something caught my eye! *ABCD (Any-Body-Can-Dance)* for a small fee levied for the tourists to participate in the dancing tutored by a dance master to do eight different steps with the seven apsara beauty dancers around you and you just have to follow the dance master's actions. I grabbed the opportunity to join the troupe paying $1 US. Harmonizing with their light, delicate movements and taking cues from the instructor, I soon blended with them in their rhythmical sequence. They gave me the benefit of occupying the center stage, dancing around me like a clam. As a part of the dance steps, I could grab and roll over the dancers. It was a fascinating experience, though short-lived. Honestly speaking, I thoroughly enjoyed it. To top it all off, as I finished the dance, a stunning-looking young lady with all grace and beauty came and shook hands with me, congratulating me. She just said, "Awesome." Then I opened up a conversation with her. She said that she had come from Nevada, USA. She was accompanying young friends from various parts of America. As we parted, she hugged me, leaving behind a critical thought for life. Embarrassed though I was with this undeserving adulation and her waxing eloquence about my quick understanding of the nuances of the dance form in a short period, I felt elated!

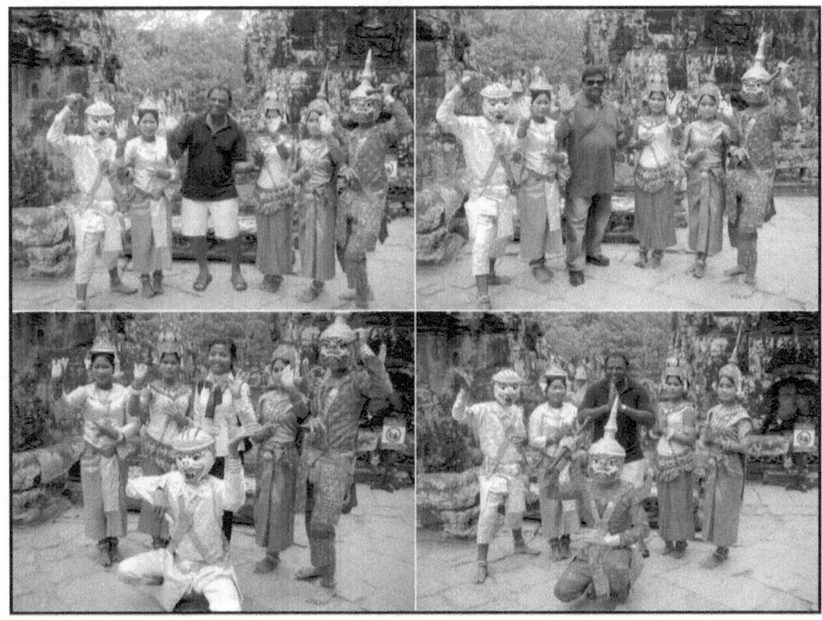

Dancing with Apsara Damsels

Angkor Wat Climbing Up

After completing the first and second stage of our visit, we ventured climbing up to the top of Angkor Wat. I fully endorse the view that Angkor Wat is not only the world's most substantial religious abode but is also the best preserved. Access to the vertigo-inducing height was by a steep ladder with no common landing platforms whatsoever en route. With one misstep, you will find yourself in the abyss below. As we approached the steep steps, the guide pulled away Gerald from us saying that he may not be fit enough to climb up. Gerald also was reluctant to climb up the ladder, since it had claimed many lives by tripping and falling down, but I was not perturbed at the forbidding height. I kept on encouraging him: "Yes, you can." I grabbed Gerald's hip with my right hand and helped him. "Do you really want to climb up to the terrace, Gerald?" asked our guide with anguish, as he placed his first step on the ladder leading to *Mount Meru.* No! This is not the Hindu mythological mountain of yore! The half conical structure housing the 'Vimana' is at the third level representing *'Mount Meru'* of Hindu mythology. Grabbing him all the way, I led him towards the top as Terry followed us. I kept instructing Gerald to keep looking up and moving forward along with me. I was panting, packed with the adrenaline-pumping moment when nearing the uppermost of the steps, my arms burnt with the build-up of lactic acid. I had to summon every ounce of my strength and braced myself to follow and be with him. The agony of my arms and hands quickly subsided, and I was overpowered by a euphoric sense of achievement.

Gerald was already panting from the effort of climbing the first two levels of the massive temple, and he was made the remaining steep flight at 70° to 80° gradient, to understand the fantastic technology fully behind this substantial man-made world heritage monument. We had to take a pause for some time before reaching the top. I held Gerald, we stood for almost three minutes to liven him up. I opened up his insight and knowledge of Hindu philosophy and its profound principles. I asked him how one should act in a given situation to be free of excessive indulgence in the mundane world and strive for spiritual enlightenment of the mind. He answered, "One must practice mental restraint and yet learn to remain effective in day-to-day life. Try 'anushasana,' a type of yoga, the discipline of self-examination, which alone can help an individual overcome the temptation that surrounds him and equip him with extra strength to meet with success." In the Bhagwat Gita, Sri Krishna tells Arjuna, "When a man's selfishness, violence, and pride are gone, and when greed and anger are no more, he sets himself free from the thought that 'this is mine' then he has risen up the mountain of the highest."

We climbed on further to complete our ascent. After conquering the height, Gerald would have realized the Buddha Statue at Top Centre; View from Top of Angkor

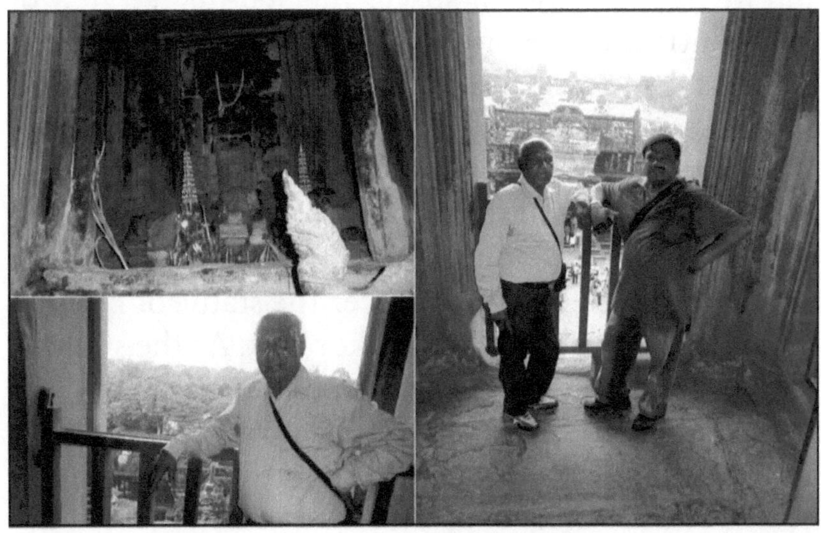

Buddha Statue at Top Centre; View from Top of Angkor Wat

Wat saying of the father of our nation, Mahatma Gandhi, "If I believe I cannot do it, it makes me incapable of doing it. But when I believe I can, then I acquire the ability to do it, even if I did not have it at the beginning."

Once Gerald reached the rooftop, he was amazed. Yes, *a-ma-a-zed* he was at the sumptuous splendor of the temple, especially at sunset! Oh! What a sight it was! No wonder it retains the honor of being one of the seven wonders of the ancient world. Excitement, thrill, with the feelings alternated when we were on the terrace. An ideal location for both a photo shoot and the heart to skip more than a few beats. No words can describe the beauty of the composite, symmetrical carvings, bas-relief with the four towers at the four corners and a lofty tower in the middle."Oh! How fascinating it is!" Gerald expressed with joy. Wholeheartedly I agreed. We were indeed at the foot of Mount Meru, reaching for the heavens, an evening never, ever to be forgotten. Crowds of tourists had gathered there, and we had to jostle for space. The 360-degree view of the countryside at sunset was absolutely breathtaking. We managed to find some quiet spot from which to enjoy the view and talked to a few orange-robed Buddhist monks. We felt that we were halfway between the earth below and the heavens above, overwhelmed with a desire to renounce all worldly affairs and endeavor to search for inner peace. The statue of Buddha stands at the top center of Angkor Wat. As the sun was setting gradually, we started descending last, and we were warned to decelerate the pace of our descent. I led Gerald in front. As Gerald stepped on terra firma, he was slightly short of breath. "Are you okay, Gerald?" asked our guide with much concern. Gerald revived after drinking a bottle of water mixed with jaggery, and I thought he would have preferred 'martini' to numb his discomfort.

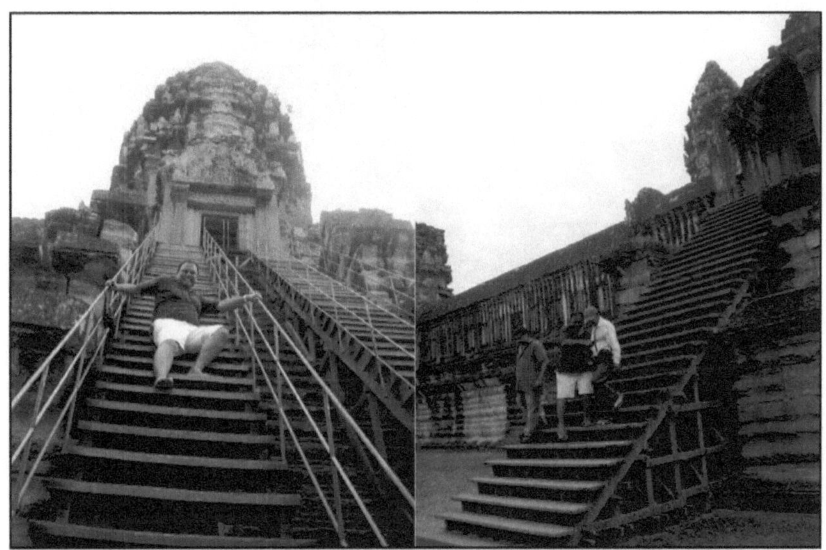

Top Tier at Angkor Wat

Angkor Wat symbolizes the belief that reaching the kingdom of gods is no easy task. (A word of warning: this steep climb, to the top level of the temple, is *not* for weak hearts, for it has claimed several victims in the past.) *Thank God for sparing us from being unclaimed.* If you decide to climb up to the terrace and throw the words of caution to the winds, my advice would be this: Drink enough water, wear good gripping shoes, and above all, charge your energy bars to the fullest. So the choice is entirely yours; whether you want to turn to history or mythology, mysticism, religion or architecture, there is plenty of everything from the remains of the bygone era.

We were exhausted; hence we took some time to ease ourselves. The sun was setting. The guide took us.

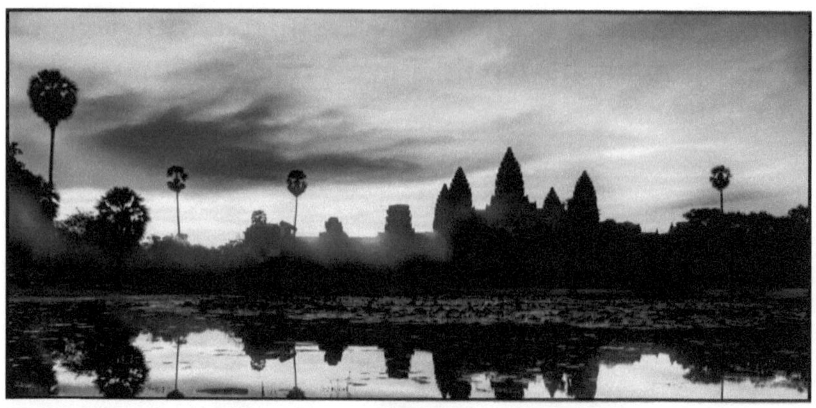

Angkor Wat at Sunset

Angkor Wat at Sunset to the exit rear gate. Before entering the Angkor Wat, she had told us that she would throw a question to us at the end of this visit to Angkor Wat. As we descended from the top of Angkor Wat, she led us to a separate podium and asked us how long each of us thought it would have taken Suryavarman II to complete this enormous structure. While Terry's guess was twelve years, Gerald's was eighteen years. Backed by my knowledge in engineering, I put it down to forty years. Immediately, the sweet guide shook my hand and said I was almost right. It had actually taken forty-two years for completion. She led us outside, and the car was waiting for us to drive us to the vantage point to view the sunset of Angkor Wat. There was quite a good crowd waiting to see the awesome spectacle; we were not disappointed like many others. We were not betrayed, we were thrilled by the remarkable beauty of the setting Sun and the glow of its kaleidoscopic colors creating silent music in the air. The enchanting vision of the sinking Sun rejuvenated us, and we reveled in its glory. Visitors enthusiastically clicked their cameras left, right and center. As we stood astounded, I started moving in haste to different vantage points, clicking my camera to record this remarkable, mind-boggling vision when I accidentally stepped into a patch of muddy clay near the water. I fell like a log hurting myself. I got up with a twisted ankle as a result of this fall. The picturesque view in front of me took over my pain initially. As time passed, we began to move forward. Our guide was considerate enough to take me to a place to change my clothes seeing my clothes muddy.

As we walked, we met a historian among the tourists who claimed to have profound knowledge about the mysterious eclipse that destroyed the entire medieval Cambodian society of Angkor, five hundred years after it was founded. The prosperous Khmer empire collapsed mysteriously by the middle of the fifteenth century, leaving a mystery as high as that of the end of the era of the Indus Valley civilization. The population estimated to be over a million had apparently disappeared and gone forever! "This is a great mystery that still challenges our mind," he said. "It had become a lost city. The artistic genius and engineering achievement were devoured by the dense Cambodian jungle!" Based on his own assumptions, he explained to us in detail that a deluge at the Mekong River must have caused the destruction. Perhaps when the river was in spate, a kind of fatal disease would have affected them. And he went on and on. We felt bored stiff soon with his pedantic 'research-oriented' lecture! We soon dashed to our waiting car with our guide.

We moved further off from there crossing the Banteay Srei area. On the way, I saw a lone, old lady taking shelter in an abandoned, dilapidated, haunted-looking cave in

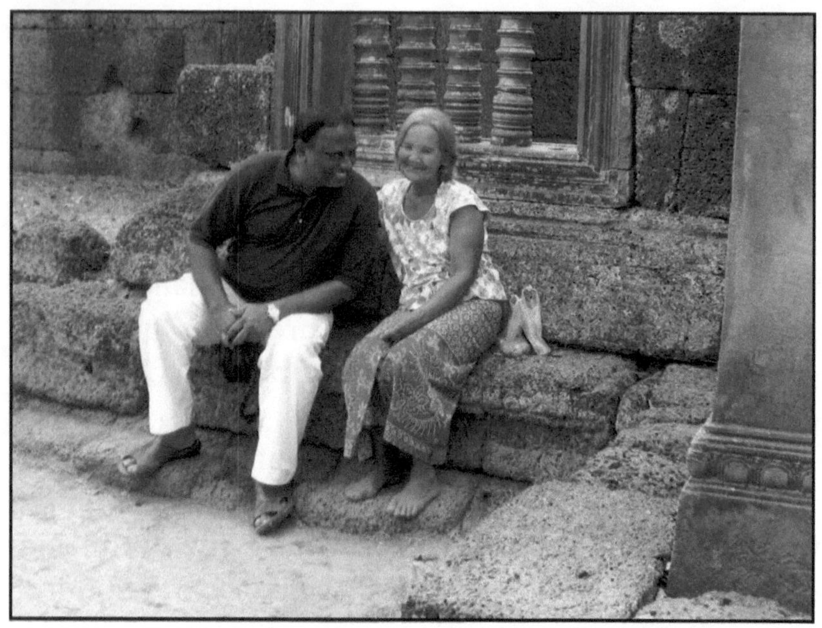

Narrating Nocturnal Activities at Angkor Wat

a corner. I stopped the car and walked towards her. The way she was staring at us gave Gerald and Terry the creeps. The stare and her look of so menacing, raising a sort of demonic feeling in them. Most striking of all was her tone of absolute authority, and it gave us a shiver, even in the heat. While it was scary for Terry and Gerald, I spontaneously stepped forward towards the old lady. I looked into her eye and held my hand out to embrace her, which she reciprocated spontaneously. I held her gently, made her sit on a small rock and both of us began to chat in sign language. She seemed to convey to me that the goddess from heaven would descend every night to perform an 'Apsara' dance ritual to the god, making a thundering noise that would echo through the place. The woman told us that she used to hear terrible noises together with fits of laughter and sometimes the sound of hooves. She would see an apparition of soldiers riding in their combat uniform brandishing blood-soaked unearthly hours. This mystery keeps human beings away from this sacred place at nights. I had always been interested in knowing about ghosts. (I was reminded of some fascinating Gothic tales of mythical messiahs waking from their thousand years of sleep, of vampires and the castle of Dracula, being reincarnated, as something surreal and strange around the neighborhood.)

I readily believed every word of the woman's description of the paranormal events, pushing the boundaries of my knowledge of the unseen world beyond the limit. Dismissing the duo who were jeering at me for my gullibility, I trusted every word of her spooky and spine-chilling narration. I am a guy who loves to walk into the hall for classic horror movies (*The Vampire Diaries, Haunted Nights*). Paranormal series are the favorites that let me feel a kind of shiver run down my spine while watching the scary scenes projected on the screen—*with my eyes covered, of course!*

As it was getting darker and night fell upon us, we went shopping at the *Noon-to-Night* market set on the river bank. It was excellent fun bargaining with good humor for the handicrafts and souvenirs with shopkeepers, who too reciprocated our joyous attitude. Later, we befriended a Cambodian family, who regaled us in the company of their children with folk music and dancing. They became so friendly with us within forty-five minutes that they offered us Cambodian coffee, brewed with the secret of their family recipe, that lingered in our taste buds for many days to come. When offered money for the coffee, they graciously refused to accept.

While we were on our way to the great temple of Angkor, I could feel a sense of foreboding that I had never felt before. A strange premonition of a distant time and remote world of lost cities came back to life in front of me as I stood transfixed, gazing at the statutes of Khmer gods, many of them appearing to be terrifying and fiendish!

Incidentally, a plan is afoot to build an enormous temple dedicated to Lord Rama in Bihar, India. When the main facade of the proposed temple was made public, it was claimed to be a replicated version of Angkor Wat. The Cambodian government, reacting to the 'plagiarised' version of its own iconic twelfth-century temple, conveyed their displeasure to the government of India. Though the proposed structure bears a striking similarity, the Indian government, averting a possible diplomatic row, said that the existing one at Cambodia dramatically differs from that of the proposed temple with eighteen shikaras (spires), whereas Angkor Wat has only nine shikaras. The proposed temple will also be more massive in size with the central tower (gopuram) inspired not only by Angkor Wat but also by the Madurai Meenakshi Amman and Rameswaram temples. Moreover, there is no international law prohibiting replication of any architectural monuments. A few years back, a plagiarised version of the Taj Mahal in Agra was being built in Bangladesh, and the government of India did not raise any objection (from the report that appeared in *The Hindu,* September 2012).

In my opinion, Siem Reap is a place that refrains from being duplicated. It is a 'postcard' town in the country of Cambodia, the handiwork of erstwhile builders from the early Khmer settlers. It has now become a hot spot for globetrotters.

It is interesting to know that as a contrast, the striking similarity of the heritage town of Hallstatt in Vienna was attempted by the Chinese in building a Siamese twin of this heritage town in its Southern province. Being smitten by its Baroque style where at every turn and glimpse its architectural elegance would amaze the visitors, the Chinese went ahead to create the duplicate version of this town down south of their country. This might give a chance to the Austrian government to start with 'Town Patent' to avoid further 'Made in China' adventure.

I began to feel the pain from my sprain; hence, I retired to bed while Terry and Gerald carried on with their personal work. Later on, I understood they had a wonderful Khmer massage followed by a visit to a pub where they had come across many multi-national tourists and had the pleasure of the company of beautiful, fun-loving Cambodian girls.

Banteay Samre

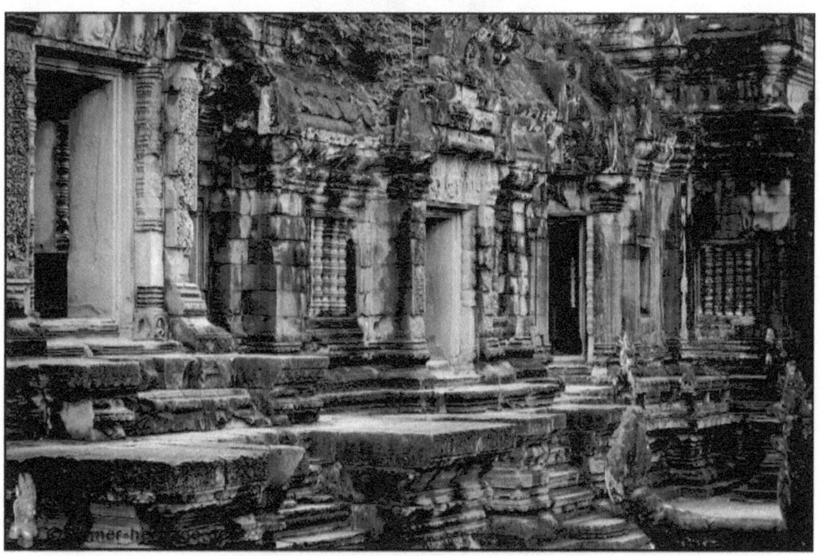

Temple of Banteay Samre

The following morning, we went for an hour-long drive to *Banteay Samre* combining with a visit to *Banteay Srei*. Banteay Samre dates around the same period as Angkor Wat built by *Suryavarman II* and *Yasodhavarman*. Due to meticulous renovation, preservation is at its best. One had to walk through a long five-hundred-foot-long Processional Avenue, lined with a 'naga-headed' balustrade, leading to a staircase flanked by seated lions. The central temple has four wings preceded by a vast hall. The whole complex is enclosed by two massive laterite walls, with a deep and wide moat all around (now dried up). The wings consist of a library, mandap, and parterre. Unlike Angkor Wat, it is horizontal in layout rather than vertical, architecturally looking more like Angkor Wat.

Banteay Srei

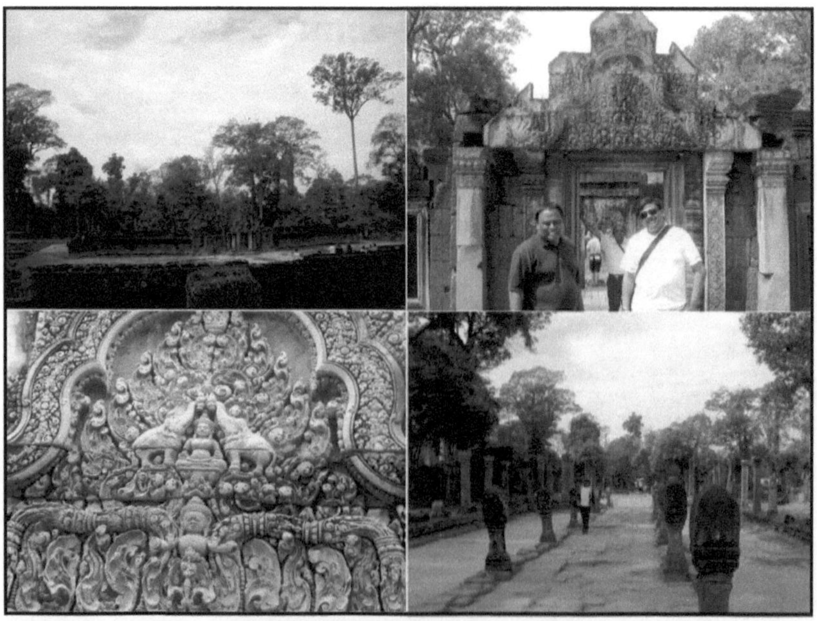

Banteay Srei Hindu Temple - Dedicated to Lord Shiva

Continuing on a dirt road about four hundred meters to the east, we were proceeding to visit *Banteay Srei*. It is a Hindu temple dedicated to Lord Shiva, his consort *Uma*, and *Nandi* (the bull). Sculptures of voluptuous Devadasis adorn the wall niches. Hence the temple is known as 'citadel of women.' The smooth touch and filigree work in bas-reliefs reflect the feminine touch. The temple is square in plan with entrances from the east and west with two intermediate entrances on either side. The central towers are decorated with male and female divinities, especially with scenes from the Ramayana. The masonry walls are of sandstone. Pink-hued, the surface is receptive and reflective of the changing colors of the sunlight. Sandstone is a soft material lends itself for intricate carvings that are profusely seen on the exterior as well as interior. The sizeable sculptural ornament exhibits impeccable craftsmanship. Banteay Srei is a masterpiece and jewel in the crown of Khmer art and architecture! As we completed the visit, I found that though the entire Angkor had the characteristics of the stone works of the Tamilian style, it had, besides, massive structures that involved hard physical labor. Banteay Srei is a tiny temple built with soft red sandstone. It also seems to have the Brahminic influence during *Rajendravarman II*.

Just after this visit, the pain that had started the day before began to increase. This was due to the strain of walking excessively to visit *Banteay Samre* and *Banteay Srei*. While driving across the village, we were surprised to find scores of vultures perched on the trees and rocky places. It was a fantastic gathering of these long-winged birds of prey on the face of a steep slide. This species is on the brink of extinction across Asia. We felt the vultures of Cambodia would have given hope to the conservationists.

Since my pain increased and my ankle started swelling drastically, I requested the guide to stop the car at the wayside village. I saw some small street vendors and a tiny tent shop selling natural herbal oil and also various silk scarfs and handicrafts, which were the handiwork of the local people. As we got down from the car, I saw to my surprise that the layout seemed to resemble southern Tamil Nadu with palm trees, other plantation, and bushes. For a moment, I thought I was visiting my native place in the southern part of Tamil Nadu. I struck a kinship with these people sentimentally, as we Tamilians are also very simple, straight, kind and soft-hearted. One elderly lady, seeing the plight of my feet, offered to give my feet a herbal oil massage for a meager amount. It was everything. Terry and Gerald bought a lot of handicrafts from those poor vendors who were also prepared to get palm toddy drawn directly from palm trees.

Since the guide said it was time for our lunch, which had been arranged in a pleasant Cambodian environment decorated with all ethnic curios, we drove to the restaurant. It was indeed the most delightful place for a little relaxation. As usual, we were treated warmly. We were given two chopsticks. The waitress faithfully taught us how to use them, though we failed many times. She could do it with ease, and I had promised her I would come back especially to learn this art. I felt Cambodia was a home away from home. I was touched by the warmth and hospitality of the people. The lunch was delicious. We were served with all courtesy as usual. We started with a couple of beers followed by a pretty good spread of Cambodian cuisine, ending with a lovely dessert.

As we stepped out of the restaurant, I again noticed my feet had swollen severely. I requested the guide to take me to a pharmacy. And we drove to the marketplace in town and took me to a pharmacy. I saw charming young ladies at the counter. They were unimaginably beautiful with bodies in perfect proportion. I noticed they did not have the same Khmer features. Hence, it is my opinion that the main cities in Cambodia consist of different ethnic groups from neighboring countries. The moment I looked at the youthful beauties, my pain seemed to diminish a wee bit. I explained my problem to the staff at the counter. Immediately she came out, looked at my feet and suggested some medicine. I also requested her if she could arrange for some physical treatment and a bandage. After I bought those medicines, I was made to sit on a stool. Another lady took the medication and knelt down in front of me with her thighs crossed. She was wearing a short, black skirt with a white shirt stuck to her body. As she knelt down and started cleaning my feet with the cleansing solution, moved from left to right and her knees seemed to move in rhythm. The process brought me great pleasure, and the pain vanished in no time! I was engrossed looking at her through and through. My emotion seemed to pass through my leg. After cleaning my legs, she probably got startled and gently looked up to see me gazing into her eyes. With a slight grin, she went back to her operation, started bandaging my leg with medicine and got up. As she juggled her body with constant movement, the top button of her shirt slightly gave way. I sat mesmerized, staring at her even after she had finished her work and moved off. Terry stood next to me muttering, "Must you come and flirt here also?" While I was happy and chirpy, he was annoyed. I was helped to get up to thank the staff at the counter. I looked for the attendant who dressed me, but she had gone to the next shop for some purpose. I waited. As she came back, I gave her a good tip. This incident brought an end to my pain throughout the entire trip away from home.

Prea Khan

With renewed vigor, we set out to visit Prea Khan (sacred swords), one of the largest complexes at Angkor with rows of vaulted corridors with exquisite carvings. It was built during the reign of Jayavarman VII but was later completed by following rulers. It has its past shunting between Hinduism and Buddhism and vice versa. It is located northwest of Angkor Thom. The structure has a central tower for Buddhism with satellite Hindu temples. But most of it is destroyed and needs renovation. It was once a center of religious learning and doctrines modeled after the ancient Buddhist Nalanda University in Bihar, India. Though it consisted of Buddhist and Hindu temples, it also had libraries and places for academic pursuits. As per Indian history, Nalanda was ransacked and destroyed in 1193 by Ikhtiyar ad-Din Muhammad Bin Bakhtiyar Khilji, a Turkish military general. The complex was so vast that it burned for three months. (Pity! Burning down educational institutions, library, museum, etc., had been a tragic, lamentable and lunatic part of human history.))

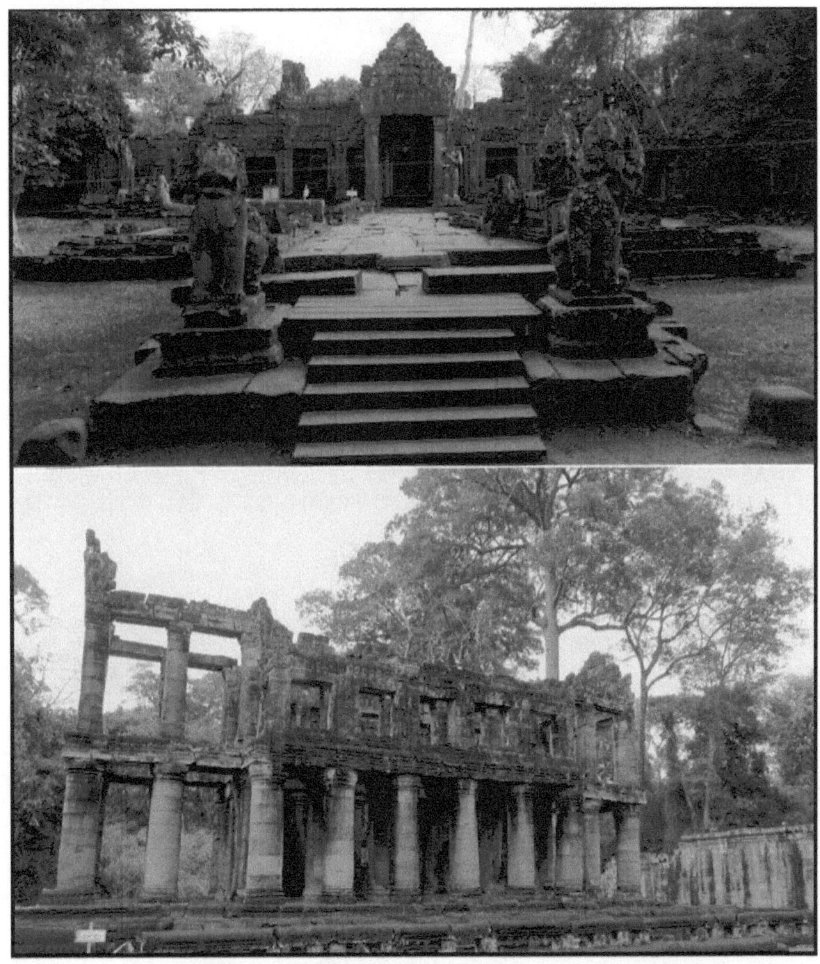

Prea Khan Temple and Library Building

Ta Prohm

On the way back, almost at sunset, we visited the Ta Prohm temple. Like Prea Khan, this was also built by Jayavarman VII and later completed by other rulers. It is not only a Buddhist site but also dedicated to Hindu gods. A visit to this place is an absolute must for tourists. Looking at the temple, we see it has been left to be swallowed by the jungle through centuries. We were choked with emotion as we clambered over the fallen pillars and saw the giant roots of the trees and their trunks embedded on the walls. We stood there aghast by the awesome power of the jungle with its muscular system embracing and intertwining the monuments with its roots and vines showing its triumph over man-made structures. It is deliberately left to be choked by two trees, evoking memories of scenes from the movie Raiders of the Lost Ark. The sight of the roots of the temple trees, embracing large stone blocks of the ruins is truly spectacular. It is a rare scene of nature in combat with human endurance.

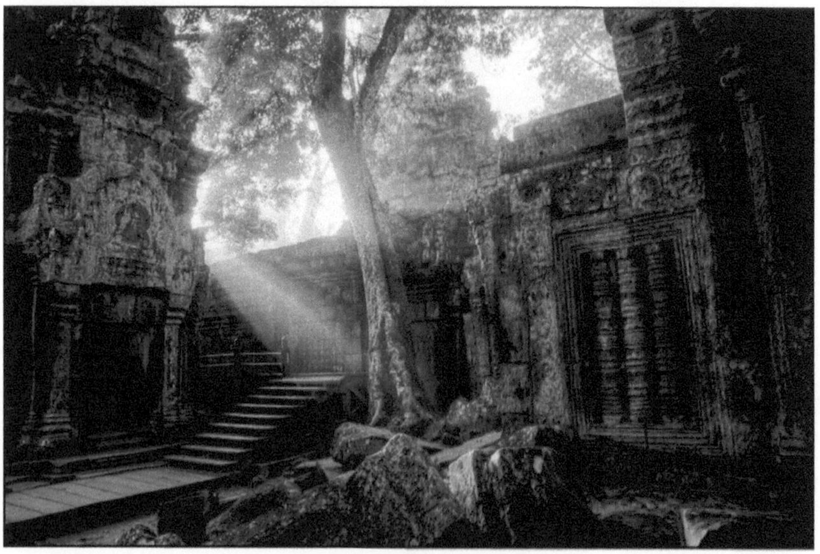

Ta Prohm Temple

Standing still, looking at the plight of the temple, we felt that our cameras and handy cams would want to freeze this image eternally.

Massive silk cotton trees had gradually grown on the 'vimanas' of the shrine which had been built around 1181 AD. A bunch of international tourists had been queuing up from early morning to see the ravages of time. Some trees grow over the complex are more than forty meters tall.

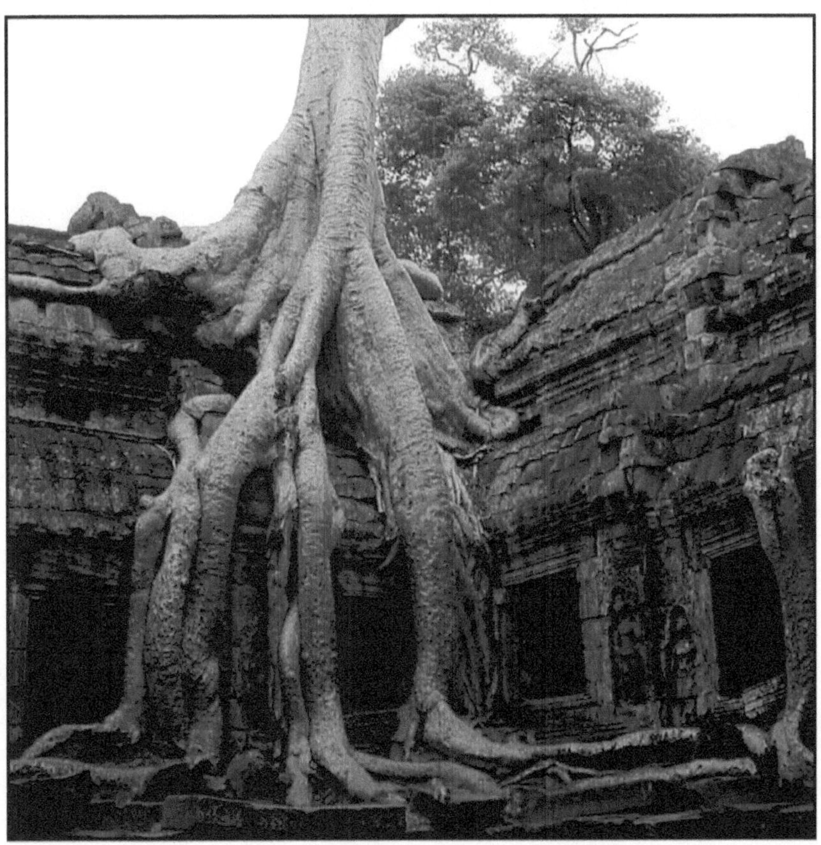

Ta Prohm Temple

Interestingly, the restoration work of the heritage building had been entrusted to the Archaeological Survey of India under the aegis of UNESCO. Safeguarding the architectural authenticity of the monument is of utmost importance.

UNESCO has strictly prescribed cutting of any tree to point out to visitors the significance of the co-existence of trees and man-made structures. This temple is an outstanding monument built of sandstone blocks, interlocked without any binding material. The Indian Institute of Technology, Madras, is helping ASI (Archaeological Survey of India) to resolve the structural stability of the monuments.

Neak Pean

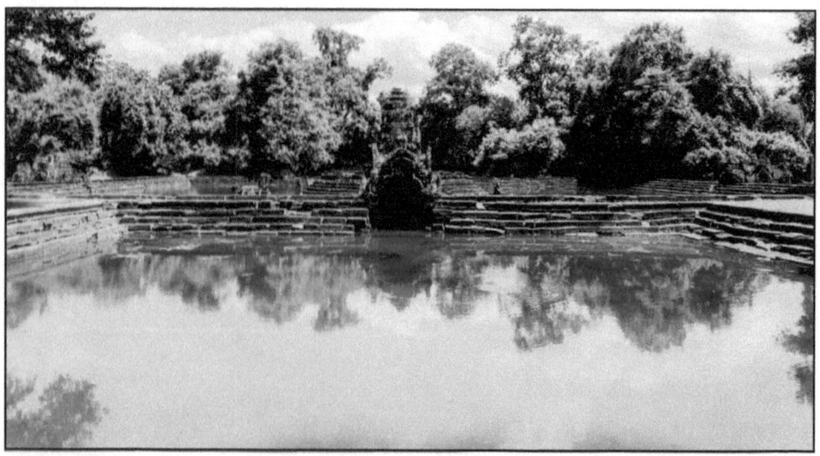

Neak Pean Temple

As Ta Prohm and Prea Khan, this is also built by Jayavarman VII conceptually for medical purposes. Four artificial ponds were created at the center of the Buddhist Nagas which were set to go around these ponds and induce a mythical medicinal effect. Bathing in these ponds would help the people get rid of their illness. This structure served mainly as a hospital. After visiting all the traditional historical places, we proceeded to visit Theam's house.

Theam's House: Training Centre for Artists

Theam's House, the home-cum-art-gallery of the Cambodian artist and designer *Lim Muy Theam*, was started in 1995. Lim Muy Theam is a restlessly creative individual, and this can be seen in every aspect of his self-designed studio/home. His media include lacquers, painting, and sculpture with pieces that are uniquely expressive of Theam while maintaining a strong Khmer ethics. He has created a new aesthetic art incorporating both Khmer tradition and contemporary international styles, hoping to breathe new life into Cambodian handicrafts.

I find the Cambodians living abroad show a lot of interest in their home country; some of the overseas educated Cambodians with proper training in art and interior designing have started the *Theam's House* to help the young Cambodian artists develop into great artists. This is a perfect training center for budding artists. The founder seems to have been educated at *École des Beaux-Arts de Paris in France.*

The gallery is located off the main road to the Angkor temples surrounded by a lush, green garden. The art studio offers training in painting, fine arts, sculpting and lacquering. You can buy handmade products made by locals, thereby supporting and nurturing young Cambodians.

Being our last night stay in Siem Reap, we were driven to the hotel to freshen up. And then we were taken for a prearranged dinner by the tour agent at a top-end restaurant, offering a wide range of international flavors with classical Apsara dance, very dear to the tourists. We were led to the center table since it was a special dance arranged particularly for us. We included our guide also for dinner. The stage in front of us slowly got filled with musicians. As the music started, the seven apsara dancers began to fill in one by one. The rhythm and sequence of the dance were beautiful beyond description, and every step and expression had a mythical meaning. The Apsara, a woodland spirit, was played by a beautiful woman, seen in a tight-fitting traditional dress, as though she was poured into the suit, rather than wearing it, and whose sinuous gestures were codified to narrate classical myths. 'A masterpiece of oral and intangible culture,' as eulogized by UNESCO in 2003. The costume of the leading dancer was a faithful reproduction of an apsara, as found on the bas-relief at Angkor Wat! We found it to be a rare opportunity to learn more about the people and their ancestral culture. The Khmer apsara dance, dating back a thousand years, fuelled our excitement about the beautiful apsara dance in its many forms. The Cambodian classical dancing is always graceful, and the sensual movement and footwork of the girls attired as apsaras can only be seen to be believed. They related the folklore in a unique presentation of their graceful dance movements. This artistic extravaganza, elevated by classical music, was so vivid and enthralling that we fell in love with it. The dancers looked like Apsara goddesses coming back to life to give a live performance. I could recall all the sculptural faces that I had observed earlier in Angkor Wat. The Khmer god and goddess had a special smile in sculptural form, and this was replicated on the faces of the Apsara dancers.

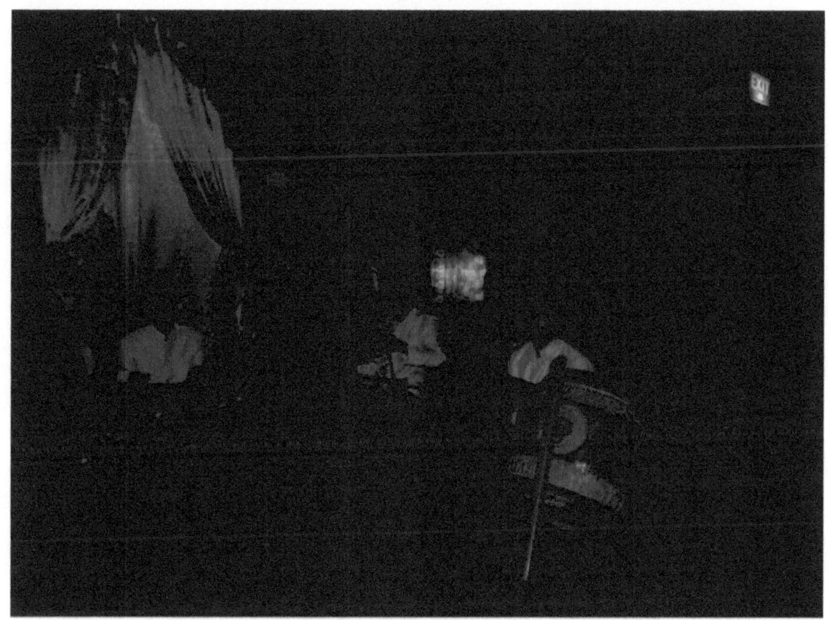

Cambodian Orchestra

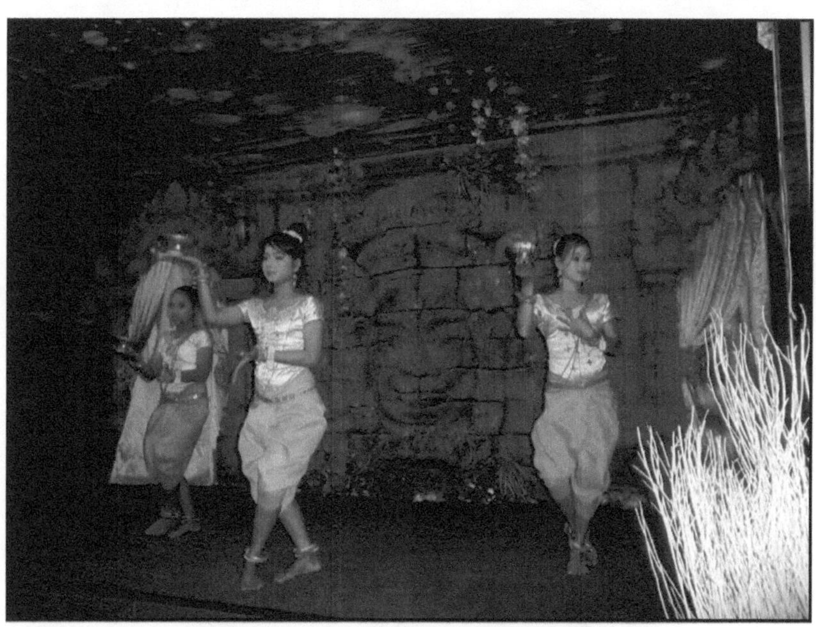

Special Dinner with Apsara Dance

While we were watching the live performance, dinner was served in true Cambodian style. It was delicious with different spreads. We were served soups, lamb and fried rice followed by delicious desserts of wobbly caramel puddings, pineapple slices and cheesecake on top. One of the best desserts we ever had in the city! We then drove back to our hotel.

Our guide was a typical Cambodian, and her knowledge of the historical and ancient culture seemed to be authentic. During our drive to the appointed hotel, we asked her how she chose her profession as a tourist guide. She told us that she was basically a stay-at-home daughter, but this present work of her choice was not only challenging and rewarding but also exciting. Mingling with strangers and sharing the greatness of her place gave her a sense of achievement. Most of the visitors were endearing though some were exasperating, she added. But during the off-season time (monsoon period) when the number of tourists trickles down, she used to take a big chunk of her time off to get back into her sweatpants and return to her old times, helping her mom in the kitchen, playing with her siblings and friends. While engaging in general conversation, Terry enquired about the status of her hotel where she was lodging. As she dropped us off at the hotel, which was a 4-star one, she quietly turned around to Terry and said, "Million stars! I sleep under a million stars and enjoy Nature in all her majesty!" She was a perfect picture of contentment, no cringing, no self-pity, no feeling of remorse, and not even striving to reach for the stars on the surface of the earth! This seemed to hang over her head all the time. We then retired for a complete rest since we had to start early in the morning.

Tonle Sap Lake

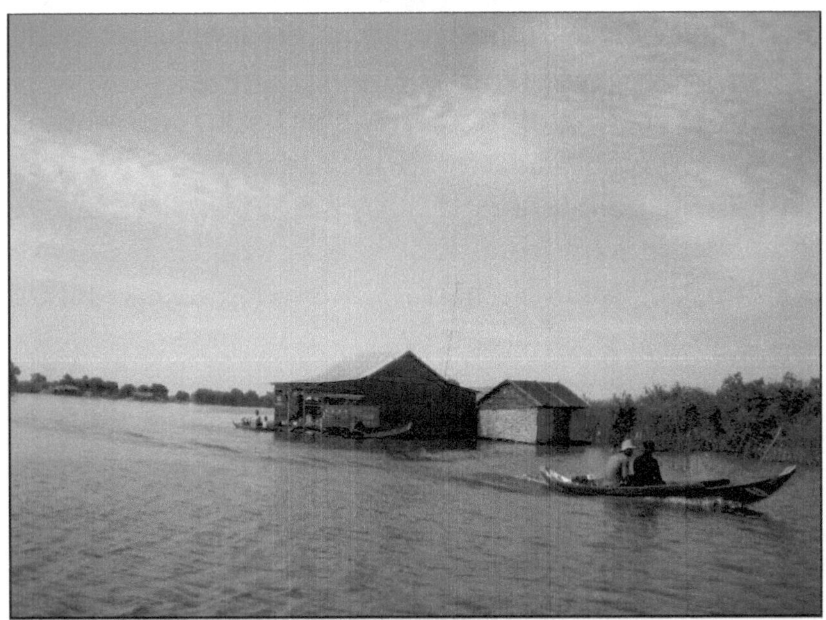

Tonle Sap Lake

In the early hours of the misty morning, we drove towards the great lake Tonle in a sylvan surrounding. Before getting into the boat, on the way we visited an informative exhibition regarding Tonle Sap Lake, its environment and life system around. The Tonle Sap Lake is linked to the sea via the Tonle Sap River, which converges with the massive Mekong River in Phnom Penh. Water has always been an important resource for Cambodia, as it is the origin of its creation. According to legend, the Khmer people were colonized in the first century by peaceful neighbors from India, and the combination of the two cultures eventually formed the kingdom of Cambodia.

Tonle Sap Lake sustains all forms of life human beings, birds, sea mammals, and wild animals. The *slow* boat ride on the lake was gentle and pleasant. We saw people living in stilt houses just above the water. The people in this village are eco-friendly and live in harmony with nature. I feel, we, modern citizens are greedy, and in striving for betterment pollute and destroy the environment. We should learn a lot from these simple people. They have even floating schools, markets, villages, various culture farms and so on. I find they lack only medical facility, which has induced me to work collectively with like-minded people to start a free mobile hospital on the boat through which one could serve these people at all times even during maternity and other critical emergencies. We stepped out to visit the *Floating Market*, a value-based shopping center. We bought a lot of stuffed dolls, souvenirs, etc.

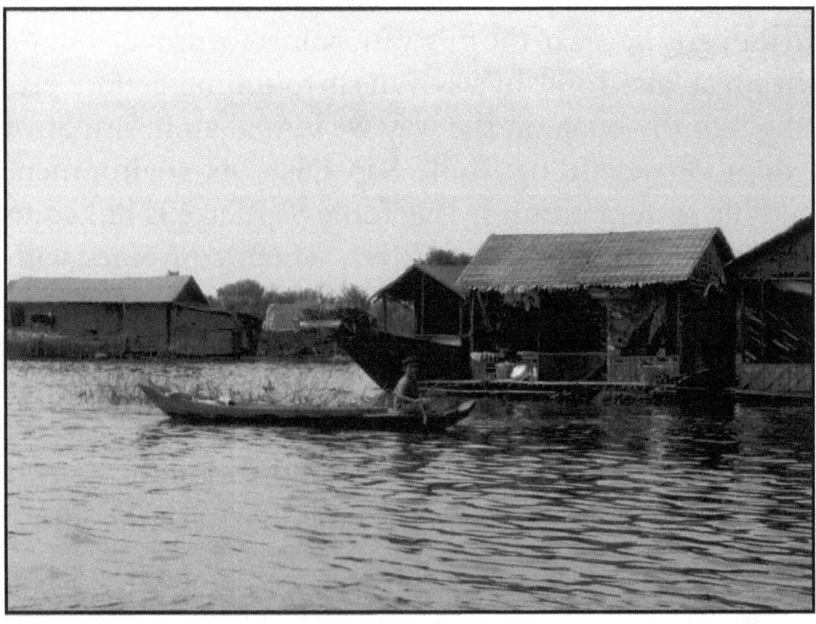

Floating Village at Tonle Sap Lake

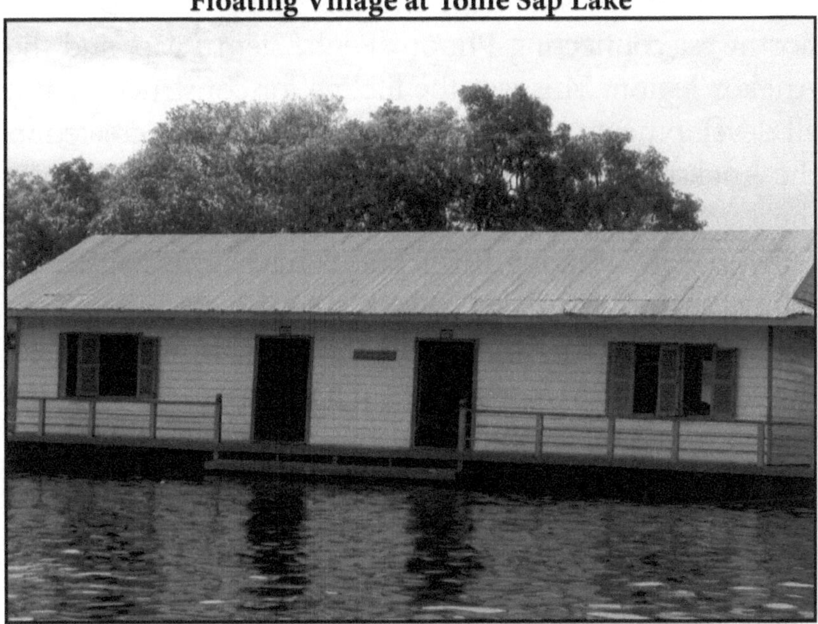

Floating School at Tonle Sap Lake

I find the ancient traders from South India had contributed much to develop this entire region. They had blended with the local people taught them various ways of trade and an eco-friendly lifestyle. The South Indians were very advanced in their irrigation system. Their engineering knowledge in all fields was par excellence. Even during the Stone Age, they had thought ahead of the times, and as a result, during the Middle Ages, a great Chola king *Karikalan* had built a dam and named it *Kallanai* because of the stone masonry. This dam has survived and is in use even now. It is said to be the oldest dam ever built. Thus the Tamils merged with the Khmers to create one of the greatest irrigational resources in Cambodia. This was the beginning of Tonle Sap Lake. Tonle Sap Lake was formed by connecting craters made by nature to the Tonle Sap River and Mekong River, which lies in the southeast and fills up the lake up to the northwest connecting Phnom Penh, Siem Reap, and the Angkor region. This was the lifeline for construction and all developments of architectural wonders ever created in the Angkor region in the past. This is the only lake where the water flows both ways according to seasons. During the rainy season, Mekong River floods into Tonle Sap River, filling the Tonle Sap Lake, which creates a catchment area of about 16,500 sq. Km. During the dry season, water gets flushed into the Mekong River in a reverse direction. This creates a natural cleaning and flushing system for a new life. During the dry season, the lake shrinks to 3,000 sq. Km only, the depth is a little less than a meter high; in the rainy season, it rises above twenty-nine meters, the water source being the Tibetan Himalayas. Accordingly, people living in stilt houses also fabricate their dwelling units, and this is an engineering marvel. Besides the architectural wonders, this phenomenon impressed me the most—nature at its best. After this visit, we proceeded to *Les Artisans d'Angkor,* 'the Artisans' Village.'

Visit to the Artisans' Village in Cambodia

We had a fantastic, great time visiting 'Les Artisans d'Angkor,' which has developed from the ambitious belief that it is possible to revive the ancient Khmer arts and crafts while improving the lives of thousands of people living in rural areas.

The artisans of Angkor have dedicated themselves to the preservation of the traditional Khmer skills in silk weaving, stone, and wood carving, lacquering, and painting. They also promote the development of individuals and secure their future through technical education and welfare.

Today, there are over 1,500 employees involved in keeping the Cambodian handicrafts alive and more creative than ever. The artisans try hard to be a timeless showcase for Cambodian crafts with pieces inspired by the Angkor heritage, as well as fashionable handmade clothing and decorative items that suit even contemporary lifestyles. 'Les Artisans d'Angkor' provides craft training to young Cambodians. We proceeded on to visit the Killing Fields, a grim reminder of the most horrifying history in the recent past.

Pol Pot: Demystified

Choeung Ek: Infamous Killing Field (a one-time beautiful orchard), now the site for communal graves where thousands of skulls are visible behind a clear glass-fronted memorial stupa.

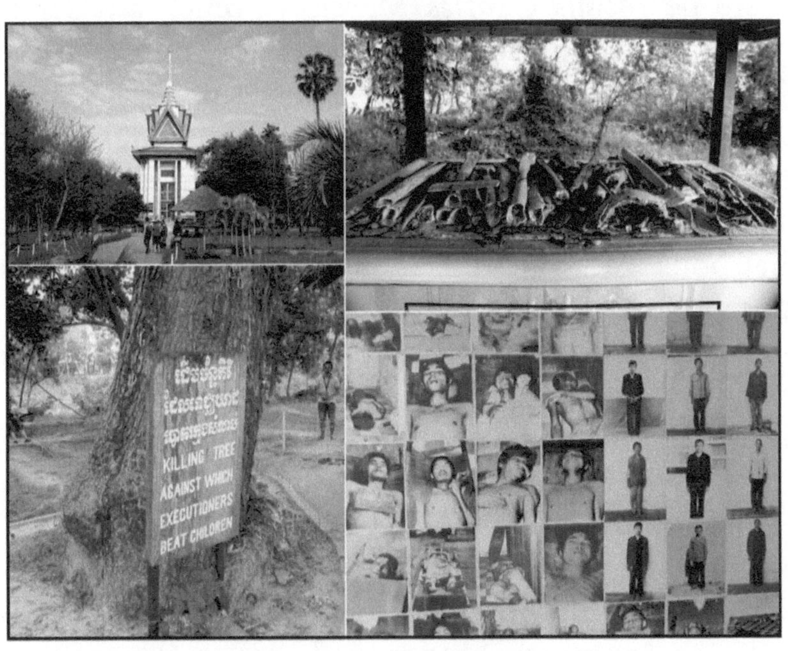

Pol Pot Killing Field

We drove to Choeung Ek, a much-talked-about and visited the site: the *Killing Fields*, the national symbol of heartbreak and horror. Visiting this site sobers you up. The fragrance of the lantana was overpowering as we approached the spot. It was here that the bodies of nearly 9,000 people were exhumed from eighty-five mass burial grounds. There are still about fifty more, left to rest in peace. Many of the graves are yet seen strewn with the remnants of the victims' clothes. Many of them died after slow and prolonged torture. This site is dominated by a tall hollow glass-fronted stupa filled with the skulls of thousands of men, women, children, and infants. We could see splits and cracks in many of the skull was a horrifying sight, to put it mildly.

Suddenly my mind sped back to my preparation days when I read a book authored by Philip Sorts. There he recalls *Charles Meyer,* a French adviser to Prince Shanonk, remarking that the characteristic Khmer smiles, an indefinable half-smile that floats across the stone sculptures of the gods at Angkor. The dictatorial ruler Pol Pot too sported the same smile *(Pol Pot: Anatomy of Nightmare, 1975–79).* Reading that book gave me goosebumps. Learning about the macabre and the gruesome genocide detailed in that book stirred up my anxiety to visit this place. A single man, Pol Pot was the leader of that terrible dance of death! According to this book, between 1975 and '79 more than 17,000 men, women, children, and infants, including foreigners, were detained and tortured, finally to be transported for extermination at *Choeung Ek.* The most chilling detail of the bloodbath was, the victims were mostly bludgeoned, to save the cost of a bullet. The book, I should confess, had left a substantial and profound impact on me. *Pol pot* was a moon-faced inhuman monster as portrayed in the book.

Incidentally, our guide and driver gave us an exciting version of his brutality. They said that Pol Pot also had the same Khmer smile, as seen etched in the faces of the ancient Khmer gods, with half-closed eyes, as depicted in their sandstone sculptures. Every atrocity committed during his regime is found graphically replicated, preserved for the forthcoming generations, to be condemned in hell, expressed on the stone friezes sculpted in the Angkor Thom temples, a sort of prediction to forecast the trial and torture, ending in the gruesome death of the poor innocents centuries later!

This massacre was one of the most brutal exercises in human history, under the ruthless dictator, Pol Pot. Although Pol Pot was educated in Paris, he was also a communist. But I cannot visualize where he developed this ideology. There is an underlying rumor that there was a section of people called the Red Army infected with various odd doctrines from all parts of Europe, which could have been the trigger for the negativity with Pol Pot. He began to strive to establish equality among his fellow citizens; he hated the idea of the disparity between rich and poor, affluence and poverty. His objective was to transform Cambodia into a Maoist, peasant-dominated society with his ruthless collectivization drive. The currency was abolished, as was the postal system. Only barter deal was permitted. The country was cut off from the rest of the world. The massacre and brutalization of neo-intellectual professionals and the community at large faced the threat of extermination.

Why were all the people silent? Why did they not resist? I could not help recalling what *Napoleon Bonaparte*-te once wrote, *"The cruelty engulfing the world could not be so much attributed to bad leaders,* as much as to the silence of the majority of good people." How true it is! Societies crumble, collapse, not because of the misdeeds of a few 'bad men,' but because of the apathy and the silence of many 'good men' remaining narcotized into inaction. When the situation becomes too painful to bear, even a worm will turn, so goes the saying.

This brings to my mind an old fable: A sage with his mastery of tantric powers was able to command all living creatures. One day, when he was in deep meditation, he was aroused by the cries of the nearby villagers, who implored him to save them from a ferocious serpent causing them great misery. The sage with his tantric power was able to conjure up the reptile, restraining it from causing anxiety and harm to the people. Encouraged to find the snake remaining calm and docile, the villagers soon started pelting it with stones and battered the poor snake with sticks. Later, when the sage revisited the village, he found the snake battling for its life. Listening to the serpent's sob story, he said, "I had told you not to kill, but had I ever told you *not* to hiss?"

Now there is a ridiculous argument floating around a particular section of people that *"the only thing that stops a bad guy with a gun is a good guy with a gun!"* I do not endorse this argument, remembering what Gandhi said, "Eye for an eye makes the whole world blind." From the arguments above, it appears we are caught in a Catch-22 situation. Only intelligence, prudence, and good judgment would prevail in the long run in any given case. It is a universal fact that life is given by God, and it can be taken away by God alone. But who gave the hardened, cold-blooded criminals the right to take away the lives of thousands of innocent people? In the United States, in 2008, the Supreme Court ruled that Americans have the right to own guns according to the Second Amendment while the First Amendment is the freedom of speech. It was reported that between 2006 and 2011, 56,439 people were murdered by firearms in the United States. To the best of my knowledge and understanding of the American Constitution that was adopted in 1791, citizens have the right to own arms but not without limitations. I also find this ideology could have been absorbed by the English as an auxiliary right given to citizens only for self-defense, which has to be proven authentically by a proper court of law.

Now getting back to Cambodia and the Khmer Rouge, had it not been for the Vietnamese invasion, the country and its culture would have gone into oblivion. On 25 December 1978, Vietnam launched a full-scale attack of Cambodia, succeeded in overthrowing the Khmer Rouge regime and helped to restore sanity and sensibility to a country gone mad and demonic. (Pol Pot died on 15 August 1988 in exile in Thailand.) Even in death, he had the mysterious Khmer smile.

Our cab driver was a courteous guy with abundant knowledge of Cambodian history, especially of the Khmer Rouge era. He seemed to be well-versed in the political narration of Cambodia during those trying years and had a reasonably good command of the language. On the subject of the Khmer Rouge's regime and its image of brutality, he squarely blamed Cambodian society as the root cause for giving birth to the mindless barbarism that had engulfed the country.

He explained that before the advent of the Khmer Rouge, the society was polarised into the haves and have-nots, the latter increasing in number as the days went by. The rich were becoming more prosperous, flaunting their ostentatious lifestyles. The farmers and the rural people were frustrated and found themselves in utter despair, especially in their part of the country bordering Vietnam to the east. Its economy was already in a shambles, augmented by the relentless war in Vietnam and the aftermath rebellious fury, slowly spreading its tentacles into the central part of Cambodia. Day-to-day survival posed a problem for them. President Nixon and Kissinger maliciously planned an attack on Cambodia to destroy and annihilate the state by employing carpet-bombing. Under an irrational idea that it would give a resounding blow to the Viet Cong's operating from their base in Cambodia to buttressed by the arms aid from Russia and To disable the Viet Cong's who had regrouped themselves and formed a core in the neighboring country of Cambodia, buttressed by the arms aid from Russia.

Americans, with an imaginary conquest of South Vietnam, supported the unpopular regime of Lon Nol to establish a sort of puppetry rule, as directed by the United States. But the plan misfired. They then resorted to the ruthless mission of sending B-52s as a form of retribution from *Guam and Da Nang* (Vietnam) in thousands, dropping one and a half million tons of bombs, secretly without any authorization from the Congress for several years. The blitzkrieg served to steel the Viet Cong's even more and induced the peasants, both men, and women, to join the Khmer Rouge as volunteers.

It was untold misery for the poor peasants, who not only hated the rich and now the Americans with utmost bitterness. They had grown up experiencing chronic poverty and pathetic living conditions in the remote border areas. Deprivation and alienation spurred the marginalized people to join *en masse* and identify themselves with the Khmer Rouge ideology. It could even be said that the Americans were partly responsible for creating this Frankenstein monster, Pol Pot. Their anger erupted into looting and mass killings of the privileged, professional and the wealthy people by these underdogs, who had nothing to lose. Free-For-All combat emerged. A large number of teenagers joined with Khmer Rouge group willingly. Armed to the teeth with unstinted support from the Viet Cong's, who supplied them with heavy weapons captured from the Americans, these youngsters were wildly revengeful. After tasting firepower, the killing and looting were rampant, targeting the neo-literates, professionals, officers of the civil services, the rich and the privileged.

After explaining the root cause of the emergence of the Khmer Rouge and its vandalism, the driver continued saying, "Sirs, *Pol Pot was not the sole villain,* as the media alleges him to be. But it was a spontaneous and justifiable reaction of the desperados who plunged themselves into the warpath." According to him, Pol Pot was nothing but an insignificant personality. He was an educated person, seldom made his presence felt, and least of all, he did not issue any form of the command to the Khmer Rouge to avenge the massacre by American bombing in Cambodia. This gentle opinion of Pol Pot was endorsed by almost all the weak and helpless Cambodians. They blame him for nothing. They say nobody ever saw Pol

Pot either killing anybody or ordering for the massacre. According to them, it was a proxy war created by some foreign force or secret service to cover up their own faults with the help of the mass media, press, and false propaganda. In the meantime, the Americans could not sustain this prolonged war against the Viet Cong's.feat and to justify their inglorious exit, they signed a phony peace accord with South Vietnam and withdrew from Southeast Asia. The vacuum was filled by neighboring Vietnam, who finally liberated Cambodia from the clutches of the terror groups. With the help of Soviet artillery, they re-established peace in Cambodia. In short, it was a thought-provoking tale of the *Rise and Fall of Khmer Rouge.*

Late in the evening, we spotted an Indian-owned handloom emporium in the main commercial street in Siem Reap. Terry bought some hand-embroidered silks, scarves, Kashmiri carpets, etc. We did some window shopping in the neighborhood where we found an eye-catching, gold-braided bedspread with matching pillow covers from an Indian-owned store. The country, being an ASEAN member was a contributing factor for a step forward, both economically and politically. Signs are there, for the encouragement of foreign investments, giving scope for long-time benefits, etc. Cambodians take pride in their lucrative business of tourism, its abundant resources, youthful, and beautiful biodiversity. Now the country keeps its door open to the economic superpowers, which are hungry for the Cambodian market.

Angkor was a prosperous city; its rich soil yielded three crops a year. Fish were plenty; the forest supplied all the teak wood for construction of temples and buildings of galleries. The sudden decline of the Khmer civilization, which flourished from the ninth century until 1431 with such resources, still remains a mystery to the historians. When the Thais and the Khmers were in combat, and the victorious Thai army revisited the vanquished city a few years later, they were intrigued to find the town abandoned and the one million inhabitants had just vanished! Why and how? It is still steeped in mystery. It reminded me of what Albert Einstein said: "The most beautiful thing we can experience is the mysterious. It is the source of all true art and science."

We were absorbed in deep thought. Perhaps, we three had suddenly become conscious of the stark contrast between the ascetic lifestyles of the Buddhist monks at Angkor Wat and the comfort and convenience that we enjoy in our urban setting.

Although we surrendered our senses to the sublime beauty of the wilderness and the spirituality of Angkor, it was time to return to the material world. It was no gainsaying that Siem Reap had become the force to revitalize the Khmer cultural skills that were forcibly kept under wraps by the Khmer Rouge through the many years of hibernation, and subsequently by the harsh blow dealt by its erstwhile rulers. Later, we drove to a school named *Les Chantiers Ecoles* where the master craftsman of the school imparted skills in wood and stone-carving techniques to the younger generation from an impoverished background. An excellent-stocked shop called *Artisans d' Angkor* was selling the exact replica of the beautiful stone or woodwork of the Angkorian era statues, household furniture and silks with different ancient royal Cambodian designs and alluring modern designs. These come from their own

Silk Farms specialized in dyeing and weaving. As all the sales proceeds would be used mainly to uplift the living standards of these underprivileged people, we contributed willingly and bought their high-quality silks and handicrafts. Another shop we were recommended to visit had 'made in Cambodia,' products specializing in quality products such as wallets, handbags and other crafts. We came to understand that the profits are plowed back into training the disabled for useful employment.

Despite the terrible years of brutalism, during the reign of Khmer Rouge, which left deep scars on the psyche of the Cambodians, they still preserve a degree of dignity, a certain gentleness, and pride in their past and culture that overwhelmed us.

As we were strolling in and around Siem Reap, we found something strange that we can never see in India. In this booming, flourishing destination for tourists, we found even beggars showed dignity. They did not cry out for alms with outstretched arms. They hardly muttered a word. Moved by their solemnity and the dignified way of begging, we readily unzipped our wallets. One more fascinating character I observed was the Khmer people formulate and perform everything to order. There are a few hospitals and medical dispensaries all over the Siem Reap area, to which the people converged from all around and nearby villages for treatment. They sit in a line, although the line seemed to extend very long, right up to the platform or walkway. They sit in order, with patience. Most of them carry their offspring, even siblings with them. If they do not reach to get their turn for treatment, they are sent home to come back another day. With absolute tolerance and order, they abide by the norms. This observation truly touched my heart, which has ignited in me the desire to work collectively towards establishing a mobile hospital to reach the poor and needy in and around Siem Reap Angkor and the surrounding villages. I am still working on the programme and looking for collective participation.

In the evening, we walked at a leisurely pace around Siem Reap which has retained its rural ethnic qualities and the old French-style shopping arcades with tree-lined boulevards, cobblestone pavements, etc. Due to the influx of foreign tourists, Siem Reap is fast becoming a gold mine for investors. Hotels are coming up every month, and the skylines are changing quickly. The Godzilla-like mutation of this sleepy town to almost a megacity is not being done gradually. The old residents still retain the memories of their recent past. It seems like the transformation itself is taking place overnight!

Onwards Ho! The next visit, according to the route map we had chalked out, was *Laos*. Driving towards our hotel, along a highway and right next to it, we saw a lonely farmer ploughing his field behind a team of oxen. The twenty-first century meeting up with millennia-old farming tradition! That is the state of the rural scenario in Cambodia today. Tomorrow things will be different. We hoped and prayed for a 'better tomorrow' for them.

While we were seated in the departure lounge of the airport in Siem Reap to leave for Laos, I could not help recalling my observations about Angkor, the high tourist spot. There were numerous unregistered guides, a dime-a-dozen. Many tourists visit the ruins in a hurry, clicking pictures of the temples, not sparing even a little time to pause and personally feel the magnificence of its archaeological wonder. The visitors could have spent a little more of their time to gaze at the monuments, to savor the sheer beauty, hang around for a while, ponder and admire the intricate figurines carved in such fine details on the pillars by the diligent sculptors with hammers and chisels in an age long gone by!

Khmer Architectural Genesis

Having expressed in detail the awesome wonder of the architectural excellence and evolution of creation of a masterpiece throughout 450 years, I was induced and lured to seek more answers; this led me to open up the arcade of knowledge of history with additional inputs by scouting for more authentic information. I could easily compile the history of the Khmers from the beginning to the present troubled recent past and the current status of the local people. While they do not beg, I can still hear their cry from within, expressed outwardly with their Khmer smile.

Khmer Dynasty

The Khmers ruled a significant part of Southeast Asia from 800–1325 AD. There were many rulers of that dynasty starting from *Jayavarman II,* ending with *Jayavarman Paramesvara.* The primary, profound rulers and builders were *Jayavarman II, Rajendravarman, Udayadityavarman II, Suryavarman II, and Jayavarman VII.* Angkor was once a seat of the mighty Khmer empire. Khmers were architecturally profound with deep Tamilians roots, and the extent of their power seemed to be vast, right from *Java* to the entire region of Southeast Asia. The same architectural and cultural epics were an extension of *Mahabalipuram, Kanchipuram*, and other parts of *Tamil Nadu, South India*. In Tamil Nadu, in India, the temple tower at the entrance is known as *Gopuram*. I find in Cambodia these are called 'pagodas' placed at the center. It could be that South Indian Tamils as a warrior race could have played a significant part in the development of art, culture, architecture, and the rule of law with great grace all around Southeast Asia. It was found that a considerable part of the Tamil literature was part of the southeast Asian culture, which is slowly diminishing due to subsequent influence from Sanskrit, Pali and other local languages. Recently, an old Tamil inscription dating back to 300 BC was found in China. *Cholas* from the Tamil kingdom traded with China from BC 300–1200 AD. Their maritime trade route from Tamil Nadu, South India, extended up to China, connecting present Thailand, Cambodia and the areas around that, further on, to present day Indonesia proceeding to the Chinese port Canton (Guangzhou). This subsequently was connected to the arteries of the then Silk Routes. Old Chinese coins were excavated in areas around *Pudhukottai and Tanjore of Tamil Nadu.* Some of the ancient Tamil artifacts were even excavated from *New Zealand.* The Tamils had extended their influence over that entire region. Their cultural mix with the local people had created many kingdoms. This evolution resulted in many wars and subsequently intermarriages. The Chola kingdom traded even with Rome; they extended their influence all over *India, Sri Lanka, and most part of Southeast Asia* up to *Java* and *Sumatra.* This is how the Tamils made their presence felt in most parts of the world. The internal conflicts among the Tamil kings brought about their downfall.

Origin of Khmer

The Chenla kingdom of Cambodia could be an off-spring of the *South Indian Pallava dynasty*. It originated from Tamil Nadu as the offshoot of the great empires of the *Cheras, Cholas, and Pandyas* who were in existence even earlier from 300 BC to 1200 AD, during and after the Maurya Kingdom. Subsequently, the Chalukya Kingdom also came to power. There were many wars between the *Cholas* and *Chalukyas. The Pallava* kingdom is said to have an origin from an illegitimate offspring of a Chola king with a *Naga* princess. The rulers of the *Pallava dynasty were Simhavishnu, Mahendravarman, Narasimhavarman, Nandivarman, and Paramesvaravarman.* They developed sculptural monuments in *Mahabalipuram* and *Kanchipuram* during the span of their regime for almost seven centuries from 200–800 AD. The South Indians played a significant part in all administration, sculptural and artworks in the Pallava kingdom. One could study more from unbiased authentic history and events of these proceedings.

The *Chenla* rulers unseated the *Funan* kingdom, who were rulers from some parts of China, peacefully. A Chinese scholar named that territory after the then rulers, the Funan which means 'Khmer,' and the same name was transferred to the Chenla rulers as well. The Chenla kingdom ruled the region from 600–800 AD starting from *Bhavavarman I* and ending with *Mahipativarman,* and the intermediate rulers were *Mohendra-*

varman, Isanavarman I, Bhavavarman II, Jayavarman I, Queen Jayavedi, Sambhuvarman, Pushkaraksha, and Sambhuvarman. During this period, the Khmer ruled the area as a small kingdom. There were battles between the ruling class to take possession of power. This is how the Chenla rulers ruled for 200 years. This was the beginning of that origin of the chequered past of the Khmers until the emergence of *Jayavarman II.*

Ruling Descent of Khmers

It was *Jayavarman II* who united the Khmer as one kingdom and made *Yasodhapura* the capital, and the region was known as *Cambodia.* His descendant *Yashovarman* I subsequently made *Angkor* the capital of Cambodia, and development in that area started dramatically. *Rajendravarman* built *Phimeanakas,* which was continued and completed as a three-tiered structure, with every detail given by *Suryavarman II. Udayadityavarman II* constructed the *Baphuon,* while *Jayavarman VII* undertook the massive project of the south gate entrance and *Bayon Temple* and other parts of *Angkor Thom.* The rest of the rulers built secondary structures and irrigation networks.

It is said that *Suryavarman II* (1110–1150 AD), who became a Khmer ruler, took an army from South India to Cambodia and fought a war with the then queen and won the battle. Later he married her, and it was he who built Angkor Wat, the modern architectural wonder and marvel, and also completed *Phimeanakas* and *Baphuon.* His descendant *Jayavarman VII* constructed the Angkor Thom. It is a city within the city of Angkor. From here, the Khmers extended their power over *Vietnam, Laos, Thailand,* even up to *Java and Sumatra* in their prime. But there was always war among them to take over control. This was how their rulers survived from the 9th to the early 13th century AD.

General

It is the opinion of the local Tamils that the influence of the Pallavas in Tamil Nadu brought confusion from 300–600 AD until they were routed out from rule by the Tamils. Although the Pallava dynasty originated from the Chola rulers, the mixed-race thus formulated to rule this area brought other linguistic influences and infiltrations of the outside into the social fabric of the Tamils. These caused chaos and confusion and resulted in disharmony to the locals; their ethnicity and culture were getting eroded, and this caused total unrest and finally the destruction of the Pallavas, but Sanskrit and their cultural influence still remain in Tamil Nadu. These were the dark ages of the Tamils from 200–600 AD where their history and records slowly disappeared from the archives. Subsequently, it got revived in the seventh century. After the Pallava kingdom, the Khmer seemed to flourish in their territory in Cambodia.

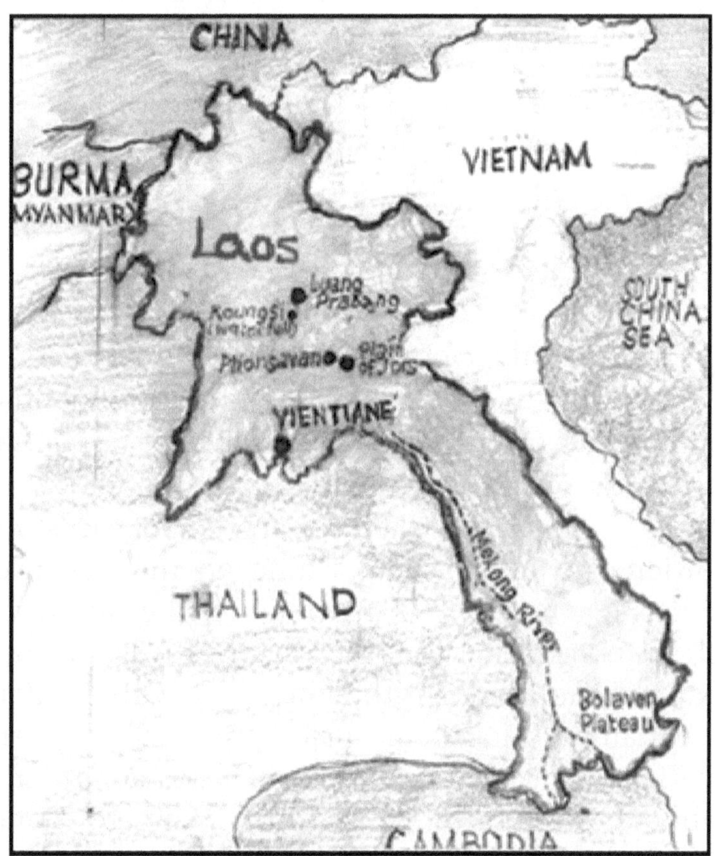

Vientiane:	The 'low-rise' capital of Laos, near the Mekong River
Bolaven Plateau:	A pleasant retreat for relaxing or meditating, boat trip to scores of islets dotting the reservoir—Spectacular view of the sunset—Drive along the Mekong River bank to Bolaven Plateau

Luang Prabang:	An ideal city, affording the joy of strolling down the bylanes, absorbing the un-harried rhythms of Laos' culture—A UNESCO World Heritage Site and the spiritual capital of Laos—Unforgettable experience with an intrepid conservationist
Phonsavan:	Exploring the prehistoric plain of jars and the longest thoroughfare of a bygone era—the Silk Route
Royal Palace:	A museum of the royal trappings of Laos' abolished monarchy
Kuang Si:	A picturesque multi-level waterfall, a picture perfect picnic spot

Laos: For Nature Lovers

We soon wended our way towards the international airport to catch our flight to Vientiane (pronounced as 'Wiang Jan'), the capital of Laos. It was almost midnight when we landed.

Laos, the only landlocked country in Southeast Asia is bordered by Burma and China on the northwest, Vietnam to the east, Cambodia to the south and Thailand to the west. While the Mekong River and Luang Prabang mountain form the boundary with Thailand, the Annamite Mountain forms the eastern border with Vietnam, while the southern plateaus border on Cambodia, which enjoys a tropical climate. Fondly nicknamed 'a million elephants under one parasol' Laos is a beautiful slow-moving non-commercialized country.

I was astonished as I went through the history of this landlocked country. Laos has a history, like Cambodia, of originating from Southern India and China after the fall of Khmers in the thirteenth century. The Khmer warriors joined hands with Prince *Fa Ngum* and took over Laos and formed the Lan Xang kingdom. This reveals that the Chinese and South Indian Tamils played a significant role in the development and governance of the whole of Southeast Asia. Buddhism had slipped into the system and culture of the people perhaps due to Theravada Buddhism, as the Naga Princess might have been influenced by the philosophy from the central plateau region of India. Buddhism emerged as a different religion among the rulers of that area. Slowly, it gave way to communism because it could not take deep root into the people's convictions. The confusion and chaos led to the advent and invasion of the European race. I find, from my knowledge of the background of world history, wherever the Europeans had stepped in, be it the Middle East, Asia Minor, Southeast Asia, Northern, and Southern India, Africa, or South America, the trouble never ends— it is continuous. I think the Western influence upset the mindset of entire people groups, thereby uprooting the rhythm and harmony.

This country, with only 92 square miles in area and with less than seven million people have undergone many changes under many rulers for many centuries. It was ruled by the French, briefly by the Japanese, and then reverted once again to French rule. It got its independence in 1953 from the French. Subsequently, civil war broke out; finally, it came under communist control. Due to disturbance caused by the varied interest of the different groups of rulers, the country has not improved economically, and fair distribution of wealth is still a far cry. More than a third of its people live far below the poverty level. The International community needs to turn its attention to the pitiable state of these people.

Vientiane

Vientiane is a quiet sleepy town on the bank of the Mekong River. We were greeted by the fresh and surreal identity of this capital city. It looked more like a rambling collection of numerous villages interspaced with a few grandiose monuments, attractive to backpackers and beachcombers. Shops were devoid of activity and almost empty and colorless. Although Vientiane is the capital of Laos, the city did not seem to us, the tourists, as vibrant as the cities around the world usually appear! There were no chaotic traffic jams associated with most ports. The people we met were friendly, ready with disarming smiles. Its glory lies in its numerous temples, and triple-pitched roofing, a unique character of Laos' architectural style. The scented smoke of the incense sticks wafted all around the temple complex.

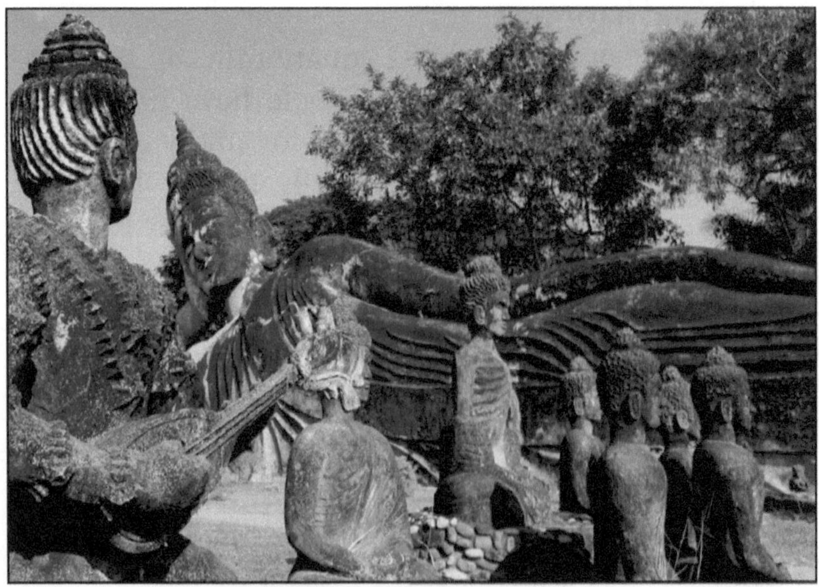

Buddha Park at Vientiane

Laos is a land of sparsely populated plateaus, mostly mountainous and thickly forested. They are inhabited by myriad animal species. Even today new species of large mammals are being discovered, such as the slow-moving Soala. Freshwater dolphins live in the Mekong River. It is an ideal destination for nature lovers. Far from the hurly-burly city of Bangkok, Laos offered a haven of tranquility and serenity, a beautiful slow-moving and non-commercialized country where tourism is still a novelty.

We had a friendly chat with a Lao officer of the tourism department, who said, as a result of the high ratio of foreign expatriate workers in Vientiane, and the booming tourism industry, the city, is rapidly reaching dizzy heights. Vientiane boasts a cosmopolitan touch, people with Chinese, Vietnamese, a limited number of Indians, as well as the natives of Laos. We checked into a hotel located in the heart of the city with all the comforts of a swimming pool, restaurant, and other facilities.

Sauntering along the bank of the Mekong River in the misty morning after, we were drawn to a riverside restaurant famed for Laos' coffee before returning to our rooms. Late in the afternoon, we selected a restaurant for lunch, offering both covered and alfresco seating. Some tables were placed beside the waters. Birds, the bold ones with a flap of their wings, gracefully glided across the sky. After a moment of contemplation, one of the birds perched first on the top of the chair, then taking courage with both hands (sorry! wings), finally nose-dived to share our lunch. We did not mind it, at all! Where else could we savor the great food while enjoying the mid-noon cool breeze of the river and have birds as our lunch-table companions! This experience showed that Laos is an ideal destination for nature lovers.

We met a friendly cocktail-jugglery bartender wearing a Panama-hat who fixed an iced 'Margharita' especially for us. Rumbling on, we had a friendly chat with a lady sweet-corn seller. Fascinated, we observed her shaving off the cob expertly and rotating the handle of the corn toaster in slow motion. A spray of orange sparks flew out, glowing briefly, before fading out. Later in the evening hours, our hotel manager directed us to take a walk towards a particular place along the bank of the Mekong River, saying, "I bet it is one of the few places in the world offering you a spectacular view of the sunset. Don't miss it, for heaven's sake." We headed toward the place, immediately. The riverbank was lined with rows and rows of comfortable chairs, full of men and women tourists, holding fishing rods for angling. Terry and Gerald were in a mood to follow the sun setting, walking along the bank, leaving me to be comfortably reclining in a comfortable chair with a fishing rod and bait. A fish basket was by the side of my chair, while the spectacular sunset, the fiery orb, lighting up the waters. Sitting there (not standing!) spellbound at this panoramic view, with a feeling of gratitude to the manager's thoughtful suggestion, I reclined comfortably in the chair. With the cool breeze rocking me gently, I soon dozed off.

Both of them returned to find me, fast asleep in my chair, snoring rather gruffly, but clutching the fishing rod soon, and they jolted me up from the slumber. No wonder my fish basket was empty, as were the comfortable chairs on either side of mine. *Laugh, the whole world laughs with you. Snore! You sleep alone.'* Walking along the *Fa Ngum Road,* for the next two kilometers, we found rows of beer garden huts with wooden floor decks overhanging the riverbank built on wooden stilts to avoid visits from wild dogs and monkeys and the overhanging deck, affording a serene setting of the river, which calmed our senses. We could help ourselves to a mug of draught froth straight from the pitchers, defining the quintessential Vientiane pub culture. Conversing half in English and half with actions, we placed our order for dinner. Vientiane boasts some of the best restaurants in Indo-China. The local menu is mostly French-influenced. We had dinner in a posh restaurant—a merely superb and sumptuous meal. There were dishes of baked potato, peas, salami, mushroom, preceded by hors-d'oeuvres of delicious crunchy crabmeat.

The darkness of the night slowly engulfed the neighborhood, and when shops, cafes, restaurants lighted up, we sauntered into one of the shops, displaying a huge banner saying 'Sale.' The salesgirls in the stores leaped up, squealing with delight to welcome us like long-lost friends. Posted on the racks were silk scarves in bright colors, silver articles, handmade embroidered bags, appliqué bed covers for the taking, and before we knew it, we had succumbed to the temptation of opening our wallets.

"Excuse me, sirs! Where you from? Oh! India! You look like Amitabh B." Then with a forced smile, looking at the bald pate of Gerald, she said, "You look like Yule Brynner." But Gerald was not too happy, pouting at this remark. I comforted him by saying, "You know, Gerald, baldies are not harebrained."

And that's that! Feeling proud and self-centered, believing every word she said, comparing us with the iconic actor, Terry and I readily fell for a time of full-scale shopping!

Later we came to know from one of our 'desi' tourists from Bangalore that the content of this spiel was prepared well in advance, memorized by the salesgirls, and used on every customer they interacted with! Needless to say that our inflated egos soon got deflated. After hours of wandering along the neighborhood, we were back to our hotel in the wee hours of the following morning. The receptionist did not raise her eyebrows at this unearthly hour of our return. After breakfast, we took a long drive along the bank of the Mekong River, heading towards *Bolaven Plateau.*

The *Mekong River* is one of the great rivers of Southeast Asia. Gentle yet impressive, it rises at Za Qus in Tibet and is 4,900 kilometers long. Half the way of its course is through China. It forms the border between Myanmar and Laos for a distance of 200 kilometers. As it flows on, it also divides Thailand and Laos, and a significant stretch of it passes through Laos, making it a right Mekong country. From Laos, it meanders into *Cambodia* and then to *South Vietnam,* and finally, through several mouths across the vast fertile delta creating one of the world's great rice-growing regions, to eventually empty into the South China Sea; however, it is not as enormous and forbidding as the *Sundarbans,* the delta of the Brahmaputra, and the Ganga in Bangladesh. The islets provide ample rice and fish—the staple food of the people of the Southeast Asian regions.

The river offers a natural habitat for the freshwater dolphins. There were regular 'river navigations,' and we could hire an individual boat or a river cruise with a multitude of tourists. We chose the latter, it is quite compact with a restaurant and a bar, in the company of foreigners, chatting in their own language. The seats were so dense that we had to sit cheek by jowl with our co-tourists, like the best of chums. The long-tailed boat we sailed on was appropriately named *Boat Chummy.* We did not mind the angle of the vessel as it was speeding and spraying water on us, tickling our skins. I was fascinated being in the midst of different nationalities. Looking at each of them into their eyes, I could understand their language and share the excitement of being in that environment. I soon became friendly with some German ladies among our co-travelers. While sailing, I had the good fortune of seeing dolphins in their natural habitat, and I feasted my eyes on their playful antics, slicing out of the water with the sun resplendent on their backs, watching them disappear with a splash into the deep blue sea. "Ashok! Do you know that humans and dolphins are the only living beings who have sex for pleasure and have no mating season?" asked the fellow German traveler who was an anthropologist. She added that she had watched male bottle-nosed dolphins forming a gang to harass the female dolphins violently. (Some of you, the learned ones, may debunk this claim, but I, being an ardent believer in UFOs, readily accepted her statement on the analogy of the sexual traits of dolphins vis-à-vis human beings).

In history, we read those great dynasties of ancient times had successfully used the sea route to traverse oceans, to reach other countries for propagation, as well as for the establishment of economic, religious and cultural ties. History also tells us the Cholas and Pallavas of ancient Tamil kingdom had encouraged sea voyages to Southeast Asian countries, even sailing along the Mekong River to reach the ports of Cambodia and Thailand for overseas trade and commerce!

Bolaven Plateau

As we reached the *Bolaven Plateau,* the landscape began to change gradually. There were coffee estates, pineapple farms, sugarcane plantations, rice fields, and lotus ponds. We saw the most vivid cannas in deep red and alluring yellow, thick ferns and hundreds of butterflies flitting about. As we walked further, we could see tumbling water, cascading with an ear-deafening roar. The fragrance of the Champa flowers filled the air. It is an 'absolute must' for visitors. We sat there marveling at the rare and rich heritage, the essence of our Laos experience. We saw the hummingbird and had lost ourselves in the idyllic settings and the chirping of the birds, timed with chirring of grasshoppers, enthralled us with their 'avian orchestra.' We had lunch at an eco-friendly restaurant. Swaying palms, a wooden rafter pergola, and a water cascade. A setting where you instinctively tend to unwind with the experience being enhanced by the aroma of the food wafting up your nostrils from the pantry. You'd put your mobile on vibration mode and hang loose to enjoy the visually-soothing impact of the greenery all around.

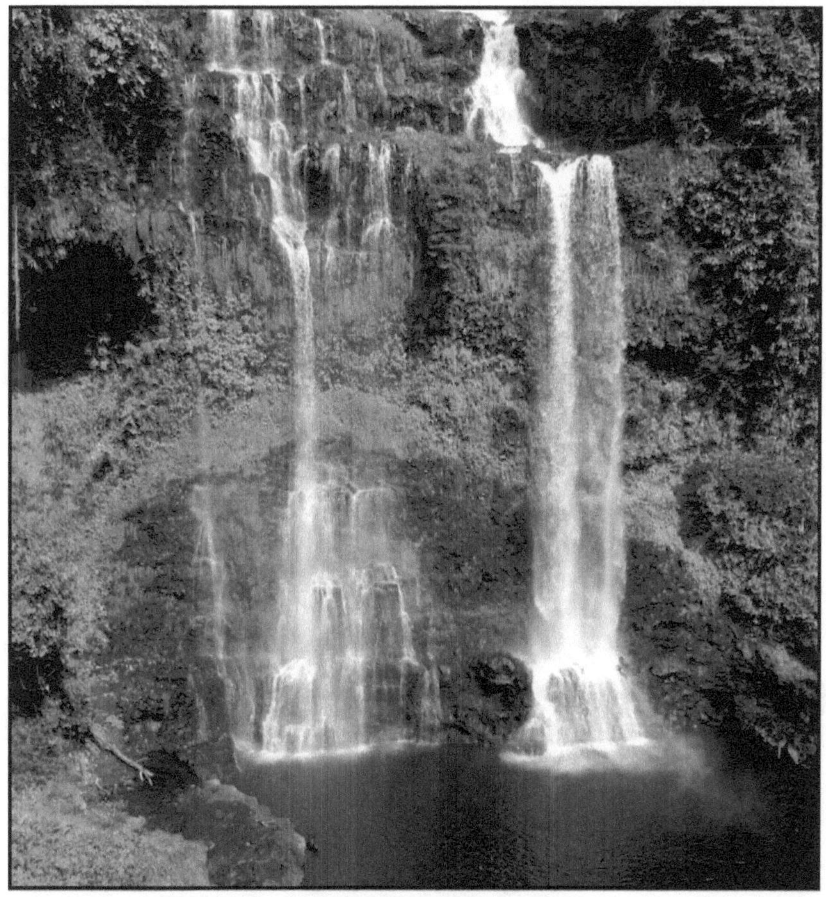

Bolaven Plateau

Luang Prabang

The following day, we boarded a domestic flight from Vientiane to arrive at *Luang Prabang,* a great tourist spot in Laos, exuding grandeur. Finding a place among UNESCO World Heritage Sites, preserving the French Laos-style architecture, the site offered us dreamy serenity along with the most vibrant culture and the most refined cuisine. The deafening silence, quaintness and the slow pace of life seemed to come from the pages of well-loved Ruskin Bond novels. Located at the confluence of the Mekong and Nom Khan rivers, the French-style villas, Buddhist monks in red robes and markets appeared unique. The cafes and boutiques, bakeries and roadside stalls merge effortlessly with the majestic Buddhist temples to make this place the spiritual capital of Laos. Most of the temples sport the classic *Luang Prabang* styles of architecture with elaborately gilded columns, holding up the tiered roof, which seems to sweep down gracefully. Cluttered mosaic and gilded carvings on columns, glistening in the fading sunlight, the bas-relief on the wall depicting some scenes from Ramayana appeared quite familiar to us.

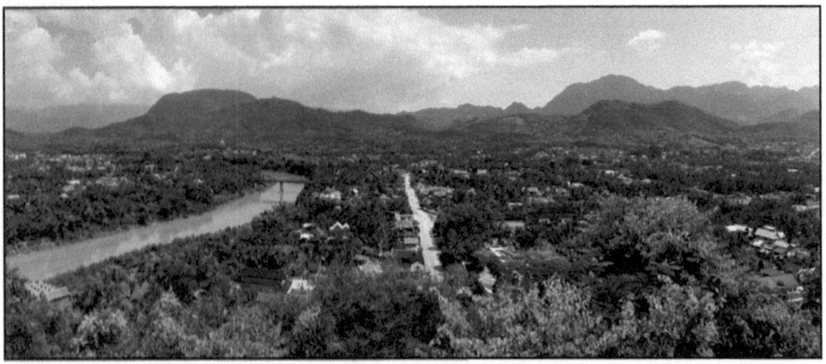

Laung Prabang in Vientiane

We chose to visit a monastery, one of the oldest in *Luang Prabang*. Devoid of any activity, time seemed to have stood still, and even an old man sitting outside the monastery seemed to be there for the past eighty years! While entering the monastery, we felt the solemnity descend on us as we heard the monks chanting almost monotonously during the solemn ritual.

Walk-a-Talk with a Conservationist

While having lunch in a restaurant, on the borders of a dense jungle, we met a guy looking almost weather-beaten, bare-bodied with unkempt hair, a European sporting a beard, who gave us a broad smile, greeting us with outstretched arms. Assuming him to be a sort of rag picker, we felt reluctant even to reciprocate his gesture. Had we done so, we'd have missed an opportunity of meeting a great guy, a conservationist at his best!

He was an intrepid biologist and accompanying him with our local guide, we went trekking into the jungle. Despite being warned that the forests were home to tigers, leopards, snakes and elephants and the trek difficulty level were 2/5, including steep inclines, we were excited. Our leader, the explorer, advised us to pop dates into our mouths but not to chew them, producing capsules of sugary energy needed during the trek. He had traversed Greenland's ice caps, ventured on numerous research expeditions in the jungles. *Indiana Jones in passé.* An adventurer who had cycled into the thickest of forests, coming face-to-face with many ferocious animals. We felt humbled in his company. He was also a health freak. He was keen on keeping his physique in good shape, doing a lot of exercises, pull-ups, run around trees and rock-climbing. "The fitter you are, the harder you'd be killed," he laughed.

The canopy of trees shielded us from the blistering sun, inviting us to his tree house. The green mountains and rocks were clothed in the warm glow of the glorious evening 'orange Sun.' He warned us that the animal movements would start around 6.30 p.m., and we should be out of bounds by then.

Wildlife conservation was very close to his heart. The numerous adventures he related were exciting, and they were supported by photographs, which he showed us in his tree house. Venturing boldly into treacherous terrains to photograph animals and reptiles and still emerging unscathed bewildered us. He had trapped and radio-collared a male leopard, receiving via GPS information about their whereabouts, mating seasons, etc. He had studied the ecology of wildcats. He told us that leopards are solitary animals, as are also the other big cats, except lions, which become social only when they court the lionesses and have cubs. At other times, they avoid meeting each other.

"Do you know that lionesses wield greater power in the animal kingdom than their male counterparts?" He added that lionesses, for instance, strike fear in the hearts of lions when they were nurturing their cubs. "Although the lionesses are slightly smaller than lions, they become ferocious and combat-ready when protecting their young ones. I've seen powerful, grisly maned lions when I was on an expedition in the Congo, I had seen the lions meekly back off from the lionesses. Even while hunting, they have proved themselves clever in strategy manipulating their chase to zero into the kill, when compared to their large, sluggish male counterparts."

He also said that it was incomprehensible that an adult male leopard, which he spotted, was babysitting the newborns, while the 'mom' leopard was away, on a hunting expedition all night, to provide meals for her family. He told us that (male) tigers are more.

family-oriented than the tigresses. There was even an instance of an adult tiger being an affectionate 'father.' When the 'mom' tigress and the cubs met their 'father,' the little ones ran forward competing with one another to greet him, to nuzzle with him like pussycats.

The numerous adventures he related to us were incredibly fascinating, and I could fill the whole book with our delight for arousing our interest in the big animals. Thanking him profusely and saying "adieu" to our Indiana Jones, we had to race against the time of the setting sun.

Phonsavan

Leaving this charming town via the domestic airlines to reach Phonsavan airport and a rough ride to the crater-ridden landscape of the *Plain of Jars,* which is also a famous tourist spot, we saw scores of jars lying scattered around the perimeter of the plain, which presented the background for beautiful scenery.

We drove to a guest house upmarket, with a clean suite of rooms with TV, WiFi, hot showers, and a communal balcony. It was love at first sight, a view of vast greenery with high range. The bases of mountains presented different hues, ranging from red, brown, to purple and blue. The landscape changed within the course of a few hours from green to a palette of colors that would have made Van Gogh reach for his brush. Pine and eucalyptus trees were scattered all over. We were told that the plain was reminiscent of parts of Southwest Australia or central British Columbia and would be a paradise for horse riding or motocross riding whichever you may choose!

Plain of Jars and Silk Route in Laos

The *Jar Site* in Laos is one of the most important prehistoric, archaeological sites of Southeast Asia. Clusters of jars, shaped out of solid rock, apparently two thousand years old were found scattered across the plains. These jars were used to hold decorative glass beads, bronze bracelets and cowries seashells (which were used as money in the ancient times, in India, China and some regions of Southeast Asia). Most of the contents of the jars were looted by robbers. One interesting aspect is that the jars are found along the pre-historically-acclaimed Silk Route trade. We were told that the Plain of Jars led towards the West. The same kinds of pots, identical in make and size, have been found in Myanmar and in South *Assam's Cachal Hills* District. According

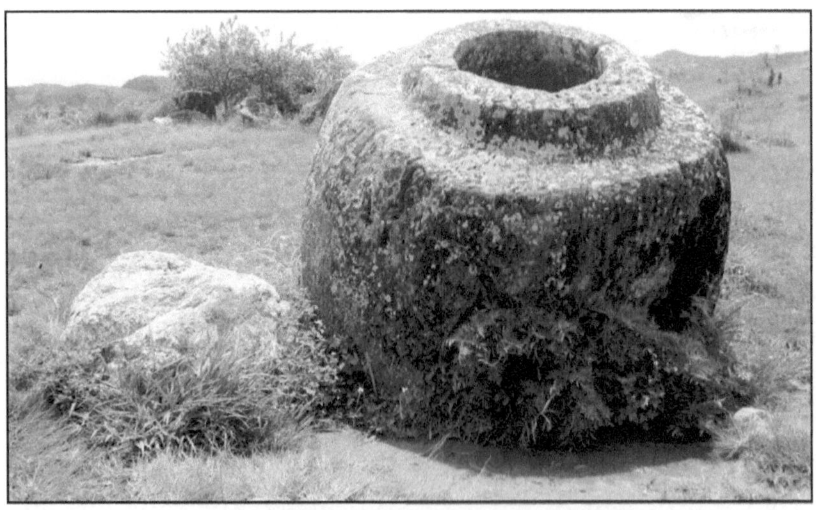

Plain of Jars in Phonsavan

to archaeologists, these jars could also have been used for storing and supplying potable water for the caravans along the Silk Route.

Next morning was dew-fresh. We arranged with a hotel manager for a cab driver to a less-traveled destination. We drove towards the village *Hai Hin Lat Khai*, where we saw well over a hundred jars scattered all around. This place is noted for a small wooded-built monastery, housing a Buddha statue damaged by a bomb. Behind the monastery, there was a path leading up to a hill passing through several fields. The journey to the quiet zone was bumpy and bone-rattling, but it was worth a visit.

We camped in a desolate place enjoying waterfalls at a distance, enjoying birds, butterflies, and silence. It was a place where we could deepen our connection with nature, and the penetrating silence was interrupted by the sweet twitter of birds.

We did not need the pair of binoculars we carried to look at the avian delights. The sun was playing hide-and-seek with the clouds. Giving us company were egrets, eagles, magpie, robins, woodpeckers and jungle fowls. We returned to our guest rooms with recharged energy in our mind and body.

Apart from the *Plain of Jar* site, the other most exciting chapter in the ancient history of the Southeast Asian region is the Silk Route, the wealthiest and longest trade route of the ancient world. The name given to the 'road' was a general term for all the overland passages between China and the West. Essentially every caravan track and the mountain pass that threaded its way between the two points was part of the Silk Route.

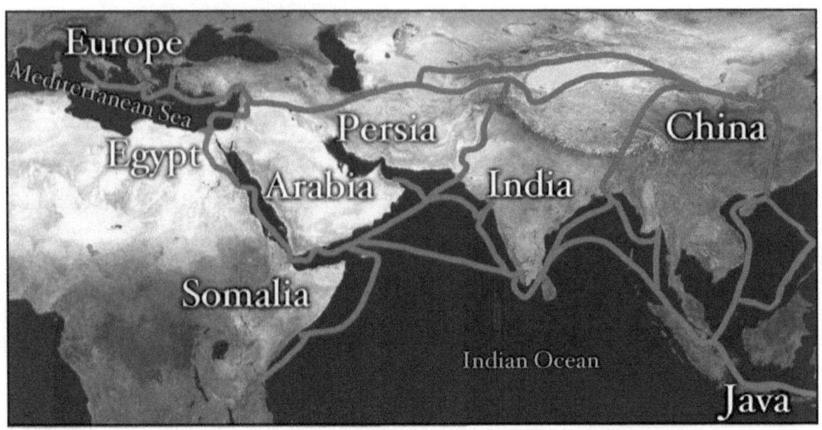

Silk Route Connecting Maritime Route from South India

Silk Route Connecting Maritime Route from South India recognized as the longest thoroughfare on earth, extending up to 12,000 kilometers long, it was opened for commercial and cultural exchange between East and West, they were strategic highways that not only shaped history but were also a conduit for conquest and commerce, cultural contacts with the foreign countries, whichever it passed through.

The Silk Route was first used approximately 2,000 years ago, well before Marco Polo documented his journey some 700 years back. It became an interconnected series of ancient caravan routes through various regions of the Southeastern countries, connected to 'Chang An' in China with Asia Minor and the Mediterranean over land, as well as sea. It is a trade route map, which played a significant factor in the development of the civilizations of China, Egypt, Mesopotamia, Persia, North Eastern regions of India subcontinent and Rome. The Silk Route helped in the formation of modern cultures. It acquired its name because it was the route used by those ancient merchants to distribute silks of the Orient in the pre-Christian era 316–209 BC. It was a trading hub for quality silks, produced in China from the cultivation of the mulberry to the dying and weaving, and the whole production process was shrouded as a closely guarded secret! Not only the silk, the bronze, ceramic wares and handmade papers too from China met with spices, ivory, and gemstones from India. Wine, cotton, and fruits from Central Asia and glasswork from Europe were traded.

Silk Route

The first documented journey began about 2,150 years ago when the Han Emperor sent his envoy Zhang Quan on a secret mission to the West. He aimed to secure western allies to fight against the threatening hordes to China's north.

In his travels, he found the kingdoms of Central Asia and learned the potential of the trade from the great Empires of Persia, Indian subcontinent and Rome. Upon returning, he inspired the Han Emperor to commence trading with these people. Thus, the Silk Route was established and for centuries trade between the East and West was carried on along the route. The dominance of the Silk Route was reduced due to the emergence of maritime trade during the sixteenth century.

At the end of the nineteenth century, Central Asia regained its importance when the British and Russians struggled to establish their power in the region. Along with the military came the spies, adventurers, and archaeologists. They uncovered many lost cities rich in culture and treasures, which they greedily plundered for their own use and also as exhibits in their own countries' museums. Now many Silk Route treasures are only seen outside China.

Many Silk Route tours began in *Xi'am in Shanxi* province and proceeded to *Lanzhou, the Jiayuguan Pass, Dunhuang, Turpan, Urumqi,* and Kashgar. As borders opened up, barriers were lowered, and side trips from *China to Pakistan, Kazakstan,* and *Uzbekistan* were also possible. Significantly, the recent opening of the rail link between Iran and Turkmenistan makes it possible to travel from Istanbul to China.

Lanzhou, the capital of Gansu Province, situated on the Yellow River, was the principal link on the ancient northern part of the Silk Road and is now a thriving industrial center. Some distance from the city, the *Bingling Si,* Buddha caves are carved into stones, and one can find many such caves above the reservoir on the *Yellow River* where stone sculptures, frescos, terracotta statues dating back 1,500 years can be seen in abundance.

History records the power of the Chinese empire during the Tang dynasty, and the former city of Chang'an commended as the largest city in the world. The unearthing of the army of terracotta warriors in 1974 is one of the most important and significant discoveries of our times. Thousands of life-sized terracotta soldiers and their horses were the highlight of the Silk Route. These 6,000 entombed soldiers were assembled along the Silk Route to follow their emperors after their death to immortality.

The Chinese traders took their produce along the Silk Route and handed them over to the caravan teams from Central Asia as a barter deal in exchange for their food.

At Dunhuang, the road splits into three main routes. The northernmost path passes through *Hami, urumqu, Alma-Ata in Kazakstan* and on to the *Caspian Sea.* The intermediate course goes through Iran while the southern pass goes through *Kashgar Afghanistan, Pakistan, and India.*

The small town of Dunhuang has sizable drifting sand dunes, where one could go on a camel safari early in the morning to watch the sunrise—one of the highlights of a Silk Route journey.

Not far from town, the Magao Caves are a rich trove of Buddhist statues and wall paintings from the fourth to tenth centuries. They are the most significant accumulation of Buddhism's remnants in the world and, in 1987, were recognized as a UNESCO world heritage status.

The creative genius was a lone monk who had the vision to create 1,000 Buddhas. Some 1,600 years ago, he began to carve Buddhist images in the sandstone caves along the Yellow River bank, and many of them have different layers of frescoes from various dynasties.

There is an excellent interest today in reviving the Silk Route (not that it has ever declined in its archaeological importance). Thanks to the cooperation from all the countries, people are moving freely along the route to discover the many archaeological treasures found there. Caravans of yesteryears had long ceased to traverse the Silk Route. Tourism is the new industry bringing life back to the bazaars and oases of Central Asia to revitalize the nations and stimulate the prosperity and wealth generated during the times of Marco Polo, Genghis Khan and many Chinese emperors of a bygone era!

Along the Silk Route, through the Central Asian regions, almonds were discovered growing in the mountains. Eventually, they spread to the *Middle East, Africa, and parts of Europe.* It was *Father Junipero Serra* who brought almonds to America from Central Europe. They took 'root' in the Central California Valley, which proved to be an ideal growing region.

Recently, its plan of setting up a $1.6 million fund to take forward its ambitious maritime Silk Route, a road plan to build ports and boost naval connectivity with the Southeast Asian countries and the Indian Ocean littoral region, including Bangladesh and Sri Lanka. A massive project was planned to revive the ancient maritime Silk Route, connecting China with territories including India, Sri Lanka with Malaysia, Singapore and the Gulf countries. Although already involved in port-specific projects in Pakistan, Sri Lanka and Bangladesh, Gwada, Hambantota, and Chittagong, respectively, the plan was envisaged to extend beyond to include Kolkata (India).

Rewinding our tour to Luang Prabang, we checked into an eco-resort run by two cheerful and lively sisters. It is found on the bank of the river *Nam Khan*, consisting of deluxe Laos-style bungalows with wooden floors, well-furnished and with a well- maintained garden. From the balcony facing the river, you could spend hours sunk into a plush leather chair watching the villagers tending the garden, against the backdrop of *Mount Phou* (a sight to be treasured in the niches of your heart).

The backstreet and bylanes were paved with cobblestones, an early morning walk. A pale orange sun appeared, and the birds squabbling became intense due to their calling out each other. When I heard the collective sounds of 'mee, mee, honk, and musical whistle,' it said clearly, that the bird language has no equivalent in my minimal range of vocabulary. Mountain ranges, silhouetted against the rising sun and our walkway flanked on either side with palm trees of uniform heights swaying gently with the cool mountain breeze, made our walk a walker's delight.

Royal Palace

After a hurried breakfast, we were to drive to *Royal Palace,* a mammoth building, built by the French. It was home to the Lao kings until the abdication and exile of the last king in 1975 when *Pathet Lao* took over the monarchy government after a protracted civil war and established a Democratic Republic Government the emperor and his descendants. King had been exiled to a cave—a journey from which he and his royal entourage never returned. The palace was classified as a museum, open to visitors, presenting the royal trappings and the paraphernalia of Laos' extinguished monarchy. The reception hall and the throne durbar were well preserved and impressive, especially the latter, with imposing high walls, spangled with the mosaic of multi-colored mirrors, dazzling even in dim light.

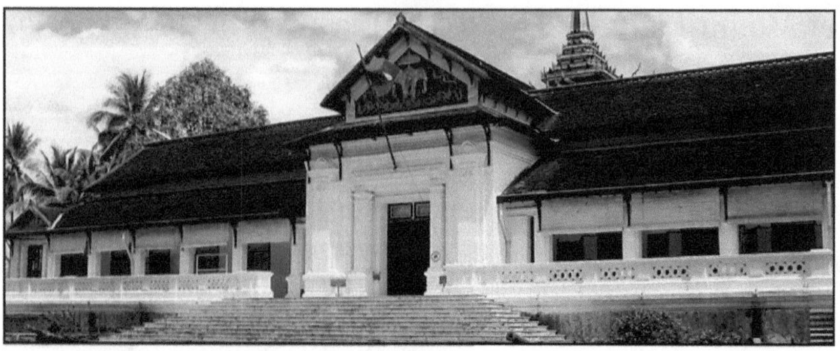

Royal Palace at Luang Prabang

As a part of our schedule, we watched a live dance performance of the Lao version of the Indian epic tale of *Ramayana* (a forty-five-minute show). After lunch, we were off to a most picturesque waterfall thirty-five meters high. It is a multi-level waterfall tumbling from this height, spilling and creating multiple crystal blue water ponds. The day was refreshing, and it was an ideal picnic spot, with vendors offering fresh fruit juices, sweetened with honey. The whole place is surrounded by green meadows and with multi-colored butterflies.

The French influence is still noticeable, the tree-lined boulevards, the baguettes, and the strong aromatic Lao coffee. We had breakfast in a classic restaurant when we spotted a (boy) waiter serving us breakfast. He was seen wearing lipstick, mascara-clumped false lashes, eyeshadow, brushed eyelids, rouge powdered on his cheeks and topped with a wig to stylish disarray. *(This must be one of Lao's mysteries and let the world solve this riddle!)*

Kuang Si

From *Luang Prabang,* we were ready to tour the countryside to drive towards the *Kuang Si* waterfalls. A panoramic view of hillocks was seen, some green and some black. The clouds made lovely patterns, and there was a nip in the air. A cornucopia of smell hit you. The sun peeped through the floating clouds. The frothy white water broke the color scheme of greenery and dark rocks. It went down in streams, spreading a cool mist in the midday heat. We stood there transfixed, with the sight of rock pools and the waterfall awash, cascading over the stone tiers like champagne spilling down to a pyramid of glasses!

We must add that this was one of the best parts of our itinerary of Southeast Asian travel. The spectacular waterfalls, about which nothing, neither the traveler's guidebooks nor our guide, prepared us for! Huge sprays of water were gushing down furiously, tumbling down to about forty-five feet over a bed of basalt. The fall happened in segmented cascades. *Kuang Si* has the highest volume of water in the entire world's waterfalls. We were told that the liters of water per second which is almost double that of *Niagara.* It was not part of our itinerary, but visiting this place happened impromptu, thanks to the last-minute cancellation of our earlier schedule.

Rewinding our trip to *Phonsavan,* a small town that had been obliterated during the past twenty-five years of conflict, wholly devastated in the second Indo-China war, but rebuilt in the aftermath of

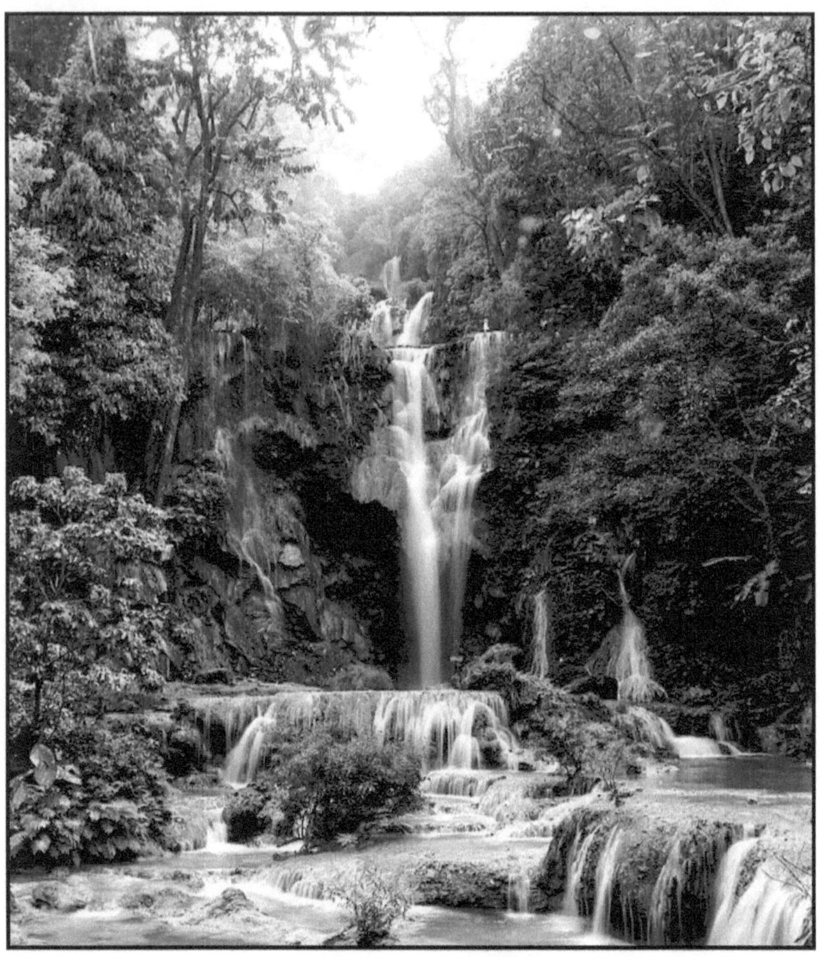

Kuang Si Waterfalls

Fighting is now beginning to recover. Thanks to the archaeological interest, especially in the *Jar Sites,* a place of great natural beauty and the surroundings were well worth exploring. International tourism had given the town a new lease of life! After lunch at a French restaurant, which commanded an outstanding view of the neighborhood, the fresh fruit salad and pâté were well worth a try. Later, we reached Luang. Prabang airport in time for an international flight to Hanoi by Vietnam Airlines.

Backtracking to Laos. Our visit to this country would not have been complete without recording our experience at the famed *Lao-herbal sauna.*

Being of a monastery, we were told that it offered a genuinely ethnic steam bath, consisting of many rustic wooden shacks (separate ones for men and women). Beneath the floor of the cabin was a drum containing water, heated with firewood, with medicinal herbs (mainly eucalyptus) releasing their juices into the boiling water, intermixed with the steam jets spurting into the shack. The temperature inside was rising abnormally. We had to come out and lounge in the cool shade of a tree, sipping green tea (to replace the water that our bodies lost due to the profuse sweating). This process of 'in and out' was repeated as long as we could physically endure. But the most impressive part was the whole place was shrouded in silence except for the chirping of the birds, and we had to talk in whispers. No doubt, even the silence was calming!

As I leave from Laos, I cannot forget the worst happenings of the recent history of the Lao people. The people of Laos formed an army to fight against the monarchy and the Royal Lao Army. Prince Souvanna Phouma supported by the Thai Army and the Americans fought a war. This civil war lasted for a long time. During this period, from 1964 to 1973, America bombed these countries: Laos, Vietnam, and Cambodia on a daily basis. Every eight minutes, B-52 bombers would unload their cargo from the sky above onto the people of that area. Probably the then political leadership of America wanted to empty all.

The stockpile of their ammunition as new advanced technology had begun. This horrifying incident is recorded as the 'Black History' of the world, which is discussed in greater detail during my visit to Vietnam. After a prolonged war, with help from the Vietnamese army, the Lao People's Army took control of their country. Since then it is under the communist party rule under Laos People's Revolutionary Party.

The cab drove us to the international airport where we checked in on a flight to advance with our journey to Hanoi, Vietnam.

CHAPTER 4

VIETNAM

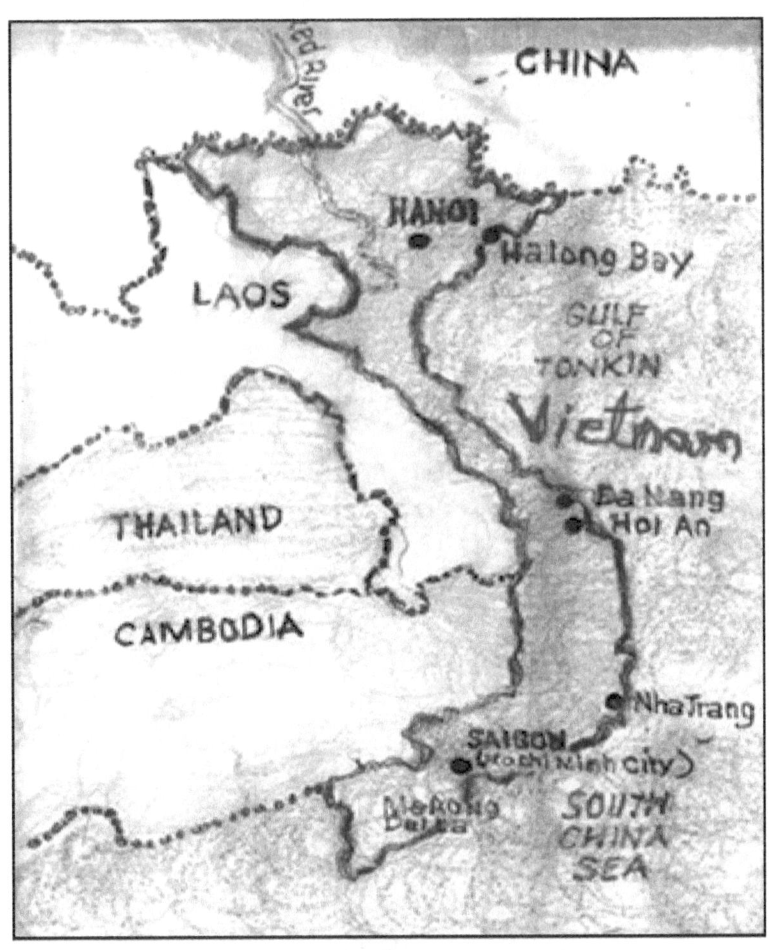

Hanoi:	The capital of Vietnam, a most attractive city, worthy of being dubbed the 'Paris of the East'
Ho Chi Minh Mausoleum:	Amidst traffic-free area of parks is the monumental marble edifice, where the embalmed body of Ho Chi Minh is kept

Military History Museum:	The trophies of battle are displayed. St Joseph's Cathedral: Neo-Gothic architectural style with twin bell towers
Halong Bay:	One of Vietnam's most spectacular natural wonders with over 3,000 bizarre limestone formations
Ho Chi Minh City:	Lively bustling city, formerly the French colonial city of Saigon
War Remnants Museum:	Displaying US armories, artillery pieces of bombs—Notorious tiger cages to imprison the Viet Cong freedom fighters, etc.
Cu Chi Tunnels:	One of the few remaining monuments of Vietnam War — Network of 200 km of tunnels built manually
Mekong Delta:	Glimpses of rural life in Vietnam's rice bowl—Colourful central market — Cruise along the river, passing fishing villages, rice paddy, and fruit farms with a visit to the floating market
Notre Dame Cathedral:	A neo-Romanesque architecture with twin spires dedicated to the Virgin Mary
Old Post Office:	In the neighborhood of the Cathedral—High-vaulted ceiling—a colossal building by the French colonist
Nha Tarang:	Prettiest coastal city, unrivaled for its sheer beauty and ambiance
Da Nang:	an Economic heart of Central Vietnam—A popular tourist destination
Hoi An:	Noted for its pristine palm-edged beaches, a UNESCO World Heritage Site

This is a charming country rich with enchanting ruins, lush landscapes and coastal plains stretching 1,200 miles to the North Mekong Delta. We landed at Hanoi—Noi Bai International Airport late in the evening. Little did I realize that this tiny little country about which I had heard and read in my youth had so much to offer with vast feats of heroism and determination by its small few people. Although it may seem that some of the contents are repetitive, I have deliberately touched upon its various contexts to emphasize the basic fabric of its people and the beauty of nature of Vietnam: Once a war-ravaged country, today the Vietnamese have rebuilt it from shambles. Saigon, renamed 'Ho Chi Minh City,' with the gracefully maintained churches, built in the style of the French Renaissance period by their former colonial masters. Old post office, schools, convents, and handsome villas, grand old opera houses, tree-lined boulevards with central medians dotted with colorful potted canvas of various hues are the remnants of the French culture.

Many American visitors had remarked, "How happy we are to see the prosperity of this nation and how sad we feel to have carpet-bombed it. We wereresponsiblefor causing cancer in many peasants by spraying millions of gallons of Agent Orange on the people and their vegetation and forests." The 2, 4, 5-T had been used, although it was banned in 1979 by the environmental protection agency as potentially dangerous. This defoliant, employed by the US forces in Vietnam, caused untold suffering to the veterans and their children. "At least the French colonists had left boulevards, imposing buildings, monuments, opera houses and cultural centers, but we had left nothing, but a multitude of the searing trauma of a miserable decade, full of terror, raining seven million tons of bombs and napalm, causing craters and planting landmines," they said. "You cannot be held responsible for what your government did to us—let bygones be bygones!" was the average Vietnamese stoic reply. a place I loved to visit was *Halong Bay*—one of the seven wonders of nature, like the Table Mountain range in South Africa.

A Phoenix Has Risen from the Ashes

Texts blazing '*Welcome*' greeted us while boarding the blue-streaked body of Vietnam Airlines as well as '*Make yourselves at home*' on board. Truly, we felt comfortable with the push-back seat and the seating arrangement. It was indeed relaxing moment and we were impressed especially by the gracious faces of the staff and their service with a smile, accompanied with the muted but melodious Vietnamese music.

Hanoi

On landing, as soon as we checked out, aftercompleting our initial formalities, we were greeted by a slim and smart tour guide. When I approached her to get a local SIM card for communication purposes,she immediately obliged us and took us to a mobile store. Although she was very helpful, I found her quite stern and uptight. Most of the North Vietnamese, it seemed to me, were less expressive, choosing to stick to the job at hand, and stay focused. An hour's drive, along with the highways to our appointed hotel, after finishing up our initial formalities, we moved into the rooms allotted to us. We didn't want to waste any time and so we went out for a stroll. Although the country had been colonized by the French for nearly one hundred years, the locals prefer English to French as the language for communication. We

Three Men in Sea could 'wade' through all over the country conversing in English—shopping, money exchange and inquiry for directions, etc., everything was in English! English with an American accent was more pronounced.

We found Hanoi to be a really graceful capital city of Vietnam and one of the most exotic cities in all of Southeast Asia. It is also one of the two biggest cities in Vietnam and very densely populated. Most of the political and military activities were initiated from here. The town is on the move, and the energy here is super-charged. Its appeal is instant, with sweeping boulevards, lakes, and pagodas that are best explored on foot. We walked around the *West Lake*—it is the largest freshwater lake, almost ten miles long, in the center of Hanoi, offering recreation and excitement to tourists. Many restaurants are found scattered around this lovely lake.

Ho Chi Minh Mausoleum

Next morning, we reached the most important place of pilgrimage—the *Ho Chi Minh Mausoleum*, A monumental marble edifice. The roof and peristyle are said to be evocative of a lotus flower. Set deep in the center of the building, in a glass sarcophagus, is the frail, pale body of Ho Chi Minh, the man credited with creating the nation as it exists today, just as George Washington is considered to be instrumental in establishing the *United States of America.*

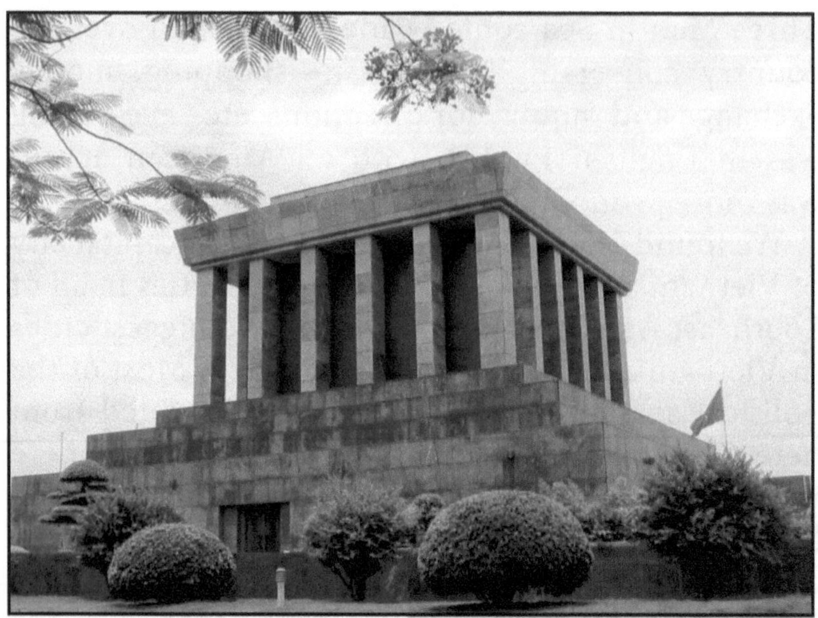

Ho Chi Minh Mausoleum

We joined the long queue and quietly filed past Ho's embalmed body. Guards in snow-white military uniforms were posted inside and outside the mausoleum. Many Vietnamese visited Uncle Ho, giving him great reverence.

Uncle Ho

Ho Chi Minh was well-educated, having studied in France and other foreign countries, including China. Initially, he embraced the Confucian philosophy. He appears to have changed his name many times, for reasons unknown. Finally, he turned communist, believing in the socialist governance. This probably due to the disparity, he saw with his fellow

Vietnamese. He was joined by General Giap, and together they roused and stirred up the emotions against the French rule, again for reasons unknown. It could have been a personal vendetta. Ho Chi Minh led the war against capitalism; the war went on for many years, even after his death. He was loved dearly by his people, so much so that they affectionately called him *Uncle Ho*. Although it had been his wish to be cremated and his ashes buried in the north and south, the political leadership decided to retain his body and preserved it for future generations. *Uncle Ho* always lives with pride in the memories of all Vietnamese.

As we walked out of the Ho Chi Minh Mausoleum, we saw the changing of the guards, with the pomp and ceremony of a magnitude that would rival the British equivalent at Buckingham Palace, London.

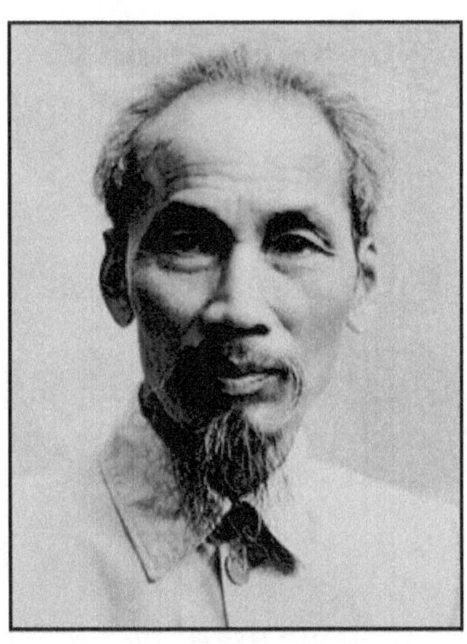

Ho Chi Minh in 1948

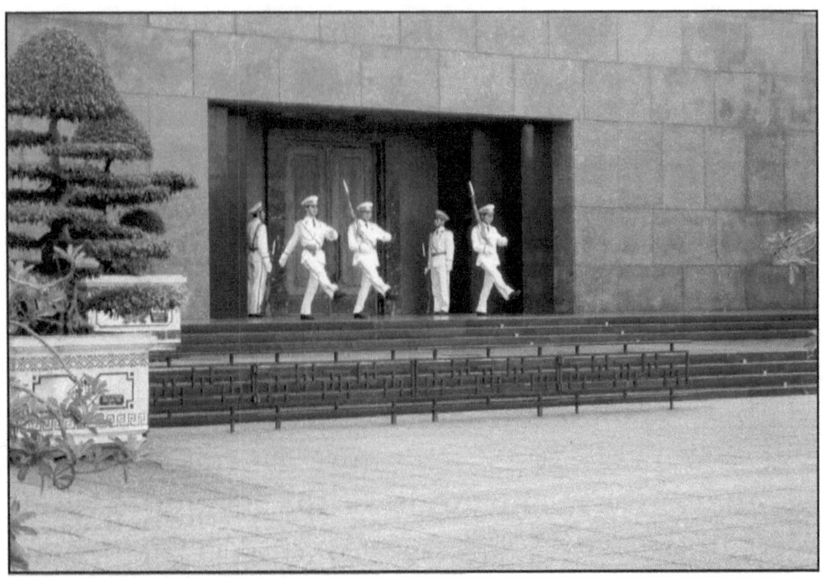

Changing of the Guards at Ho Chi Minh Mausoleum

Later, we strolled through the stately parks and water bodies nearby, window shopping in some of the tiny streets, evocatively named *Silk Street, Jewelers Street and Basket Street,* a fantastic browsing paradise for take-away souvenirs, quite inexpensive for their quality. We then went on to visit the *Presidential Palace.*

Presidential Palace

Our next stop, on the way to the airport, was the *Presidential Palace.* Initially designed by a French architect, built in the colonial French-style, it had been constructed during the French rule in Vietnam, in 1905. The French governor lived there, enjoying a stately and lavish lifestyle until the French were thrown out of Vietnam. After independence from foreign occupation, Ho Chi Minh refused to live in this palace. He chose to stay on in a traditional stilt house, living a simple life. Only state lunches/dinners were held there for foreign delegates or any dignitary coming on a state visit. This was the inherent simplicity of *Uncle Ho.*

The atmosphere in Hanoi was one of reserved, cautious tranquility. The tree-lined avenues host balconies, spilling over with splashes of colorful bougainvillea. Mute, broken shutters still hung from old colonial villas. In short, *Hanoi still* exudes a subtle charm—a shining example of culture, as opposed to the brutality of war and we noticed cerebral beauty reigning supreme.

During our stay there, we could not but help recalling the disturbing scenario that this bustling city once endured—the 'Christmas bombing' by the B-52s in mid-December 1972, an unabashed genocidal act of wickedness just a couple of weeks before the signing of 'ceasefire' by America. Amidst the worldwide celebrations commemorating the birth of Christ, these B-52s were busy raining death upon unwary peasants, newborns and even babes-in-arms!

We returned to our hotel to freshen up. Then, we proceeded further, after passing through rows of shopping malls are displaying tempting goodies. Although quite physically worn out, we ventured out to do some window shopping and admire the elegant designer silk that Vietnam boasts about! We went on foot to explore the city that day. A legacy of French the rule had seen the setting up of some excellent and moderately-priced French brasserie-style restaurants, offering delicious baguettes and croissants. Before the lunch, we were directed to the *Hoan Kiem Lake* for a walk around that enchanting water body, the soul of the city dwellers, where we saw many families and young lovers strolling around us. A squat three-tiered pavilion occupies the center of the lake.

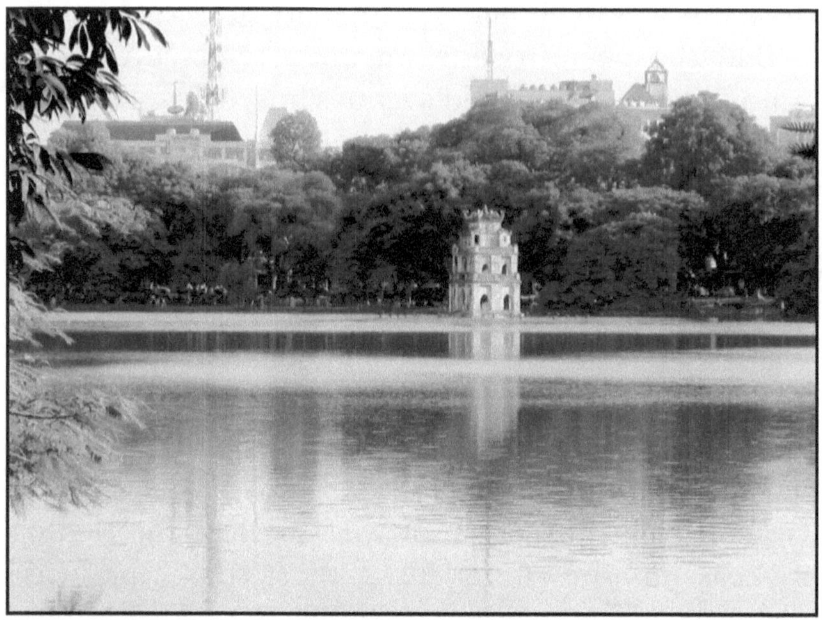

Hoan Kiem Lake

A pristine glamour was evident anywhere we walked. Well-laid boulevards gave the city an additional dignity. I fell in love with the city; more Europeanised than any of the other towns we had visited thus far. *It did not look like a rebuilt or restored place; instead, it appeared to be a reincarnated one, risen from the ashes!*

Then we went on to a much-sought-after afternoon siesta, reclining in the inviting, comfortable chairs, under the cool shadow of the palm-fringed bank of the lake, with portraits of Ho Chi Minh observing us from the many walls of the city. We visited the *Fine Arts Museum,* housed in two buildings, which had served as the French

Ministry of Information and Broadcasting during the colonial regime. We stood there, amazed at the outstanding collection of artworks, superb textiles, as well as furniture and ceramic wares. In the main building, there were rare artistic treasures of Vietnam of a bygone era, including ancient Chapa-stone carvings of the effigies of their Goddess of Compassion. There was also an extensive collection of contemporary art displayed for sale.

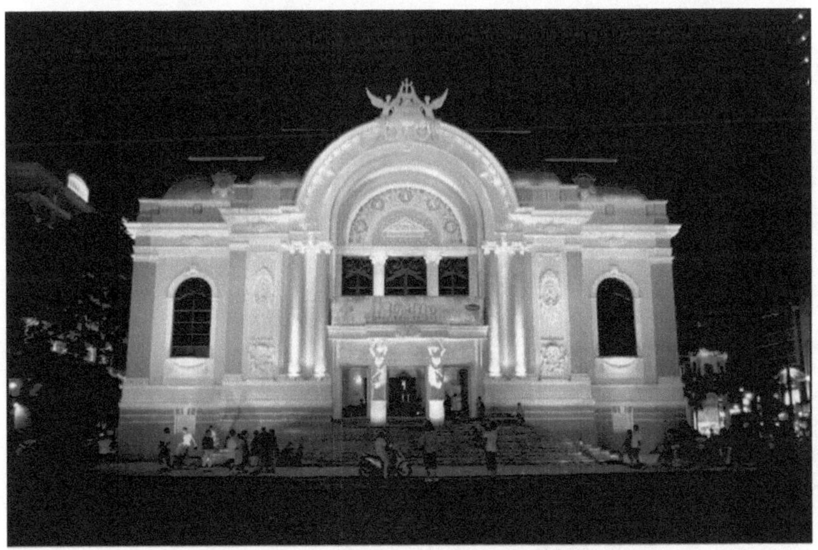
Fine Arts Museum at Ho Chi Minh City

It was late in the evening when we visited *St. Joseph's Cathedral.* This ancient church, built in the eighteenth century, had been constructed in the striking neo-Gothic style, with its soaring facade facing a little plaza. Its most noteworthy features are the twin bell towers. The interior boasts an ornate altar and French stained-glass cathedral windows. Being a Sunday, we participated in the evening mass service. To our surprise, we found the congregation spilling out onto the treet. Hymns were beamed across and the 'congregation,' seated on their motorbikes, was listening intently! An apparently

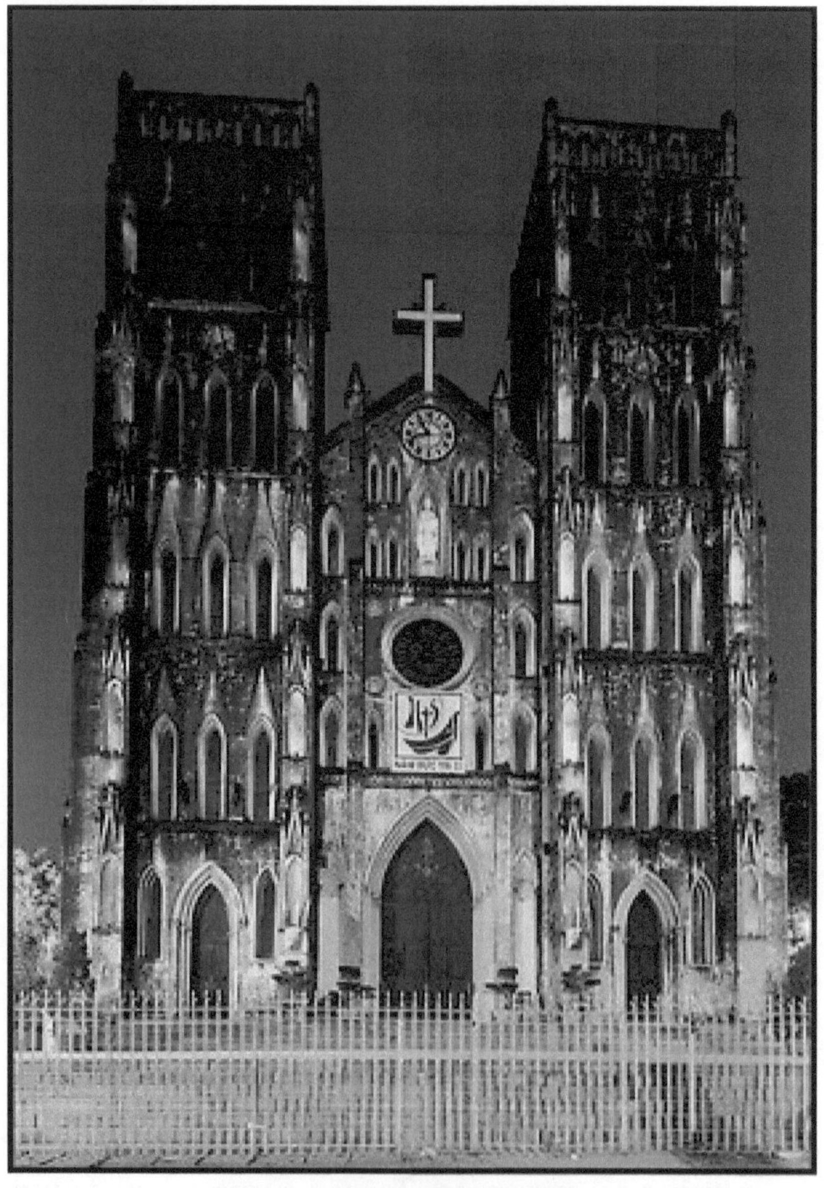

St. Joseph's Cathedral at Hanoi

effortless weaving of Western and Vietnamese classical music gently streamed out from the church and all the four voices, *soprano, alto, tenor, and bass* delivered the song in St. Joseph's Cathedral at Hanoi pitch-perfect rendition. Outside, a serenity of silence enveloped us like a comforter, and not a whisper, save the chirping of birds could be heard. Two soloists ended the solemn service, with the male's rich tenor, mellifluously blending with the bell-like soprano of the female.

While returning to our hotel, after dinner I could not help but think of the hunger, the death, severed limbs and above all, the gallons of Agent Orange poured upon this small country during the war of the liberation.

'I love the smell of napalm in the mornings,' says Kilgore a character, symbolic of the American excesses in Vietnam, in the iconic film *Apocalypse Now,* directed by *Coppola,* retelling Joseph Conrad's *Heart of Darkness,* set against the backdrop of the sheer madness of the war in Vietnam. The iconic opening scene hit us with a hiss-and-ominous throb of the choppers, spraying gallons of Agent Orange. The arresting visuals with quotable quotes and the terrifying action, shifting from the Belgian Congo to Vietnam, vividly portrayed the horror of the 'uncalled for' war! The movie was a poem in celluloid, and brought forcefully to my mind, pertinent questions about this self-assumed, self-righteous attitude of a nation to launch unwarranted aggression into other territories. America appeared to be masquerading as a modern avatar of the age-old Crusaders who had asserted that their beliefs were right and that the non-believers needed to be exterminated and wiped off the face of the earth!

Military History Museum

After our lunch on the *Hang Go Street,* we sauntered through the brilliant displays of the Vietnam Museum of Ethnology (enjoying a glimpse of the different lifestyles in the mountains) and the hard-won trophies of the battles at the Military History Museum.

Vietnam has about seven museums situated in various locations. The important ones include the *Military History Museum at Central Hanoi located in the vicinity of Lenin Park, the Ho Chi Minh Mausoleum* and the *War Remnant Museum* at Ho Chi Minh City (Saigon). After visiting these museums, one could clearly, understand the military genius of a few of its leaders who had transformed the untrained peasants into great soldiers. These soldiers became a marvelous fighting force, supported wholly by young Viet Cong women along with their families. The museum contains displays of all the armaments used, the ones indigenously made by the Vietnamese, along with the military hardware supplied by the *Soviet Union and China.* At the center of the Military History Museum, you can see the MIG-21 Jet Fighter. Next to that are the wreckages of the French and American aircraft. This was the highlight of our visit. After literally scratching our heads to shake off the confused status of our minds after having seen the awful wreckages and military hardware, I really wondered if the war had ever been worth it. Did war have a purpose of achieving? Could any type of army might win over the human spirit and willpower? With such confusion spinning in my mind, we chose to retreat for some relaxation. Before returning, we stopped for dinner at the Metropole's Le Beaulieu restaurant, where we encountered an almost an endless line of couples, just beyond the street-side bar, clicking photographs of themselves against the back a drop of Metropole, the icon of a more glamorous age. Hanoi, like Saigon, is changing fast.

Halong Bay Visit

The next morning turned out to be quite disappointing. Our plans for a long leisurely stroll to unwind and relax in the shade in a park nearby went awry, as also our eagerness to savor the Vietnam-centric cuisine for breakfast, because our guide emerging from nowhere asked us to sign off by 7 a.m. Sadly, we needed to miss our meal too. We were ill-prepared for this sudden turn of events, sans any prior information from the tour operators. It was a bolt from the blue! Admitting the futility of exchanging any barbed comments with our guide, we quickly packed our bags and baggage after our morning ablution, etc., at break-neck speed. But in the melee, Terry left behind one of his bags, packed with his personal clothes, etc., in the room, which he realized only during our long drive to *Halong Bay*. Halfway through the journey, I got really rattled, and straightaway called the local representative of the tour organizers and gave them a piece of my mind regarding this early morning mishap. Slowly, things began to change; the guide and the driver became very cordial and even chivalrous! They also willingly stopped en route at a small place where we could nibble a little something along with our coffee.

Cruise at Halong Pier

The 160-kilometer drive to reach *Bai Chay/Halong Pier* was interesting. When we reached Halong Bay, we saw a luxury liner waiting for us. It had about twelve cabins, of which we occupied two, and the rest was for the Germans, French, and other nationals. I found it easy to get along very well with everybody. A couple of them were lovely to me, especially the German ladies who were very courteous and friendly towards me.

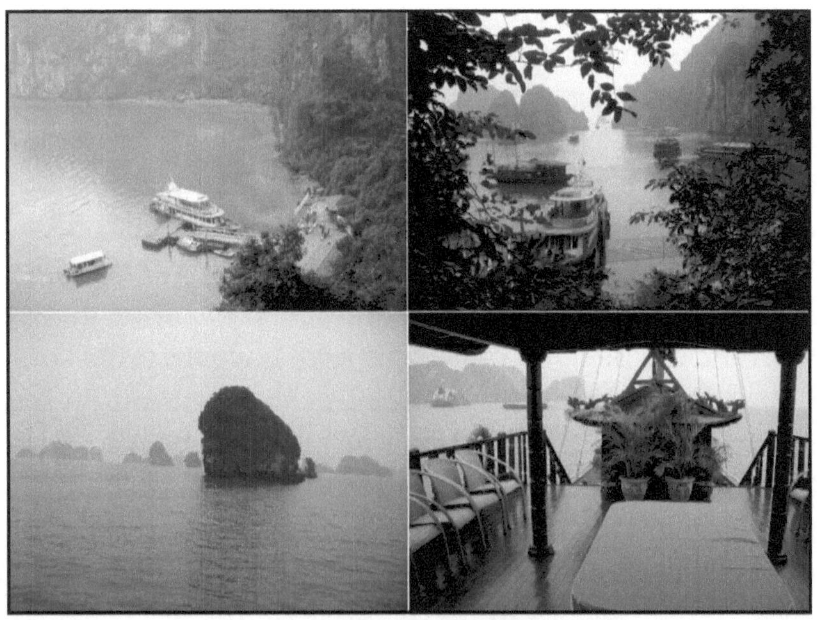

Halong Bay – Hanoi

Halong Bay boasts one of the most beautiful natural scenery and is a topnotch destination for any visitor. Also known as the 'Bay of the Descending Dragon,' it lies on the coast of the Gulf of Tonkin. It includes around 2,000 islands and islets. This has recently been designated as a UNESCO World Heritage Site and one of the New Seven Wonders of the World.

These limestone formations are bizarrely shaped, putting their noses out of the still waters. Our minds were at total peace with the world Cruising in the bay in a luxury yacht with reclining seats,. Four hours of sailing on the bay offered us a quick-paced change of unforgettable scenery of hidden coves, needle-sharp ridges, and caves.

Surprise Cave

We berthed at the Bo Hon Island. While crossing the wooden bridge, we encountered several other cruise boats that had already docked at the entrance of the enchanting *Sung grotto*, otherwise known as the **Surprise Cave.** It is right at the center of the World Heritage Site and one of the most beautiful and most extensive caverns ever to be seen in that area. You ascend up sizeable paved stone blocks in the middle of an avenue of trees and foliage. The climb is like the vestiges of a prehistoric era, where you can admire a textbook display of sparkling stalactites with the floor being covered by what has been described as a 'forest.' The cave has two chambers, one of which is square, and which serves as the waiting room.

As you move forward, you are visually surprised with the stalagmites and the entire interior panorama of the caves are very aesthetically and dimly lit up in shades of different colors. Eroded over millions of years by the trickling of water, to its present fantastic form, it is mind-boggling to set foot into one of the most massive caverns. The interior is thirty meters high and looks like a palace or opera hall. Stalactites hang from the high ceiling, with numerous impossible forms and shapes. It seems like a cavalry of animals of different shapes and sizes led by the general going to war or remaining alert and on foot to protect their kingdom. This hidden world of exotic geology is revealed as the ranks of dripping stalactites give way to a myriad of tunnels and pools. We had a thrilling and unforgettable experience when we set foot in the cave, although the jagged floors demanded careful navigation. But first things first: It is advisable not to go off wandering by yourself as you could easily get lost, and no one would realize it, even if you yelled at the top of your lungs! So as safety and precautionary measure, follow the crowds of tourists and explore the ambiance that will literally and figuratively take your breath away. We saw, in some places, water seeping through the rocks, dissolving the limestone, and also the little drips from the ceiling twinkling like numerous stars reflected by the focusing lights placed at strategic locations. The cave by natural formation was divided into two parts—as the first part of the exit narrows down, it opens out into a more significant second part. You can walk into the new world of the more massive cave, the illuminated beauty of it, highlighted with different colored neon lights is simply breathtaking; it is a 'must visit' for anyone. You almost walk for about half an hour through the extent of the twin caves. As we exited, we had to climb 55 steep stone steps up to a height of 22 meters. We reached the grotto area of the exit. This cave is pretty unique, about the eight thousand square meters, naturally decorated with stalactites and stalagmites; it has also human-influenced unique lighting decoration. *This marvelous masterpiece of na-*

ture stirs one so deeply, one can even feel like the divine authority overall human beings and mastering the demonic evil spirits as we come out of the small exit stand on the canopy pedestal overlooking the Halong Bay. The marvelous sight of Halong Bay is one that would really fill the heart with deep contentment with the travel experience.

After our visit to the caves, we returned to our cruise ship. The cabins were comfortable and cozy, with attached toilets. Equipped with an in-house pantry and kitchenette we could have food on demand A la carte, either continental or Vietnamese. We opted for the local cuisine, mostly of root vegetable (Tapioca), an abundance of fruits, roasted pumpkin seeds, with less meat, and less spicy than Thai cuisine, all washed down with the locally brewed but excellent 'Tiger' brand beer.

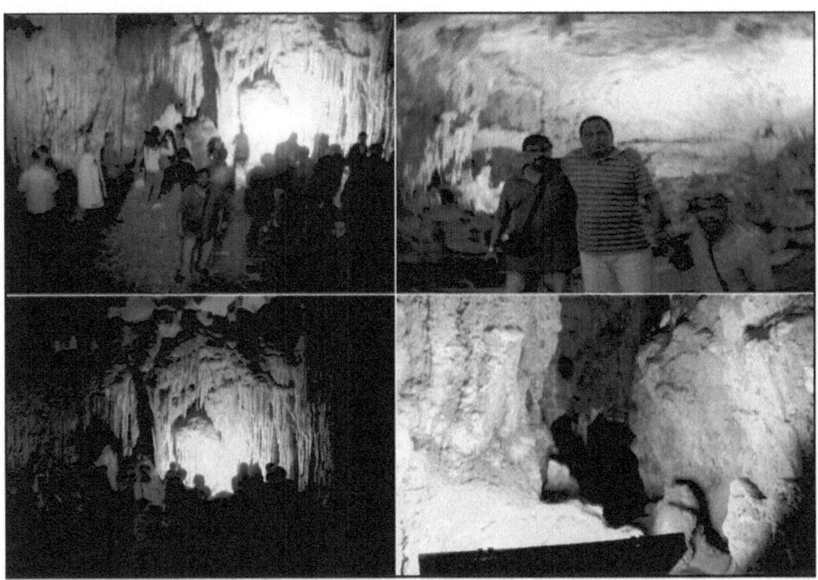

Surprise Cave at Halong Bay

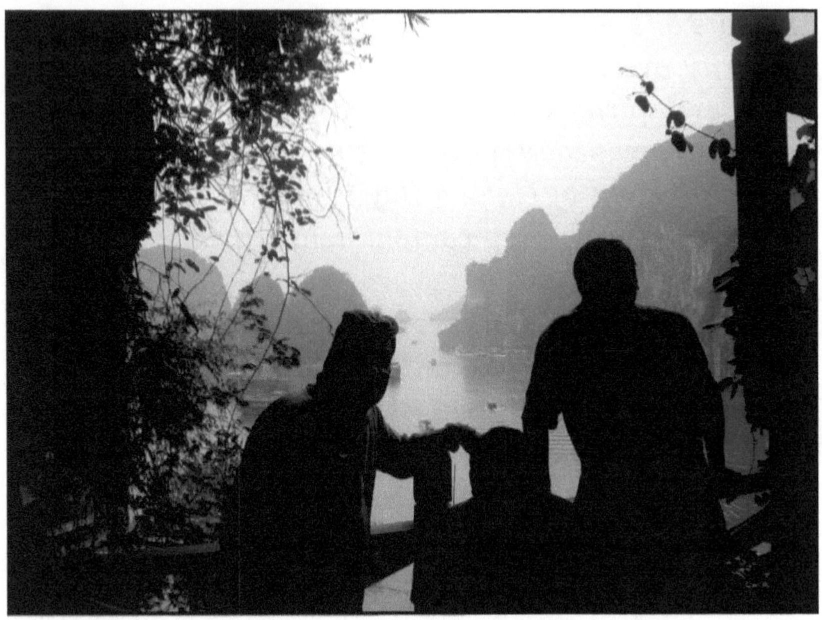

Exit at Surprise Cave

Bat Cave

After lunch, while a few chose to sunbathe, I along with some young ladies decided to kayak to Bat Cave. Bat Cave is otherwise known as cave *Hang Doi Hang Bat Cave*. There are eight such caves, which are actually water caves, with a clearance level to the ceiling of about two to three meters, depending upon the water level. Here too one can see elements of stalactites hanging from the ceiling. They look like BATS hanging from the ceiling! These deposits remain on the roof, which consists of gravel and breccias, cemented by carbonate. As we kayaked through the *Bat Cave,* we also came across Luon Cave.

These caves are about twenty-five meters long, and a new world opens up in front you. There are clusters of islets, most of which are currently being studied from the environment and nature. Scientific research is also presently undertaken for their origin and formation. Gazing upon this amazing wonder of nature we wondered why the French and Americans had wanted to go to war against these poor natives of Cambodia, Vietnam, and Laos! Why on earth should humans land on moon or Mars? There is so much to study and learn from Mother Nature's wonderful offering, I am sure God would have unraveled more its secrets if we were to explore these areas. Kayaking with the young foreign ladies was a most interesting experience. I seemed to find a lot in common with them. In fact, I could handle their wit and excitement, and I am sure I will stumble across them in another travel experience.

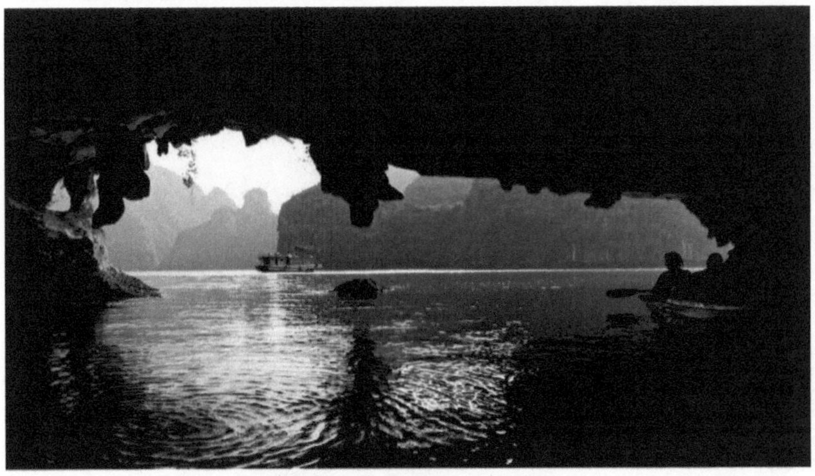

Bat Cave at Halong Bay

Ti Top Island

Our cruise boat was on the move after our visit to Bat Cave. We were on low cruising speed and the change in scenery, regular intervals were quite dramatic. After cruising along for about forty-five minutes, we disembarked at Ti Top Island; as soon as we landed, I asked the local guide why it had been named Ti Top Island. The guide narrated the story that gave it its name. It is said to have been named Ti Top Island by Uncle Ho in honor of *Ghermann Titov, a former Soviet Union hero,* who was an astronaut. After their visit to the island, it had become very famous! Its white sand and calm waters with gentle waves attract many tourists for water sports and other beach activities. If you like rock climbing, there are plenty of places for that too. On the shore, we walked towards a well-tended garden with greenery and a water fountain. Smitten was I, at the

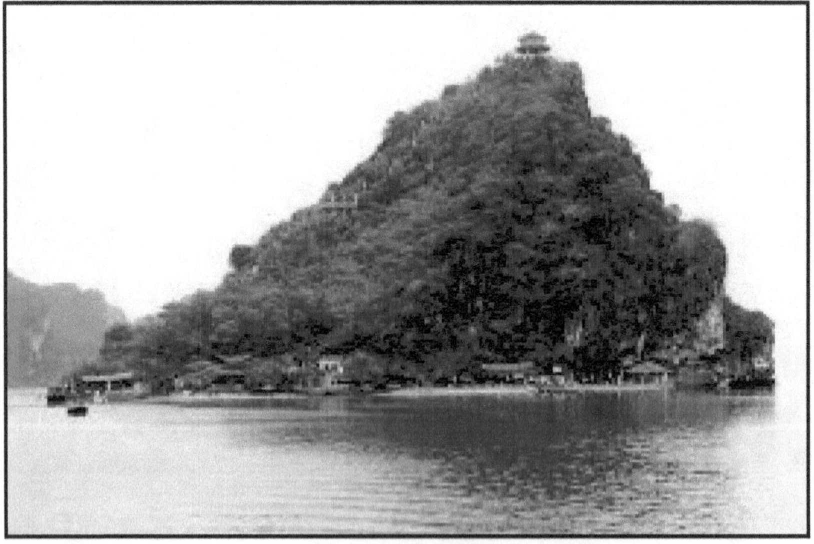

Ti Top Island

beautiful setting, my mind recalling the well-known words of Jehangir, *'If there is paradise on earth, it is here! It is here!'*

While Terry and Gerald were enjoying the evening hours, lounging in the garden, I (caring little for my feet) climbed up a rather steep hillock on the rock-cut steps. The view from the top unfolded deep blue water, white limestone peaks, deep-green mangroves, making it well worth the trouble of my labored climbing! When I finally reached the top, the other tourists clapped their hands to welcome me! After a while, I climbed down, spent some time in the water and played volley-ball with a Russian tourist. Soon, it was time to leave, and the guide took us back on board. We had to clean our hands before getting on board really. The time was right for us to leave, and as we set foot on the deck, the captain of the yacht kindly invited us to the Captain's Dinner on board. Dressed to the nines, we climbed up the floor to be greeted by the captain.

We were sailing along for quite a while. When we reached the Luon Bo area, the cruise ship was anchored for the overnight stay. The night party and dinner were memorable; it was quite a lively, glitzy party with an annoyingly chirpy emcee, pounding with music and couples dancing on the deck under the starry night with foot-thumping 'fast numbers' and incessant chatter. The singer was a dainty damsel, not a plain Jane the crooner, but sporting the haute couture look, wearing chic Western gear dress to match her robust physique. Her bee-stung lips, rendering seductive super hits, both in Caribbean and Vietnamese were outstanding. *(Not only mellifluous was her voice, but also her looks combustible enough to set the yacht on fire!)*

After quaffing an avalanche of cocktails and chatting with our fellow tourists, we lost track of time. Then we proceeded to the main buffet spread. My choice was smoked salmon for starters while the main course was beetroot salad, spaghetti with lamb balls and green peas in a red wine sauce. The dishes were light and fresh, leaving a little tummy space for a sinful chocolate fondue cake and delicious mango ice cream. We returned to our cabin only in the wee hours of the morning.

It was invigorating to see the rays of the sun casting a golden reflection on the still waters and the jagged limestone outcrops, silhouetted against the rising sun, presenting us a sight to be clicked for posterity! After doing a bit of breathing exercises and yoga on the upper deck, I returned to the cabin. Later, we Freshwater Pearl at the Cruise climbed up to the dining deck for

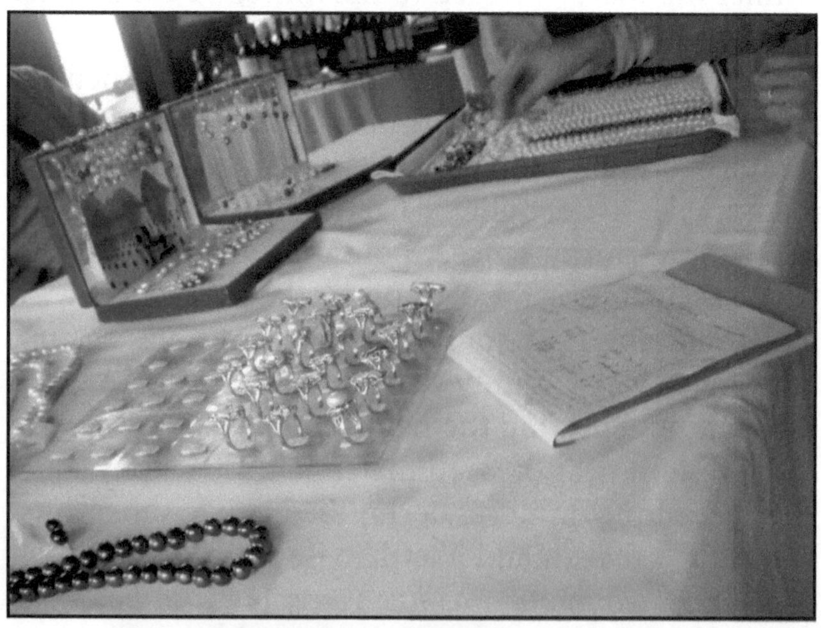

Freshwater Pearl at the Cruise

our breakfast. It was announced that the lunch would be served early as the passengers needed to disembark by the forenoon. The the lady who was managing the kitchen pantry brought a a tray of pearls strung together in a chain or necklace in an ornate pattern (white, pinkish, and black) for sale. These pearls were from freshwater oysters, and compared with the seawater ones, they were cheaper but less radiant. I bought a lot of stuff from her to be given away as gifts.

Aquaculture Farm

We then transferred to the smaller boats, each accommodating about five. Later, we sailed towards a floating aquaculture farm made of waterproof ply lined with mesh at the bottom. These compartments were Floating Fish Farm immersed in water, where shrimps,

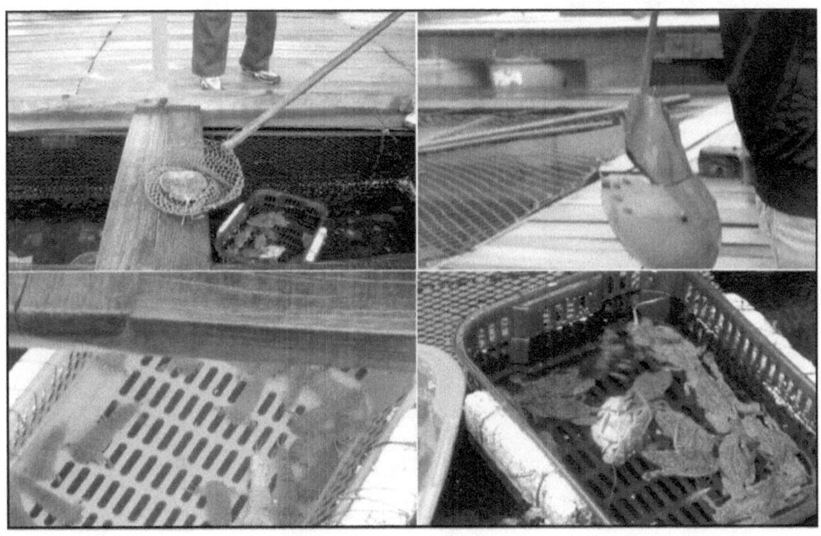

Floating Fish Farm

crabs, squids and oysters were cultured. We saw several floating cages to rear fish, keeping them confined while also allowing them to swim freely in their own natural surroundings. These sets were referred to as 'batteries,'

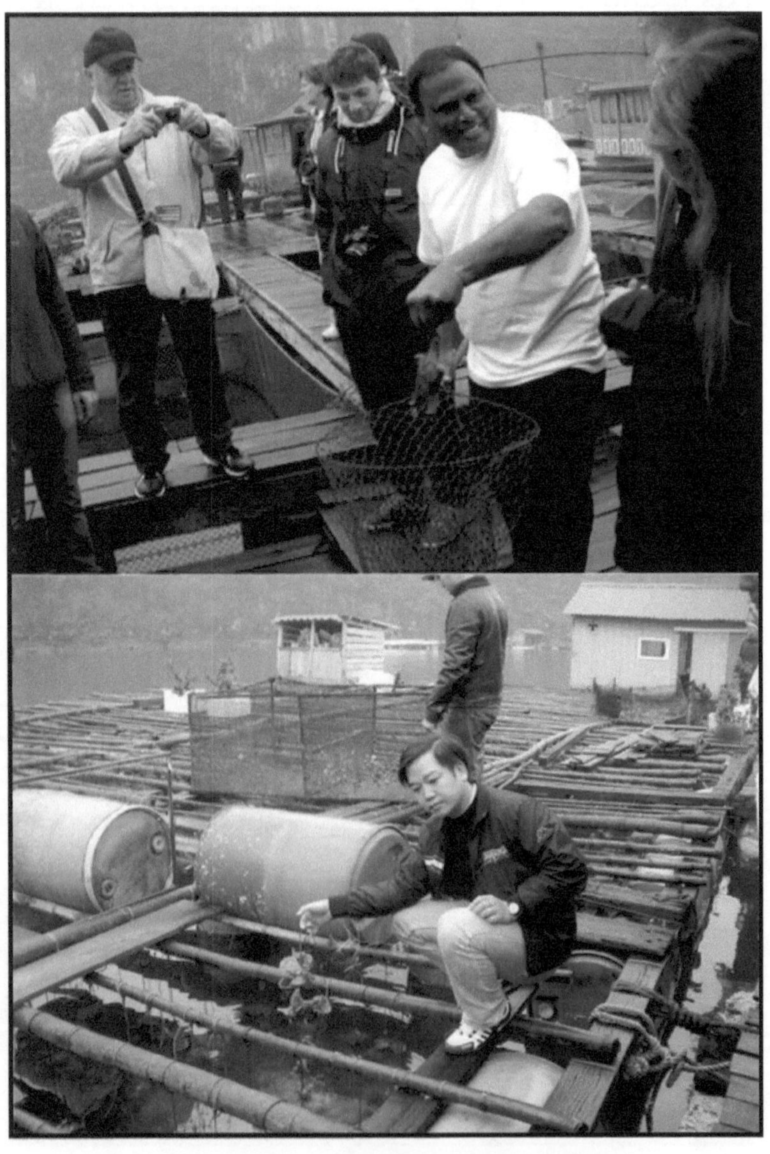

Floating Fish Market – Halong Bay

and the first battery was used to grow fingerlings from the seed. The other ones were meant for rearing regular fish. Similarly, these batteries were used to rear baby crabs as well as the king-sized ones. A few 'batteries' were present for prawn culture too.

We befriended some tourists hailing from Austria and France. While I was engaged in conversation with them, they froze in their places when they saw me holding a king-sized crab in my hand as I displayed 'fearless valor.' by pressing a monstrous crab with my bare hands! The crab was slowly opening its pincers to latch onto my fingers. "Oh boy!" Terry and Gerald were waiting eagerly *(with a malicious look on their faces)* to watch me dance and writhe in pain when the crab accomplished what it had begun. But alas! I was alerted by a German lady, one of the tourists, and to their dismay and utter disappointment, I hurriedly threw the crab back into the compartment! We were told that a baby crab would need two years to grow into a king-sized one. The whole farm was managed by an old man. Then we were whisked off to see the floating fish markets. Abundant varieties of fish were displayed, and many restaurant owners came rowing in canoes to buy the seafood in bulk quantities. No bargaining and no short supply of produce. A well-oiled system of marketing!

Cua Van Floating Fishing Village

After the aqua farm, we visited the most massive floating village that houses almost six hundred people who spend their lives and work there. They live on these floating houses, anchored in sheltered coves found in the bases of the tall mountainous islands, thus deriving some degree of natural protection from Mother Nature's wrath during the typhoon season. Although there are several floating villages, Cua Van is the largest one, with 130 houses. Many of the residents have never left this village; they have Cua

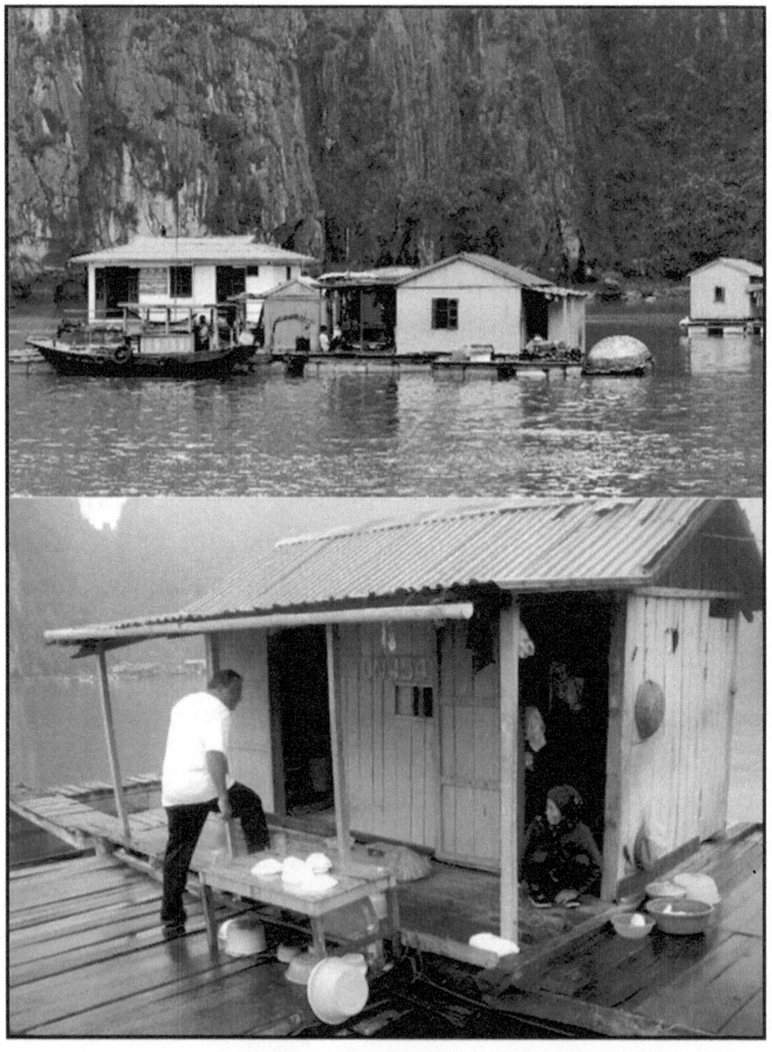

Cua Van Floating Village – Halong Bay

Van Floating Village – Halong Bay spent their entire lives here. This island has a school, clinic and public utility facilities, and the people always enjoy the nature around them during their entire lives. Professionally, they are all fisherfolk with a unique fishing style. A newborn learns to swim even before he/she can walk. They row little bamboo-basket watercraft on their own, amazingly deftly, at only about 5 or 6 years of age. We were lucky enough to visit this village and were captivated by this extraordinary little community and its distinctive way of life.

We shared our contact details with co-travelers from Germany, France, and other nations. My popularity graph peaked among the tourists whenever I shared details regarding my business with them. Our boat passed through two islets protruding out of the water called *Kissing Rock*. On reaching the bank of the river, we trooped out, bidding farewell to our fellow travelers. Carrying our bags and baggage, we walked to the shore.

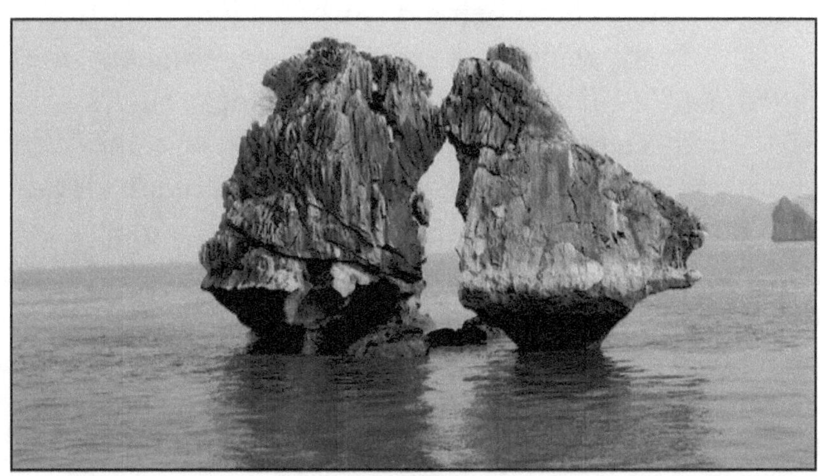

Kissing Rock

It was lovely to walk barefoot through the crystal-clear water and along the sandy banks of the Kissing Rock river. Our cab was parked and waiting and the driver welcomed us with a broad smile. We were soon driving back to Hanoi.

En route to the airport, we stopped at a pearl research center. We were shown into a swanky retail showroom where authenticated seawater pearls were on display. (We gave our freshwater pearls to verify their authenticity and were greatly relieved when they were certified as genuine). Terry bought a delicate *'Sea Pearl'* necklace. Next, we visited a lacquer workshop, where we met, face-to-face, with the artisans, mainly young women having some physical deformities. These children had been born to parents affected by Agent Orange and other chemicals sprayed during the war. It was a government-sponsored cooperative store, and the net profit from the sales would be shared among the artisans. They never looked pathetic nor craved anyone's sympathy. They appeared to be confident and proud of their skills in handicraft. Here too we bought crafts and other curios, without being disturbed about the price.

On the way, we visited a temple (a very ancient one) called *XA Tac Temple,* built by the Chinese rulers who had ruled Vietnam for more than 1,000 years? Well preserved and beautiful, the temple stood on an elevated rectangle platform (215 x 175 m), with a manmade lake (now devoid of water) in the foreground serving as the core *feng shui* element. The outer temple walls were painted in the five primary colors, signifying the five directions, with yellow in the center, green indicating the east, while the west, red the south, and black the north *(prerequisite color code for Feng shui).*

One Pillar Pagoda

On the way to the airport, we stopped by One Pillar Pagoda, which is said to have originated in the mid-eleventh century, during the rule of the Ly dynasty. The ruler who had no children had chosen to undertake a penance by sitting on a lotus flower. A divine power would initiate him to marry a peasant girl who bore him a child. As a devotee of Bodhisattva Avalokiteshvara, he was launched in a dream to build one single stem, as a memorial of thanksgiving for the child. This is believed to be the story behind the One Pillar Pagoda.

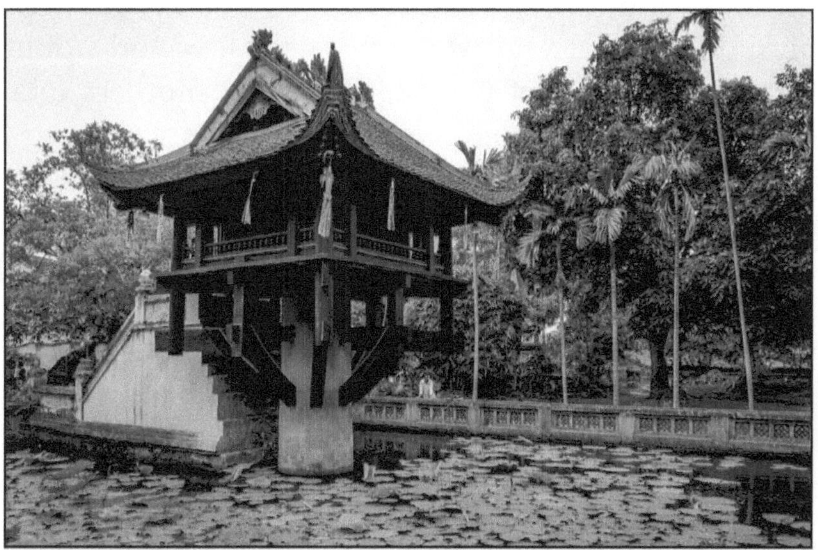

One Pillar Pagoda at Hanoi

One Pillar Pagoda at Hanoi We were a little hungry, so we entered a catering center. It was packed to the maximum! Finding a table, we placed our order for beer and cheddar cheese sandwiches. A chic waitress, maneuvering herself adeptly, among the throbbing humanity walked towards us elegantly balancing a tray laden with beer mugs and sandwich with her palm held aloft. When she approached us, we felt sorry to see that she was in an advanced stage of pregnancy, but she hardly betrayed any physical discomfort. We were quite bemused to find several ladies 'in the family way,' bravely toiling in the kitchen, working as waitresses in restaurants, and sometimes staffing departmental stores. According to their beliefs, babies born during this year would be blessed with strength and vitality, under the sign of the Dragon, (Chinese New Year – 25 January, 2012). The same phenomena held true in all the four countries we visited. It is believed the children born during that year would be very lucky and would turn out to be great people. Therefore, mothers take this opportunity to conceive during this period.

We found, to our surprise, that the Vietnamese are very orderly, even in times of crisis or emergency. Most of the hospitals (well-maintained by the civic authorities) looked spick and span and the maternity wards were overcrowded. One could see hundreds of expectant mothers seated patiently in the open space in front of hospitals, waiting for their call for an appointment with the gynecologists. The same trend was noticed in Cambodia and Laos.

On the way to the airport, the guide took us to the Temple of Literature, which is almost 1,000 years old. It was built during the period of the Ly dynasty. It is said to be the first national university with the Imperial Academy. It propagates the philosophy of Confucius; The scholars also shared the same ideology. One ought to relieve oneself of all attachments and possessions to get admission into this learning process. This is unique by itself with royal profundity. We were lost in its scholarly ambiance knowing about the philosophy of Confucius with its blend of multiple feeds for physical, mental and spiritual, in absolute simplicity! The guide had to wake us up and remind us of our journey ahead as she dropped us off at the airport.

We landed at the Hanoi Domestic Airport; the airport was very crowded because of several flights were taking off at that time. So it took us a while to check in; while we were waiting, we saw rich and affluent mothers who was in the family way, although they already had three or four young offspring, in sequence. It is my understanding that the Vietnamese are having more children to make up for the hundreds of people who had lost their lives during the war. Temple of Literature in Hanoi As we observed

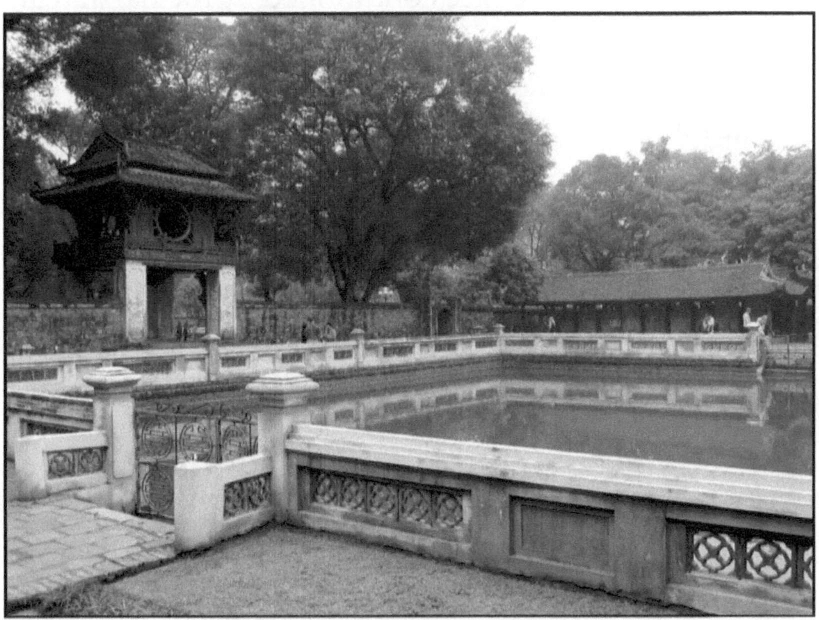

Temple of Literature in Hanoi

the people and their styles and mannerisms, we found some women wearing the traditional 'Ao Dai' dress and the conical hats like their counterparts in the 'countryside.' Our hand baggage contained some toys which were protruding out, and which caught the attention of some of the kids! They promptly began to ransack our bags, tearing off the packing and rummaging through our bags with happy abandon! When we objected, their mother did not even bother to control or check them; this type of intrusive behavior was rather encouraged! This irony was that it was happening in most of the major cities of Vietnam, and most often in public places. We were annoyed and took the toys back from the boisterous kids. But this was not an isolated incident. Chiding the 'never-mind' attitude of their moms, we retrieved our toys and we encountered similar situation in Saigon too! We wondered whether this behavior could be a genetic outcome of the psychic trauma of the race conditioned by the harsh reality of earlier times!

Finally, we checked in, and after completing the formalities and security check, we boarded the plane. It was an hour later, quite late in the evening, when the plane touched down in Ho Chi Minh City Airport, and after collecting our bags and baggage, we checked out to drive towards our prearranged hotel.

Ho Chi Minh City:
Frenzied Cousin of Hanoi

Saigon as the locals prefer to call their city more than Ho Chi Minh City retains its 'Parisian chic' ambiance. A bustling city, with an industrial and commercial centre is marked by a hundred years of French colonization and twenty years of American occupation and war. A living museum of broad tree-lined boulevards with the French kind of pavement cafes, it was full of bicycles, tuk-tuks, and two-wheelers everywhere. Our guide was an English-speaking Vietnamese girl, knowing all about the glorious Vietnam culture and a brief history of the area. Spontaneous by nature, she had the knack of putting a smile on our faces with her bubbly presence, her pixie smile, and bright look. She must have had the X factor that counted. *(I had to check the overwhelming feeling of packing up my baggage and moving over to Saigon!)*

After settling ourselves comfortably in our suite following a refreshing shower and a body massage at the hotel's parlor, we set out on a walk along the shady bylanes, avoiding the main thoroughfare. The sidewalks were beautifully decorated and illuminated with Chinese lanterns. What a fantastic sight it was, especially during the Chinese New Year (Year of the Dragon). Monstrous, marionette dragons in colorful papers with silvery scales, glistening, and snaking their way, oh so life-like! We were walking at a leisurely pace, trying out the new food joints and cuisine. After much scouting around, we located a Punjabi Dabha in the middle of nowhere. Wood-fired rotis, chicken tikka, and tandoori, preceded by steaming hot soup of chicken and noodles—Ah! What bliss! Returning to our rooms in the wee hours of the morning, we slept barely three hours. Our wake-up call came promptly at 5.30 a.m.

Mekong Delta (My Tho): Canoeing, Vin Trang Pagoda and Proone Praince

After a light breakfast, we drove towards *My Tho* (the fertile Mekong Delta), south of Saigon. We went through village roads, gravel-topped, and arrow straight. Flanked on both sides were rows and rows of rubber trees and paddy fields. After reaching the delta, we took a speedboat towards *Ben Tre Island.* The boat passed through Orchards of Islands, which boasts a Coconut Workshop and a Bee-keeping Farm along with a lot of floating markets. Finally, we landed at *Ben Tre Island.* Canopied with leaves and branches, the area was so dark that the headlights had to be switched on. We then set out on foot to explore the island; people were friendly, greeting us with spontaneous, warm smiles. Feeling physically tired, we lounged on the comfortable chairs bordering a footpath. Then we saw a savannah-type grassy field, and we walked towards the ground. "Do not get closer, "we heard our guide shouting at us. She warned us that area was infested with snakes, including rattlesnakes. Conceding our defeat to nature, we backed off. We purchased some beautifully crafted stuffed Vietnamese dolls (a tad cheap) and mother-of-pearls inlay workpieces. Lacquer-painted flowers were available at almost in every nook and corner of the island.

Later, we sailed in a canoe exchanging 'namastes.' with our folded arms and bowing our heads with a broad smile to the country folks who reciprocated our greetings in their language with simple gestures. Driving towards *Quoi Son village,* we saw tiled-roof

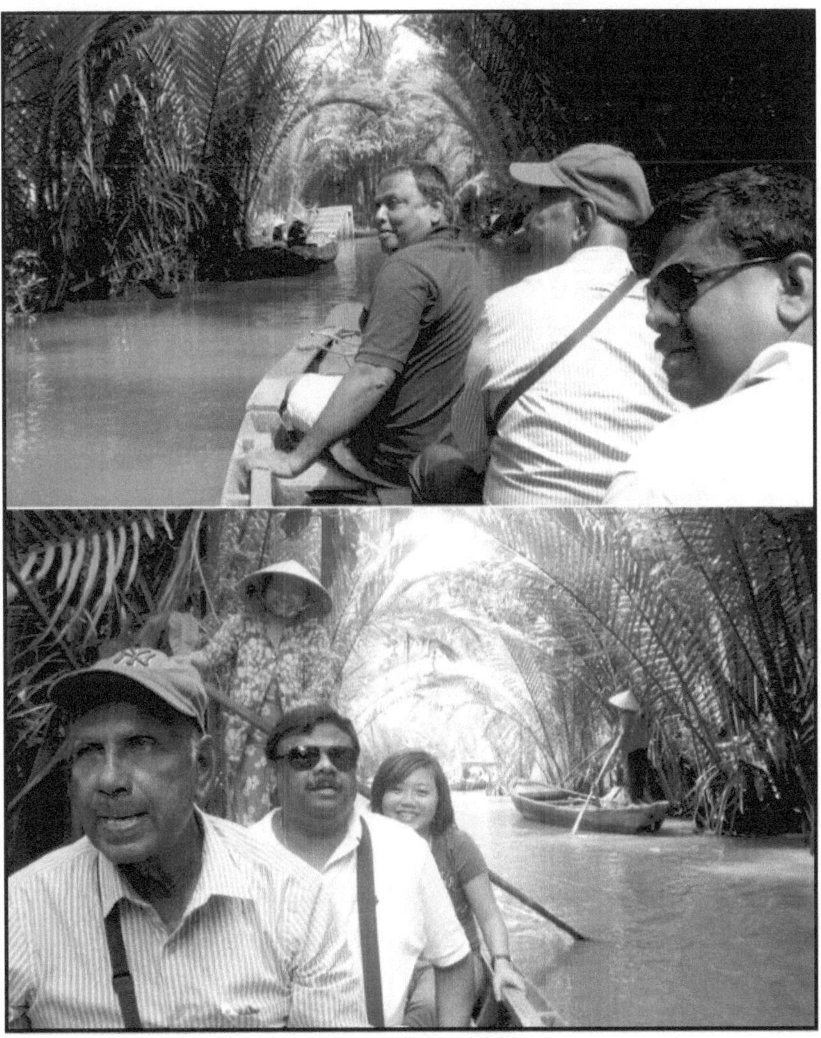

Canoe Ride at Canal

ranch-type houses (or weekend cottages) built among sylvan surroundings. We strolled towards an elevated platform with a thatched roof made in the midst of sprawling trees from where we watched a variety of life performances by a group of traditional men and women singers setting the tone with trombone-like musical Canoe Ride at Canal instruments. *The piece de resistance* was the 'Lotus Fragrance' dance. It was an unexpected joy both to our ears and eyes!

Lavishly tipping them, we walked a short distance to a cottage industry, where coconut toffee was being manufactured using a mechanical device manually operated by old women. Most of them had been widowed during the war of liberation. Each toffee was lovingly wrapped in wafer-thin rice foils. The uniqueness of the toffee was one could chew it along with the wrapper. This industry produces about 10,000 pieces a day. Work begins at 9.00 a.m. and ends at 6.00 p.m., except for festival days, when they have to work extra hours due to the demand. During those days, their daily wage would be doubled. Then we saw, to our horror, bottles of home-brewed rice wine soaked with live green-colored snakes writhing in the solution. We politely declined to taste this concoction when it was offered to us in small wine glasses. I bought a small bag of coconut toffee for my mom. It took us about forty-five minutes to reach *Vinh Trang Pagoda,* one of the landmark structures ever to be built; this is an important marker for any visitor traveling In that area. This is a combination of Chinese, Vietnamese and Khmer culture. This structure is a blend of European and Asian architecture. It has several sections— the front department, main department, worship department and back department. The pagoda has a design of equal spacing with netlike horizontal panels connected with rectangular panels. It has five pagodas with numerous towers. On this visit, this was one of the oldest buildings we ever saw in that area.

Then we went on to another island called *Proone Praince.* The beautifully well-laid-out garden flowers of a variety of hues, bonsai, evenly manicured greenery, glistening under the sunrays seemed to rival even the biblical Garden of Eden! Amidst the luxuriant growth, there was a substantial circular podium erected with thatched roofing, at the peak of which a monitor roof is built to allow for the natural convection breeze to circulate. The texture of the laterite material, thatched roofing with spider-web bamboo framing increased the ambiance of the restaurant. A lily pond with a gently bubbling fountain and a courtyard encircling the building with lush greenery enticed us with its 'come-hither look.' Then we made our way back for lunch.

As we walked into the dining hall, we spotted a bar in a corner looking slick and chic. 'Shooters?' Asked the petite lady behind the bar. Tequila seemed too sordid for lunch, and we settled for a pint of beer. The dinner was perfect and balanced. Instead of kowtowing to the local preference, the menu had a mix of exotic and the familiar, offering us a meal that could merit the description *toothsome*. The restaurateur said, "Had it not been for the inflow of tourists, I would have had to shut down this business." It is located in a far-flung place too far away to be frequented by the city dwellers. A pity indeed!

> *Full many-a-gem of purest ray serene*
> *The dark caves of the ocean bear:*
> *Full many a flower bloom unseen,*
> *To cast their fragrance in the desert air.*

After lunch, it was a long drive back. I slumped in the backseat of the tourer and soon sank into an afternoon siesta. Terry and Gerald also had their own forty winks! But they accused me of disturbing them, with snoring away to the high heavens! Terry jokingly asked our guide, "Was there any breaking news of any wild bear escaping from the zoo? We could hear the growling of a bear within earshot inside the van!" Sensing that they were sarcastically referring to me, she replied, "Physicians! Cure thyselves!"

Later in the day, we visited a lacquer factory where we purchased lovely souvenirs. We were told the proceeds were mainly used to support the Vietnamese boys and girls born with genetic deformities, caused by the toxic, lethal, chemical bombing by the Americans. Though differently-abled, with guts and determination, they were crafting lovely *objet d'arts*. It was exquisitely artistic work, of the highest order! Overwhelmed with pity and struck with horror at the sight of these hapless young boys and girls working nimbly with their deformed hands, we asked whether they had felt a sense of revenge for being victimized for no fault of theirs, against the perpetrators of mindless crime. *They emphatic answered a "Nope! It is history. Moreover, we do not want to be trapped as prisoners of the past, but emerge as passengers of tomorrow!"* There was no remorse or self-pity in their replies. How could a nation that had been subjected to an undeclared war by American 'carpet bombing' as well as the spraying of lethal gas polluting the atmospheric oxygen, breaking down the 'O_2' to 'O' survive? However, the nation has survived regardless!

We were shocked to know that during the Agent Orange attack, the poisonous herbicide used in Vietnam (1961–67) covered an area of 20,000 square kilometers of forest. Vietnam has estimated that about 400,000 people had been killed or maimed due to its use; about 50,000 were born with birth defects.

We bought some lovely flower baskets and a lacquer-painted vase. *A piece de resistance* work of art to adorn my drawing room. Terry and I bought a lot of handicrafts, especially the artistically done mother-of-pearl inlay works, more out of a humanitarian feeling to help them financially. The patronage and proceeds of the sales would go a long way towards mitigating their sufferings and raising their living standards.

Later, on the move again, we walked into a government-sponsored 'high-end' fashion boutique, where we had a friendly chat with the conductor of the expo. She was also an expert on weaving techniques. Prancing around like an elf, "I love giving interviews. If it is okay with you, we can do it, straight away!" she said. She then explained to us that there is a clamor for retaining the traditional Vietnamese styles, however, with a contemporary fashion twist, a sort of conventional aesthetic appeal to satisfy both the young and the old.

"But I should not look overtly ethnic. What works here in Saigon must work in New York too. Of course, it has to bear the subtle touches, carrying our brand logo, 'Made in Vietnam,' but at the same time, it must appeal to a broader market transcending geographical boundaries," she added.

"Today's youngsters have too many distractions: BBM, social networking sites, cafe, disco, kiosk, etc." She explained that Saigonites were becoming very fashion-conscious, day by day. Textured black, vibrant teals and aqua are part of our repertoire. The creations come in comfortable fabrics and free flowing silhouettes. Young and old revivalists prefer to go back to their roots with traditional textiles, indigenous to their culture and heritage. A noteworthy piece on display that she showed us was a printed cotton ensemble, embellished with shimmering crystal and pearls, ideal for evening outings. Words flowed like water from a designer's faucet: "We are suffocated with orders. The response is fabulous and we, the designers, are the creators and we do a lot of things *ad hoc*." She also added, "It is not just the women alone who are conscious about their looks, but men also have become quite aware! In my opinion, it has a lot to do with how a man's style quotient has changed over these years. He is becoming more 'metro secular.' Keeping up with this trend, we have a men's apparel section, an avenue for men of different age-groups and we have also created a separate zone and we know for sure what'd work best for them." Being fed with this information, we readily ought some trendy designer shirts with matching accessories as recommended by her.

After this hectic whole day trip, we were also tired, and our guide gently told us that we could for the rest of the evening; we were too eager to spend the night out in Saigon style to take us back four decades. This had been our lifestyle ever since we left home for Thailand. Each country offered us its unique company in its own dissipation, and we didn't want to miss out that from Saigon. We were not disappointed after having had an exciting time with a beautiful female company, drink-ing, and dancing. We returned pretty late to our hotel. Night at Saigon did not seem dangerous; we could walk about quite freely.

Visit to Cu Chi Tunnels

The next day was one of the most important visits in our itinerary. The bubbly guide arrived with her charm and beauty which quickly revived us of all our fatigue.

Bright and sunny, in the early hours of the morning, we drove just after a refreshing shower to Vietnam's most-talked-about site, the *Cu Chi Tunnels* used by the Viet Cong guerrillas as living quarters, stores, hospitals and escape routes. Though the cab-drive was considerably long, covering 75 kilometers, we did not feel the passage of time, thanks to our guide and her effervescent chatter. She asked whether we had seen the Taj Mahal, Himalayan range, Everest Peak, Bodh Gaya, and all things connected with India, including the Bengal tigers! India seemed to her figuratively at the other ends of the earth. Reaching the *Cu Chi Tunnels*, 75 kilometers northwest of Saigon, was a long drive through the forests and a network of these subterranean passages which stretch from the gates of Saigon to the Cambodian border.

The road was a scenic route, cutting through the thick jungle foliage. At the end of the way was that famous landmark, *Cu Chi Tunnels*, and we happily joined the crowd of tourists taking photographs of themselves beside the signboard. As we were on foot moving towards the tunnel site, we saw the town was divided into two parts—one New and the other Old. The latter had a strong flavor of French-style mansions with the typical mansard roofing on either side of the tree-lined pathways. We felt literally transported into old times—a feeling that was reinforced when we encountered free-ranging ducks, hens, and chickens confidently wandering all over the place. This scene must have charmed some of the French colonists so much that they became long-term residents as well! The old town was typical of the Saigonite peasant tenements.

We walked towards an open-air amphitheater in the midst of a mangrove we watched a thirty-minute detailed video show with a close-up view of cross-sectional maps of the hidden passages and the network, the purpose for which it was executed, followed by a lecture in English, on finally how the excavation itself was done. No machinery, no bulldozer had been used; only a primitive method of cutting the earth with a pickaxe and a shovel to remove the excavated earth. An incredible underground network bored into the universe manually by Vietnam's motivated guerrillas during their long struggle for independence. The tunnels, accommodating a hospital, a conference hall for military discussion and a school were there, waiting to be physically explored by us. During the video the show, I found, to my surprise, the network of tunnels extended up to 250 kilometers long. It had four decks interconnected by a cobweb-like formation leading to the main stem; the fourth deck would ultimately lead to an exit at the mouth of the Red River. This is how the Viet Cong guerrillas refurbished the stocks they required from the North. Their knowledge of the terrain both by waterway and land route was immense; their navigating skills by sighting the celestial bodies were unique; in fact, they could pinpoint and figure out any location without depending much on modern gadgets, whereas the Americans needed satellites or other Global Positioning Systems. The soil also was conducive to convert their concepts into reality as it was elastic and clayey in texture and, hence, naturally waterproof. It could withstand water pressure. The sealant lid manufactured by the Viet Cong's was super airtight with camouflaging features. The Americans had even tried to flush them out of these tunnels but failed due to these factors.

The tunnels thus formed were used by the Viet Congs against the Americans in their tactical war. Their tactic was to capture the American tanks, grabbing and wearing the enemy's helmets to conceal their identity and approach the American soldiers (masquerading as fellow Americans) and then turn the cannon on them. We were shown a demonstration of some primitive but highly effective forms of traps and how efficiently they worked. Covered with grass, pivoted in the center when their enemies pursued them, the Viet Cong's would lead them to the traps, which swung like a see-saw and plunged their pursuers into the pits filled with sharpened wooden spikes.

The prime strategic plan of the Viet Cong's was to maim the enemy physically, instead of killing them, thus making the American government arrange for their transport, hospitalization, rehabilitation, which would eventually cause a drain on the country's exchequer, and this strategy paid off!

As I listened to the short lecture, supported with video clippings, I later wondered how a tunnel with so many layers could actually exist. As we were walking along, our guide asked us to identify the entrance to the shaft. We looked around sheepishly, but could not find it. Our vivacious guide smiled and said that was standing right on the top of the entry. It was not easy to locate because the trap door was covered with dry leaves to mimic the surroundings and it was smaller in size than that of a standard manhole. We were shown different kinds of booby traps, defused, of course, lying around the entrance, assembled from scavenged American ordinance duds.

"Guess what this is?" asked our guide, pointing to a sort of termite mound on the forest floor. Before we could make a wild guess, she said that it was a ventilation duct cleverly built to admit fresh atmospheric air into the tunnel below. Cooking posed a problem, but the ever-resourceful Viet Congs worked out an elaborate way of ducting the smoke out while cooking. While we were debating among ourselves how the tunnel roof could withstand the load of the moving military trucks and heavily armored tanks without crumbling, she said that the soil was naturally so sticky that it bound the roof and kept it from crumbling.

The history of the Cu Chi Tunnels is fascinating. During the Vietnamese struggle for independence from the French rule in the 1960s, these tunnels were connected to villages, districts, and various guerrilla support bases with living quarters, do-it-yourself ordinance factories, kitchens with concealed chimneys, hospitals, theatres and even movie halls, not forgetting schools! The tunnels were dug as hiding places for the Viet Minh, the nationalist guerrillas fighting against France, in the 1940s, until the ceasefire in 1954. After gaining independence from France, Vietnam was provincially divided into two, North and South Vietnam. The former was governed by communist idealists headed by Ho Chi Minh who had been educated in Paris,

Moscow and China. The South became an independent Republic, led by the anti-communist Catholic leader, Ngo Dinh Diem, buttressed with American support. Washington had to do so, out of fear of a communist victory in the South, amalgamating Vietnam into a unified nation, thus bringing most of the Southeast Asian countries within the an orbit of Soviet-Chinese influence!

The American and the Soviet Union became warmongering nations after the fall of Hitler and surrender of the Japanese Emperor. The cold war between communism and capitalism commenced then. This started out as a war in Korea, but the North Koreans outsmarted the Americans and took over almost the the whole of Korea until the multinational UN Army went in. As the UN Army advanced, fearing they would reach up to Yellow River, the Chinese physically got involved with volunteer fighters. They joined forces with the North Korean fighters and the Soviet Armament and fought a great battle. The war ended abruptly without any side being benefited. Hence, it was termed a purposeless effort, which made the North Koreans more adamant and frigid. Till today, it remains an uncooperative nation. I feel the whole matter could have been handled differently and with greater diplomacy.

Now, in Vietnam, when the war between the two halves began in 1960, the first move by the Viet Cong was to expand the underground tunnel network. The the unpopular regime in the South could not cope with the guerrilla-type warfare by the Viet Cong's, who was morally and physically supported by most of the peasant farmers in the South and the people at large. In 1965, the American army arrived to augment the forces of the Southern regime against the onslaught by the Viet Cong's. Despite its advanced devices, intelligence inputs, and its massive engagement of troops with firepower and modern weapons, the United States found themselves completely isolated, as the local people regarded them more as invaders than liberators. Seeing the odds were stacked against them, they had no other option than to retreat, in 1973. The victorious Viet Cong troops finally took control of the South in 1975, thus uniting Vietnam as a single nation and under a unified rule of governance.

The History of Cu Chi Tunnel

Travel to Vietnam will not be complete without a visit to the famous Cu Chi Tunnels. Classified as a relic on a national level it is indeed a relic worthy of a visit—a monument to the will, determination, wisdom, pride and heroism of the Vietnamese. It was amazing to read that the tunnel cobweb, consisting of multilevel layers, extended over 250 kilometers in length including places of accommodation, a conference hall for military planning, theatres, and a hospital for a primitive degree of emergency surgery. It had withstood the attacks during the war with the French and American invaders for about 30–40 years. It is a an immense interconnecting network of underground tunnels expanding to a total length of 250 kilometers which began as an individual hiding place as a dugout for each peasant.

We felt sad to know that before the war, Cu Chi had been a lively area with luxuriant fruit-bearing trees in all four seasons, with fertile soil close to the Red River. But everything had been callously destroyed by the bombing and spraying of toxic gas 'Agent Orange.' We were looking forward to physically setting foot into the tunnel, to experience a little of the hardships and the endurance of the Vietnamese freedom fighters.

Unraveling the history of the tunnel! It had served as an efficient hiding space for the Viet Minh guerrillas to wage war against the French rule till 1954, and later for the Viet Cong guerrillas under the leadership of Ho Chi Minh. Uncle Ho's popularity extended as far as the South, so his goal was to amalgamate Vietnam into a unitary country under the communist regime. The peasants in the South supported the Viet Cong's in pride of their own motherland. With the help of local population, the tunnel was extended to about 1,200 meters long, almost knocking on the door of Saigon.

Despite its primitive method of tunneling and construction of this hidden structure, several stories deep in parts, with a roof which could withstand the massive load of live military trucks, heavy armored tanks, and other vehicles without caving in, defied our knowledge of structural design! Moreover, the whole tunnel complex had endured the Americans' firepower and gassing. Historians have acknowledged that Cu Chi had been the most targeted area facing untold devastation in the history of modern warfare.

Failing to locate the entry or exit points to gain access to the tunnels, the Americans engaged tens of thousands troops. To deny the Viet Cong's supply of food, the rice fields were defoliated by spraying chemical toxic gas aerially, and as a result, the trees, paddy fields, plants, and all types of vegetation withered and became tinder-dry. Further, the area was systematically ignited with gasoline and napalm. What a demonic way of punishing the helpless people in the country of their birth! But the VCs stayed put and remained safe inside the tunnels for weeks and months together with their limited stocks of food. It was physical endurance stretched to the utmost limits.

Hanoi and the central heartlands of the industrial regions had also been bombed by the Americans. They were also found guilty of using Agent Orange, a toxic, deadly chemical bomb. Not to be deterred, the embittered farmers, especially the women, exposing their rice fields thus devastated, ploughed and tended their fields during the nights under cover of darkness.

The tunnels were working efficiently and strategically well for prolonging the civil war. While the terrified young GIs with acne and M16s hacked through the jungle with machetes and canned rations, the Viet Cong's hid silently in the tunnels and lived on grubs and wild roots. After a lot of hits and miss, the Americans located the foxhole to gain entry inside the underground tunnels. Those GIs knew as Tunnel Rats physically crawled down the tunnels but most of them were shot dead or maimed by booby traps. While they were trapped inside, the oxygen supply from outside was sealed, subjecting them to suffocation. Incidentally many of the Viet Cong guerrillas were women foot soldiers, who were given training for camouflage and concealment techniques, digging and hiding in trenches, patrolling and attacking the enemy posts unawares!

Not to be deterred by this different type of warfare, the American soldiers let loose German shepherd sniffer dogs, trained to inspect and find out the enemy's secret hideouts in the tunnels. Down-to-earth in their philosophies, one of the smart alec Viet Congs said, "These dogs are color blind, and they are led only by their sense of smell. If we could change ourselves into Americans, we can outsmart these canine-sniffers." Yes, but how?

"Yes, we can," retorted the smart alec. We have piles and piles of their uniforms from the dead, as well as those in captivity. We will wear their unwashed uniforms, use their own toilet soaps, and soon we will turn these canine adversaries into *fidus Achates,* meaning 'faithful friends.' The trick paid off. The Sniffer dogs soon found wagging their tails in the company of Viet Cong! The American Tunnel Rats were so furious finding this switching of loyalty by the dogs that they felt so betrayed (the dogs were quite literally biting the hand that fed them!) and fired a salvo of bullets at these 'traitorous' dogs. The Viet Cong's, capitalizing on this the situation as well as in an attempt to change the color of war into a psychological one, soon circulated video clippings of the American soldiers shooting the dogs, the world over. This mindless massacre quickly stirred up a hornet's nest, arousing the fury of all animal lovers and Blue Cross activists, who implored the Americans to stop such atrocities, perpetrated on these helpless animals that had now become the hunted rather than the hunter! Protest rallies were held around the globe! This episode had not only raised the conscience of all animal lovers, but it also tilted the scales in favor of the Viet Cong, and they became the beneficiaries, forcing the Tunnel Rats onto the back foot. *(Crime Pays … to the lawyers!)*

The massive ramp-up of the American troops had little effect on the Viet Cong, but it led to serious unrest in troubled America. Anti-war movements gained momentum. It was evident that an incalculable the damage had severely affected the American social fabric, like the GI drug addiction, bitter domestic discord was bleeding the nation's finance totaling about 146 billion dollars. Sadly, the poor American soldiers, returning home, found themselves ostracised and branded as Baby Killers.

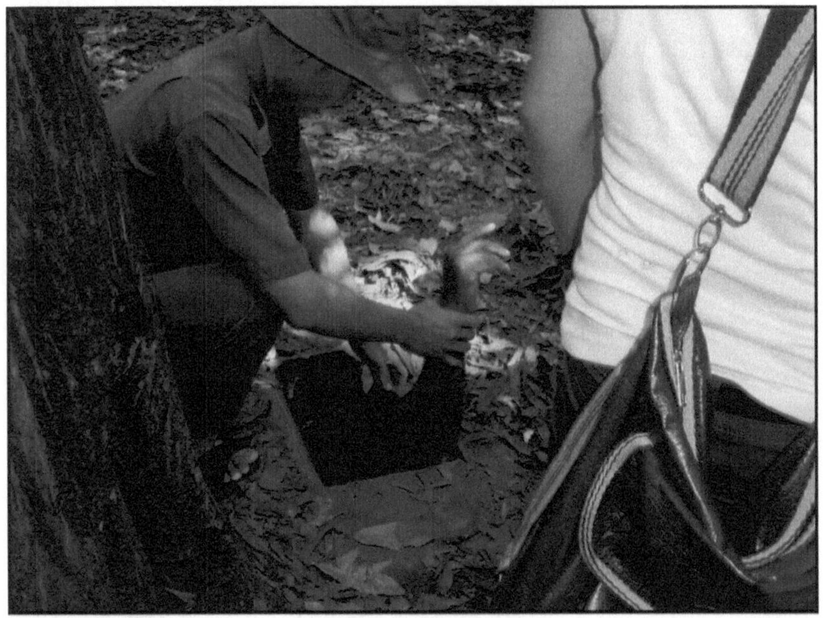

Ashok in Foxhole

Gerald narrates the adventure of Ashok at the Cu Chi Tunnel. *"Listening to the episode of how the Viet Cong men, women, and children would have endured this sub-human lifestyle, steeled by their motivation and determination to gain liberation for their country, Ashok, posed as a reincarnated Viet Cong, wearing the chappals used by them [sold as souvenirs]. Wriggling his torso and amidst the chanting of 'Bravo! Bravo!' by the onlookers,* *he slid into a tiny foxhole pit, paying scant regard for his shapeless anatomy at that moment, about ten feet deep, access to the tunnel made only for the sleek Viet Cong guerrillas. He miscalculated in his enactment of a local Viet Cong sneaking into the hole, pulling the lid down on top of him with leaves on the top, which concealed the existence of any rat hole there and he came up effortlessly. This inspired Ashok to jump into action to get into the foxhole, as well. Ashok came back to place the lid and top, everyone looked with surprise and wondered how Ashok's profile would be affected! While we were waiting for his reemergence with bated breath, horror of horrors, he got stuck in the mouth of the rat hole due to his rather large gut as he struggled to climb out. Halfway between the earth and sky, his body posture seemed very hard and crooked. He started sweating profusely. The guide was stumped! Then with the help of two well-muscled men, he tried to pull him out but failed. Terry suggested that the guide bring three elephants to pull him out! There was a section of tourist onlookers who became worried. Then Ashok took a moment, composed himself, and without getting perturbed, peeped out and asked the local Viet Cong helper and the guide for three or four more lids of the hole. Then slowly taking the covers inside down below in the hole, he arranged them into a systematic self-engineered structural platform. Using that as a foothold, he stretched both his arms outside the hole and slowly wriggled his way out without anybody's help by shaking his body first from the front and back and then from side to side! The excess flesh around his tummy slowly became elasticized and slipped out. Finally, he could come out by himself. As he sat proudly with both his thumbs up, he shouted, '***Yes, I could,*** where the Americans failed,*

I could be out to enjoy the serenity of the land and the beauty of these wonderful people!'

"His heroic feat would propel his popularity graph upwards, soaring to giddy heights and several admirers flocked around him clicking pictures. Later, he confided to them. **It's hard to appear fit as a fiddle if you're shaped like a cello!** *It proved to be nothing short of a mare's nest for him.*

"However, we were greatly relieved as Ashok was finding his feet. Terry raised roars of laughter with his quick remark: 'One should not bite off more than one can chew.' I agreed with him in toto, 'Ashok! One's narrow waist and broad upper change places when you are past the mid-age!' In fact, he resembled a gorilla more than a [Viet Cong] guerrilla, with his battered shirt, shredded trousers, and blotches of mud all over his face! Our guide, together with Terry, sprayed a water cannon on him." (Here ends Gerald's account of Ashok's adventure in Cu Chi foxhole.)

We then walked into a small factory, where the remnants of the bombshells, odd pieces of armor and other military leftovers by the Americans were collected and recycled as rocket launchers, etc. We also saw footwear made from damaged tyres from the abandoned military trucks. It was an ingenious display of recycled armories.

After a cup of refreshing green tea, we walked towards the tunnels. While Terry and Gerald hesitated to crouch into the shaft physically, I egged Gerald to follow me by telling him, "Let us leave Terry, he is too lazy and frightened, but I will be your leader, you just have to follow me." After stepping down to a depth of 5 to 6 meters from the ground level, we had to traverse a tunnel measuring about 3/4 meters wide and 1.5 meters high. *(This width and height was deliberately selected so that the American soldiers of standard height would find it difficult to walk with their heads and shoulders bent.)* I could not take one step forward for it was pitch dark, except for a small beam from the torchlight flashed by our guide. It was also sweaty, with little oxygen, and claustrophobic, but nevertheless a thrilling experience. Understanding the gravity of the situation, I coaxed Gerald to bend down slowly and crawl on his knees. Crawl he did, paying obeisance to the brave soldiers whose mission was only to be free of the foreign bondage! Even though the guide told us that we had to traverse a distance of just less than thirty meters, it appeared to me, that we had moved a gazillion miles! The time to pass through the passage would generally take less than fifteen minutes, but it was like an eon to me! As we were crawling and moving, I kept Gerald engaged in conversation so that his mind would not entertain any negative thoughts or indulge in self-pity or defeat. I even narrated the incident of the catacomb that I had visited earlier on in Rome, of how I had gone down to two to three decks, where the early Christians who had been persecuted under *Emperor Nero* had taken shelter, buried their dead and worshipped as small congregation, etc., all of which kept Gerald occupied. As a slight light began to appear at the end of the tunnels, I said *"Phew"* and finally shouted *"Wow!"* The lovely warm sunshine at the mouth of the exit above our heads shone down at the end of the tunnel. I made Gerald sit down for a couple of minutes and take a deep breath to refresh himself. A steep climb up a ladder to the opening helped us to crawl out. We were puffing like a couple of steam locomotive engines! But this physical feat of us was well worth the trouble. Gerald said, "If this is the end, we have endured it," after coming out. Then he hugged me and said, "Bravo!" "Gerald, you have conquered the world," he patted himself on the back while Terry was fearfully sitting outside and ridiculing us for our bravery and achievements after we came out.

"Thanks be to Ashok," said Gerald. "It was he who inspired bd pushed me to endure this venture at my ripe old age of 82! Traversing through the Cu Chi Tunnels on my knees is equal to the conquest of Mount Everest!", he said with modesty. I made Gerald stretch out on a mat. I could not help but salute the Viet Cong's—both men and women, including 'school-going' children for their grit, courage, determination, and dedication to stand against the Americans and ultimately to scuffle them out despite their brutal onslaught. Their spirit, mental strength, and the willpower defying all odds will always be hailed as an inspiration for millions of youth throughout the world!

On our way back, we spotted thick smoke oozing out of the earth in a remote corner of the bank of Red River. This was a demonstration of how the smoke from the cooking platform was innovatively ducted out. How grueling it must have been to stay below, huddled together for weeks on end for twenty long years, a bolt hole where the inhabitants had to lie on the floor to get enough oxygen to breathe!

After our lunch in mangrove and an hour-long drive along with a mud path amidst thick greenery and flowering shrubs, we came upon tree houses and weekend resorts, salons, spas, etc., mainly catering to international tourists, as Cu Chi Tunnel has now become an important place of visit for all visitors and locals. Situated within the Cu Chi battlefield is *Ben Duoc*, a substructure complex, where the VC military commanders' headquarters was housed, and is now classified as a national-level relic. A photographic exhibition was set up there and the most eloquent ones and the highly publicized ones during the Armageddon was the photo images of the intense Viet Cong firepower (armed with Russian armaments) against the US troops at *Bao Trai* near Saigon in 1966, captured by *Horst Faaz*, a combat photojournalist covering the Vietnam war, as mentioned earlier. But the one that stayed in my mind was that of a peasant woman with an agonized look on her face, carrying her infant in her arms with two of her other children with terrified looks on their faces escaping from the blazing fire of their village, wading through murky water, hurrying away from their burning hut. It was a tear-jerker which won him a coveted prize.

Mr. Horst Faaz, while receiving the honors, said that his mission was to record the sufferings, personal sacrifices and emotions of both Vietnamese and American soldiers, especially the latter in a blood-soaked country so far away from their own homeland! There exhibits of sand models, pictures and sculptures that eloquently illustrated the revolution, the stalwart, resilient characteristics of the Vietnamese campaigning for the liberation of their own country, spanning a period of about one hundred years of tragic history against the French and American invaders. While the American and French armies led by *generals with military genius* equipped with heavy military hardware and excess firepower, supported with banned chemicals and defoliant, the Vietnamese, especially the women (Viet Cong guerrillas), relied on only their own grit and guts with their instinct and knowledge of the environment, nature, and soil and used the excess firepower of the invaders to their own advantage to beat them back. Most of the bombs and shells dropped by the Americans did not burst; instead, they got buried in the sticky soil.

These were dug out and moved to their own factories, cut open and refurbished hs smaller arms which were used or hit-and-run tactics. Thus, the American hardware was indigenously converted into a Vietnamese weapon to be used against them itself. This was how the mighty Americans lost the war by their own weapons.

It is relevant to recall the famous saying of Carlos Fuentes, the Mexican author and a visiting professor of Princeton University, who was a nominee for the Nobel Prize for literature: *"There must be something, beyond slaughter and barbarism to support the existence of mankind and we must all help to search for it!"*

No other war for national liberation was as fierce and intense as this war, causing so much human misery, brutally extinguishing so many innocent lives, causing so much agony and heartbreaks as recalled by Vietnamese General Giap on the eve of the thirtieth anniversary of the fall of Saigon, in a press meet in 2005. "But we fought because of our love for our country. Nothing to us more sacred or precious than our independence and freedom from the clutches of the ruthless invaders, to unify our nation, amalgamating the South and the North."

General Giap

Vo Nguyen Giap, the legendary General, who lived on to see the fall of Saigon, was a self-taught military genius and quite ruthless in his approach. He was second in power to Ho Chi Minh. From his childhood, he seemed to possess precocious intelligence. He had been educated along with Ho Chi Minh and the future President of South

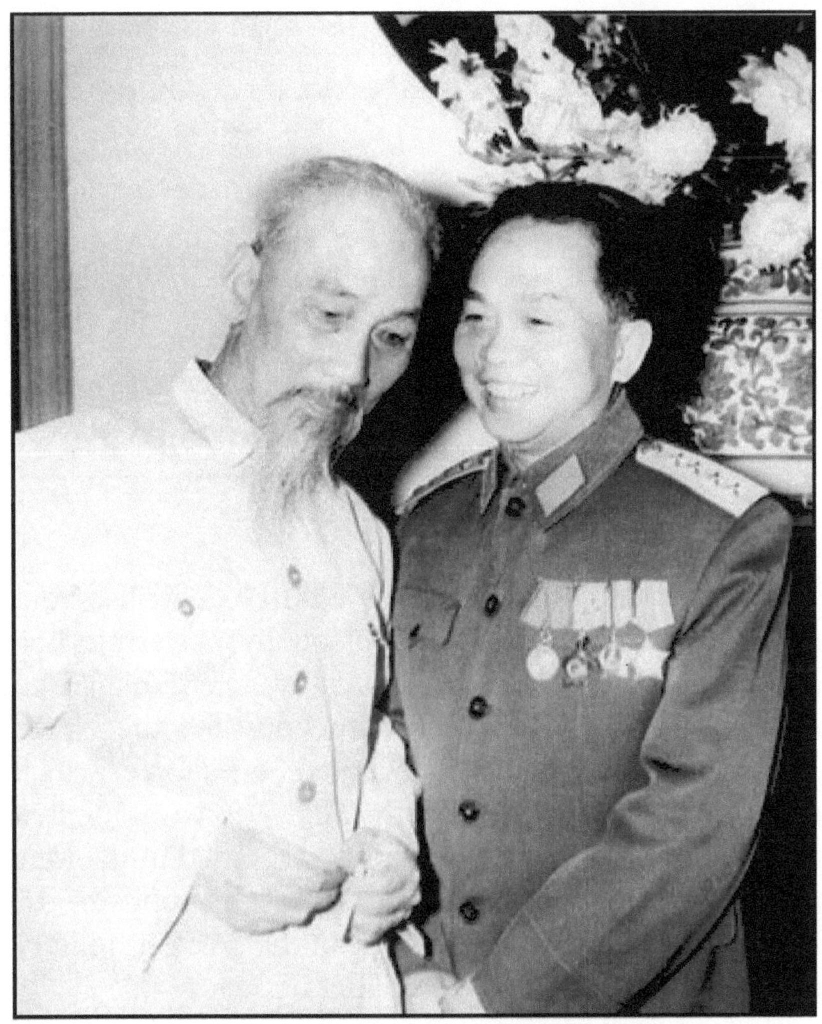

Giap and Ho Chi Minh

Vietnam NgÔ Đình Diệm in a Catholic school in Hanoi. General Giap too had lost his father and sisters due to the imprisonment by the French during his youth. He also lost his wife in prison during his exile in China. He was later married to another high-profile lady by Ho Chi Minh. He lived to the ripe old age of 102. He was the one

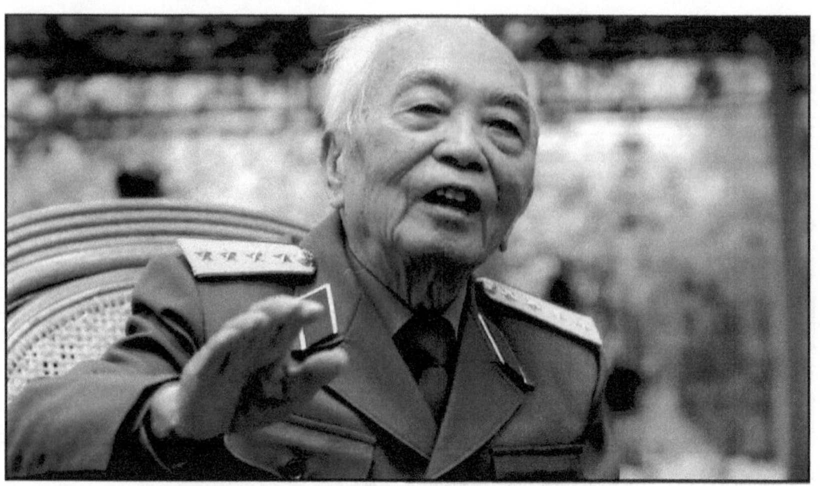

Legendary Military General Giap

who formed and organized the Viet Minh guerrillas from the high northern mountains. Personally masterminding the defeat of the French military at Diem Bien Phu near the Laos border, he subsequently led the North Vietnamese army against the United States forces which were entrenched in the South. His action was ignited by the sufferings of his own family, who had undergone untold agony and subsequent death at the hands of the French. He was acclaimed as one of the greatest military general of the post-World War II era.

Known as Red Napoleon, he was revered as a national hero, second in position to the President Ho Chi Minh. It was under his able command that the Viet Minh forces endured the grueling two-month the long battle of Diem Biem Phu, in which he managed to surround the French troops, bringing them to their knees in a bloody engagement, and ultimately triggering the inglorious exit of the French army from Vietnamese soil in 1954. After a fiercely fought battle utilizing modern armory supplied by the Chinese he has been immortalized in *Bernard Fall's* Legendary Military General Giap book *Hell in a Very Small Place*. Fall was an Austrian, who moved on to France and finally to the USA. By career, he was a correspondent and great writer, a person who was an absolute authority on the Indo-Chinese history and its people.

Later, General Giap and Văn Tiến Dũng went on to vanquish the US-backed South Vietnam government in April 1975, reunite the country as one country, named the Socialist Republic of Vietnam (SRV).

General Giap from his childhood was an outstanding strategist, a genius who possessed the ability and greater impulse to foresee events that could occur both militarily and politically. After the war, he met with several political and military adversaries including Defense Secretary, *Robert McNamara*. Although General Giap was revered in his own country, his military foes saw him as ruthless and ruthless. The US General *William Westmoreland* acknowledged General Giap's prowess on the battlefield, but not without criticism. He said, "Of course, he was a formidable adversary, but let me add that although Giap was trained in small-unit guerrilla tactics, he persisted in waging a big-time war incurring terrible losses to his own men with scant regard for human life. He may be a formidable adversary, but that does not make a military genius." I do not swallow this argument. General Giap along with all the Vietnamese fought for the freedom of their own motherland, not to prove their private individual military ability, which was any day superior to their opponent's, whereas the Americans were prepared to exhaust all their arsenal on the opposing army without incurring a loss of their own.

After the exciting trip to Cu Chi Tunnels, we were in a combative mood to fight a war among ourselves. The conversation began for and against the United States and West. While I stood firmly for my Asian kin, Terry, being a naturalized American, stood up for the United States. The argument began to get heated up and quite a ferocious. Sensing the high-strung tone of the argument, the guide suddenly stopped our vehicle where a large crowd had gathered in one village en route. We spotted a group making loud noises and our curiosity got the better of us. A cockfight and a wrestling bout was simultaneously going on, the local folks' favorite sport. *(In fact, to call it a mere sport would be such an unfair understatement that the participants could take immediate umbrage at it being so termed!)* Saigon's hinterlands and even the urban spaces are home to several cockfights conducted very discreetly. These fights enliven the *quotidian* humdrum lives of especially the youths who were carrying their roosters with beautiful plumage in great pride! After gently caressing the bird and bouncing it up and down, and patting it vigorously to provoke anger against its opponent, they prodded the birds in the center of the ring. The cocks flew almost instantly at each other, with high speed and fury, trying to tear into each other with their sharp beaks. These fights roused a lot of fanfare excitement and a great response from the crowd. It were an intense sport and a not-too-healthy pastime! By the way, fights are often recognized as a metaphor for masculinity and martial sports. Being fired up by what I had just seen, I returned back with more vigor and continued arguing with Terry! I was still strongly condemning the American and French as merciless killers and supporting the Vietnamese as brave and committed to save their own land. They were prepared to go to any extent, and kept their morale high to fight to the end! Terry bravely defended America and the West with the statement of the general ideology that it was just a full-scale war—capitalism versus communism, while Gerald was a mute spectator! However, the driver and the guide too got extremely excited. They were laughing and chatting in their own language. Finally, Terry had to withdraw. After a lull, the driver turned and gave me a broad grin and the guide with her sweetest voice said, "Let bygones be bygones." She continued, "We don't want to be slaves of the past–we would rather travel on to a brighter future."

On our drive back, we saw many men and women peasants tending their rice fields, clad in colorful sarongs! Bare-bodied men were revving the motorbikes that seemed to us a part of the slumbering and peaceful pollution-free village. We then headed towards a bird sanctuary. The constant chirping of the wide variety of these feathered delights called out to remind us 'not to get too obsessed with the drudgery of living in the concrete jungle of the city'. Every tree was teeming with birds, some trees thick with bats hanging upside-down and enjoying their siesta. Along with a crowd of bustling tourists, we trooped into a restaurant. The guide led us to a lovely lunch with wonderful Vietnamese cuisine. After this hectic trip, we were famished. With our animated conversation and the pleasant company of the guide and the driver, we hardly felt the passing of the travel time. The lunch was quite filling, ending with a wonderful dessert. We then went for a stroll into the nearby garden surrounded by bountiful natural beauty and doling out an equally sumptuous fare were many operators inviting us to try several activities—shooting, outdoor and indoor games, trekking and rafting. We opted for a boat ride instead, down a sparkling stream. Indeed, we felt the intense atmosphere of tranquility. An unsuspecting bird might approach you for a *tête-a-tête* or a woodpecker or a kingfisher may play hide-and-seek while some of the bolder birds came swooping down on you while drifting midstream.

Many islets were dotting the midstream, with different species of storks and cranes, striking them characteristic pose, as willing partners, to coax us into clicking unforgettable pictures of them. As we sailed, we witnessed a spectacular aerial display of painted storks, touching down in the shallow regions of the river after a glide, as smooth as the movement of butter in a skillet. Our guide suddenly said, "Do you see the boulder there and a hump next to it? Well, the hump is the back of a monster crocodile." We were horrified to find ourselves, slowly approaching the aforementioned 'hump.' "A swing of its tail on our boat and you'll find yourselves airborne!" she chuckled. Before we could kneel down to say our last prayers, the guide calmed our nerves, saying, "Don't get too panicky about the croc. It'll make no attempt to devour you. It is well pleased and happy with its own staple menu of fish and the odd small bird." The crocodile lazily paddled near our boat nonchalantly without caring to give us even a sidelong glance!

After the boat ride, we were heading towards the city, driving along a mud path through the rice field. We reached a beautifully landscaped garden right in middle of a well-laid pathway bordered with lovely flowering shrubs. There were rows of cottages, built on stilts, with bamboo-framed thatched roofs. We paused from our drive, went to the cabin, and comfortably stretched ourselves out on the lovely mats spread on a wooden floor with cushions for our heads! We were then gently massaged by trained masseurs to soothingly soft melodious instrumental music played by a local artiste. We had been aching for such a relaxation, especially our poor tired legs! After this nice relaxing and refreshing massage, we freshened up and got dressed; we were offered Chinese black tea. We paid them generously and got ready for the drive to the Chinatown area in Ho Chi Minh City.

Chinatown

Chinatown is part of Ho Chi Minh City, also known as Cholon. It is on the bank of the Saigon River, forming a maritime trade passage. Small Chinese settlers had lived there from ancient times as traders. During the Vietnam War, some part of Chinatown had been used as a black-market area for foreign goods. Thus, it slowly grew to become a huge market! Now, of course, everything has been regularised. We visited *Bin Tay Market* in Chinatown, one of the biggest markets in Ho Chi Minh City. Vendors, here, prefer to sell in bulk quantity. Due to its proximity to China,you can almost buy any Chinese product here at a bargain. As in other international markets, the tourists needed to be little more careful about their belongings. Later, we reached a supermarket.

This double-storied market had small shops and boutiques, chock-a-block. It tops the 'must see' list for any tourist. Before you begin, here is one thing you shouldn't do. I repeat, don't look for any coherence concerning what you should see first or which shop, to begin with. Just follow your instincts, brace yourself with money, hone your bargaining skills, allow your heart to decide and you won't regret your choice of clothes, shoes or anything! There is just no end in sight. The dreams you have ever had of owning high-end branded items will come true in a few minutes, for a fraction of the cost, to raise your style quotient!

As we began shopping, the urge took over us. A shop literally drew Terry and me to step in. Adorable and fashionable, a one-stop store for men and women, with beautiful apparel on display. The concept of the fashion mainly East meets West *(not the other way about)* and the designs combined both simplicity and elegance, drawing inspiration from the Chinese women of the '60s. It was a good collection of dresses, maxis with patchwork, long sleeves or sleeveless dresses in printed cotton, jumpsuits, scarves, shirts and trousers. We were surprised at the very affordable price tags for these quality goods. An array of T-shirts for men was stacked on the shelves, and we bought some branded ones at a good bargain. The store had another compartment where exhibits of exquisite leatherwear, Mary Jones ballet shoes, kitchen heels, sneakers, and large-sized handbags, striped and polka-dotted were displayed!

Coinciding with the celebration of the Chinese New Year, every shop had a banner announcing discount sales. (As the global recession in the economy had a direct impact upon Vietnam, the sales index touched nadir, and customers had dwindled. It was an all-time low for the country as the cost of living had spiked up and the buying power of people had significantly reduced). We hope the bilateral trade between India and Vietnam would benefit both the nations for the revival of the economy. Although the trade between them has not taken off as yet, it may shift gears in the coming years.

Vietnam and India have not cooperated as closely or maximized their potential in their economic relationship. If you walk into any shop, you will be mobbed by the saleswomen. (I bought a good number of shirts and ladies' bags.) We met some Vietnamese entrepreneurs who had made some kind of mark in the social fabric.

Leaving the supermarket, the guide presented with us a tray full of fruits; they were unattractive to look at with a kind of thick hair-like outgrowths. With a blonde or red exterior, the fruit resembled lychee. Seeing our hesitant looks, asked us to peel off the skin, and the kernel was a treat that every visitor to Vietnam should taste. The fruit is aptly called *Chom-Chom,* meaning messy hairs!

Then we proceeded to the *Chùa Quan Âm Pagoda.* This is quite unlike pagodas we saw in Cambodia and Laos, with only Chinese features. Many inscriptions were in Chinese, and now Vietnamese words are being added as well. Then we proceeded on to the Ngoc Hoang Pagoda.

Ngoc Hoang Pagoda

Ngoc Hoang Pagoda is otherwise known as the Emperor Jade Pagoda or the Tortoise Pagoda. This is one of the most beautiful pagodas housing a lot of statues and wooden carvings. The style of this pagoda is unique with a typical Chinese or Taiwanese style roofing featuring Chinese dragons and a phoenix made from multi-colored ceramic tiles. This is dedicated to various. Chinese-Vietnamese divinities. Two colossal statues with names guard the main gate. The pagoda attracts many pilgrims in the first and the fifteenth day of the lunar month. The guide suggested our trip would not be complete if we don't visit the lacquer workshops.

Lacquer Workshops in Ho Chi Minh City

There are four or five main lacquer workshops in Saigon. The war veteran Vietnamese turned from manufacturing small indigenes ornaments into products of intricate workmanship, beautiful artifacts, excellent handicraft, and artworks. They excelled in all kinds of inlay and lacquer works. These workshops are most transparent. They are willing to train any interested parties in their skills. You are given a video lecture on all kinds of the process done there. You are conducted on an on-site visit to the entire workshop of the artisans. I was amazed by the items that are being produced with eggshell inlays. These Items could be purchased in bulk, which then the society would be shipped by itself directly to your home address. For ready reference, I can spell out some names, Phuong

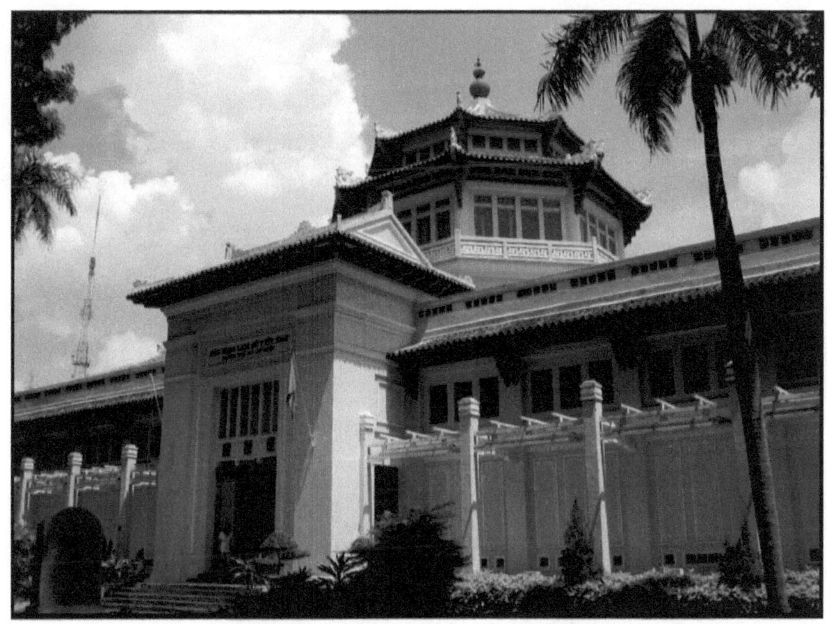

History Museum at HCMC

Nam lacquerware and Tay Son lacquerware workshop, Mac Thi Buoi showroom factory at Thu Duc District. The cheaper variety of lacquer can be purchased in Benthanh Market too. Actually, I found all over Southeast Asian countries such types of cooperative stores in cooperation with the government. You are given a free ride to these workshops. Don't hesitate to bargain to a minimum of 30% to 45% of the net cost. The negotiation skills lie with you. After an exhausting day trip, we were finally dropped off at the hotel. Terry, as usual, a night bird, did not let us rest in peace! After freshening up, he poured us each a peg of double black, which he forced us to down, on the rocks. As we charged ourselves, we were on the move looking for pleasant Saigon companions as partners for dinner. We never failed in this attempt throughout History

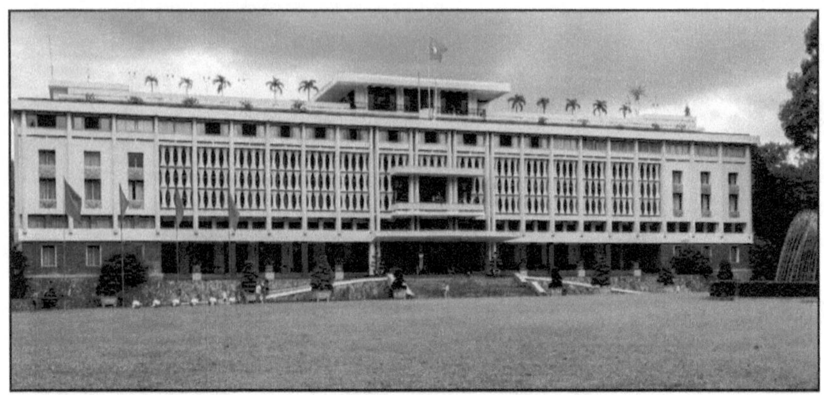

Reunification Palace in Ho Chi Minh City

Museum at HCMC our entire trip. The thought of the next day never arose in our mind until we reached our room in the wee hours of the morning.

History Museum

Later we drove to the *Museum of History*. Royal antiques, dating back from the eighteenth century up to 1945 were on display. Excellently preserved, arrays of guns, swords and knives were seen mounted on the walls. It will be interesting to know that the ancient rulers followed a type of 'patriarchal' regime, relegating the 'matriarchal rule'. Only the male members belonging to the royal family and their personal apparel was on display, without even a semblance of the queen's attire. The mummified body of a 40-year-old man who had died about 4,000 years ago was there in a glass coffin dressed in all the funerary accouterments. A meticulously carved bronze receptacle dating back to 204 BC with a capacity to hold forty liters of anointing Reunification Palace in Ho Chi Minh City

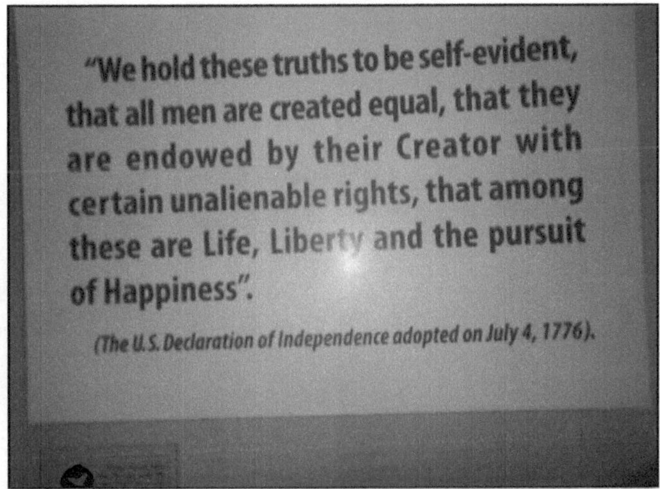

Displayed at the Entrance of the War Remnants Museum

oil was the highlight of the exhibit. It was amazing to see displays of prehistoric relics of the human race dating back to several centuries before Christ. Fortunately for us, this was not part of the conducted tour, and we were allowed to wander free, to explore at will and browse as much as we could! Taking a guide would have been even better as it would have given us more information and insight regarding the displays. Later we moved on to visit the Reunification Palace.

Reunification Palace

Reunification Palace was initially built by the French as a Palace for the Governors who represented France, governing the Indo-China area during the nineteenth century. Later on, in 1962, the South Vietnamese President Diam built a new palace although he did not live to see its completion; it was completed by his Displayed at the

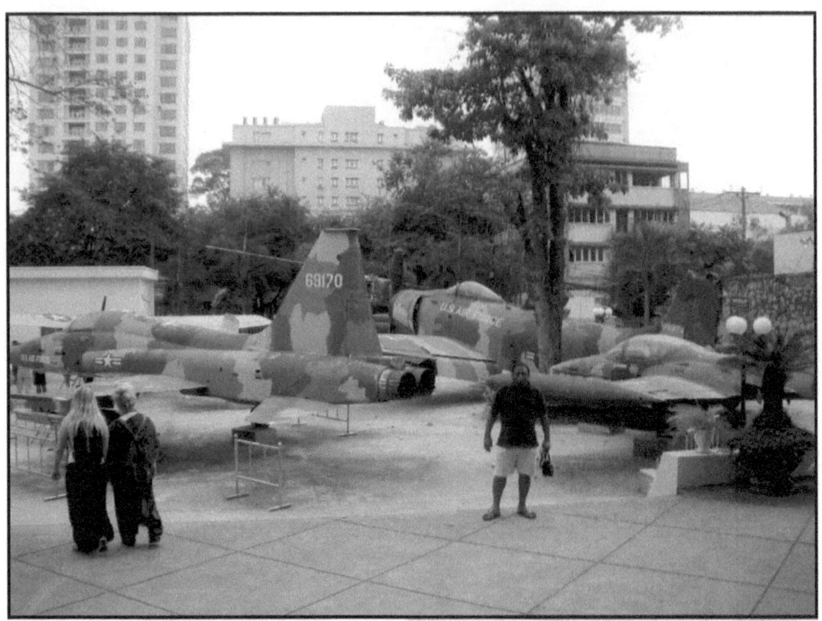

Open Foreground at War Remnants Museum

Entrance of the War Remnants Museum successor! In 1975, as the war was coming to a close, a North Vietnamese tank blasted through the main gate of the palace, and the entire South Vietnamese army surrendered and the country was unified. The castle was named the Reunification Palace, otherwise also known as Independence Palace. Then we proceeded to the War Remnants Museum.

War Remnants Museum

After bidding farewell, we rushed to taste the spectacular coffee with sweet condensed milk at Trang Nguyen, a nationwide coffee shop, a necessary kick in the synapses, before visiting the War Remnants Museum. Open Foreground at *War Remnants Museum.*

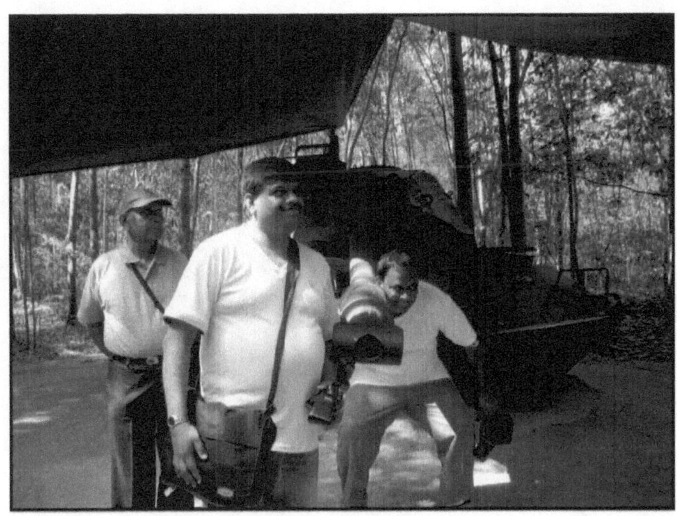

War Remnants Museum

I did not realize that I was actually going to see for myself some of the events that had happened in Vietnam during the horrors of the war. As I stepped in, I read a bit of the history about the place, which appeared to be located at the former the *United States Information Agency building* from where various intelligence activities had been taken. This museum was opened in September 1975. Initially, it had been named the US and Puppet War Crimes Museum followed by Exhibition House for Crimes of War and Aggression. After normalizing their relationship with the United States, the name was changed to War Remnants Museum. Visitors from the West\ have varied reactions to this museum—some brush it off saying it is only war propaganda while others really feel the agony the Vietnamese went through. The photographs are really touching and are supported by facts and remnants of the arsenal used during the war. We spent a few hours watching a slide show of Vietnam War accompanied

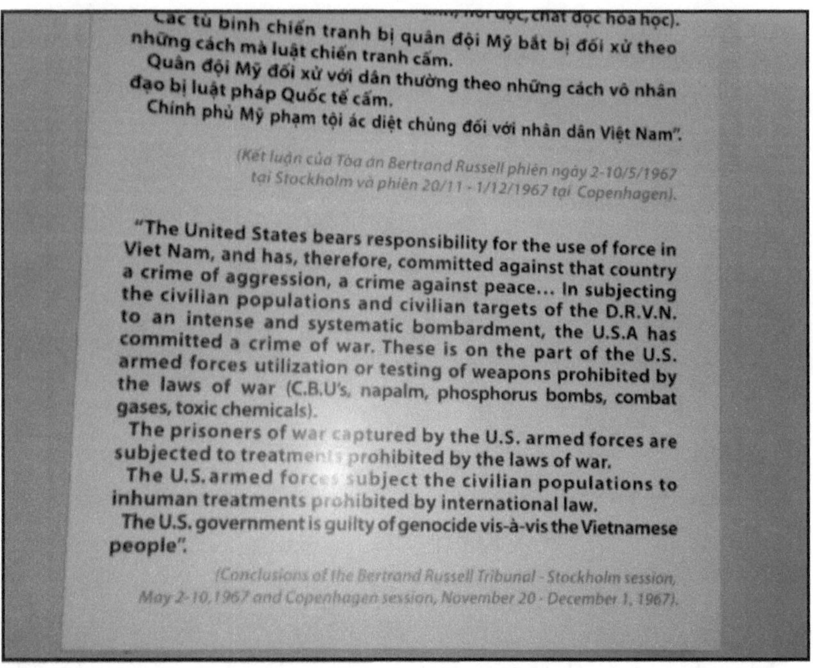

Photograph Displayed in War Remnants Museum

by lectures. In fact, the exhibits of this museum speak volumes for themselves regarding the distressing nature of the ruthless horrors of modern warfare. The grim tragedy of the war was presented without censorship. We saw the photographers' work of the conflict along with tales of the chemical atrocities inflicted by the United States on this land. It was a resounding cry for world peace! Everyone visited would have heard this cry! It had carefully researched, collected, preserved and exhibited the remnant proofs of the war crimes and their consequences. A war-weary American howitzer had been captured intact by the Viet Cong's, complete with self-propelling long-range cannon and a twin-rotor jumbo helicopter that had been used for the transport of American troops into the jungles—a ghoulish collection of bomb parts and

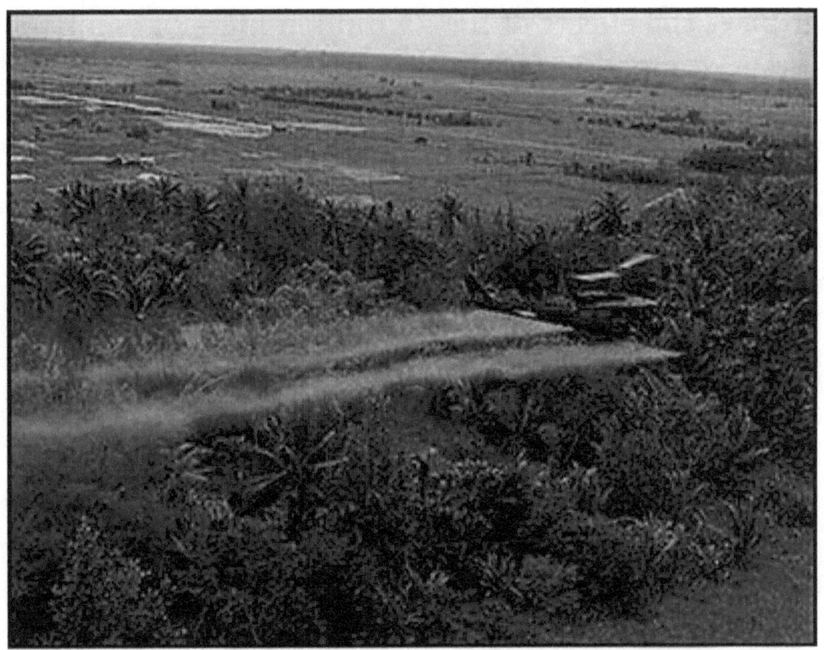

US Force Sparing the Agent Orange during Vietnam War

a renovated Douglas Sky Rider plane sit on the vast open the foreground of the museum!

The heart-rending images of this pointless war and its atrocities were clearly displayed. They cry out aloud to the nations of the world to shout in the chorus "No to war and yes to peace, solidarity, and co-existence!" *It was here that the early growth of the modern Republic of Vietnam was crystallized.*

Declare Victory and Run US Formula

Declare Victory and Run US Formula One section of the vast hall presented a grisly portfolio of photographs of mutilation, napalm burns, and torture. One gallery displays the effects of the 75 million liters of defoliant sprays dumped indiscriminately US Force Sparing the Agent Orange during Vietnam War across the country, including hideously malformed foetuses preserved in pickling jars; another section reveals the international opposition to the war, as well as the average American citizen's peace movement against the meaningless and brutal involvement of American soldiers in a far-flung land. There is also a moving exhibition of children's artwork on the atrocities of war, photographs taken by the countless photojournalists showing people who lost their lives during the French and American wars. The museum rounds off with a horrible mock-up of the tiger cages, the prison cells of Con Son Island.

Among the many photos exhibited on the second a floor of the building are the photos that continue to haunt our memories, like the chilling photographic image of a 9-year-old girl, *Ms. Phuc.* She was seen in the center of the frame running naked with both her arms outstretched, crying with terror and pain and her clothes and tender layers of her skin melting away by napalm, as she was fleeing from her burning village. *Mr. Nick Ut,* a Vietnamese photographer, won the Pulitzer Prize, and more than that, this iconic photo helped to change the direction of the war. This photograph also raised some ethical questions in the minds of many! Should he (*Mr. Nick*) not have put his camera down and run to help the little girl instead of remaining as an objective observer? And that had posted a more significant moral dilemma! Although I am not a journalist, recalling the iconic image of that young girl fleeing away from the scene, I am convinced that the photographer's primary purpose had been to capture that very moment. People panicking, starving animals running helter-skelter and the landscape littered with hundreds of dead was one among many of the photographs that still haunts my mind. It was like a vision of hell. An unforgettable, surreal experience for the photographer who needed the patience to numb his skill and move forward, stay focused on the subject, without being distracted by compassionate or any other types of thoughts. He focused, concentrating on his motivation to tell a story at a deeper level to the world devoid of any ethical niceties.

Mr. Nick Ut later explained, "I want to show the world, through any medium: a photograph or hand-drawn sketches that would hit on something to which we would all respond—to strike a universal chord!" Further, the worldwide publicity it gained communicated the utter state of despair and horror, the sheer madness and the futility of this war, sullying the image of the United States internationally, triggering the pace of the withdrawal of American troops from Vietnam!

Incidentally, have we ever noticed whenever the US armed forces launched an attack against Korea, Afghanistan, Iraq or Vietnam, it is always dubbed as the Afghanistan, Korean, Iraq or Vietnam wars, etc. But back home, the wars between any other countries always termed the Indo-Pakistan war, Franco-German war, Iraq-Iran war and so on. The United States media had played up in the minds of their people that their sending out combat units against any other nation was a sort of 'crusade' to bring about peace and order either in Iraq, Afghanistan, Vietnam or any other country. The role of 'God Almighty,' perhaps!

President Nixon who succeeded President Johnson promised to end the war in Vietnam and withdraw the

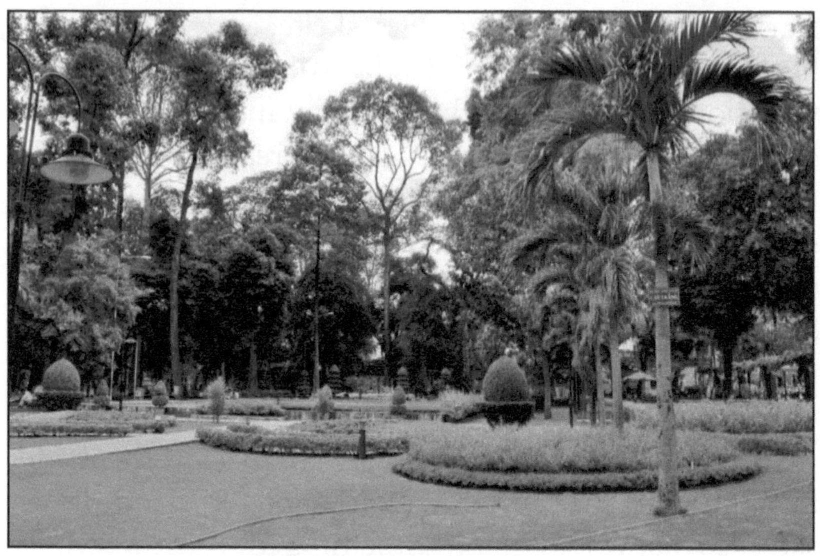

Tao Dan Park in Saigon

American troops as the primary emphasis of his election speech. But after he was elected as the President of USA, he continued to support President Thieu of South Vietnam, buttressing the war with US funds, arms, military personnel, a supportive bombing on a scale surpassing that of World War II. These moves provoked intensive dissension and a mass demonstration in the United States. The anti-war sentiments and protests held in front of the White House by young Americans aroused a wake-up call to the United States from its torpidity. With utter disaster and defeat staring them in their faces, they hurriedly devised a sham formula: '*Declare victory and run*'. They withdrew their combat troops from South Vietnam in 1973, leaving South Vietnam to face the wrath of North Vietnamese and the Viet Cong's who marched unopposed into the capital, Saigon. Saigon was later re-christened, Ho Chi Minh City, thereby unifying their country as one under the leadership of their popular hero Ho Chi Minh Tao Dan Park in Saigon (the glow of the US victory during World War II was dwarfed by their inglorious exit from Vietnam in 1973 and before that from the Korean War).

This undeclared war, too, finds a parallel in the annals of American history! Fighting in an alien environment against the committed local forces, the US army found itself in a similar position to that of the British army during the American Revolution.

Tao Dan Park

The guide saw the depressed expression on our faces after the visits and suggested that we take a walk up to Tao Dan Park. Strolling leisurely along the streets of Ho Chi Minh City, we could feel the calmness and the non-agitated demeanor of the people. As we were leaving against the backdrop of the visit to the museum, we found ourselves in front of the beautiful Tao Dan Park. The entrance was the most welcoming sight with lush green meadows and tall avenue trees. A picture-perfect therapy for our fatigued eyes! We had a ride in the park on pony-driven open carriages. Although our bones were rattling after the rough ride, it was sheer fun, and we were wearing their special cone-shaped straw hats. During every Lunar New Year, an annual Tet flower festival is conducted there. The flower display was gorgeous. We also saw many displays of rock sculptures. The guide walked us to an open-air multi-cuisine eat-out an area where you can find almost authentic Western and Asian foods served by the locals, including delicious ice creams. Lunching in the outdoor ambiance was exciting and thrilling.

Water Puppet Show

After lunch, our guide whisked us away for a water puppet show, as it was almost shown time. It is a novel kind of puppetry with the puppets dancing on top of the water accompanied by music and narration. Co-sponsored by the National Tourist Bureau, it has been nominated for the highest mention in the International Cultural Show held in Geneva. The show was performed twice a day, drawing full-house crowds. Unlike the conventional ones, the water puppet show was performed in water, where the hands animating the marionettes, present an illusionary effect of floating. Puppeteers stand waist-deep in the water, manipulating the colorfully painted wooden puppets attached to long underwater poles.

It was indeed a spectacular show worth watching. The background music was lovely with the solo voice of a female singer, adding to its richness. Her voice was musical yet powerful, sometimes mellow and also melancholic. Her voice would soar to a crescendo effortlessly, leaving us quite breathless. The instruments mainly string ones, blended with her voice so well that the sounds you heard were those of the audience gasping with delight! The choreographer used to appear on the stage at the conclusion of every episode to relate the next item in English.

The theme of the episode was about lovers rowing in a boat, when a sea dragon rising from the depth of water, spewing fire tries to devour them. Suddenly, a team of mermaids emerge from the seas to protect the lovers from the ferocious dragon, subduing its killing instinct. In the end, the dragon soon disappears into the deep waters, much to the relief of the lovers and the triumphant mermaids. In the second episode, the recidivist sea monster reemerged from the water, opened its jaws to bare its fearsome fangs, and finally devoured the lady-love. The third and final episode showed the male lover in a fit of rage. With an utmost vengeance, he hunted for the dragon, which ultimately provided him a chance to avenge the death of his sweetheart. He fought a fierce battle (it was almost realistic) and managed to outsmart the dragon and kill it. The show was so meticulously performed, stupefying us, making us almost believe they were real and life-like with suitable lighting and background music, lending the perfect support, appropriate to the mood of the show.

Later we learned this episode was inspired by the poem 'O, Captain! My Captain!' by Walt Whitman, a metaphor for the American Civil War, which talked about the death of Abraham Lincoln after the victory in the northern states. With a sorrowful modulation of voice, the singer rendered a melancholic song at the grand finale of the episode and the two girls seated next to me were sniffling and crying. The whole play lasted for seventy-five minutes. At the end of the show, the performers came on the stage to take a bow before us and were given a standing ovation. The singers, too, followed them to be greeted with thunderous applause!

General Post Office

Later, we moved to the General Post Office and Notre Dame Cathedral. The next on our agenda was a visit to the old Central Post Office Building built during the French colonization in 1868. Well preserved after

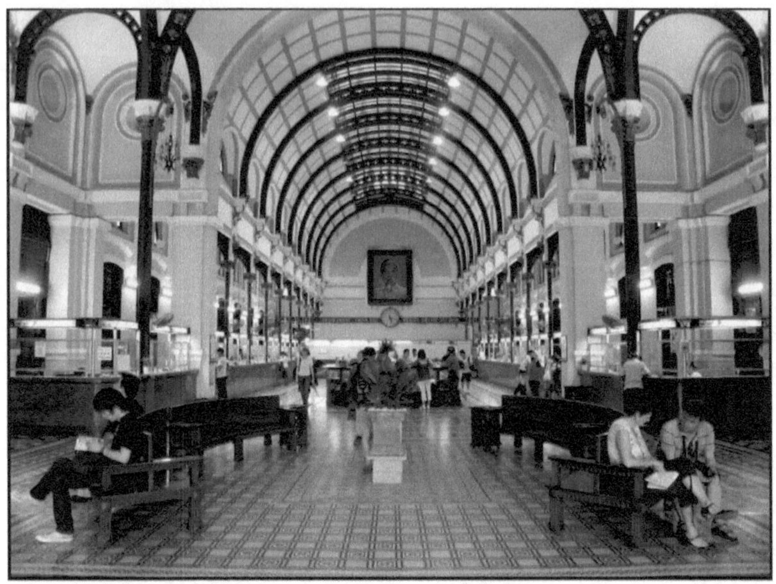

Old Central Post Office at Saigon

careful restorative work, it evokes the style of the French Renaissance period. We walked inside the spacious hall among a multitude of tourists thronging there.

Notre Dame Cathedral

The past a quaint square shopping area, was the famed *Notre Dame De La Basilica.* Admiring the cathedral, located at the corner of Le Duan and Dong Khsi (built from 1877 to 1880), we were clicking pictures of the church from many angles. According to our guide, who was well-versed on the details regarding the beautiful cathedral, it had once stood, nestled in the vast area of among the coconut groves and green fields but now the surrounding area of the church had metamorphosed into one of the main shopping destinations for chic fash-ion boutiques and also had a rabbit warren of flats.

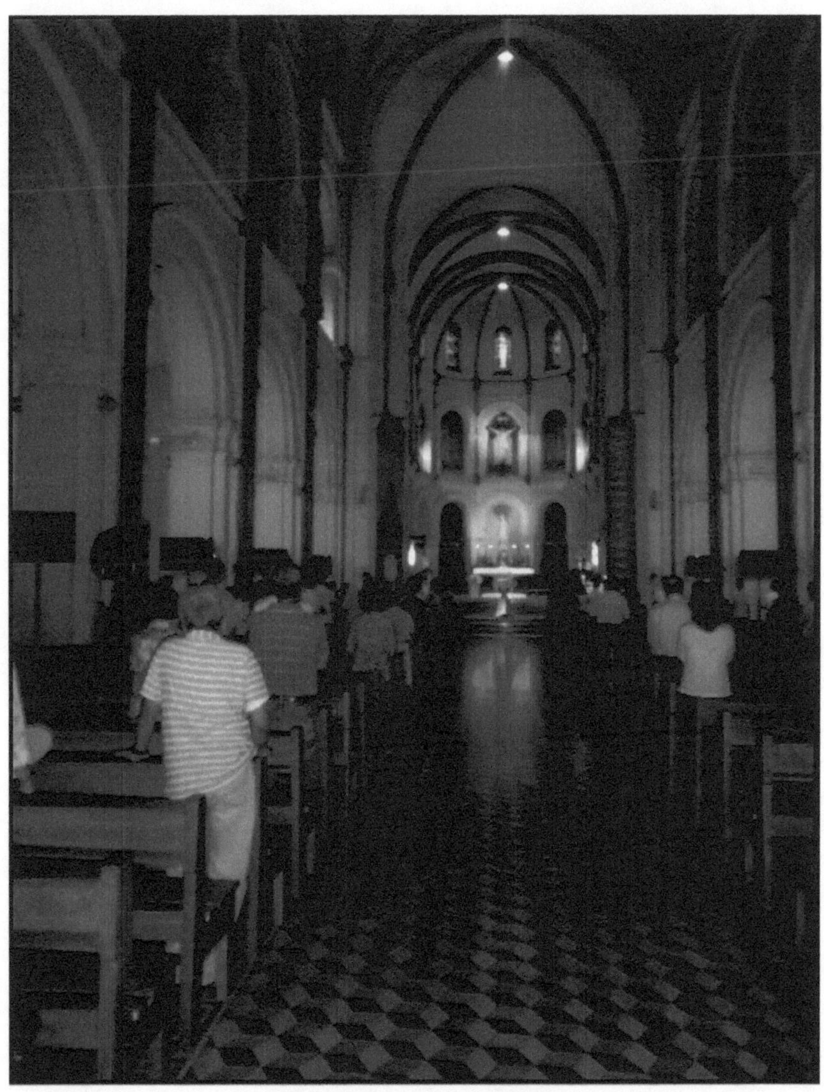

Notre Dame De La Basilica

Being Friday, there was an evening service being conducted in the church. Gerald and I\ walked down the main aisle towards the congregation. As the Friday evening mass was going on, a nun with a stately walk stopped us. When we expressed that our intention was to kneel down and pray, she gracefully led us to a pew. As we genuflected and made the sign of the cross, we started praying. The interior was sublimely lit up with eighteenth-century stained-glass cathedral windows. Incidentally, a keen observer could perceive that the central line of the nave did not align with that of the main altar. With my little knowledge of architecture, this non-alignment was a deliberate action to proclaim that we, human beings, are imperfect in the presence of the Almighty. And to eloquently express our humility in His presence, the imperfection was demonstrated physically. This could be a factor could turn out to be merely fluff *(and if it were so, we are not to be blamed)!*

Once inside the church, listening to the choir music and the gentle breeze, carrying the strains of the hymns sung by choristers swirling around, you'd say to yourself, yes, I can always go to whichever place I am headed for, but later. Let me now be seated in the pew and listen to the choir for some more time! The choral evensong began to encompass the whole area with softly sung hymns, lifting our souls. The timbre and reverberation of the soul music were so soft that we felt we were being carried on the wings of angels to the heavens above. The vast cathedral looked ecumenical and filled with peace!

Returning to our hotel and to the relief of Terry, the baggage that he had inadvertently left behind at Hanoi had reached him. This was as a result of me having contacted the travel agents to express my displeasure for having caused us so much mental anxiety due to the last-minute change of our travel schedule in Hanoi sans prior information. A bottle of choicest port wine was also gifted to us. Jackpot!

Late in the evening, we took a stroll down the streets and bylanes. The roads were brilliantly illuminated with festoons, etc. While walking along, we ground to a halt when we stumbled upon a live rendering of favorite English folk songs. Listening to the live music helped us to overcome our fatigue, and be energized once more to face the world. The fusion of rock, jazz, and Caribbean music capriciously drew us inside the pub. A lot of tourists lined up along the wall, sipping mugs of beer and swaying deliriously. They used their cameras and cell phones to click pictures of the singers who must have felt that they were performing on the main stage in an opera house! We walked further, sauntered into a pizzeria, and had a cheddar cheese pizza along with red wine to wash it down.

We met a 70-year-old American, a war veteran, in the downtown market who had been a combatant in what the Vietnamese call the American War. He was surprised how Saigon had changed in the decades since he left for home after the war. To his surprise, he found the people friendly, warm, and gentle. "They harbored no rancor against us Americans and seemed to have moved on," he said. He had found that Vietnam, despite having undergone a lot of changes due to war ferociously fought had retained all the attraction of the beautiful old landscapes, great beaches, historic structures and all the comforts of Thailand, yet more welcoming than the Thais. It is also more accessible than Myanmar. He advised us to visit Da Nang, Hoi An, and Na Thrang. We were really interested in attending those places. He said that he had been based in Da Nang North of Saigon along the coastline. He extolled the serenity of Da Nang, the third largest city in Vietnam, and eulogized the virtues of the town. Good for whiling away a few days off our tourist trail. He stirred up our imagination regarding what the city would offer to us if we did choose to visit. He advised us to take the *Reunification Express.*

As we were tired, we didn't want to move immediately. Our bodies needed rest, so we stayed back in Saigon itself. We reached back to the hotel and rested. The following day, as we believed that when you visit a place, although you might be interested in the historical monuments and statues, you must still want to get to know the local people, find out about the life they lead and how they enjoy their day-to-day life.

No sooner had we expressed our desire to visit a Vietnamese family than our guide promptly arranged for a meeting with someone at their residence. "Are our lives better now?" The head of the family repeated the question we posed to him. "Today, we don't lack anything. We eat meat and fish every day." Pausing for a while, he said, "But if I had to answer your question, I'd certainly say that those days were better, though grim. We had less, but the motivation within us to attain our freedom from the invaders was uppermost, negating our physical discomforts and hunger. Everyone was poor, but not like these days where there is so much of disparity and inequality and the spirit of capitalism thrives in the fiber of people. It has truly become the survival of the fittest." As the old man was warming up to pour out his heart, his son soon cut in! He told his father off for giving us foreigners a wrong impression of the country. Then the father, with an endearing smile, gave us a warm handshake. It was the briefest interview we ever had and our eagerness to solicit more 'down to earth' information took a beating. We put on a bold front with a broader smile to conceal our disappointment, we shook hands, and that was it. Nevertheless, it was comforting to talk to the sons of the soil who are passionate and proud of their city and they wanted to showcase it.

In the evening, we hired a cab to go to a German-restaurant, *Garten Stadt*, at Dhong Khoi Street. We walked in (there was no dress code) to a long teakwood bar counter, and seated on the cane barstools, feasted on sliced walnuts and mugs of draught beer. Then, we chose a private dining spot on the second floor with a balcony commanding a panoramic view of Dong Khoi Street, overlooking a beautiful scene. We were recommended by the chef to taste the tender juiciness of a duck cooked in the German style. For the appetiser, we had apple salad. Our main course was a pan-fried duck with ginger sauce and schnapps.

Da Nang

We were recommended by the chef to taste the tender juiciness of a duck cooked in the German style. For the appetizer, we had apple salad. Our main course was a pan-fried duck with ginger sauce and schnapps. Da Nang We took the overnight Reunification Express from Ho Chi Minh City to Da Nang and arrived there in the morning. Da Nang is situated on the Central East Coast of Vietnam. The train connects from the North to South along the coast. It is at the opening end of the Han River is overlooking the South China Sea, which decorates it with natural beauty. There are many soapstone islets. This enhances the beauty of the bay. It is the main economic and educational center. Although train travel was not very comfortable, we enjoyed it. It was well worth it, just for a glimpse of the countryside, rice paddy fields, Chinese-style tombs on the edge of the tracks and chrysanthemum gardens.

We stayed at a villa resort, sitting on the beach sands on the east coast of Vietnam offering both Vietnamese and French cooking in a lazy setting. The Da Nang Museum of Cham Sculpture is a 'must visit' for tourists. It has an extensive collection of relics from the Champa Kingdom.

The French created the museum in 1919 to house the sculpture salvaged from the ruins of Champa. The masterpiece of the exhibit was a two-foot-high statue of Lady Tara cast in bronze with her clothes tied at her waist, her breasts bare and her palms up forward, an image of great elegance and beauty!

The Cham kings worshipped the Hindu gods way back in the fourth century and their artisans recreated the stories of Vishnu, Lakshmi, Shiva, and Parvati and scenes from *Ramayana in stone.*

As we were preparing to leave from Da Nang, we crossed a beautiful park. We stepped into relax a while, where we met with some old "goodies" of Vietnamese. As we engaged in conversation about the distant past, especially during the days of conflict during the American intervention in Vietnam, they frankly narrated the horrifying happenings during their time in Da Nang. It is from this very serene location that all kinds of American bombers along with another military forces along with South Vietnamese forces committed merciless atrocities all across Vietnam, including parts of Cambodia and Laos. Every five minutes, a bomber took off fully loaded to return empty after its task was completed. While the commander-in-chief and others in command ordered these executions, the actual performers might not have known the consequences of their implementation. Thus, they explained the war without any remorse.

Hoi An

Later in the day, we drove along the coastal road (a breathtaking view of a palm-fringed beach on our west) down south of Da Nang, a thirty-kilometer drive to *Hoi An City,* where we found the pristine beaches which were as good as any in Thailand.

Hoi An is a UNESCO World Heritage Site, where cars and motorbikes are banned, and the only mode of transport is the bicycle. It has the oldest port in Southeast Asia, where the Japanese, Chinese, and Indian traders transacted business with them. The Tamil kings with their maritime power influenced this area in ancient times. You can find Indian settlers there. Architecturally they have introduced design patterns and craftsmanship in this area. When we visited the city, the feeling of stepping back in time was enhanced. By chance, our visit coincided with the Full Moon Festival (on the fourteenth day of every lunar calendar month), when the street lights were switched off, and candles were floated down the river, akin to numerous stars twinkling in the sky! It was a sight to be treasured.

On our first night at Hoi An, we had our dinner at a restaurant (recommended by one of the locals) priding itself on the authenticity of its Viet food: seared tuna with mango sauce and fried spring rolls. It tasted heavenly.

Hoi An's pristine palm-edged beaches are as good as any in Bangkok-Pattaya, home to the sort of sophisticated resorts you'd expect to find there. But unlike their counterparts in Thailand, where one has to pay a hefty sum for comfort and excellent food, these amenities all come together at a moderate price, and apart from this, the main reason to stay in Hoi An was the alluring charm of the city itself.

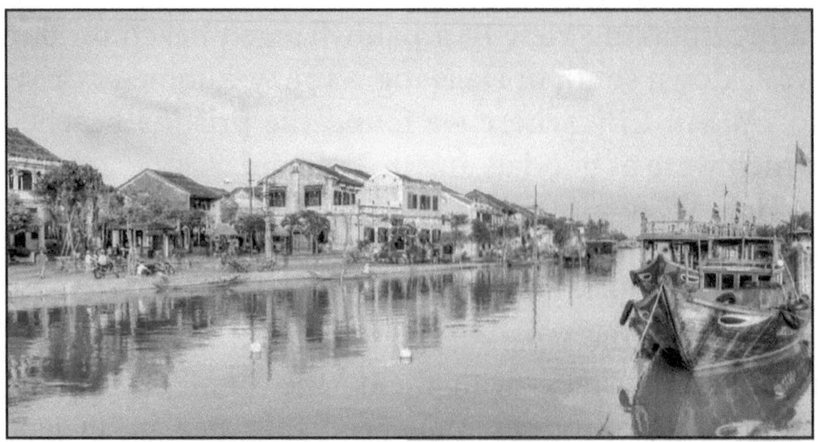

Hoi An – Ancient Town Cum Port

We would have happily spent a week in Hoi An, traveling into the countryside and lazing on the beach. However, as we had a tight schedule of travel, after a hurried visit to the Hoi An Museum of History and Sculpture where the exhibits recorded the centuries of rule by Cham and other Vietnamese dynasties, their artifacts, ceramics, etc., were on display, we drove back to Danang and took the train onto *Nha Tarang*.

Nha Tarang

We boarded the train at Da Nang and reached Nha Tarang in the morning. We took a long drive through the city. It seemed to us again the natural beauty of this country was revealed in its excellence! Later we found that it even hosted Miss Universe and Miss Earth pageants in 2008 and 2010. It conducts the Sea Festival every year, bringing in participants from all over the world. This prettiest of coastal cities remains unrivaled for its sheer beauty, lined with seafood restaurants and pubs. Along the shores, many luxurious hotels were overlooking the azure blue sea. The beach was worth the long drive, and it set the tone for a good holiday. The sun had already set, the beach looked un-spoilt, pristine with yellow sand. *If God were to appear before me, to ask Him for a wish (a greedy one), I would say, "Please, God, grant me a beach house in this spot!"* The beach was clean, and the water had the shimmering effect of the reflection of moonlight. For seafood lovers, the shacks right by the sea was like a dream come true. Eating some of the most exquisite dishes made with fish and prawns, accompanied by a glass of wine and the sea breeze and the murmur of the waves for company, aligned with our idea of ultimate fun. A range of aromatherapy and body massage services were also available there.

I am longing to revisit this paradise on earth some-day to just spend an entire day in solitude, simply watching the endless dance of the waves on the shore and the huddle of boats bobbing silently nearby. Later in the night, there were impromptu gigs and a jamming session on the shore around a lovely campfire. As you enjoy the riot of music and dancing, you detached yourself from the fast-paced world outside. We were sold on the idea of spending the night out there until the following morning and fortunately there were shacks available for the night stay. It was not the type of beach holiday we were familiar with. This one was effortless, merely waiting for you and ready-made! With its proximity to the beach, the quiet chill, and the palm trees swaying every now and then, Nha Tarang beach presented a view that bordered on the ideal.

The monotonous sound of the waves lapping on the shore lulled us to sleep. When we woke up in the morning, the beach was empty, offering us a panoramic view of the azure blue sea. It was a relaxed morning, and nobody seemed to be in a hurry to go anywhere! We waded into the toe-chilling waters of the pebbled beach, and at the deep end of it, we watched the orange sun rising inch by inch turning the sky into a canvas of orange and pink! Soon the sun was glowing in its splendor—an ideal location for a vacation with your family and friends. We returned to the railway station to leave for Ho Chi Minh City.

After arriving in Ho Chi Minh City in the late afternoon, we drove to our hotel. Late in the evening after freshening ourselves and munching on something we stepped out for fun and frolic. En route we stopped at a place where the air was rich with music, and it was actually the din that made us take a peek inside. As we stepped inside, we were delighted at the spectacle of quite a lascivious dance! People mostly foreigners dancing with the locals! We had to sit in a corner like wallflowers and watch this merry-go-round of all kinds of music and riotous jigs (Hindi, English, and Vietnamese). The words were inconsequential as the rhythms do not call for the knowledge of any particular language. The gongs, hand drums, guitars and the verses were punctuated with whistles and whoops. We sat at a vantage spot to enjoy the view of STD (short, tight dresses), pretty faces adorned with more beautiful smiles, dazzlers in cute outfits, and the *cheer quotient* threatened to go through the roof. We (once a band of merry men) could now only feast our eyes on the svelte models sashaying stylishly on their stilettos on the ramp. It was time to call it a day. We returned back and tossed ourselves into bed after a hectic day.

We woke up in wee hours in the morning filled to the brim with happiness for the beautiful companionship barring minor glitches, but with the fulfillment of joy during our unchartered destinations. Was I happy to return home to the drudgery, routine and yet the comfortable homely life! Being our last day in Saigon, we took a morning stroll to make in the presence of the city. To sense the pulse of its heart and soul, one has to walk along the narrow streets, lanes, and bylanes. Although it was early in the day, the streets were noisy, active and alive. Conical hats and brightly patterned pajamas set the oriental scene. Bowls of noodle soup, seafood, and other tasty items were expertly dispensed with steaming stock from large wok by the samplers of street food. Yes! Saigon is lovely, retaining its characteristic Parisian charm and chic and makes a riotous assault on the senses.

I took leave of both Terry and Gerald midway, saying that I would venture out in the neighborhood alone on foot to explore a little deeper. Terry and

Gerald returned to our suite to have a cuppa. While walking along a cobbled bylane, the scented smoke of incense sticks and the ringing of small bells the Hindu style of 'pooja' was in progress at a small shrine adorned with a 'vimana' at the portal. As I lingered there out of curiosity, I found to my joy, coming face-to-face with a descendant of the South Indian Tamil community who had settled there (from time immemorial!) with his two children, wearing the sacred ash on their foreheads! After the customary introduction, he greeted me with folded hands and invited me to his house. Immediately, I rushed back to the hotel to fetch Gerald and Terry. Upon our return, we were wholeheartedly accepted by them. We were interested to know from him about the settlers from Tamil Nadu and the migrants from Madras (now Chennai). The present generations are the descendants of trading families who had followed the tradition of sending their menfolk to amass their fortunes mainly in Burma (now Myanmar) and almost all the regions of Southeast Asia, as far as Hong Kong and the entire Indo-China, awaiting their periodic return home.

(Although we could find that he was not very comfortable in conversing in Tamil, his enthusiasm to speak in that language was really great.) "Our ancestors came here from Madras." He showed us an old framed photograph of his great-grandfather's wedding. "We still carry on the traditional rites of special poojas to venerate them on the appropriate day of their horoscope. The Tamil families staying a few kilometers away and we have formed a small group, he said, refilling our cups with more coffee. "Why did they choose to come here?" we asked. "My ancestors were traders, bringing gingelly (sesame) oil, onions and fishing nets from the coastal areas of South India. Some of them were involved in the money-lending business too."

Tracing the history of Vietnam from the days of the Portuguese, he said, 'The Portuguese sailors came to Vietnam during the fifteenth century, established commerce along with the Japanese and Chinese. With the advent of the Dominican missionaries, the Catholic Church had a more significant impact on Vietnamese then in other countries in Southeast Asia. We liked the Portuguese descendants who were very friendly. There was a mutual help between us settlers in the field of commerce and we built a cultural relationship with them; one of my aunties was married to a Portuguese and they have children who have become Catholics and we have no problem with them. A few members of the older generation like me still remain Hindu and follow similar rites, as practiced in Tamil Nadu.

"Vietnam in those ancient days had a distinct division between the North and South. The Dutch established their influence in the North, and their weaponry and firepower were matched by the Portuguese armaments in the South. Later on, in the eighteenth century, the French colonized Vietnam amalgamating the North and South. Our ancestors were working as clerks in the administrative offices under the French rule. The ethnic equation prevailing in our ancestors' culture-custom and even our mother tongue gradually became distorted, blurred and almost forgotten in the alien environment."

"Did your ancestors bring their wives to settle down here?" we asked.

"No! Never! They did not. Perhaps they would have found it too expensive to go back and forth in those days and it took months for the navigation and the frequency of the mode of travel was minimal. Hence, many of the settlers married the Vietnamese, Japanese or even Chinese to raise their families in their newfound land. They never went back! They quite figuratively burned their boats!" Ransacking through the almirah, he fished out some old dusty photographs framed in glass. The grainy pictures of his ancestors showed men in skull caps sporting wispy beards and other strange features.

"I come from Sumatra," said his charming wife in her mother tongue, pronouncing it with pride! "The people of Bali are not as pure Hindus as the Indians are! My husband taught my sons and me some of the fundamentals. From the age of 6 to 12, my husband brought up my children according to his ancient Tamil culture." Then her husband intervened to say, "I teach my sons the Hindu rites, perpetuated by my father using a few Tamil words. We celebrate Veetu Pongal and Maatu Pongal. We offer prayers to our parents and grandparents a day before Deepavali, but we also participate in the Buddhist festivities and celebrate the Chinese New Year by lighting lanterns. The ceremonial edges of our neighborhood festivals and faith often merge with our own customs and culture, amalgamating effortlessly and we live in a peaceful co-existence. In spite of their richly merged bloodlines, the Vietnamese Indians erected selective, sequestering, ethnic barriers around themselves!"

Now that we have arrived almost at the concluding part of this narration in Southeast Asia, I must narrate a unique episode that happened.

I was fortunate to meet a newfound friend in Saigon. This Mr. Know-All person rattled of his sales pitch with accuracy. He offered to be our tour guide, too, to roads less traveled. "Are you on a tour package too?"

"Oh! No, it is nothing but a glorified form of bondage. You would be awestruck at the sites I'll take you all to which you would have never, ever, have dreamt of, I'll bet!" We were overawed, at the description, in chaste English, of the places in details. "You'll carry back home a really pleasant memory of this tour." he added. He gave us the impression that he would make our lives worth living. " I shall lead you to every part of the city. I am familiar with all the places of interest like the back of my hand." "Truly, O Master", we said in chorus, "lead us, O kindly light, please show us the way, and we'll meekly walk behind you, and help us to see the eternal light." As he was rattling on with an air of self-aggrandisement, we felt that he was slowly baring his teeth. His verbiage, tall claims, exaggeration and verbosity, and other gestures caused annoyance to well up within us. Paragliding, para jumping all over the place, wrestling with leopards, holding a 2.5 meter-long boa constrictor in his bare hands, etc., his claims were tall!

Moreover, he must have mastered the technique of re-maining calm, collected and composed with confidence. We felt overwhelmingly sure that this guy could sell a ton of brass as pure gold with ease and also could do so with no expression of guilt or remorse! He scoffed at our idea of snorkeling. "Bah!" He said, "I would always opt for scuba diving in South China Sea, right in the middle of man-eating sharks swimming around me."

"Did we hear you say in the company of sharks, that to man-eaters?" we asked.

"Yes! I have refined the technique of telepathy, sending my thought-waves, my friendly feel to them. It is a form of psychic technique that I have mastered the art of conveying my feelings telepathically to others, even to sharks. Do you know that I can tame a tiger shark and make it as lovable as a lapdog and…?" Before he could utter his plan of publishing a book entitled *How to Win the Friendship of Sharks and Influence Them to be Vegans,* we cried out, 'Enough is enough,' and we politely but firmly bade him adieu!

Living It Up: More of Saigon

The following day was a well-earned rest for us. Towards the evening, we headed on to the beach, along cab ride away from Saigon. During our drive, we spotted an old chapel, again reflecting the characteristic French-style of architecture. After visiting the church, I saw our guide standing in a remote corner. Forgetting all personal nicety and manners, I spontaneously asked the guide which religion she belonged to Christianity or Buddhism. She replied, "No! I do not identify myself with any religion. In my opinion, there are no organized forms of worship; they also do not unify people. Belief or no belief, being merciful and kind to the fellow human beings are the only religion. I found, on the pretext of religious rights, religious leaders show their utmost love for power. Certain sects of all the major religions manipulate and grab the power of governance calling themselves God's own people, misusing the potential for political and material gains to tarnish humanity and tear down other sects of people. Such an attitude of arrogance will never go unpunished. For all, that is life! They will have to face judgment someday or the other for all their doings. One who causes misery to others will face suffering for generations to come. I believe in the power of love and compassion, not the desire for power! Only the power of love can empower the powerless to scale great heights. As a humanist, I believe all are equal, irrespective of caste, creed, and race. We should be wary of the one-point agenda, of the so-called self-styled god-men and gurus who boast of themselves as superior human beings and expect you to remain sycophantic to them." *Gosh! What a treatise on religious dogma!* I stood there perplexed at the underlying philosophy which the guide professed and followed.

At the fag end of our stay in Saigon, we walked along the well-paved roads, instead of getting ferried by a taxicab. You can truly experience this city when one's feet meet the ground, and the town (no one we had met so far had used the name Ho Chi Minh City) was a walker's delight. We saw families replete with little kids with glowing faces walking along the pavements. It was very peaceful; children were playing among the fruit trees. A bright display of goodies in a departmental store, confectionery, music, charming mums, smiling dads, everyone was well dressed, looking chic. If there was an image of peace, tranquility, prosperity, and rejuvenation, this was the opposite of the Vietnam War and for that matter, of any war, this was it! Whatever you choose to do, Saigon will encourage 'you' to be you. It was heart-wrenching to bid farewell to this charming city. But like a warm-hearted friend, it will invite you back and you'll be happy to oblige with a return visit soon!

The upcoming generations in Vietnam showed high interest in learning English and speaking it with an American accent. It is not uncommon to find advertisements appearing in the newspapers with the names of private institutes offering English language courses to acquire both written and spoken skills. We even spotted a hoarding in a shopping complex, announcing, 'Admissions open for spoken or broken English'! The consequence of the 'broken' English could be hilarious at times. Once during our walk, we noticed a hoarding on a hairdressing salon, confidently announcing, *Heads are cut here in American style!* I stood and gazed at that billboard while Terry and Gerald looked confused. I stepped into the salon to check out the details. The hairdresser in broken English showed me photographs of different styles of haircuts, one of which had a specific name followed by 'American Head Cut Style' as well as a pattern number.

Recapping our tour of Vietnam, we found a vast divergence in the culture and behavior between the people of North and South (although I cannot exactly express it, one had to experience it as the understanding may differ from person to person). The capital city Hanoi in the North exudes charm and placidity, the people are more rigid and less expressive. This is somehow different from its frenzied cousin, Saigon where the people are more friendly and at ease with anyone. In this unified country of 90 million people, there is still a tale of two cities being written, fortunately not in blood now.

Saigon is clearly a land that Mother Nature looks upon kindly. Vietnam is full of Russian, Chinese and Japanese tourists; Americans and Europeans show a lot of interest in that country. Many of them come back for the second or third time. Big-spending Russians were flocking to Vietnam, providing the much-needed boost to the country's present economic recession. Moreover, there is a direct flight from Moscow to Hanoi and Saigon. The lighted up 'Happy New Year' signs on the main streets had greetings in Russian, besides English. Many Russians come here, partly because of the long historical and economic ties between the two countries and partly for the shopping. They enjoy pleasant weather, sandy beaches, and historical monuments.

Seafood is favorite in Vietnam. It is said that the women, in particular, eat three servings a day, which will give them lower chances of having colorectal polyps, which can trigger cancer. True, it had been found that the omega-3 fatty acids in fish can reduce the incidence of rectal cancer.

In the vicinity of Saigon, we found several high-rises residential apartments following the 'green design,' as an integral factor of architectural planning, together with function, budget, and aesthetics. The green approach maximizes the use of natural elements with solar power to create a healthy environment. Saigon has a climate very similar to that of Chennai. The 'green' facades of the horizontal louvers were designed to protect the inhabitants from direct sunlight, street noise, and pollution, encouraging natural ventilation, thereby saving on power consumption.

Saigon dispelled many stereotypes about Vietnam. We observed that the cities are fast, losing their ethnic flavor and resemble any other world-class town with chrome and glass skyscrapers. I am sure that the present generation of Indian tourists is bound to move eastwards, as opposed to the older 'Swiss Alps' generation!

Urged by the desire for last-minute shopping, we sauntered into several malls including the government sponsored handicraft emporium where I bought a bamboo crafted figure of a nymph with a harp in her hand. It was a beautiful piece of artwork, lacquer polished, to a mirror finish, a suitable adornment to the entrance foyer of my house. But Terry discouraged me from buying it, expressing his apprehension about whether this kind of delicate stuff would reach Chennai intact, it also being extra baggage, he would have to shell out more for the airfare. But I wouldn't take no for an answer, justifying that a similar one would cost me more back home.

Ridiculing me, for my foolish decision, Terry and Gerald recalled to my mind, the famous Chinese proverb: *It is not economical to go to bed early, just to save on the cost of a few candles, if the result is a twin!* On my request, Gerald carried the prize package of the nymph to Chennai. Somehow, I wanted the nymph to reach home, come what may.

I had the piece neatly packed and sealed. When I unpacked it after reaching home, as I had been forewarned, I found it had cracked in several places and even the lacquer finish was scratched. I was crestfallen but nevertheless, I got it restored by a local craftsman after spending a fortune to get it back to its original shape.

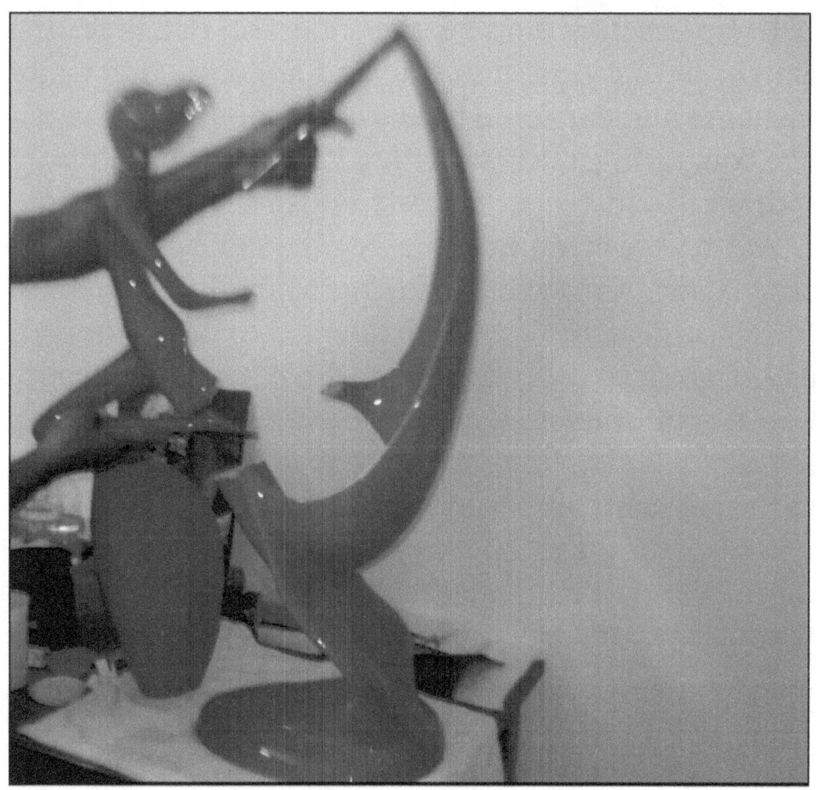

Broken Sculptural Artifact

After our breakfast, it was time to wrap up our thoughts and get down to packing up. Our guide was there to bid goodbye! She was quite comfortable in our company. A word of praise for the van driver who accompanied us during our stay, duty conscious, effervescent, and also a sporting personality! We reached HCMH City International Airport and our return tickets to Bangkok and Gerald's to Chennai were in order.

As Thai Airways connects Bangkok to Chennai from Saigon, all three of us were boarding the plane from Saigon to Bangkok.

If I were to compare the cities of Bangkok and Saigon, both are good for fun and holidays. Every moment of your stay could be enjoyed. Comparing them is like comparing a Ferrari with a Lamborghini. Both are sports cars, and super fast, but both are very different.

As we were about to step inside the cab, bound for the airport, my newfound friend, Mr. Know-It-All emerged from nowhere and asked whether he could accompany us as a guide and a companion, also a source of inspiration for all of us, to places wherever we were heading for! Terry bluffed him saying that we were on our way to the police station. "Any problem, sir? I can sort it out for you, I know the top brass in the police force" was his reply! We said that we needed to go to the police station to collect our passports which had been left there in safe custody, and added whether he was willing to join us. There was no answer, and when we looked around we could see neither hide nor hair of him anywhere!

After our 'byes' to the guide and the van driver, who had become great friends with us, we exchanged pleasantries. We checked into taking the flight. After landing in Bangkok in the forenoon, Gerald, being the transit passenger had to remain in the sanitized lounge until late at night. He was going on to Chennai first.

After Gerald's departure for Chennai and taking leave of him at the Bangkok International Airport, we drove towards our appointed hotel for a few more extended days of holidaying in the city of Bangkok. We rested our feet for a whole day, feeling a bit of a void in our hearts due to Gerald's absence, our dear old companion, who had embroiled himself in all our activities. On the penultimate day of our stay, we visited many street markets, explored the trade circle, shopped for Thai silks, a traditional product, wooden carvings and precious stones, costing a fraction of the price, compared to the upscale, high-end shopping malls. I allowed Terry to freak out to the maximum as I knew his days to go back to his own home were numbered. He began to count the days of leisure left literally.

Being the last day of our holiday with the time of departure around the late hours of the night, we had a little time at our disposal for a long drive in the misty morning to Hua Hin, a quiet spot in the Gulf of Thailand, a beautiful beach with excellent restaurants, unspoiled by tourists. We had lunch under the shade of a big beach umbrella. The food was just right—hot and spicy, with the characteristic Thai tang. Then we returned to our hotel to pack up for our final departure to Chennai, bidding farewell to Southeast Asia.

I must take a pause to narrate the real story behind this book. Initially, it was never meant to be a book. What started as a jolly good ride to have all the fun to free ourselves from all mid-life crisis and stress turned to be soul-searching and emotionally overwhelming. I could not resist but pour out and share these excellent experiences with all. This book is the outcome of that. Here I find that though we had the proper equipment to take photos and videos, we did not tune them to the required levels for print or digital media. I am told, one should take pictures at least 350 dpi for copy and 150 dpi for digital media. The crawling experience inside the dark Chu Chi Tunnel and the underwater snorkeling experience could have been recorded with suitable equipment like a night shot camera. If you don't carry these types of equipment, your guide can hire them for a short time for you to take these shots.

One more special incident that happened in Cambodia flashes in my mind. Our hotel laundry bills were excessive. I asked my Cambodian guide if she could help me to have clothes laundered outside. Smilingly, she helped us to drive to a place where the attendants immediately took our clothes and washed them manually. The attendants were smiling and welcoming. They made us comfortable to sit around their work area and even served us with a nice cup of black tea laced with lime. Upon return from our scheduled visit, we collected our clothes. Except for the quality of ironing, the job executed was equal to the service offered in the lodging house but was much cheaper. The hospitality of these simple people lingered in my mind.

If this chronicle of mine can help me qualify as a writer and gain patronage from readers, it only goes to prove that anyone who has the courage of conviction to share experiences freely with others can also aspire to become one.

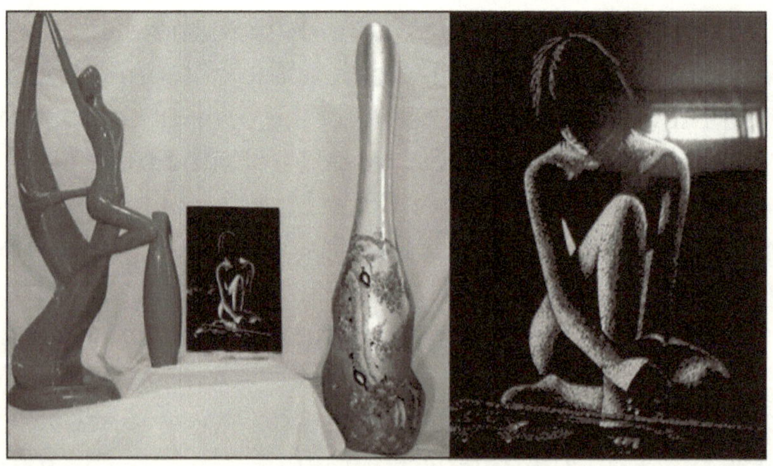

Some Artifacts from Southeast Asia

CHAPTER 5

SRI LANKA

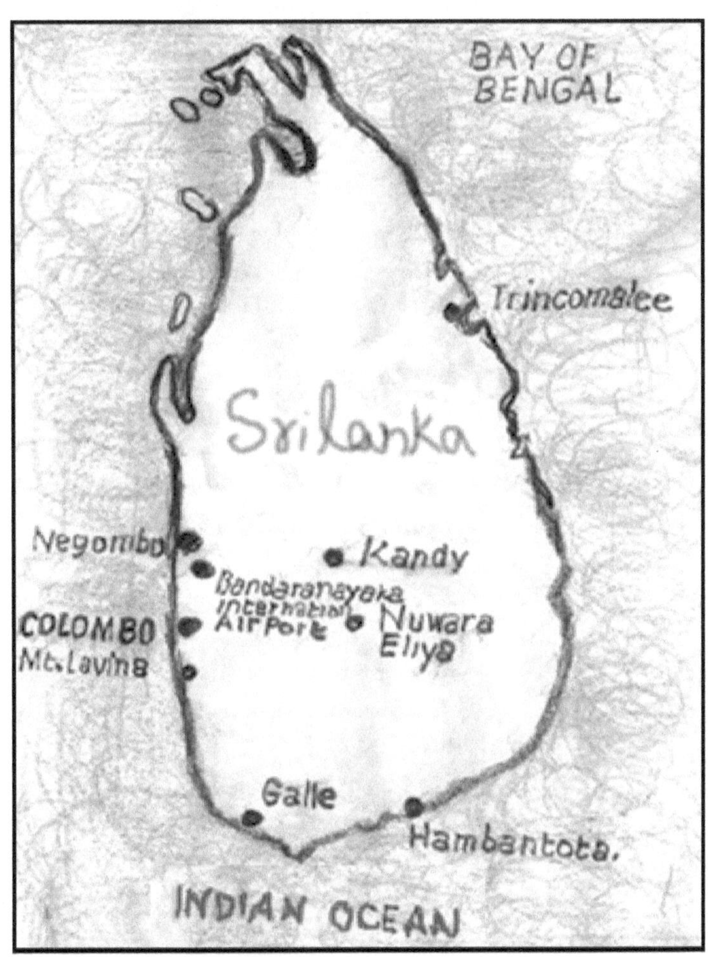

Colombo: Commercial capital of Sri Lanka, with the main port of call for ships from Southeast Asia, Australia, New Zealand, to the West, and vice versa

Independent Square:	Typical Kandyan style of architecture with a sweeping roof erected on a podium with monumental steps leading to the structure
National Museum and Town Hall:	Worth spending a few hours exploring the ancient the culture of Sri Lankans
Mount Lavinia Hotel:	Most reputed resort in Sri Lanka, former residence of the British governor, set on an imposing headland.
Negombo:	Bewitching coastal town, 30 km north of Colombo. Dubbed as 'Little Rome,' an apt name given to the town for its Catholic population. Beautiful seafront famed for the seafood
Kandy and Peradeniya:	Visit the elephant training camp at Pinnawela, near the hill town of Kandy. Sri Lanka's second largest city, a cultural capital. Home to the royal palace and the sacred Temple of the Tooth (Dalada maligawa)
Bentota Beach:	Betwixt a picturesque freshwater lagoon and a long stretch of a fine white sandy beach
Nuware Eliya:	Nestled among the tall trees, emerald green meadows, some 6,000 ft, above MSI. Summer resort for Sri Lankans and a favorite destination for international tourists. Worth visiting the tea factory and enjoying a gentle initiation to the art of tea making
Trincomalee:	This northeastern province of Sri Lanka has natural harbor. Main attractions are the natural hot springs
Galle:	The Dutch fort town is home to the booming boutique hotel business. Wander around the ramparts. The fort is the seventh UNESCO World Heritage Site
Lankan History, Civil War, and Tamil Eelam:	Chequered history, ruthless conflicts, war crimes, and genocidal acts Three Men in Sea

After returning to Chennai, we took a couple of days' rest, while getting updated on the work at home. Terry had to complete some procedures on his tooth implant. During that time, we were discussing our future plan of visiting Sri Lanka as planned earlier. Unfortunately, Terry felt too tired, and fatigued. Hence, we concluded Gerald alone would visit Sri Lanka and thus the plan was changed from three men to a single man. Gerald had spent his childhood, youth and early career in Sri Lanka. I was not personally inclined to travel there, for the atrocities committed by the Sinhalese fascists against the Tamilians were still fresh in my memory that I felt it would be better to stay away from the place. Further, the grief that engulfed me, after witnessing the plight of the Sri Lankan Tamils, through the media, day after day, was so profoundly to be far away I am there, the better. The irony was that the whole world kept quiet when the war crimes and genocidal acts were being showered upon the innocent and defenseless Tamils. I will narrate the sufferings of the Sri Lankan Tamils, while Gerald recounts his journey in Sri Lanka.

SRI LANKA: Formerly known as Ceylon, offering breathtaking scenery, golden sandy beaches, and above all, friendly people, except for the ruling class. The emerald tea plantations from colonial times, fronds of coconut palm elements, miles, and miles of beaches, paddy fields, precious gems, sari, and sarong-clad locals, whose genuine warmth and hospitality especially that of the native Tamils are all bound to impress.

Destination: Sri Lanka

Gerald packed his travel kit and personal knick-knacks and we were ready to leave for the Trichy Airport after a quick breakfast. I accompanied him to the airport. It was time for his flight. I left him at the airport wishing him a safe journey. Further on, Gerald narrates his experience in Sri Lanka while I intrude with snippets about Tamilian history, torchieres experiences, and sufferings in Sri Lanka.

Gerald's Narration

'Ayubowan' is the unique way of the Sri Lankan greeting, by the sari-clad, slim air hostesses with folded palms and smiling faces as I was trooping onto the tarmac. It was sheer music to my ears, hearing the Sinhalese language after so many decades!

The duration of the flight across the Palk Strait was only an hour or so. Landing smoothly at Bandaranaike International Airport, I hired a cab to drive towards the south to Colombo, the commercial capital of Sri Lanka.

This beautiful island, Sri Lanka, formerly known as Ceylon is resplendent with lush greenery, a magical kaleidoscope of history, culture, eye-catching scenery, golden sandy beaches and friendly people. Just 240 miles long from the north to south, intertwined with the legacy of 3,000 eventful years, including a brief spell of the colonial rule for a few years there are Buddhist temples, fronds of coconut palms, elephants, fishing hamlets, coastal towns, miles, and miles of beaches, paddy fields, precious gems, charming sari-clad women and sarong-wearing men who are friendly and generous. If you are wondering how I know all these, I must tell you I grew up on this island!

Sri Lanka is a tangle of ethnic movements and settlements, right from the date when the land was a protectorate of the British. There was a century-old migration of shopkeepers and manual laborers, white-collar workers and others from the coastal regions of Tamil Nadu who came seeking their fortune in Ceylon. The northern province of Ceylon was inhabited by the Tamilians who migrated from South India many centuries back, during the dynasty of the Pandya kings of the Tamil Kingdom. These native Tamils are as many sons of the soil as are the Sinhalese in the south and the central provinces. A vast majority of Sri Lankans are Buddhists who speak Sinhala, and with their unique culture, according to history, they migrated from North India centuries ago. While the migrants from South India are Hindus and their mother tongue is Tamil, they follow the typical South Indian Hindu culture and their fete champetre! There are also a sprinkling of Muslims termed as Moors, Burghers (descendants of the Portuguese, Dutch, and English) who form a minor proportion of the population. Pearls lured the South Indian Tamils across the sea. They liked the land so much that they fanned out, specializing in trade, especially coconuts. Some of them moved to the interior parts like Kandy and Kurunegala. There are also third or fourth generations of Tamils who were recruited to the island during the British rule and most of them worked in the tea gardens in Hutton and Nuwara Eliya, forming a community of their own, confined to the tea estates of the central province.

Most of the Tamils integrated themselves into Sri Lankan society, followed their customs and speaking Sinhala, yet managing to retain their distinct culture and identity. But the vestiges of Hindu culture still remain for they continue to tie the *Thaali* around the bride's neck during the marriage ceremony. As many Tamilians living in the coastal areas of Sri Lanka and Tamil Nadu had been converted to Catholicism by the Portuguese during their trading period, they carried Portuguese names. But they still, follow the Indian tradition for important ceremonies.

The population grew and the divide between the two major races—the Sinhalese versus the Tamils in the north and eastern province—became wider, mainly because of the economic pressure and financial crunch. Ultimately, with the introduction of the Sinhala Only Act as the official the language of the island when the late Solomon West Ridgeway Dias Bandaranaike was elected Prime Minister (the ruling party, he was heading Sri Lanka Freedom Party and was defeated in 1957), the ethnolinguistic separation of 'Tamil Eelam' flared up in the north and eastern provinces in the form of civil war, resulting in untold sufferings, death, and misery. When SWRD Bandaranaike of People's United Front became the Prime Minister, he brought about a major change. Sinhalese, the language spoken by the majority in the country, replaced English as the official the language of the country, and Buddhism, the religion followed by the majority, was given a prominent place in the affairs of the state. A disgruntled Buddhist monk shot the Prime Minister dead, in September 1959. His wife, Srimavo Bandaranaike succeeded him to become the first female Prime Minister in the world in 1960. What more, she was elected the Prime Minister during the next three subsequent elections as well!

Colombo: Riding in a Tuk-Tuk

Colombo, the commercial capital of Sri Lanka, has a chequered history from the eighth century when it was founded. Invaded by the Arabs, followed by the Portuguese, Dutch, and finally by the British, Sri Lanka (then known as Ceylon) finally got its freedom on 4 February, 1948. Democratic government was established.

Being the hub of commercial activities, the city is densely populated with a mixture of Sinhalese, Tamils, Indians, Burghers, and Moors were competing with one another.

After freshening up, I was sipping that world-renowned a cup that cheers, after which I sauntered out for a leisurely walk down the bylanes of Colombo towards the sea wall. There I strolled along, around the heritage building, *Old Dutch Hospital and visited the beautiful Cathedral at Kotohena and Old Parliament House* in Galle-face Court. I wanted to experience the feel of the city and what better mode of transport could it is done in than by hiring a 'tuk-Tuk'. Then I went on to visit the famous Independence Square, formerly known as *Torrington Square,* gifted by the Chinese, with the traditional style of Kandyan architecture with high-pitched roof. Although it had been built more then sixty years ago, it remains well preserved on a high podium, reached by great steps!

Riding in a *tuk-tuk* is entirely different from any other mode of transportation. It is a bone-shaking ride; shock absorbers seem to be considered an excessive extravagance. I had experienced a similar ride back home in Chennai. Hence, we are quite used to this hair-raising the rough ride. Unlike the drivers back home, most of the tuk-tuk drivers in Sri Lanka were cheerful and loquacious, talking nineteen-to-the-dozen as they take on any heavy-loaded oncoming trucks or buses with casual insouciance which could prove both baffling and terrifying to the uninitiated, but for us, the stoic Chennaites, it was quite part of the game! Incidentally, many drivers preferred to be addressed as 'Bajaj' drivers using the Indian brand names for the three-wheeler, rather than the onomatopoeic 'tuk-tuk.' drivers, as they are commonly labeled in the parts of Southeast Asia, we had just visited.

I understand that these three-wheelers were introduced in Sri Lanka by Bajaj India in 1979 and just two sold in that first year of launching. The popularity of these workhorses steadily grew, providing direct and indirect employment to almost 1.5 million of Sri Lankans, who depend on businesses directly linked with the drivers, dealership and service centers within a decade. Compared with the taxi fares and other modes of transport, travel fare by tuk-tuk is comparatively cheap and the most convenient way of getting around the city. Further, there is no parking problem involved. Just a thumb up for a pick-up at any location on your way and they stop the vehicles by your side from out of the blue, addressing you with the endearing word 'Mahathaya' (sir).

As per the programme, I joined the joggers along the Galle face green the following morning, negotiating with a friendly tuk-tuk driver, who would act as our guide while taking us to the National Museum and Town Hall. First, I visited the *National Museum*. It had been built around 1877, in the British colonial style of architecture. It was well maintained and one could spend hours at the museum, following the evolution of civilization until the present. The archives were full of old scripts in the ancient Pali script on the palm leaves. The throne of the last king who had ruled the island was on display. The history, migration of people from the neighboring countries, intermix of culture and the advent of Christianity were on display with well-defined photographs, serving as a source of inspiration, especially to the historians. There is also a separate section for nature lovers. There were arrays of stuffed prehistoric animals, birds and marine creatures on view. *The Old Town* Hall presented a picture of an ancient Greek Senate House with a massive colonnaded corridor and an imposing entablature at the main facade with manicured greenery all around. It is a landmark building in the very heart of Colombo.

The driver guided me to the fort area where I could buy Sri Lankan green tea, handicrafts, and a charming gem-studded pendant at the high-end departmental store 'Lakasala.' From the fort area, I was taken to Pettah, the central hub of shopping where I could shop till I dropped—Majestic City, Liberty Plaza, Crescat to name a few, where one can find garments of all kinds, leather jackets and varieties of canned food at real bargain rates.

Then I got myself dropped off at Fort Railway Station and took the train to Mount Lavinia, which is about eight kilometers south of Colombo. The railway must have seen the golden days of Ceylon and it puffed, pulled and rolled through the outskirts of Colombo and rumbled along the coast down to the south. Just as our tuk-tuk driver had said, it happened to be one of the best train journeys that one could ever experience. At sea level, just bordering the beach, the blue sea, the gently swaying palm groves and the ocean breeze engulfing our compartment added pleasure to my joyful train journey.

Mt. Lavinia Hotel perched on top of a hillock commanded a panoramic view of the blue ocean, private swimming pool, open-air restaurant, and bar. Reflecting upon the affluent and the rich tapestry of the residence of the British governor, the interior walls of the lounge were wood-paneled, with chandeliers and sofas and beautiful leather upholstery. The guests were also pampered with 24/7 attendance. Freshening myself up after a shower, and clad in casual wear, I walked towards the beach. There were reclining chairs, beach umbrellas, and an open-air bar.

Sri Lankan musicians, sporting hot pink shirts, dark blue shorts and oversized hats played some lovely music— Mexican, Caribbean, Hindi, a popular Tamil number, and later, on our request, 'Surangani,' a popular and foot-thumping Sinhala 'Baila.' I enjoyed the company of a few Sri Lankans who shared a conversation with me. They were a bunch of happy-go-lucky guys born with the proverbial silver spoons in their mouths!

Cricket, cricket and more cricket! This is the passion of an average Sri Lankan, apart from all other activities including local politics. Cricket plays a very significant part of their lives. 'Thanks to cricket, England had never been at war with nations that played cricket!' *(You can check it from the history books if you doubt it.)* While having a few drinks, the conversation mainly orbited around cricket, punctuated with jokes, along with numerous wisecracks. I remembered two as the most hilarious and rib-tickling ones!

During the England-Australian cricket match, Merv Hughes, the Australian pacer, found the tail ender, English batsman Robin Smith missing to make his willow connect with the ball, but standing like a rock just blocking the ball without scoring a single run. So exasperated Hughes said, "Robbie, if you turn your bat over, you will find *'Teach yourself how to bat step by step'* written on it! You'll find it useful to learn it."

When Ian Botham, the English batsman, trotted up to his crease, 'So how are your wife and my children?' was Rod Marsh, the Australian bowler's message of welcome. But Botham was totally calm. He replied without batting an eyelid, 'The wife is fine, but the kids are mentally retarded!'

It was a beautiful way to end the day! Taking leave of them, I sauntered back to my room. I was left with just a couple of days to spare for my stay in Negombo.

Negombo

The next morning, I was on the move from Colombo northwards and in an hour and a half I was in Negombo, famed for its beach, now peppered with luxurious hotels, set among the palm trees, along with the ocean-front of Negombo.

In Negombo, I also visited an ancient fortress built by the Dutch in 1682 and a spacious bungalow amidst a large palm grove. The people were friendly and many of the older generations, though Sri Lankan, conversed in pure Tamil.

Kandy: A Paradise within a Paradise!

After visiting Negombo as per our itinerary, I was moving on to Kandy in a hired cab in the early hours of the following morning. I reached the Fort Railway Station in Colombo with a reserved ticket to Kandy. It was around 7.00 a.m. Most of the trains in Sri Lanka were small and slow, possibly the same rolling stock of days gone by. Kandy was only seventy-five miles from Colombo and the train passed through many tunnels, gardens and villages along the slopes. I could see rice terraces, full of still water mirroring the blue sky. As I was enjoying the scenery, changing from the green carpeted gardens to the swaying coconut plantations, neat vegetable farm, and pineapple fields into the cooler air and taller trees, the ascent was steadily rising steeply and I reached my destination by noon.

Kandy is Sri Lanka's second largest city, at an elevation of 1,500 ft above sea level, with salubrious climate. It is the cultural capital, a gateway to the surrounding lush hills and plantations. The train journey is highly recommended as the winding track goes through a panorama of verdant jungle and picture-postcard beauty of green paddy fields cascading down to you. While you are moving at a slow pace, enjoying the scenic beauty, the air gets cleaner. I checked into a lodge, billed as Kandy's luxury-budget hotel, a few minutes' walk from the station. The rooms were spacious enough, equipped with air conditioning, attached toilet with bathtubs, etc. An empty fridge allows you to store whatever you want, rather than tempt you, stacked with mini-bar goodies.

The manager of the hotel guided me to a lake in the heart of Kandy. The lake is a man-made one, with a white stone parapet that runs along the north shore of the artificial lake built by the last king of the island. It resembled the one at Kodaikanal in South Tamil Nadu. There is an islet right in the middle of the lake. A walker's cobbled pathway was laid out, skirting around the lake, where one could go on a walk for an hour or so... and it could be really refreshing. Then I was off to an auditorium, where I was entertained to the traditional classic dances of Sri Lanka. There were nearly twelve types of hops. The hall was modestly spacious with the full complement of almost three hundred spectators. With eight male and female artists, the dances were continuously performed—snake dance, peacock dance, Kathakali, a traditional Kandyan vigorous dance, as well as a sword-wielding dance. The admission was free and late in the evening I stood apart from the crowds going about their daily lives and were warmly greeted by these gentle, friendly men and women with their beautiful, expressive faces in saris, dressed in a different style from that of South Indians. Moving on, I reached the ramparts of the Royal Palace of Sri Wickrama Raja Singam, the last Pandyan Tamil king (1798–1815) when the British clandestinely overthrew him in Kandy, and thus, the whole island of Ceylon was subjected to their rule until 1948.

I walked to the famous, sacred Temple of the Tooth, known as Dalada Maligawa. Two red-robed monks-in training shyly led us into the temple. I kicked off my shoes and rambled inside the 'vihara.' Inside, the walls were covered with murals, blanketing every inch of space. The whole interior of the Maligawa echoed with the continuous, monotonous chanting of the monks with a swirling fog of warm incense.

There were tuskers caparisoned in their finery. I wanted to take a snapshot of the temple elephant at a close range. But the mahout did not allow me to come close saying '*Palayalla*' (Go away). But to me, the elephant appeared to be harmless and docile, in a good mood after her staple diet of bananas, fruits, and jaggery. While the mahout was talking on his mobile phone, I had a chance! I walked too close to the animal to stroke her love when all of a sudden she trumpeted loudly. I ran away in mortal fear like there was no tomorrow for me! After calming the elephant, the mahout called out, '*Mang kivva nay*' (I told you so).

There were milling crowds of visitors, along with the local devotees carrying trays of flowers, etc., to offer Lord Buddha.

At the entrance, flanked on either side were rows of elephants sculpted in stone. In the upper level, I visited an ancient library built by the last king, where manuscripts of Buddha's teachings were found inscribed on old palm leaves and now preserved in glass-fronted cases. I had a 'darshan' of the Buddha's tooth kept in a gold casket. I saw a golden statue of Buddha, about two feet high, placed on a pedestal in the seated posture. Looking at the statue, I felt as if the figure was gazing at me with half-closed eyes, whichever direction I stood, like the celebrated *Mona Lisa by Da Vinci, displayed in the Louvre Museum, Paris.*

I sneaked into the library again to discover more antiques of printed books, to browse through all the ancient history of Sri Lanka. Except for a very few, the rest were stacked in locked cupboards and most of these were inscribed on the fan-shaped palm leaves (Talipot leaf) Preserved in silver foil. Most of the scripts were written in the classical Tamil language and some bits were said to be Pali, which nobody can understand today, contemporary to Latin, and as I could not decipher any of these, I did ponder over the civilization in the remote past!

It was rather late when I returned to the hotel, too tired to go to the dining hall, I then rang for the room service and ordered string-hoppers and tea, and then, headed off for a good night's sleep. The morning was pleasantly calm and serene. A Sri Lankan watched us getting ready to visit *Peradeniya*, the world-renowned botanical garden. Noticing I was on tour with my binoculars and cameras slung across my shoulders, he cautioned us to be wary of touts and self-styled guides.

After my breakfast, the Sri Lankan said it was too far to walk to *Peradeniya*, and he kindly went out of his way to find us a taxi and even negotiated the fare. The drive from Kandy to Peradeniya was quite scenic and the air was perfumed with blooming wildflowers that could capture any heart!

The Royal Botanical Gardens were devised by the British, where many of the trees were ancient, some of them having been planted in the nineteenth century. The bamboo groves at Peradeniya were dense, many of the cane shoots were gigantic, and the old palms stood tall. Walking amidst the lush and beautiful gardens was great. They were spread around six hundred acres, founded by *Mr. Alexander Moon*, the chief of staff of the British Ministry in 1821. There were licensed guides who explained the genesis of the trees, their age, and botanical names and taxonomy. In the vast area of the gardens, there was a greenhouse where flowers of various kinds and hues were artistically arranged. The garden was maintained by in-house horticulturists and the most impressive segments was a cactus garden with a remarkable variety of cacti with showy flowers of white and purple.

Just a short drive from Kandy, and home to almost one hundred elephants are the *Pinnawela Elephant Orphanage*. In a shed, I saw a mother elephant cuddling her four-month-old calf and few more baby elephants that were found quaffing vast volumes of milk. The sanctuary was built in 1975 on six acres in a palm grove, and it attracts a lot of tourists across the world to see the elephants with their calves, rambling about freely, feeding on palm leaves. It was well maintained, and I was told that the minimum birthrate of an elephant was one calf every two years. The elephant orphanage center has set a benchmark in the propagation of Asian elephants and their healthy upbringing for other countries to emulate! The majesty of the elephants' forehead and the symmetry of the curving tusks and the unique trunk that touches the ground created a visual feast for the avid elephant lovers. The Hindus worship the elephant-headed Ganesha as the auspicious remover of all obstacles.

The other attraction was the walking of the elephants, one behind another in a self-disciplined manner for about a half-kilometer distance to a shallow river called the *Mahoya*, on a ten-foot-wide mud path for their regular bath. I was standing on an elevated balcony of a restaurant run by the Department of Tourism. While munching on some short-eats, I enjoyed the sight of the elephants spraying water among themselves with their trunks in a playful mood. I was told that elephants have many capacities that we human beings don't have. Elephants have large ears that help them to perceive a wide range of frequencies inaudible to human ears. They can communicate with one another of their species through infra-sonic waves. Their memory is powerful. It is believed widely that the elephant can recognize people by their smell even after a lapse of several years.

It was a chilly, misty morning when I took a train to Nuwara Eliya from Kandy. Some six thousand feet above sea level, Nuwara Eliya is aptly known as 'Little England'—Sri Lanka's tea-growing country and home to horse racing—a vibrant place to welcome the dwellers of the plains during the summer months.

The lobby of the hotel I had checked into was bright with air-conditioned sunshine. I opted for a conducted tour of the town, visiting the fabulous golf course set amid the rolling hills, horse-racing tracks and the beautiful garden *Hakgala*. A brief time was allowed for shopping. I found many of the shops, although overpriced, offering pretty trinkets and in-vogue outfits that rekindled our buying spree!

The Hills are Alive with Fragrance of Tea

The Hills are Alive with Fragrance of being in a hill station, dusk descends early in these parts and darkness engulfed the region by 5 p.m. The tourist van dropped off the passengers at the doorstep of their hotel. As I was stepping into the lobby, which was converted into a bar during the evening hours, I ran into a long-lost cousin of mine, whom I had met a decade back in Chennai. I found him nursing his mug of beer, seated in a lounge chair, munching on cream crackers and cheese. After exchanging pleasantries, I had a wonderful time with him. He was the proprietor of a furniture shop in the main bazaar area and he booked me a seat on the *Ceylon Tea Trail,* a conducted tour, offering a leisurely stroll into the tea garden and a visit to the tea factory. He then left for his home.

The next morning when I woke up and was getting ready, I saw the Land Rover parked at my door ready to take me on the *Ceylon Tea Trail* to visit a tea garden and a tea factory.

The concept of the tour is to take a step back in time and re-live that wonderful 'golden era' enjoyed by the British tea planters of yesteryears, 'a throwback.' to the wonderful 'days of wine and roses' when life went on at a leisurely pace and one had all the time to enjoy. Tea is one of the main export products of this island. It is here that the crème de la crème of Sri Lanka's tea, the fragrant and delicately flavored high-grown, flourishes.

Nestled among the *Bogawantalawala* region are the four British colonial era bungalows, impeccably restored and offering the visitors accommodation of an international standard, as well as a chance to unwind in The beautifully tended gardens. Besides this, an instructive visit a tea factory, with a lesson on the correct art of tea-brewing threw in. The chef's job was to make us understand the concepts of brewing tea in his inimitable esoteric language of tea experience the differences among the tea leaves, brewing time and procedure, etc.

This was a charming exercise washed down with several cups of tea, ranging from green, white, and red, flavored or non-flavored. It was an excellent place for the cuppa, even with or without lessons.

The bungalows are isolated from one another, perched high on the mountain slopes, surrounded by fragrant emerald green tea bushes at an altitude of about five thousand feet. Each bungalow I visited was unique. The one I stepped in last was a 100-year-old villa nestled in a densely wooded area close to the waters of a beautiful lake, offering us unique views of the lake and the surrounding garden. A sixteen-kilometer drive through tea plantations and beautiful scenery with a picture of the lake kept us visually satiated all along the *Ceylon Tea Trail*.

I enjoyed the sight of the traditional English way of serving tea on the lawns by the correctly clad *Apoos*. In fact, the high tea was a ceremony itself, complete with cucumber sandwiches and scones.

When I returned to my hotel, it was the strange time of the night, too late to make a 'plan' and too early for the pyjamas. Besides, I was in the summer retreat house in a hilly station wondering what to do in the next three hours, when my cousin, Cross Moraes, walked in like an 'angel incarnate' to enquire about my trip to Tea Trails.

"Take me somewhere, anywhere, please!" A ten-minute walk, I was knocking at the door of a brewery, arguably Sri Lanka's most excellent micro-brewery. What is the difference between the micro one and the ordinary one? I quizzed the innkeeper and a roly-poly gentleman with an endearing smile explained, "The beer I brew here is exclusively created to be consumed, right here from the barrel. It is bitter, fresher, and frothier than the average bottled ones and the fact is that you don't burp after drinking refreshing beer."

Soon he disappeared into the cellar soon to re-appear, carrying a massive mug of golden frothiness. "Drinking or gulping this fresh beer, you'll never get sick or indigestion." He said that bottled beer contains all kinds of additives, including glycerin. (Glycerin is added to stretch the shelf life, but it affects the beer in the bargain.) Beer lovers are sure to have a ball too! The micro-breweries, where beer is brewed, is made in small batches and completely handmade.

It was a night well-spent in the company of my cousin and the innkeeper, and I took leave of him. The next morning, I woke up thoroughly rejuvenated and awaited my cousin's arrival. He took me to tucked away in a plateau, still retaining its hundred-year-old charm against the stunning skylines. Amidst the perfectly manicured greenery and the old-world sublime charm of the landscape, untouched by anything crudely modern, the church was completely in sync with the land on which it stood. Surrounded by a vale full of clematis trees towering majestically to disappear into the clouds it looked simply superb.

St. Xavier's Church looked stunning against the blue sky. Even a photographer with zero skills could click the church against this backdrop, and the photograph would still look like the work of an expert. I walked into the church where I heard a mesmerizing recital being played on an organ.

The following day, I left for Kandy and went on to Dambulla junction by train via Matale. It was about five to six hours' journey. I stayed overnight in a hotel at Dambulla.

In the morning, I drove through a highway leading to Trincomalee. The road passed through a densely forested area with a lot of Palmyra trees, swaying in the sea breeze. Driving for nearly five hours from the junction of Dambulla was a treat by itself. Traffic was sparse, and everything seemed quiet. There were a lot of safe, clean campgrounds to choose from, especially on the banks of a lake built in the third century by King Maha Sena. The man-made lake was a mile long and about seventy to eighty feet wide.

It was late at night when I reached Trincomalee and my hotel, which I had booked via the internet, was worth the money. The hotel staffs were very courteous. I felt at home and comfortable in conversing in Tamil after many days of trying to choose the correct word in Sinhala to strike a conversation, albeit my smattering knowledge of the language.

In the morning, I walked towards the sandy beach and the ocean remained still and calm. Trincomalee has a natural harbor similar to the one at Vizag in Andhra Pradesh. The sandy beach was littered with conch shells and star-shaped ones too. After a sumptuous lunch served on plantain leaves in South Indian style, I walked into the main tourists' attraction of bathing in the natural hot springs. I could soak in the water for hours, and with the geological curative properties it possesses; naturally, I found myself refreshed and invigorated. Most of the houses that had been devastated by the tsunami were being rebuilt with financial aid from all over the world. I found some 'Trincomaleeans' sporting rather expensive, high-end apparels, gifted by the philanthropists.

A Coastal Ride to Galle

The following day, I took a flight from Trincomalee to Ratmalana Domestic Airport near Colombo. The next morning, I went to Fort Railway Station. I traveled by train to Galle along the west coast of Sri Lanka, south of Colombo, parallel to the glittering seashore lined with abundant palm trees and the rushing of the ocean breeze into my compartment. This journey will be treasured as one of the loveliest I ever enjoyed.

While journeying, I struck a conversation with a fellow traveler who spoke in Tamil fluently and the talk, somehow or the other veered around the tsunami. He had been an eyewitness to the fury of nature at its worst. He gave us a graphic account of the devastation:

On the morning of 26 December 2004, the tide on this coast receded dramatically revealing the weird sight of water being sucked off the ocean, exposing the seabed gleaming in the bright sun. A milling crowd of people attracted by the strange news of this unusual phenomenon ran wildly into this 'new found land'! Many fishing boats found themselves, sitting on the strange waterless dry land. After a lull, the catastrophe began, with the tidal waves rising more than twenty feet high or so, like a wall of foam. Figuratively speaking, it was like numerous giant-sized king cobras lined together looking at you with menacing eyes, raising their hoods, rushing towards you, crashing on to the land, crushing the houses built along the shores and drowning cattle and people alike with demonic fury!

As ill luck would have it, a train leaving for Colombo from Galle packed carrying around 1,500 passengers, the day after the Christmas holidays was hit by the waves, knocking it on its side, and mercilessly sweeping the coaches away from the track, drowning almost everyone. Only the palm trees withstood the ravages of nature, standing undisturbed, although the fortress-like thick walls and the paved roads were extensively damaged. The irony was the palm trees stood like sentinels along the coast, preserving the characteristic serenity of the coastal region and did not portray the knocked-flat aftermath associated with the hurricane. Many lives were saved as they clung fast to the trees, until the waves retracted, sucking inside their belly the scores of people who had been fleeing from the scene with fright!

For thousands of years, the sea has captured the imagination of man, its flooding and ebbing tides, gentle breeze, gale winds, crests and troughs of the waves, and the surreal sunsets. I just could not come to terms with this scene depicting the sudden fury of the sea sucking up the lives of so many thousands in a matter of a few hours.

I was heading towards Galle, and all along the line, there was hardly any evidence of tsunami-induced damage. Many villages and houses had been rebuilt, new bridges in addition to the old ones had been relaid, roads repaved, and the restoration work was going on in full throttle. Amongst the clusters of palm trees and mangroves, Galle appeared to us, suddenly a town on a big blue bay, an old Dutch fort just outside the station and also the market square.

Galle Fort has been included among the UNESCO World Heritage Sites. A fortified city built by the Portuguese, it is described as an urban ensemble that illustrates the interaction between European Ashok architecture and South Asian tradition from the six-teenth to the nineteenth centuries on the South-Western tip of Sri Lanka. Galle had been colonized and was home to the Portuguese, Dutch, and finally the British until 1948 when Sri Lanka won independence.

It is a small town, immaculate, spic and span, with everything ship-shape, pretty and cosmopolitan. Fort Galle is home to artists, writers, poets, dancers and sing-ers. There is a grid of clean cobbled streets bordered by the typical Golan style of residential buildings, single or double-storied, with pink bougainvillea spilling over from the front courtyards. A big gate guards the town with a network of roads leading to a lighthouse and the ramparts on the sea.

The town still bears the imprints of its colonial past in its architectural style and town planning. The fort area was an exciting place to walk about aimlessly. It offered a view of the Indian Ocean, and as the Sun was setting, leaving its golden orange trail on the water, my eyes were fixed on the beautiful scenery. The lovely aquamarine color of the ocean looked even better from the height. The Galle International Stadium is so stra-tegically positioned in the vicinity that if some prefer cricket to sea, the choice could be theirs.

According to the historical records, *Lourenco de Almeida,* captain of a Portuguese fleet, finding himself lost in the sea, heard a cock crowing, which to him sounded like 'Galle.' He sensed that the shore was quite close and he anchored. Boats were lowered, and these men were the first foreigners to set foot on these shores. Although the Portuguese were legendary travelers, they were entranced by the scenic beauty of the place and found it fitting to settle here. The Galle Fort was their first landmark.

I was fortunate enough to find a cozy guest house perched on a small hillock. I hired a tuk-tuk to the top of a winding road. I did not have the heart to explore the town on foot but enjoyed the surroundings, seated on the roof-terrace garden captivated by the sloping tile-roofed houses. From this vantage point, I could see the multitude of lamps of the fishing boats berthed in the harbor under the full moon and the town below glittered like crystals in a tiara. I considered this one of the best evenings of my trips. There was no event, no earth-shattering news from anywhere, no drama, no nothing. Just contentment and peace with the world!

It was a mild sunny morning! While I loved the ever-present glorious vegetation of the coast, and although I was inclined to stay indoors the whole day, I felt the need for doing justice to my sightseeing assignment of my trip. Soon I was on the road to the bazaar lined with hawkers, selling clothes, kitchenware, and some antiques. Just as I was walking out, the sky was overcast and it started to drizzle. I spotted a Sinhala lady and shared her table for a cuppa and our conversation drifted towards the catastrophic event of nature that had happened about eight years back.

Galle took the brunt of nature's fury at its worst. She recalled those tragic moments riding tandem with self-loathing, regret, and pain, virtually expressing all these emotions. I was also enthralled at her felicity for description, punctuated with subtle humor.

"It began in the early hours of the morning on Boxing Day." She had chosen to spend the Christmas holidays with her husband, two young sons, her newborn baby daughter, and their parents. They decided Galle, being an ideal spot to celebrate Christmas in Yala National Park.

Their mid-morning walk along the beach was quite a languorous one. Then a white foamy wave, much to their horror, rose above the rim of sand where the beach fell abruptly to the sea. Then chaos let loose with a massive sheet of water finding its way into the mainland out of nowhere. Then the chase began.

With the tidal waves literally on the heels of fleeing people, leaving them at the mercy of an angry sea, the poor lady lost her parents, her husband, and all her three children. She miraculously was the lone survivor of that sudden catastrophe. It was the most gruesome and horrifying moment of her life, coping without her family, who were all lost to her suddenly and at an unexpected time. It was a struggle for survival when her dear family had been taken out of her life.

She is now living in the UK, doing research at Cambridge University. 'I had come out of past event though many a time a phrase, 'unprecedented tragedy' kept recurring in my mind. Nobody could have predicted these sudden savage moments. I remembered a news item which appeared in the newspapers at that time, Mr. Taro in Japan had just built a thirty-four-feet-high sea-wall land and the city acquired the name of Great Wall of Japan. But the wall had been swept away hopelessly by the tsunami in 2011. Later I hired a tuk-tuk veered around the tsunami-hit area and drove back to *Weligama* in the deep south.

Weligama is as lovely as any of the South Pacific islands with the same limpid beauty, the blue sea and a white sandy beach enclosed by groves of palms and clusters of bamboo huts. The driver took me to a crowd of foreigners milling around some fishermen. A friend of my tuk-tuk driver approached me saying, "Mahathaya [sir], I can arrange for a visit to the scene of the tragedy, the very spot where the tall monstrous waves swept away the train, swallowing around two thousand passengers. I could set sail in my catamaran and return to the shore in time for lunch. It would cost you just rupees 1,500 per head."

I said no emphatically. Inwardly, I had chickened out at the thought of a remote possibility that those very same waves, then seemingly, mere blimps, might suddenly become furious, on a monstrous scale, and toss my catamaran up in the air and catch it, repeating the action over and over again!

After a couple of days during my vacation in Galle, I visited Hembantota by bus. The climate was soothing, and my body badly needed some rest. I chose a modest budget hotel, inexpensive but satisfying my comforts. It was time to call off my travel experience and I observed that one of the happier and more helpful delusions of the trip are, that one is always guessing, and being overwhelmed with surprises—"expect the unexpected!" I was back in Galle and reached Colombo by train. My travel agents had reserved my flight from Bandaranaike International Airport to Chennai through the courteous service of Sri Lankan Airlines.

Here ends Gerald's narration on his Sri Lankan travel.

I will continue the narration on the Tamilian history and the suffering they regularly underwent and still experiencing under the ruthless and the harsh leadership of Singhalese. I sincerely express my passion and solidarity with my fellow Tamils.

Brief History of the Sri Lankan Tamils

Sri Lanka had been ruled by many rulers in different parts. The Singhalese and Tamils had ruled different regions of the little nation. Anuradhapura was govern the Pandya dynasty before the first century BC. The northern part had always been ruled by Tamil kings, the east and central parts were also under the Tamil kingdom from early 50 AD. Thus, the country had still been under divided rule. This was the fundamental aspect of Sri Lanka, in which the Singhalese ruled the southernmost parts, and the Tamils ruled the central, northwestern and eastern parts of this divided nation. In my opinion, this country should not have been unified as one nation. It should never have been put under single governance. Many Tamil kings had ruled Sri Lanka at different periods. Some remnants of the Tamil kingdom still remain in the north, east, and central provinces. The last ruler of Sri Lanka, before the advent of British rule, was *Wickrama Raja Singam* of the Pandyan dynasty of Tamil Nadu, who reigned from Kandy. He ruled from the central plateau of Sri Lanka. Tamilians have contributed a great deal to this country in all fields. During the British rule, they were involved in the administration, teaching, trade, and development, exploring natural resources, farming, and plantation. But they did not bother to enter into the military services or that of the establishment. Thus, the entire armory was under the control of the Sri Lankan Buddhist extremists who were in power. The general concept of the British to carve out the boundary of any nation as they handed overrule proved fatal to many sections of various societies because it lacked the inclusive representation of all segment of the people. Many countries should have followed the American system of federalism, declaring themselves to be republics, and being represented by all the sections of the people, so that all could work together for the entire nation and thereby governance would have been entirely by all the people themselves, rather than the failed British parliamentary system, which was old-fashioned and manipulative. This caused many internal wars; some of them were civil wars. It was an advantage for them to sell arms to these warring parties, thereby profiting them economically. I sincerely wish that the bifurcation had been done in consideration according to the need and culture of the people. It was the Indian National Congress which played a major role along with the British giving inputs and finally carving out national boundaries around the South Asian region.

Under these circumstances, after independence, the Tamils and Sri Lankans lived in harmony, but the Buddhist fascists had other ideas using the weapon of philosophy to eliminate the Tamilians. This design of disparity was echoed in the distribution of wealth and proceeds of economic development, whenever a representation was made, it was dealt with ruthlessly by framing false charges resulting in imprisonment and torture. The first main voice and representation to take up the cause for Tamils was *Thanthai Chelvanayagam*. He negotiated peacefully on numerous occasions with the Sri Lankan government. More atrocities against the Tamils were executed. It became unbearable and the people could hardly live in peace. Hence, he called for a meeting in Northern Sri Lanka and titled it '*Vaddukoddai*

Resolution' and declared Tamil Eelam. After the death of *Thanthai Chelvanayagam*, Amirthalingam was given leadership. As he was indirectly coerced into supporting the Sri Lankan government, he was assassinated.

This kindled the idea of a separate Tamil state of Eelam. The architect of the resistance force is said to have been a group of three persons, namely, *Jagan*, *Kuttimani,* and *Thambidurai*. All three were very solid and massive. They were arrested and tortured. Later, they escaped and came to Tamil Nadu. The Sri Lankans literally forced the Indian government to deport them back to Sri Lanka, which was done during the time of the rule of one of the major Dravidian parties in Tamil Nadu. These three people were imprisoned and starved until their bodies had shrunk to an almost skeletal state. Then their eyes were gouged out and crushed and stamped under the Sri Lankan military official's feet. These were the types of atrocities committed by the Sri Lankan army when in governance. While these torturous acts were going on, the international community did not pay much attention. Out of sheer frustration, all the Tamils started taking up arms to fight against the Singhalese. In the process, various leaders and resistance movements started. The disciples of the three who suffered and died horribly deaths at the hands of Sri Lankan army formulated a separate army under *Velupillai Prabhakaran*, which became even more focused and ferocious in its commitment. As all liberation movements, it finally became unified into one force as the *Liberation Tigers of Tamil Eelam (LTTE) Under Prabhakaran.* Unable to withstand and counteract the will and grit of the United Tamils, the Sri Lankan government hired variously ruthless mercenary groups to fight against the LTTE. But every effort failed. The LTTE grew from strength to strength, day by day. They managed against all odds employing unique skills and unbelievable willpower; they built up a dedicated military force with its own sea defenses. The equipment was designed and made indigenously. They even manufactured self-made aircraft and bombers. The cadres were well educated and disciplined. During this time, Sri Lanka lured India into the picture. Unfortunately, India unnecessarily got involved in this mess. Because of the unexpected assassination of the then charismatic leader in India, a pilot turned leader was given leadership to govern India. His political inexperience led to hasty decisions. Probably he had not been advised correctly. This led to an impractical critical accord being established between the then Prime Ministers of Sri Lanka and India, without the involvement of the Tamil parties who had been the worst affected. This resulted in one-sided operations being conducted in this matter. Due to this, divisions occurred between the Singhalese, Indian army and Tamils. The Tamils were adversely affected by both sides. The Indian military invited the Tamils for a 'friendly.' talk, had them arrested and handed them over to the Sri Lankans. The political advisers in India took the Tamils for granted. They assumed them to be just a silly handful of foes that could be blown to pieces. But they were proved wrong. Although during that time all the Indian and Sri Lankan secret services were spending a fortune in collecting intelligence reports on the LTTE establishment, movements, and armories, their knowledge about them was wholly insufficient. These rifts gradually erupted into a full scale bloody war. The Indian Peace-Keeping Force (IPKF) created more chaos in this war. There was a lot of looting, rape and ruthless massacres. These war crimes are yet to be investigated on both sides (especially abuse committed on the university campus by Indian Army). This grave mistake was paid for at the high price when the Indian leader was heartlessly assassinated by the people who had suffered directly at the hands of the IPKF.

No proper representation of the Tamils was included in the governance in Tamil Nadu. Invariably other Dravidian representatives were at the helm of affairs in Tamil Nadu, although the aspirations of the local Tamils as to offer support to their brothers and sisters in Sri Lanka. No matter what they did they could not send a powerful political message to the Sri Lankan Government. Quite often, an unexpected lousy event would destroy the once progressive and constructive path. The 26 December 2004, tsunami destroyed most of the strongholds of the LTTE, although the Singhalese areas were also affected. The international community then pumped in vast amounts of funds to Sri Lankan government to be distributed for the development of the entire nation. The fascist Singhalese took this opportunity to arm themselves to the teeth making the entire Tamil population cry out for mercy from heaven above. Thus, half the LTTE force became diminished. The Singhalese heavily bribed a small section of the Tamilians to betray the cause and used them against The LTTE. The untimely desertion by India and other nations played into the hands of Singhalese to wage a bitter war against the LTTE. Almost three hundred thousand Tamils were bombed with various dangerous arsenal was causing death and terrible destruction. And one million others were wounded and displaced, many were raped, and many were starved to death. Now India took a negative side along with many other nations. These war crimes and genocidal acts despite being represented and conveyed to the United States, UK and the European Union countries fell upon deaf ears. Now the entire matter with supportive documents has been presented before the United Nations which has taken up the cause of the Tamils. The United Nations is clearly advocating for a war crime tribunal to be set up against this neo-fascist regime in Sri Lanka. The Tamils may finally achieve their goal of separation. The war crime inquiry could also bring to light the underlying intent of the neighboring nations against the Tamils who had supported the fascist regime with dangerous arsenal and modern technology, including satellite imaging and communication systems to destroy the real aspirations of the Tamil people. This act could be considered equal to the atrocities of the *Pol Pot regime or the Rwandan genocide or the Srebrenica massacre* and the one being committed In Syria. It is generally believed that all the neighboring countries, along with a few other nations are believed to have supplied Sri Lanka with advanced war and tactical armories, which was a significant setback for the Tamil Eelam Group, and as it is said, *The battle may have been lost, the war goes on!* The spirit and the grit of the Tamils will never die. It will end only after the Tamils become victors and are relieved of the Singhalese rule!

War Crimes and Genocidal Acts against the Tamils in Sri Lanka

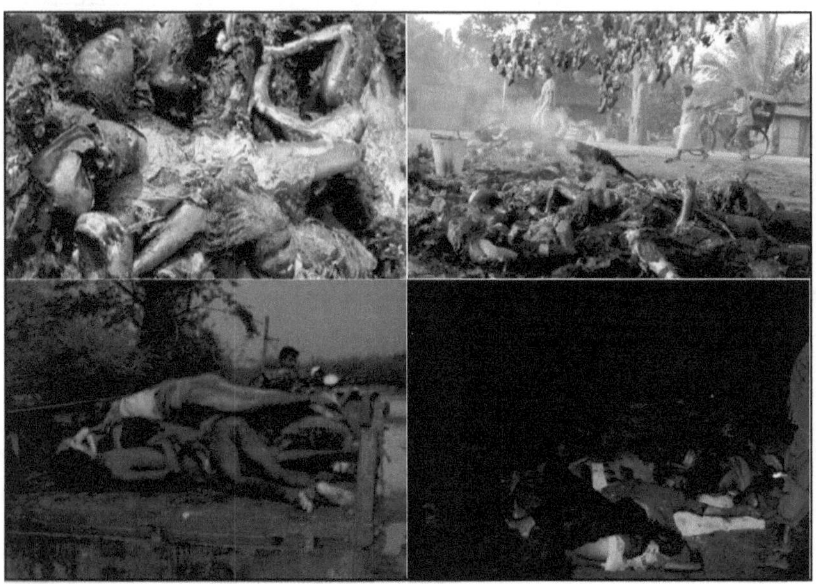

As I turn from travel mode, which includes narrations about the history of the corresponding areas I visit, I continue on with the central aspect of our travel.

Nature's Fury and Massacre

As I concluded my views regarding the genocide on the racial and ethnical fronts, I return to that Unforgettable day, 26 December 2004. It was a Sunday morning and I was attending church with my family. It was Testimony Sunday. Some intuition within me drove me to give my testimony, to publicly proclaim to the congregation the grace and mercies of God that my entire family and I had graciously been given thus far. An elder suddenly interrupted me, so I quickly concluded my speech. Later on, I understood that while the church service had been going on, our shoreline the *Marina* in Chennai was gulping down the Sunday morning walkers, players and all the rest of the people on the shore! Some had even got sucked into the ocean while still inside their cars. I still, wonder what could be the extent of nature's rage on mankind. What had happened in Indonesia had turned into a massive tsunami wiping out most part of the coastal areas of the entire South and Southeast Asia, the worst hit being Phuket, Thailand. For many years, I have been contemplating this incident within me. Later, on a visit to Mahabalipuram, a favorite coastal part of Tamil Nadu and also a tourist spot, I met a lady from Sri Lanka. She happened to be a Tamilian who shared with me the following incident that had happened to her friend and their family who at that time were living in the UK. This friend had migrated to the UK along with her husband and family on work. Their family had come on a visit to Galle, Sri Lanka, to meet up with their other relatives. They were visiting the beach in Galle on that fatal morning of 26 December 2004. When the monster wave rolled in and stood like a huge serpent in front of her before they could think, all of them were swallowed up. Everyone was sucked in, this lady included, but she happened to grab hold of a tree on the way, and she alone survived. She visits Galle every year on 26 December ever since then.

While we thoughtlessly harm and destroy nature, it reverts and hits back at us ferociously, causing untold devastation and destruction. So let us treat mother nature with great respect and not tamper too much or extract from it beyond what it can offer. Let us all deal gently with mother nature in oneness to educate the monstrous and greedy humans who indulge in the degradation of mother nature and let us save this planet from these indiscriminate destroyers… which takes me to a cameo of our tour to Southeast Asia.

VIGNETTE

A Bird's-Eye View of Adventure from Travel

Our Impressions of Southeast Asia

In conclusion, I must confess that it is nothing like being in a particular place. In person, discover for oneself, wowed and joyous with the unknown, and develop a pang of hunger to know and learn more about other cultures and share with the people and learn to live in oneness with them. This enchants you and invites you to a new life, helping you to understand and rouse yourself for the improvement of your own self-esteem, and encourages you to deal with others positively. Our travel experience drew me back in time, to the past; hence, it was a traveler's past experience and survey of the historical background of the people, culture, and history of those places we had visited. The process of unraveling historical events had burst open a Pandora's box before me, giving me an optical view of the past. History may have been written for the benefit of a few or a particular section of people, but it is high time we understand the past well enough so that mistakes could be ratified. This will help us join together to rewrite history, to thus put things in order so that fairness and justice can be meted to all mankind.

Our travel turned out to be more than what we had ever bargained for. This adventure of ours was the best decision of our life. It is indeed a different world out there! We never felt as strangers or aliens in the countries we visited. We were accepted as one among them, transcending borders and barriers. Every hour was filled with happy moments, all joyous; our conversations were punctuated with mirth and pleasantries. We never felt the hours hanging on heavy our hands. The only time we looked at our watches was to check the time of our flights! We formed a well-balanced companionship. Although we encountered a few hiccups now and then, at the end of the day, we were still in high spirits, joking and merrymaking. Many a time, Gerald teaming up with Terry would target me, and I had to grin and bear it. When Terry and I used to call each other names, when we did not see eye-to-eye with each other or whenever our conversation turned frosty, Gerald wearing the mantle of 'agony aunt' would sort out our little arguments. (Although I had a feeling that he was always running with the hare and hunting with the hound!) But all said and done, we three had a great time, with not a single dull moment during our vacation. *'It was magnanimity to all and malice towards none.'* Personally speaking, Gerald and I too had endless skirmishes, breaking into diatribes, and sometimes ending up rolling on the floor, physically fighting! However, his constant guidance and support had been (to put it mildly) splendid. "Gerald! With all thy faults, I love thee still." *(Little does he know that I have a dartboard with a photo-image of his face mounted on the wall of my bedroom.)*

It may be a matter of one's own opinion, but we felt that a conducted tour to the pre-determined destinations with a well-tutored guide leaves little room for us to explore and ponder. We found that the appointed guide would be ready with answers and explain the history of the places in parrot fashion, thus soon ending up as a willing slave to the whims and fancies of the representative of our tourist agents. It would be a sort of Stockholm syndrome. This may be perhaps only the start. In a few decades from now, we may not be able to recognize the good old values of planning the itinerary to suit our time and purses, and also, we would no longer look at the world differently! Our travel experience was unique, for although we had guides to accompany us to certain places, we also had our own freedom to explore, meet people, and have many a tête-à-tête with them.

Tips for a Traveller

If you are planning to travel and if you are interested in visiting places like Thailand, Cambodia, Vietnam, Laos, and Ceylon, and you really want to have an experience with a difference, I can offer my suggestion. One must first dump all guidebooks. Be awed by surprises. Some impressions will make you cringe, some smile and laugh, but such is the life and experience of a traveler. You could sample a country and find out what it offers! Be challenged by the unknown. It is pleasant to be overawed by surprises. We can read about the nation, their customs, and culture, etc., before visiting it, but only when you are there physically, can you absorb their culture to some extent. Keep the nomadic spirit in you flying high; traverse every nook and corner of the places you are visiting. It is fun to involve yourself in a new culture, experience, a new verity of food, and just let your hair down. It would help you broaden your outlook on the world!

To our regret, there are no credible books on travelogues, which are readable with well-written travel stories, offering entertainment, history, humorous anecdotes with up-to-date information and other details in the leading bookstores here! On the other hand, the airline-sponsored travel plan, beckons you, on the front page of the newspapers and journals with the tour packages, discounted rates, and other perks, colorfully displayed. Even though these are available by the lorry load on the internet, yet we would like to see hard copies as an introduction or enticement or a teaser trailer to any travel destination.

It is important to stay safe: From the beginning to the end of your journey, be wary of the surrounding as well as be open to people. It may sound odd, mainly because your objective is to meet and mix with people, but you will have to be a good judge of character; if not, you may end up learning the hard way. If anyone were to ask for your number, your e-mail identity or address, you take theirs and say that you will get in touch.

Wherever you go, your health must be given importance. Carry all the medicines as prescribed by your physician for cough, fever, allergies, headache, nausea, stomach disorder, and a painkiller. If any of your companions take a firm stand, waxing and waning whether to join you or not, it is better to leave him, for he will prove to be a spoilsport. *(It'd be like popping a sleeping pill and laxative together!)*

Food and Drinks

Be careful about what you *eat and drink;* once you get sick, the whole programme will fall apart. So think before you eat and drink, however good it may appear. Once, during our morning walk, we were drawn by the smell of piping-hot soup at a wayside Chinese eatery. The soup was thick and delicious. We assumed it to be chicken, but to our horror, our guide told us it was a snake. Except for the mental jolt, our stomachs remained calm, to our great relief. *Moral: Please check the ingredients. Exercise as much caution as you'd do while accepting a drink from unknown people.*

There is not much of a difference between the meal pattern and menu in these countries. It is better to stick to vegetarian food to be on the safer side. Unless you know for sure, you can try using chopsticks; in fact, you will be tutored by a waitress. They are ever friendly and comfortable for you.

As mentioned earlier, you must carry some extra passport-sized photographs. They will be useful to you. Learn about the mobile system of the country you are visiting, whether GSM or CDMA. Carry an additional cheap phone with you, suitable to accept the SIM of the places you visit. Usually, the travel offices sell you a SIM card at a nominal price. You can get a discounted offer on that too. Mostly, these SIM cards can be charged in leading departmental stores. In Thailand, 7-Eleven is the main store outlet for such a purchase. Regarding currencies, it is important to take a couple of legal tenders of the country you are visiting. You may need some upon landing during the process of immigration clearance or taxi fare to your destination.

The main problem we tourists encountered in Bangkok was the language. Save for a few, many do not understand English, resulting in a communication gap. We had to use little English and more action to convey our needs to them. But I feel the problem lies with us. We feel ashamed when we are at a loss to find a suitable word or speak fluently in the Queen 's language. In fact, most of us take pride in conversing fluently in English, whereas the Thais have no problem, and their pride lies in expression in their own mother tongue! The Thais are generally people-friendly and will smile and help when needed. The minute we point our camera at someone, they will stop whatever they had been doing and pose for us willingly, with the quintessential V sign that they make with their fingers. In short, it is a country torn between the allure of a modern 'shiny persona' and the strength of their traditional heritage!

Beaches in Thailand

We thoroughly enjoyed *Pattaya and Phuket*, tourist paradises full of water sports, water scooting, etc. Ninety percent of the foreign tourists were from Russia. Nightclub haunts, watering holes, flamboyance, licentiousness, massage parlors, and all sorts of nocturnal attractions were available for the tourists. The town has a *Dr. Jekyll* and *Mr. Hyde* syndrome—the really friendly and laid-back precincts during the day, and thumping music and partying after dusk. Walkers Street is a paradise for fun. You can give vent to whatever is bottled up inside of you; it sleeps during the day and keeps awake for you at nights. Once you go there, you will be treated as a special guest. Of course, everything is readily offered for money. Do not pack up your intelligence; let your vision run around you all the time.

As a useful tip for travelers, the men are wished Kap un cap and ladies are hoped in *Kap un ka*. For a refusal, you can say *meddai*. You will always be invited for 'boom boom' meaning she is prepared to offer herself for fun. Massage is all over, you name it, and you will have it, sometimes a one in all and all in one offer. Even for massages, you can get an offer as per the season. Aromatherapy is said to be the best herbal massage. There are well-trained masseurs, who twist and twirl along with your body while giving you the massage, so much that it really excites you. Of course, it all depends how one cooperates with them to get the best. One ought to be enriched in the art of receiving by coordinating well enough with the person who is offering. Although there is a price tag, you can always fix the price on an hourly basis. Thus, the services are provided on an hourly basis.

Thai Airways: Green Energy

With interest we learned the *Thai Airways* was taking active steps to improve its green credentials for their aircraft, with ongoing research for significant weight savings, resulting in cost benefits compared with other airlines. According to the *President of Thai Airways International*, their airlines have been the first to introduce *biofuel*. His Majesty the king's vision was for renewable energy to ultimately replace fossil fuels as the future choice of power for the world and to achieve a reduction in the carbon footprint, also striving for the highest level of passengers' safety in this demanding world of 'airborne' travelers.

While in a cab traveling in Thailand, the driver was saying some insurgencies were working from the south of the country. His statement could perhaps have been, but we must leave them to rule by themselves. That might stop the unnecessary destruction and attacks on innocent people. This was the attitude shared by the ordinary local people out there.

Cambodia

Some countries are just perfect for tourism. I would give Cambodia the top billing. Cambodia was once considered a state where *'fools rush in, where angels fear to tread.'* Now it is back on the tourist map, as an ally of *Korea and China* for economics. During the 1990s, this beautiful country remained difficult and dangerous to travel because of the presence of the Khmer Rouge guerrillas. Now that peace has returned, it is open for exploration. Its cultural tradition and its past dominance and power have become a showpiece for international tourism. It is the most visited region in Southeast Asia. The average number of tourists exceeded 2.5 million last year! Going through the Angkor ruins, we felt a sort of strange, revolutionary experience of an unexplained institution that 'we would visit again.'

The sunrise walk along almost lonely bylanes with only birds for companions in Laos is unforgettable! The French influence could still be felt along with the smell of freshly baked bread and the aroma of Laos coffee wafting up your nostrils in the misty mornings.

Traveling along the bank of the Mekong River, we were bewitched by the stunning sunset scene. The traditional Lao sauna is a 'must-visit' place where medicinal herbs in a steam bath and the green tea will rejuvenate you to face the day with extra-positive energy. Just about anywhere, wildlife means tourists, and tourists mean dollars, US dollars!

Vietnam

After the revolution, although communism had been established in Vietnam, we could observe the competitive instinct that was uppermost to do business and elevate themselves to a higher standard of living. The distinct class of the urban-rural divide still prevails. Communism appears to have been replaced by the survival of the fittest.

When I visit a country, I am not only interested in monuments and landscapes, but in the stories behind them, as well. The first thing we think about Vietnam is the 'dirty' war, too many times displayed in the movies, and a visit to *Hanoi* should not miss this tribute to *Ho Chi Minh*. I am only too willing to avoid any further comments on this persona.

While mysteries still remain regarding the sequence and origin of Buddhism. There was a belief that it was not a diversified religion but a single one. After visiting Southeast Asia, to my surprise, I find a lot of sects! Different kinds of Buddhism exist in various formats. While some are spiritual and believe in all goodness, the others' main priority seems to be only in chanting but not practice religion at all. There is a lot of disconnect from its original belief and the practices of the people who appear to profess it. Most of the countries have transformed themselves into being communistic, while others are enchanted by fascist ideals, like those of *Aryan Hitler.* Perhaps there is a link between *Aryanism* and the *Buddhist* religion. The culmination of this combination could have originated from India, which happens to be the birthplace of Buddhism, where the Aryans who came seeking shelter started creeping up into administration and tried to use all kinds of underhanded methods to progress into the assistance of governance.

We met many of our 'desi' globetrotters during our travel, honeymooners, senior citizen groups, and other species of vacationers. Due to the rapid increase in middle-class families with their growing salaries, people and places have begun, like never before! We ran into many familiar faces, identifiable languages, sari-clad ladies, and instead of the oft-repeated destinations *(Singapore, Malaysia, and Thailand)*, they now visit the unchartered, unfamiliar countries. We met a family from *Bangalore* at *Siem Reap*, who conversed in Tamil. *(It was music to our ears after so many days!)* They said that his two kids were eagerly awaiting the last lap of their journey in Macau!

We also found many 'desi' tourists who had booked their trips on impulse after spotting various airline promotion and also of resorts offering four-night stays but charging only for three etc.

Before even looking at your ticket, get all the information regarding the place of your visit, the occupation of the people there, their eating habits and their hospitality quotient.

I was moved by this country's need of the hour. I have decided to form a society to build more rural hospitals with proper infrastructure, as my heartstrings were touched by the plight of the rural folks of not only in Vietnam but also in Cambodia and Laos. I have decided to go beyond charity. Do something more profound, more sustainable, a more long-term projection, improve amenities attuned to health-specific for the rural poor. I have decided to promote NGOs to join hands with well-wishers (known and unknown) concerning physical and financial involvement. I am determined to fulfill my dreams of building healthcare buildings, dotted across the villages of Cambodia, as well as those of Vietnam and Laos, where access to the medical facilities still remains remote! My perspective, on so many things, awakened me in awareness to issues I didn't know existed. This has helped me find purpose in life, besides mere existence.

On a personal note, I found the Thai economy is purely run by women. They are at the forefront of every field. The men stay in the background and watch them like guards. Most of the men are supported by women. In Thai society, women remain subdued by men, thereby avoiding any issues of ego or conflict between men and women. They always have a smiling face! The same was fundamental and noticeable in Cambodia, Laos, and Vietnam; but Cambodia and Laos are economically more impoverished. The Thais are better off than the Vietnamese, more than those of Cambodia and Laos. While the Vietnamese are waking up to the challenge, Cambodia and Laos still lag behind. The international community should stand by these poor nations to bring them back to their feet.

All the tourists are very friendly. The Americans are full of life, willing to share their joy and happiness. The French seem a little stuck up, preferring to keep to themselves, abitaloof and non-interactive. The Russians should learn to expose themselves to other nationalities by not being secluded. Due to this handicap, they always travel in groups. They must begin to interact more and be friendly with other people. Iranians are one of the loveliest and most cultured people one could ever come across—I met a few families; they were excellent to deal with. The Chinese and Japanese are friendly; they have a language handicap. While we do not understand their language, they do not understand English. They are proud of their own vernacular, unlike us! We take pride in a borrowed common language that is English. The other Europeans are generally okay, but non-communicative. The Germans, I found them to be the best! They are very friendly and give you a warmth approach. They listen to you very carefully and take the time to understand, interact and connect with you, in depth. The German ladies especially are fantastic to move with. I must visit Germany and get to understand their culture and home life more. I still wonder how a person like *Adolf Hitler* could have ever come from this beautiful race with such a terrible motivation for his horrifying genocidal acts. A more in-depth study of German history may reveal more truth regarding this matter.

Traveling in Asia is indeed very different from touring in Europe or America. In Asia, one can visit at leisure, without really having to be under pressure for anything. The people are more accommodating and interactive, and you can ask for help from anybody.

They will be ever willing to oblige you and take pleasure in expressing hospitality; hence, travelers can visit the Asian countries without any inhibition. You can loosen yourself and feel free to interact with locals. This would remove all your stress, and you will begin to understand people and nature in a much better way. This will transform your travel into dream travel and give you total satisfaction. The memories will linger in your mind for a long time.

"The true wanderer, whose travels are happiness, goes not to shun, but to seek." Freya Stark

European travel did not seem very pleasant to me, but perhaps I am biased. Of course, you see great structures, impressive buildings, avenues and bylanes in perfection and the system is almost tailor-made. There are no surprises, no secrets and not too much of pleasantries exchanged with the people. Everything and every human is formal—yes, it is an entirely different world where one man may not quite fit into the other! Maybe the world is not designed to be so. I would not say anything about which is more productive than the other; if someone is rich in one type of wealth, others possess different other kinds of wealth in abundance, and they are willing to share it with you in Asia.

To my surprise, I was definitely told by the Thai people that they were never ruled by the European race. They are proud of it; on the other hand, I find to my surprise wherever the Europeans have landed or governed by deception in Asia or Africa or South America, there have been constant conflicts. This is never-ending and goes on and on. Some wars are continuous civil wars! The Europeans must have left behind the thirst for freedom with some section of the people, or while they ruled, they did not represent the entire community and its people, or when they left, they saw to it that the conflict would always go on, which would ultimately give them importance and benefited them in many ways. As a result, there is still conflict in *North Korea, Afghanistan, Pakistan, Bangladesh, Sri Lanka, and India in Kashmir.* Maybe confusion pays someone, but we the people are the ultimate sufferers.

Buddhism migrated from India due to the Aryans. It was uprooted entirely in India itself. This was used as a stop gap for the ultimate motive to bring Hinduism back into the mainstream in India. The Buddhism which thus spread all over could not survive for long, and finally, communism took over. On this note of being confused, I will move on to the concluding chapters.

AFTERMATH

A renowned historian in her book, "The Past as Present: Forging Contemporary Identities through History" explains why presently chosen viewpoints about the past need to be critically examined before being accepted as historical truth.
—Romila Thapar

When the past no longer illuminates the future, the spirit walks in darkness.
—Alexis de Tocqueville

Hence, it is a call for all humanity to wake up to the knowledge of real past history.

History, in its pure form, will always enlighten and enchant the future generation to their fullest glory.
—Ashok Yeshurun Masillamani

Self-Declaration

As I conclude pouring out my heart in vignettes about the excellent experience and disentanglement of the old threads, which were unraveled in front of me, oriented me to traverse into my own ancestral past. This provoked me to scavenge about the reality of the history of our different ethnicities, race, and origin. Hence, I began to explore my own inception cell. This raised a lot of questions regarding my own nativity, ethnicity, linguistic, the cultural and political affinity of the country, the one I belong to now.

This country was born as a nation only in 1947, whereas for my personal ancestral evidence, the documents of my citizenship, nativity and other records are intact from 1760 AD. My great-grandfather, who was known as Iyyamperumal, Alias Masilamani Nadar, is said to have converted to Christianity by a special calling. I am proud of my documented history as a native Tamilian, which began even before the historic American Independence. Hence, I have a strong lineage and affinity towards the Tamils and other allied races sprouted from there. Tamilian history certainly was even before the so-called Stone Age, which could be much more than 50,000 years, relative to the existing order of time and calendar years.

A Passage into History

As I continued my exploration, I found that the Tamils and its allied races were the only indigenous people of this entire continent and much more. Their extent was all over up to East Bengal and beyond in the east, Nepal, Sikkim, Bhutan and further in the northeast; Pakistan and Baluchistan in the West; Afghanistan up to Persia and the entire Middle East in the north; and entire south which was then known as Kumari-Kandam. This would be stated as a package of Tamil race's extent henceforth.

The Occurrence a time of Deluge

Due to a significant deluge, Kumari-Kandam was submerged and defragmented into parts. This caused the creation of new separate landmasses. Later these became Australian subcontinent along with New Zealand and Easter Island including parts of Indo-China, some parts of Southern, Northern and Eastern Africa. Then the Europeans named this lost continent as Limeira for their benefits and buried all truth.

All these parts belong to the cradle of the Tamil-an civilization. This event could have occurred between 5,000 BC and 3000 BC at the time of nova to nimrod, the time where many dangerous events took place by the active induction of satan. Due to this occurrence, you could find archaeological artifacts of the Tamil-an stamp in Australia, New Zealand, Easter Island, parts of Africa, Indo-China, and Chine, and so on.

Even a section of indigenous people is the descent of tamil-an race only. Modern dna test reveals the ancient tamils along with their extended human runs had asi dna, and the infiltrators were of ani dna.

Even the good god uttered words for creation only in tamil. I am certain about that. Further research with an open unbiased and qualitative work would bring out this real truth.

The sickening reality

At This Juncture, I Must Make An Emphatic Statement That The Greatest Crime The British And The West Jointly Committed To This Subcontinent, Was To Divide Our Subcontinent Into Three On The Religious And Communal Basis For Their Own Benefit. This Was Done By Lord Mountbatten Joining With Dubious Nehru Along With All Other Gujaratis, Patel, And Gandhi. Gandhi Crowned Himself As The Father Of The

Nation Due To The Innocence And Trust Bestowed On Him By Indigenous People. This Social Sickness Has Caused Significant Danger To Indigenous People Who Are More Than Ninety-Nine Percent Of The Population. The One Percent Only Are Aryans Who Came For Shelter Here. The Locals Took Care Of Them Well. The British Purposely Handed Over The Power And Properties Of The Locals To The Aryans, Brahmins, Sindi's, And Janis Who Lived In Small Parts Of Gujarat And Rajasthan Then. I Propose To Express In-Depth On This Little Latter In This Book.

Taking a moment, to look back to the beginning of this book and the remarkable experiences also brought some sorrows along with that. I opened my eyes to question myself as to why cruelty engulfing the poor and innocent around the world.

I find it brings joy to the Aryans, Fascists, and saffron sadists' like-minded groups whose religion is only that. They create chaos and confusion to bring down any orderly section of the societies by traitorous means with falsehood mirage of happiness and success. They induce poverty and prey on it. It gives them great joy and lust to enact further. Their system of operation is at the first stage is to throw a veil over their frank, and innocent people's possessions and all assets then take them over and re-engage using the same as if they own them, and place themselves as executors and commanders to disdain and desecrate the entire society at this point, I must refer to **The Bible Kings James Version;-1 Timothy Chapter 4 Verse One**;- some shall depart from the faith, giving heed **"To Seducing Spirits, And Doctrines Of Devils;"**These are those agents referred to as in the BIBLE.

Origin of Universe

Let me get into the deep-rooted assessment on this. These annoying reflections in front of me pushed me into a bottomless hole for retrospection. Then I suddenly recouped myself to gaze unto the skies with both my arms lifted. Then, comes the revelation of the entire past, adorned with Divine inference, by sector and segment.

USC library southern California

"Under its applicative nature, functional theory in the social sciences is of value precisely because it fulfills one primary purpose. To explain the meaning, life, and challenges associated with a phenomenon, often experienced but unexplained in the world in which we live, so that we may use that knowledge and understanding to act in more informed and effective ways."

As per science "The origin and development of the universe and modern cosmology is dominated by the Big Bang theory, which brings together observational astronomy and particle physics." Aforementioned is stated to be in plural noun: cosmologies, an account or theory of the origin of the universe.

The universe is believed to be at least 10 billion light-years in diameter and contains a vast number of galaxies; it has been expanding since its creation in the Big Bang about 13 billion years ago, accommodating both matter and space which considered as the whole as; "The Cosmos."

The universe has not always existed as per the Big Bang theory. It is perceived to have originated from a source of an unexplained Nebula. *A nebula is a giant cloud of dust and gas in space.* This raises a clear question where did the Nebula appear from? What is its origin? If there is no answer, then that would collapse the Big band theory.

The Nebula usually is classified as an interstellar cloud of dust, hydrogen, helium and other ionized gases so far from where a process took place which causes the origin of the universe, galaxy, and earth. Initially, that term was used to describe any diffuse astronomical object, including galaxies beyond the Milky Way followed by the process of hot and dense matter cools and becoming more or less impenetrable, simultaneously expanding far and wide. Cloud of gas and dust in outer space, are visible in the night sky either as an indistinct bright patch or as a dark silhouette against other luminous matters. To a healthy eye, this reads as defective vision.

Astrology Vs. Astronomy

Modern European and the western world always choose to annul the older documented records as myth or have no pertinence for the contemporary world. Mostly this is the Aryan style of execution to affirm their position ahead of all. There had been much higher and better institutions in different parts of the older world from South, middle, East and West India, Middle East, and Africa than the present Columbia, Harvard, Stanford, MIT, and so on...[**The ivy league**]. This is a commercial Myth to make money by big corporations and to induce brain drain from other potential parts of the world. The brain is a part created by inner cells by induction, periodically rotating in cycles from genes which naturally exchanges with celestial bodies. It does not grow at the trees of North America or even Briton and other parts of Europe.

Though the practices of astrology and astronomy have common roots, there is an important distinction in astrology vs. astronomy today as per the West. Astronomy is the study of the universe and its contents outside of earth's atmosphere. Astronomers examine the positions, motions, and properties of celestial objects. Astrology attempts to study how those positions, movements, and features affect people and events on earth. For several millennia, the desire to improve astrological predictions was one of the main motivations for astronomical observations and theories.

Astrology and Astronomy generally complement each other. Astrology denotes a set of Patton of the atoms and particles of the cherubic bodies inter-exchange with each other which includes earth and its holdings both moving and staying put{nature, trees...} includes us. These patterns are for used for astronomical studies and navigation purposes. This set of the model was later on misused for palm reading, fortune telling and soon, which is a Satan's myth to invalidate one's own intelligence to blindfold them without questioning or reasons. This is not to cancel the core message of planetary action and the relevant message nature consistently conveying to us the temporary human occupiers.

Europian Preception

There is a new school of thinking that all that was old is to be junked, especially after a newly crowned icon IN Isaac Newton. As always, one needs attention as a distraction in crisis' time. Entire Europe had gone through the war of the Crusades fought over five centuries, which resulted in the worst loss. After the fall of Byzantium Empire to Ottoman Turks almost at the same time, it became an adventure and voyaging time in Europe, The Portuguese and Spaniard were funded by Roman command. That is how Europeans stepped into occupying other areas which did not belong to them. As always destruction gives birth to construction Europe was rebuilding itself. British history had troublesome history by various raids by Viking, Saxons to Scots and Irish before settling down under a monarch. British monarch diverted their attention to making a mark in all fields by hook or by crook. There was an English man in Isaac Newton favored than finding itself. He was only a mathematician had his clout behind him. His controversy with Leibniz Gottfried, Hooke and Huygens Christian many others speak volumes. New Satan at the helm, new set of orders, and all existing validated system to be junked, and replaced with a new structure; measurements and new formulas were enforced. British and the French got the better always. That period the worst due to the bloodshed, best due to not well-defined democracy: with the flexibility that it could be converted to [**demo- mockery-see**] **"the french revolution in 18th century"** and American war for Independence.

Gottfried Leibniz was for better and more straight forward in his findings of integral calculus and much more. Robert Hooke was another genius, who's pendulum and elongated spring is un-measurable. He also found cells and gravity force. After his death, he was banished from the then scientific world. Christiaan Huygens,{ Titan, Orion Nebula} who with all greatness to his credits, had to vanish under the pull and power, of Isaac Newton. Most of these great men works and many others who were contemporaries lost due to the influence of Isaac Newton. Their credits went to them later. Till today the same phenomena occurs in all fields even today. I share to relevant links:

https://archive.org/stream/christianhuygens029504mbp/ christianhuygens029504mbp_djvu.txt
https://io9.gizmodo.com/was-robert-hooke-really- the-greatest-asshole-in-the-his-30803492

History, Knowledge Its Reading

After toiling through history, science, and cosmology, i am convinced that everything within the cosmic arena is inter-connected and acting on each other with its own time zones. Pendulum osculation findings proved that any suspended object continually trying to stay at the center which is quivering always, which is classified within the scientific world as:- star wobble or dance or even as gravitational dancing.

We are Connected with one Central Clock Outside the Cosmos" The Devine Clock."

Hence the time clock of objects within the cosmos is relative to its size and properties of force acting on it and emitting from it. Like the central bank or the federal

-reserve the meridian area from where the transfer or exchange takes place is space. Though it seems nothing is there, hectic actives are going on to keep the universe stable constantly. The buffer action to maintain humidity and supply of gas and liquid is done by neptune and uranus otherwise called icy plants. Here i would choose to discredit the theory of plants are of globe shaped, but it is like a disc {as the discus round] rotting on its tentative spiral. This movement started from the time of first nuclear incident. From then on it is either moving apart or shrinking at a relative space and speed which maintains equilibrium or stability. Hence it is my firm conjecture that earth, and other plants are almost flat with hump at the middle. As we spilt up at the beginning, we would converge to that final destination, religiously called the next world. {Scientifically called the black hole}

As per tamilian cosmology from early origin of this universe they only consist of seven planets where sun and moon are considered as stars and act as reflectors from a light source. The very light source is of life to each, and everything that of life, which means the entire universe functions from therein. All-stars are only act as reflectors like gems do only due to that very source.

With this perception i would creep into the creation of the world and its beginning. This is the overture to the following.

Vocal Crack its Multitude

The most intelligent {an iq of an implausible quotient,} the most-high was on his usual circuit with all his hosts, suddenly an argument of equality or supremacy transpired. Lucifer who was the higher of the hosts for the highest enthused by his self-illusion chooses to challenge "god almighty the most-high" citing equality or superiority over "god" using the position and domain allocated by" THE MOST-HIGH." Lucifer was the first in command for the Highest. Since his illusion motivated his action, he and his fallen troops were classified as illuminates. This is how illuminates came into being. The event of the split was unimaginable with a loud noise. That division was the occurrence of the first nuclear action, of unthinkable magnitude. That first occurrence of nuclear activity foundation of the beginning of all matter, particles of physics and chemical atom along with its parameter of electrons, patrons, and neutron. This would later be classified as the cosmos or the universe.

We as human determine and read this creation in a different direction and classify various fields of study as mathematics, science, chemistry, cosmology, and so on. This keeps us occupied. Our survival is hooked onto that. Little do us realise where we come from, and where do we go to. If nuclear action was the reason for the origin of this universe due to obliteration of some purgeable materials, then the cleansing has started from then itself. At the end of that procedure would take us back to that oneness with that supreme being by a final nuclear event. This may sound philosophical but this how the end would come about. That occurrence is round the corner.

அணுநாயகி = Anunnaki = Nuclear Heroine

To prove my point on illuminate otherwise classified as anunnaki by the ancient world, i referred back ton the origin of the only language which is tamil.

IN TAMIL அணுநாயகி, IN HEBREW תיניערג הרוביג in Hebrew

Ядерная героиня IN RUSSAN

Πυρηνική ηρωίδα in greek

English is a limited language only for modern usage. It has borrowed words literally without any meaning sense. That is why it is stated as Annunaki literally stated அணுநாயகி.

But all other older languages translate it meaning entirely, as "nuclear heroine."

One would ask a pertinent query. "Why addressed in the feminine gender. "The lord almighty is always addressed in masculine gender." That is why the religious books address the marriage as wedded to the lord, both man and woman as one wedded into the lord as one body. Man as feminine man and a feminine woman where the lord takes the he position to unite them as one, thereby declaring equality to both sex.

The satan or the annunaki race conceptually build a scenario to claim heship by subjugation of their own femail to place at the helm and also all other femails. This is the satanic race tool from its inception.

If You Go Through History, The Satanic Action Of Destruction Is Mainly To Soften A Situation Or A Rigid Set Up By Breaking Their Morality.

Then drop a veil or a blanket of their possession and trust for existence, followed by creating disorder which would necessitate reorder, in the bargain, maintain confusion to claim power to maintain order further discover more differences to stay in power to rip off. This is how the satan or illuminates stay at top always. All the heads of all institutions and states are smitten by illuminati blood. In course of time these actions become very apparent very dangerous for survival. This is that time now. Hence the nuclear bomb for final cleansing is around the corner. We are in the period of rule by force by anunnaki, enki, enlil.

One more grossly act the annunaki blood representatives implement in a disguised maner is to annul the true history and begin one at their starting point ot takeover. Now the wisdom has dawned on all communities to get to the truth of all. It is laid out in front as they excavate for archaeological findings. But the illegal set up made by the british for a country named india, where the satanic illuminati's to whom the power was handed over for governance, refuses to allow that, for fear of all truth, would spill out. The history of origin lays there, from early mankind to adem and his descendants connecting as first spread to middle east and further on. The satanic poison to obliterate entire mankind started at iran.

Modern archaeologists and scientists feel anciently found clay tablets however fragle that may be, can dramatically add to our understanding of early human civilization, data from these studies contribute to our knowledge of this dark period of evolution. Here you find some satanic race blankets those activities.

The tamil race is the first rece, the only race with greater beainpower to spread the entire world. Till today without them the world economy would collapse. [Add a picture]

One more aryan, fascist, or supremacist {all in one or one in all, as satan or anunnaki} act, is to re-write history only for their convenience as beginning time. All previous records would be invalidated by veiling or blanketing. Early women such as tamils never wore head cover or veil. They are always considered as equel.

As all tamils, i stand by the belief of seven plants, where sun and moon are reflecting stars, supported by two water or icy celestial object. The order of the planets, starting nearest the sun and working outward through the solar system: mercury, venus, earth, mars, jupiter, saturn, +uranus + neptune

Some existing information links provided herewith for ready reference:

https://www.space.com/16080-solar-system-planets.html

https://www.khanacademy.org/humanities/world-history/world-history-beginnings/origin-humans-early-societies/a/where-did-humans-come-from

One more interesting observation i made from the bible reference is number seven. Seven words uttered to reconnect humen with god. Seven heavens link :

https://en.m.wikipedia.org/wiki/seven_heavens

Seven seas, seven continents both divided as per its geometry, divided during the deluge what was once as one land portion covered by sea. Now strangely, none of the sea water mix and river water do not mix at their estuary or their meeting point with ocean and sea. You can even find freshwater brook in sea they do not mix. Seven musical notes which is nature's fundamental contribution, seven colours so on. This invites some attention to more studies and further on to the following issues: mazaca{ japhetite tribe,} and kedar {to be carried out later} The statements made so far reflects through the following narration.

Men, nature in six days

After spelling out so much of analogies on cosmos and the origin, would grant me the ascension to qualify as the author to present the formation of this earth, and to put down matters on this subject with full conviction on this topic.

In six days god, the heavenly father created all that would consist of life on this planet earth including men and women, that would co-exist here after resting on the seventh day, he made the atmosphere to churn so that there would be an interaction between land, water, and air including billows above. This brought rain, dew, and precipitation; thereby life, which already existed, began to accelerate its production of all species at a faster pace, could be including men and women. Early race could be the aborigines and allied races. They were an anaerobic. They were either dumpy with steady solid thighs or very long tiny legs and thigh and shorter upper body. Link: http://humanorigins.Si.Edu/sites/default/files/erectus_knmerwt15000_skeleton_front_cc_p.Jpg

One more strong point i want to make is that we are not of homo sapien spices evolved from apes, gorillas, orangutan or anything else. If that is so some of us are reverting back like they or all of them would have become like us or when frustrated we may prefer to sleep with those spices. There would gurth sexual activities inside the forest.

Concurrently or after a gap, adam and eve were made put on garden of eden which was placed at the east of that one entire landmass then. From there one massive river flew to the south called phison {ghrdk; in tamil}.

It branched off to the northwest to africa and one to the west and one to the north. River phison ended up at sea at kumari kandam basin after passing through the land of havilah and the valley of opher. Opher had the purest of gold. So the whole area was called the land of gold.

To proof is presented herewith. Number one with the issue of putting forth the evidence of reference to the aspect of tamil being the first and foremost language on the planet earth, and then number two to prove them to be the descendants of adem and eve, i put forth the following evidence. As per islamic belief, adam hurled off from garden of eden,{ due to deception by satan the serpent!} Landed on the land of kumari kandam, and eve fell in the middle east between iraq and saudi. They crossed over and produced children here. Their language was tamil only. Even the lord god spoke just in tamil with adam and eve including with the serpent {the lucifer} that is why the tamilan and all allied races are called the nagas since they were the offsprings of adem and eve deceived by the serpent the satan. Later they where classified as semitic and ani as non −semitic races [a serpentine race would somehow want to rule the world by trickish deception and forcing a merage of fear]

In the beginning, in all other accepts relating to time, space, size {in every thing relative to present}was about ten times more in size from that of present days. Even the galaxy was ten times bigger than that of the current time. Likewise, the lifespan of humans was about 1000 years or more as against 80 to 100 years at present times. A day then was equal to 1000 days of now, vice versa.[Theory of relativity comes in here] i mean the devin clock.

The nebula started burning out, gave out gas and vapors, etc.… The cornea had a clearer vision with its anointed power offered by divine excellence.

New galaxies said to have been born since then. Over some time, we automatically got changed due to contamination of earthly priories and miniaturized into our present size and the original power of the cornea diminished with layers of diverse cataract.

Even all animals, which were massive, got modified, and miniaturized from its original form to its present extent. This process is still going on now also. [A warning to all almighty proud, soon we all would be of the size of a dot or dust]

Nowadays we can walk at an average of about 25 to 28 km per day with rest in the middle. Then they walked about 250 to 300 km.[Logic of ten times] that is why we find main settlements [which later became major townships for trade and commercial centers in this sub-content] for rest in the middle. Mostly natural waterways crisscrossed at these points. So men moved with their flock and settled at these places before proceeding further on.

Early humans were known even for their space travel. Individual leaders maintained their connection with their heavenly contacts from where we all come from. Each of their trips took about 160 to 190 present years, which was equivalent to 50 to 60 days in their time. Heavenly dwellers also visited here and found it fascinating and started settling down here. They married local women since they saw them exciting for intercourse.

By nature, they did not give any respect to their women, unlike their counterparts of natural descent by the happenings of god first and later by deception by satan the serpent.[Lucifer a thrown out angel by god who has the inclination to dethrone god for himself to become god] thus, the heavenly dwellers also has a mixture of incomes, including some as representative of the very lucifer. Thus a bloodline of utterly inhuman and satanic god mixer along with some who came to sex settled down since they found this earth as a fascinating paradise. This is how good, and the lousy mixture of people became inundating our lovely mother earth. The natural complexion of colors got changed forever.

Adam while traveling to thanuskodi, had to cross a small bit of waterway which was called adam's bridge later the brahmins[aryan non-somatic satanic race] fraudulent called it ramar palam.

Naming as ramarbridge is for their mythical convenience to create a religion to promote themselves over others.

Here, i can cite more genuineness towards the islamic claim: as one traveling from thanuskodi to keelakarai, one could find dargahs of the descendant of adam and eve. These are of about 60-foot long. These ancient dargahs are the first burial site at the beginning for mankind. Their descendants of that race had spread all over, including the middle east and persia.

Edam (பரந்த இடம்). The title india was the name introduced by the westerners for their convenience. Neven kumari kadal (குமரிகடல்) was changed into the indian ocean. The area of tamil land was called thiraviya idam "திரவிய இடம்)" (land of riches}since tamilians are ornamented with all their holdings of fascinating assets both mentally and materially. This was ordained by god on to them. The tamils lived all over bharatham with their capital in the south. They spread into all other parts along with their great linguistic, cultural pride. Tamil is the original first ancient language that ever existed on this planet. It is stated and believed that our tamilian race had come from the very beginning of creation itself straight from children of adam and eve.

Then came the period of nimrod who was the great grandson of nova and a contemporary to abraham. Abraham was the great-great grandson of noah, came through the descendant of nova's first son shem. From shem came the elamite empire, who was in persia and syria. Nova, shem and their descendants spoke the language of their earliest forefathers tamil only. They were trading with mohenjo daro and harappa civilizations. Lot the nephew of abraham who also lived at that period. He should have moved to the greener pasture area of mohenjo daro and harappa between 3500BC to 3000BC.

It was in that period the sins of men had gone bizarre due to the infiltrations heaven dwellers sinning with lust in abundances {satanic induction} god had to intervene.

Due to this from nova's time till the period of nimrod and continued later too, there came about a lot of changes that happened on this planet earth. At this time, a significant deluge occurred. The land which was like one colossus mass combined got split into various continents, what was until then a semi-flat area changed drastically. The contour of mother earth also radically changed. New vast and tall mountains erupted along with valleys. Ravines, gorges, and canyon explored. What were green pastures became desert and vice-versa! This was due to compression from surrounding ocean thrusting upon to its sizeable coastal front created during the deluge. { Refer: burgess shale }

Another significant change was that common language tamil was smothered and split into many dialects and various vocabularies. Nimrod intended to maintain a constant link between all mankind. Due to the rapid multiplication of human dimensions, nimrod decided to have a central monumental pillar at babel, which was to the east of persia, so that all could converge at any point in time, to be under one leadership.

This concept disturbed the serpentine race above. It was lucifer' s aspiration to subjugate the human race under him. He had begun his operations at the 'garden of eden' deceiving eve. So lucifer, along with his host, came down onto mother earth using these circumstances of the deluge and began to tarnish the brotherhood of mankind splitting languages and phonetics from its fundamentals. Then he created many serpentine sects' and placed his appointees as heads. He chooses a venerable personality and his descendants. He was nova's son, japheth. He made them occupy persia far east asia, eurasia, and europe. Mostly cold places, since the illuminati has cold blood, emotion Less. They have no souls. They usually dispose of their dead person very fast. Nowadays, they put them in the freezer just for ceremony purpose. While their men are cold, their women are hot. They are a battle-ready machine to be sent as pilots for softening their targets. That is what happened at mohenjo daro and harappa where lot and his family lived. Mohenjo daro and harappa and sodom and gomorrah are one and the same as per my findings.

He planted heads of states, and all spiritual head was authorized by him and appointed. All major commercial establishments, business enterprises, money changers, communication media were to run under him only. His final goal is to subjugate all human under him in the name of globalization. This present-day super power's all a fosse. Nuclear or more of anything has no power against mother nature since it is almighty's creation. It can take care of itself. These vicious acts have been carried out through the sinuous bloodline by lucifer through their illuminati representatives who carry serpentine blood within them. They call themselves "i am god" and act that way without anyone to answer for. They create artificial wars, famine, insert stimulated fear, and so no and more; more about them follows:

The origin of all these languages was only tamil. This is how tamil, which is the father of all languages, was instrumental in parenting other words all rest exploded from there. Here, i would like to point out a quote from tamil literature expressing its existence

The burgess shale: a fossil jackpot

Fossilization is not as common as we might think. Most organisms are eaten or decay before they can be fossilized, and even then, it is usually only the hard body parts, like bones and exoskeletons, that stay intact long enough to become fossils. But of course, there are some exceptions to these rules...

Occasionally, a disaster creates the right conditions for soft body parts to fossilize. A little more than a half a billion years ago, one or more massive underwater mudslides buried a whole community of ocean dwellers. The mud protected the entombed animals from decay and delivered a fossil "jackpot" to modern paleontologists. This find, known as the burgess shale, preserved an array of fascinating animals in their entirety.

From nova's time till the period of nimrod about 5,000 Bc, a lot of changes happened on this planet Earth. It could be at this time a significant deluge occurred. The land which was like one giant mass combined got split into various continents, what was until then a semi-flat area changed drastically. The contour of mother earth also radically changed. New vast and tall mountains erupted along with valleys. Ravines, gorges, and canyon explored. What were green pastures became desert and vice-versa! This was due to compression from surrounding ocean thrusting upon to its sizeable coastal front created during the deluge.

Another significant change was that common language tamil was smothered and split into many dialects and various vocabulary nimrod intended to maintain a constant link between all mankind. Due to the rapid multiplication of human dimensions, nimrod decided to have a central monumental pillar at babel, which was to the east of persia, so that all could converge at any point in time, to be under one leadership. This concept disturbed the serpentine race above. It was 'his' lucifer'saspiration to subjugate the human race under him.

He had begun his operations at the 'garden of eden' deceiving eve. So lucifer, along with his host, came down onto mother earth using to circumstances of the deluge and began to tarnish the brotherhood of mankind splitting languages and phonetics from its fundamentals. Then he created many serpentine sects' and placed his appointees as heads. He planted heads of states, and all spiritual leader was authorized by him and appointed. All major commercial establishments, business enterprises, money changers, communication media were to run under him only. His final goal is to subjugate all human under him in the name of globalization. This present-day super power's all a fosse. Nuclear or more of anything has no power against mother nature since it is almighty's creation. It can take care of itself. These vicious acts have been carried out through the sinuous bloodline by lucifer through their illuminati representatives who carry serpentine blood within them. They call themselves "i am god" and act that way without anyone to answer for. They create artificial wars, famine, insert stimulated fear and so no and more; more about them follows:

The origin of all these languages was only Tamil. This is how Tamil, which is the father of all languages, was instrumental in parenting other words all rest exploded from there. Here, I would like to point out a quote from Tamil literature expressing its existence

கல் தோன்றி மண் தோன்றா காலத்தே முன் தோன்றிய மூத்த குடி-தமிழ் குடி

"Kal thondri mann thondraa kaalathe mun thondri mootha kudi thamizh kudi!"

This translates to mean that the Tamil civilization existed in the world even before the sand was born out of stone.

Affirming Tamil as the ancient first language, and Tamils and their extended race were known as Dravidians due to the riches they possessed. Initially, the Aryans proclaimed themselves as Aryans and titled Tamils and their extended run as Dravidians. This was later used by *Bishop Caldwell* and westerners as Aryans and native people as Dravidians, the language as Dravidian group of communications and the Aryan group of words. The Aryan languages came about after Tamil merging with Persian and other western languages. It did not have any substance or bones to stand. That is why they vanished. Only Islamic language Urdu and Hindi erupted, after many reformations much later. I have lineage only to Biblical timing. Hence, all of my references pertain to that.

Cognate of Indus Valley Civilisation

Further scrimmaging through the historical thread to unknot the distant past, I found reference of Indus Valley civilization along with Elamite and Sumerian civilizations which also belongs to Tamil extended races. These civilizations blossomed before 3,300 and 1500 BC. This era was before Christ. I could only find a subtle reference to these civilizations. Their language Brahui is almost identical to Tamil and the Elamite and Sumerian language. Even the word *Jesus* spoke, the *Aramaic* had its roots from Tamil only. The language migration was done by the *Phoenicians* who had their origin from Tamil Nadu. During the prime time of this civilization, I find nomadic and scavenging races, whose intend to live off other's efforts was on transitory for better pasture. The Tamils with a much earlier history lived with their capital in the south since the stone age had enjoyed a marvelous civilization. This aspect has been purposely ignored by the historians. Explicit historical reference is yet to be appropriately recorded. The cognate of the Tamilian civilization would include *Sumeria, Babylon, Egypt, Judaea, Mesopotamia, Persia*, and *China*. During the same period in China had the Yang-Shao culture subsequently gave way to Lung-Shan culture which in turn originated the Shang dynasty. This had a feudal system in the Bronze Age itself. Simultaneously, the Inca civilization was also thriving in South America. The Inca civilization by the Mayans also related to the South Indian Tamils. The well-known historian *Gene D. Matlock* finds out from his research these connections. As per *Matlock* it was the South Indian Tamils who had various ports all Three Men in Sea 303 over this subcontinent and left from a southwestern port, perhaps from *Gujarat* or *Maharashtra*, sailing southward, going around the African continent finally to reach *South America* or *Meso-America*. It is said that they took the craftsmen who probably were instrumental in building the Mayan Temple. According to his, all the most magnificent structures ever made around the the world had the participation of the South Indian Tamils. Their construction had the similar symmetry, geometry and the specific style of Tamil architecture, which is called *Zikharis* (tiered or pyramidal temple platforms). Matlock also explains the specific features of the Tamils. The ancient Tamils were international traders and colonizers. Wherever they went in the world, they left an unmistakable imprint of their presence, such as place names, foods, games and temple buildings. Due to their excellence, it is stated even *Cleopatra* wanted to visit South India to learn more about this remarkable race. She persistently conveyed her aspiration to her son. In the later centuries, even *Christopher Columbus* satisfied his yearning to explore the trueness of the Tamilians excellence and undertook a voyage sponsored by Italians. But he accidentally landed upon the continent of America! Since he was a Spaniard, in later years the Spanish invaders ruthlessly raided South America and razed the Mayan culture to ground. The marauding nature of the European race was unleashed on the entire indigenous inhabitants of the American continent. This is how the white race, *Europeans*, and *White Attila* Huns hold on to their possession until now. It does not belong to them; instead, it belongs to the cognate of the Tamil and its allied races, called as the *Red Indians*. The complexion of the Tamils became fairer due to the climatic conditions. This is how they got the name as *Red Indians* in America.

The occupiers owe them a lot. No matter whatever freebies were offered to them, it would not contain them for a more extended period of time. They will revive their original status sooner or later.

A lot of injustice had been meted out by the white race,just as the Aryans had done to the local people, especiallyto the Tamils. Thus, while the Asians, parts of Africa andSouth America had rich civilizations since the Neolithicperiod, the Europeans lagged pitifully behind. Afterone century, history records that a Nomadic race inEurope was on transitory all over the world in searchof better pasture. During the same period, some of themarauding runs were also on the move wreaking havocwherever they went. The more popular among thelatter of this race was the Huns. According to Europeancivilization, I question the period of Stonehenge at Wiltshire in British Territory.I only observed an oddplacement of a couple of dozen stones! Could this meanthat civilization thrived there too? As mentionedearlier, the Asian cultures had the most originalancient languages. The Tamils were profound with theusage of their word, which had in-depth expressionand meaningful values. Their scripts were excellent andpoetic; it is still in use as never lost its sheen. Here Iwould like to bring to notice a famous Tamil quote:

யாமறிந்த மொழிகளிலே தமிழ்மொழிபோல் இனிதாவது ஏங்கும் காணோம்.

Meaning: Among all the languages we know, we do not see anywhere any as sweet as Tamil.

Stolen Historical Entities

The reference goes back to the term Dravidian to mean Tamils only. Hence, Tamilians appeared to have livedusing their own language, culture and traded with othernative people in the present *Pakistan, Afghanistan, Persia*, and *China*. They also had maritime trade with *China,Rome*, and *Greece* since the Bronze Age. The historicalreferences of the Tamilian and other native races seemedto have been lost, hidden or perished. For various reasons,this loss could have been utilized by the other runs togive more importance to themselves rather than to realhistory. They probably took over the documentationand maintained records to suit and elevate their ownrace, with some ulterior motive. The Tamilians from thebeginning are known to be straightforward, frank, simpleand down-to-earth people with no inhibitions. Hence,their recordscould have easily been destroyed by theother races. Their literature could have been translated orcopied and given a different name to claim that the originof that literature was their own, by different linguisticgroups. This generates so many questions within me, andas a proud Tamilian, it is my right to know the real partof my linguistic and cultural heritage and the richnessof the society to which I belong. As all fellow Tamilians,my ancestors were also upright and straight. Hence, thefollowing narrations and analyses are based on thesepriorities that have been brought out. Those who havethus far not been correctly represented are adequately documented here. This may seem one-sided, but I am onlytrying to present some facts with the following narrations.

The Tamils—Fountainhead of All Roots of Excellence

In general, the native followed a feudal system of governance from the ancient times. They inter-traded among themselves using the barter system. At dawn were only nature worshippers and also worshipped astronomical objects. They were very religious. There was a different class of people with extraordinary intelligence and understanding levels. This genius was recognized as Cittar (rpj;ju;) Siddhar who professed and practiced an unorthodox type of Yoga powers to attain liberation. They were anointed with excellent skills of understanding of medicine, science could derive a solution to any problem. These people were leaders hence hailed as saints. After their departure, their sainthood remains, this caused the creation of God and Goddess with powers along with idol worships. This idol worship was induced by the Brahmin community for their own benefits. The original native Tamilians were only nature worshippers but not the icon. This gave them an excellent insight into all the matters they dealt with. They were advanced in mathematics, science, astronomy, sports, martial arts, music, poetry, dance, drama, medicine, and all the other fields besides. The unique creation by the Tamilians is the basis of language creation and the numerical system from 0 to 9. The value of a number to so many zillions and beyond came from the ancient period. The zero being valueless was the masterpiece of the basis on which the numbering system exists. In Tamil zero is termed Suzhiyam or Poojiyam. The Tamil, numbering system from ancient times is as follows:

Original Tamil Numerical System Since Bronze Age

Numbers	In Tamil	In English
0	Suzhiyam or Poojiyam	Zero
1	Ondruu	One
10	Pathu	Ten
100	Nooru	Hundred
1000	Aayiram	Thousand
10 000	Pathhayiram	Ten Thousand
100 000	Noorayiram	Hundred Thousand
1 000 000	Pathhu	One Million
10 000 000	Koodi	Ten Million
100 000 000	Arputham	Hundred Million
1 000 000 000	Nigarputham	One Billion
10 000 000 000	Kumbam	Ten Billion
100 000 000 000	Kanam	Hundred Billion
1 000 000 000 000	Karpam	One Trillion
10 000 000 000 000	Nikarpam	One Hundred Trillion
100 000 000 000 000	Pathumam	One Zillion
1 000 000 000 000 000	Sanggam	Ten Zillion
10 000 000 000 000 000	Vellum	Hundred Zillion
100 000 000 000 000 000	Anniyam	Not Yet Defined
1 000 000 000 000 000 000	Arttam	Not Yet Defined
10 000 000 000 000 000 000	Pararttam	Not Yet Defined
100 000 000 000 000 000 000	Pooryam	Not Yet Defined
1 000 000 000 000 000 000 000	Mukkodi	Not Yet Defined
10 000 000 000 000 000 000 000	Mahygam	Not Yet Defined

The zero and one are the basis of the binary system that is being used for all computing technology and further to many other scientific and mathematical usages. The Tamils had the remarkable astronomical knowledge, which was shared with *Babylon, Persia, Egypt, Judaea, Greece,* and *Rome.* To my surprise, I discovered, with pride, that we, the Tamilians, were the pioneers in astronomy, who actually drew the path of the Sun, Moon, Stars and the entire planetary system since ancient times. Thus, I feel proud to belong to the Tamilian race for creating the modern calendar those days itself—of dividing time into years, months, weeks, days and a day into twenty-four parts and after that into smaller chunks. This helped them to create a navigation system supported by unique navigation skills. Every Tamilian was born with a composite entity of multiple faculties. But simplicity in existence was their motto. The Wise Men who went to visit *Baby Jesus* in *Bethlehem* are believed to have gone from the present Indian subcontinent, maybe even from the South Indian Tamil region.

To continue to describe the extent of the ancient Tamil civilization's knowledge, they knew the power of the numbers in fractions, way back during the ancient days itself. They had knowledge of fractions up to 1/2323824530227200000000, while modern science and galactic scales have reached only up to 1/10,00,00,00,000 which is said to be the nanoscale. To give a more elaborate reference, I wish to present the following details:

Fraction Values	In Tamil	Phonetics in English
1	ஒன்று	onRu
3/4 = 0.75	முக்கால்	mukkaal
1/2= 0.5	அரை	arai
1/4 = 0.25	கால்	kaal
1/5 = 0.2	நாலுமா	naalumaa
3/16 = 0.1875	மும்மாகாணி	mummaakaani
3/20 = 0.15	மும்மா	mummaa
1/8 = 0.125	அரைக்கால்	araikkaal
1/10 = 0.1	இருமா	irumaa
1/16 = 0.0625	மாகாணி (வீசம்)	maakaaNi (veesam)
1/20 = 0.05	ஒருமா	orumaa
3/64 = 0.046875	முக்கால்வீசம்	mukkaal veesam
3/80 = 0.0375	முக்காணி	mukkaaNi
1/32 = 0.03125	அரைவீசம்	araiveesam
1/40 = 0.025	அரைமா	araimaa
1/64 = 0.015625	கால் வீசம்	kaal veesam
1/80 = 0.0125	காணி	kaaNi
3/320 = 0.009375	அரைக்காணி முந்திரி	araikkaaNi munthiri
1/160 = 0.00625	அரைக்காணி	araikkaaNi
1/320 = 0.003125	முந்திரி	munthiri
3/1280 = 0.00234375	கீழ் முக்கால்	keel mukkal
1/640 = 0.0015625	கீழரை	keelArai
1/1280 = 7.8125e-04	கீழ் கால்	keel kaal
1/1600 = 0.000625	கீழ் நாலுமா	keel nalumaa
3/5120≈5.85938e-04	கீழ் மூன்று வீசம்	keel moondru veesam
3/6400 = 4.6875e-04	கீழ் மும்மா	keel mummaa
1/2500 = 0.0004	கீழ் அரைக்கால்	keel araikkaal
1/3200 = 3.12500e-04	கீழ் இருமா	keel irumaa
1/5120≈1.95313e-04	கீழ் வீசம்	keel veesam
1/6400 = 1.56250e-04	கீழொருமா	keelorumaa
1/102400≈9.76563e-06	கீழ்முந்திரி	keezh munthiri
1/2150400≈4.65030e-07	இம்மி	immi
1/23654400≈4.22754e-08	மும்மி	mummi
1/165580800≈6.03935e-09	அணு	aNu
1/1490227200≈6.71039e-10	குணம்	kuNam
1/7451136000≈1.34208e-10	பந்தம்	pantham
1/44706816000≈2.23680e-11	பாகம்	paagam

1/312947712000≈3.19542e-12	விந்தம்	vintham
1/5320111104000≈1.87966e-13	நாகவிந்தம்	naagavintham
1/74481555456000≈1.34261e-14	சிந்தை	sinthai
1/1489631109120000≈6.71307e-16	கதிர்முனை	kathirmunai
1/59585244364800000≈1.67827e-17	குரல்வளைப்படி	kuralvaLaippidi
1/3575114661888000000≈2.79711e-19	வெள்ளம்	veLLam
1/3575114661888000000000≈2.79711e-21	நுண்மணல்	nuNNmaNal
1/2323824530227200000000≈4.30325e-22	தேர்த்துகள்	Thaertthugal

Thelowestfractionwasdenotedin Tamil as- "தேர்த்துகள்– *thaertthugaľ*" which means 1. Dust emitting from a celestial chariot in motion (வானரதம்/vaanaratham).

2. Minute measure of length = 4 atoms of dust in a sunbeam = 8 katir-eḻu-tukal; எட்டுக்கதிரெழுத்துக்கள் கொண்டதோர் அளவு.

Such was the knowledge power of the Tamils from ancient times to which the present world is yet to catch up, and which I believe, will take more than 3,000 years. I as a Tamil myself know for sure that these aspects are ingrained in our very fabric, make these statements proudly.

Origin of Languages and the Science of Six Senses

I must also add here that the architecture derivation of *Six Senses* also originated from the Tamilians. Due to the remarkable knowledge power of the Tamils, they derived the *Six Senses. The Six Senses* and basis of language creation and composition belong to the Tamil language alone. Refer to *Tolkappiyam*, an excellent piece of Tamil literature with a deep sense of sharing the power of knowledge with mankind. It existed from almost much earlier than 600 BC. It could even have been in existence from before 5,000 BC. This is undoubtedly the oldest literature ever to survive in this universe.

Tolkappiyam orients the basis of the creation of any language. The fundamentals are stated below:

1. Orthography
2. Phonology
3. Morphology
4. Semantics
5. Prosody

Tolkappiyam's explanation and adoption of the *Six Senses* is given herewith:

ஒன்று அறிவதுவே உற்று அறிவதுவே
இரண்டு அறிவதுவே அதனொடு நாவே
மூன்று அறிவதுவே அவற்றொடு மூக்கே
நான்கு அறிவதுவே அவற்றொடு கண்ணே
ஐந்து அறிவதுவே அவற்றொடு செவியே
ஆறு அறிவதுவே அவற்றொடு மனனே
நேரிதின் உணர்ந்தோர் நெறிப்படுத்தினரே
(தொல்காப்பியம்: பொருளதிகாரம் 571)

Ondru Arivathuve Uttru Arivathuve
Irandu Arivathuve Athanodu Naave
Mondru Arivathuve Avattrodu Mooke
Naangu Arivathuve Avattrodu Kanne
Ainthu Arivathuve Avattrodu Seviye
Aaru Arivathuve Avattrodu Manane
Nerithin Unarnthor Neripaduthinare
(Tolkappiyam – Porulathigaram 571)

328

1. Ondru, Irandu, Moondru, Naangu, Ainthu, Aaru :
   1, 2, 3, 4, 5, 6 respectively
2. Arivathu : Know, feel, realise, sense
3. Uttru : Touch, come into contact
4. Athanodu : Along with some other thing (usually when the number of objects is two)
5. Avattrodu : Along with some other things (usually when the number of objects is more than two)
6. Naavu : Tongue, in this context, taste
7. Mookku : Nose (for sense Smell)
8. Kann : Eye (Sight)
9. Sevi : Ear (Hearing)
10. Manam : Mind
11. Nerithu : The truth
12. Unarnthor : Those who realised the truth (Meignyanam-Divine Knowledge)
13. Neripaduthinare : Classified and organised the life

Translation and Full Meaning: Beings with one sense are those that have the only sense of TOUCH. Beings with two senses are those that have the sense of TASTE and TOUCH. Beings with three senses have in addition the sense of SMELL. Beings with four senses have the sense of SIGHT, along with the above. Beings with five senses have sense of HEARING, as well. The beings with six senses have a MIND, along with the above. It is the people who had realised the truth of God through divine knowledge who have classified and organised the living organisms appropriately.

Tolkappiyam does not stop with this classification alone. It also gives examples of living beings in each of these classifications: Sixth Senses of the ancient Tamils (Meignyanam). The sixth sense or subtle ability of perception, refers to our ability to understand the subtle cause and effect relationship behind many events, which is beyond the understanding of the intellect. Extrasensory perception (ESP), clairvoyance, premonition and intuition are synonymous with the sixth sense or subtle perceptive ability. Tolkappiyam is said to be the first in the world to describe the sixth sense, which is related to something external to the body parts. The explanation of the verses of *Tolkappiyam* mentioned above is truly an amazing classification and proves that our Tamil ancestors were not only well versed in literature and grammar, but had also obtained a higher spiritual knowledge that is of a more progressive universal acceptance and of lasting importance in terms of a time span of centuries. The way of life of the ancient Tamils, which was associated with nature and worship practices, is depicted clearly in *Tolkappiyam* and other Sangam literatures. From the early periods, the Tamils have always given priority to their belief in God. According to another verse from *Tolkappiyam* under Karuporul 'culture of the people', God is to be prioritised first, followed by food.

What did the ancient Tamils believe? They believed that God created all the various types of worlds from *Maayai* and gave suitable bodies to each soul to inhabit these worlds. Souls were *anaathi* before creation and God's motive for creation is to help delete the *aanavam* from souls and prepare them to attain a suitable state to receive *veeduperu (mukthi)* by imparting spiritual knowledge. Worshipping the Supreme Being, God, with true devotion is one way to achieve gnanam, which means to 'realise' God. During this period, the soul develops the ability to receive the spiritual nature of knowledge from the subtle bodies imparted by God, and the deep inner longing to 'realise' Him increases. Receiving divine knowledge from the Universal Mind and Universal Intellect (i.e., the mind and intellect aspects of God) is the highest kind of achievement a soul can gain. When the soul attains that spiritual maturity, God Himself will come as a guru and impart knowledge.

Effect of Excellence and Simplicity

Hence, proud to be a Tamilian, I want to stress that it was our language Tamil which was instrumental in the creation of many *other languages, numbers and mathematics, the basics of science, astronomy, art, culture and medicine.* The Tamils had incorporated a unique medical science with *Sidha medicine,* which was very successful to ensure a healthier life. The medicinal compositions were very simple, most frequently a mixture of multiple herbs mixed with a tint of certain metals. The knowledge of the composition of these medicines right down to their specific proportions very uniquely pertained to the disease, sickness or the necessity of medical requirement from the ancient days. The Tamils are said to have even executed dental operations, orthopaedic and internal and cosmetic surgeries. While I can make an elaborate presentation for Tamil art, culture, and other sciences, I will refrain for the moment. This gentle race was more than willing to share these abilities with anyone who would desire to have them. But the Europeans had their own plans to take away these fundamentals and possess them as their own by some means or the other. This resulted in the creation of the 'Aryans' as a race to make-believe that they as a race had greater intelligence and linguistic powers.

As I searched through old history, I understood that the Dravidians occupied the entire region of *Bharathadesam,* otherwise known as the present Indian subcontinent, which extended up to Persia. The main languages included *Tamil, Telugu, Kolambi, Kurukh* and *Brahui.* The other branch languages were *Kannada, Malayalam, Kodagu, Kurumba, Gondi, Muria, Badaga, Chenchu, Tulu, Naiki, Kolami* and *Elamite in Persia.* The real Dravidian name for this subcontinent is yet to be explored and revealed; this name could have been lost probably due to the Aryan incursion, which could have created a new name such as *Hindustan* for their own advantage. It is a very sorry state of affairs. The real history of the entire Dravidian race which had spread all over this subcontinent seems to be missing or lost due to reasons unknown to us. After several years, scholars and researchers have begun to question the records of past history and have found many projected statements on history that could not be absolutely true. On research regarding the excellence of the Tamils and Tamil Dravidians, who lived in the entire extent of the present Hindustan and adjourning places, it was found that from here they had trade even as far away as *Sumeria, Judaea, Greece, Rome and Egypt.* The Tamils have lent many fundamental words to these languages. The lexicographers have found Tamil to have been main source for many languages, including English.

King David and Solomon who traded through '*Ur*' in Sumeria, had built ships in the port of *Ezion Gebar*, which is near *Elath* on the shore of the *Red Sea*, in the land of *Edom*. From that port ships sailed to bring gold and precious items from *Opir*. This precious cargo was loaded at the seaport of *Ovar*, which is said to be the location of the present *Maharashtra* or *Gujarat*. Each trip took about three years to complete. The word '*Ur, Edom, Elath, Opir* and *Ovar*' all are Tamil words. The researchers have not found the actual location of *Opir*, which is mentioned in the Bible but it is perceived to be an extension of Tamil Nadu under the Chola and Pandya kings. This land mass is supposedly lost in the sea and is under the Indian Ocean. Lanka was also a part of Tamil Nadu and it was the Aryans who created the myth to divide Lanka and Tamil Nadu through the *Ramayana*, which has no connection with real history. Therefore, more anthropological research and more information are required to unearth the hidden facts pertaining to the lost treasures of this marvellous race, which existed even before 7,000 BC.

Western and European Design

There are lot of references and debates circling around in the literary world with information on colonial powers through the *East India Company*, paying up very big publishing houses to publish history and records twisted and twirled to suit their personal design and priorities. Many of the historical facts regarding the Dravidians, the mapping of their territory and their language skills have been suppressed and singular endorsement and acknowledgement have been given to the so-called *Aryans, Vedic people* and the Sanskrit language. The *Aryans (Vedic people)* had many ridiculous social and ritual compulsions. Their language Sanskrit said to be initially only as oral language. This is the oral language tradition transmitted to generations without proper history. One does not find any basic origin for Sanskrit. I would categorically say that the Dravidian languages and other possessions have been so powerful and profound that even Greece and the Middle East including European languages have borrowed many fundamentals from Tamil and the other Dravidian languages.

By-Product of the Ancient Dravidian Languages

To make an assertive point on this statement, relevant information has already been shared earlier. Hence, while Tamil being a living language from the ancient past until the present, Sanskrit, a borrowed language from the Parisian and Dravidian languages, is a dead one now, just like *Pali* and *Latin*. These languages were mainly used for reciting and rituals, more of a humming and reverberation, which induces one into a trance. Hence it is the general opinion that the person chanting these languages in religious rituals may not know the meaning of what he is reciting and people listening may not know the real meaning at all. Hence, this language does not have any rich or in-depth meaning that should have been the reason for the natural death of these languages. There seems to be a mystery on the part of the Europeans for suppressing the Dravidian's possession of their culture and language under Aryans. The reason is still unknown and rather questionable.

Worship, Knowledge Sharing and Governance

The Dravidians were originally nature worshippers and venerated astronomical objects as well. The only thing they feared was the awesome power of nature. They had good knowledge of the universe and solar system. In the beginning, there were no temples built, rather they assembled under a *Peepal Tree* or *Neem Tree*, where the wise men (Saadhus and Munivers), scholars, and intellects used to gather their fellow citizens in the town or village to instruct them with moral and social lectures. These trees are found in the Indian subcontinent Bangladesh, Nepal, Myanmar, Pakistan, part of China, Indo-China, and the regions of Tamil Eelam in Ceylon, and these lectures were delivered to the local people by the wise men. Religion did not occupy a central role in governance under the Dravidians. The leader of every society or group represented their people during early centuries during the BC period itself. Thus, theirs was a unified and secular federal rule. The social fabric was maintained in true harmony, when the entire Indian subcontinent lived in unison with its pioneering civilisation of *Harappa* and *Mohenjo-Daro* in the northwest and the Tamils in the south. It was also during the same period that the Dravidians ruled over Persia, prior to 630–550 BC, at which time they were called Elamites. The Elamite race was spread over most part of Middle East up to Egypt from the early centuries (BC) itself. One of the *Elamite princesses, Amytis, married Nebuchadnezzar II*. As a queen from Elamite descent, Amytis was instrumental in drafting and creating one of the ancient *Seven Wonders of the World, the Hanging Gardens of Babylon*. As she was a nature lover, she covered the entire area with a lot of greenery. The Dravidian Elamites lost their power to the Persian king Darius in 550 BC. Eelam was otherwise known as the homeland. This is how the Tamil Eelam, which is the homeland of the Tamils, should have been given the power to rule in Lanka. The Indian National Congress during the time of independence time was flooded with Brahmins (Aryans) and the main players in authority were only the Brahmins who along with the British took a decision against the Dravidian Tamils of Lanka and resolved to make the British hand over powers to the racist and murderous Singhalese. In this connection, a greater role was played by the Brahmins of South India, especially those from Kerala to suppress and divest the Tamils of all their powers and even their dignity.

Consequence of the Excellence and Genetic Identification

The fame of the Dravidian race appears to have extended beyond the borders, reaching all over Europe, Asia and Africa. Therefore, they desired to be involved with the Dravidians in some way or the other. After a lull, I observe that many research activities are being carried out by very great universities in the United States and Europe regarding the Tamils, Aryans and other races, although the Dravidians are classified as *ASI (Ancestral South Indian) genetic formation and the Aryans as ANI (Ancestral North Indian) genetic formation. The research scholars discovered that the ANI* gene did not belong to India at all, but rather to the European gene. Although it is being termed ASI, the people with this genetic stream spread all over Indian subcontinent right up to Persia, the Middle East, Tamil Lanka, and other subcontinents, even as far as South America. The Dravidians are believed to have assisted in the building of the *Egyptian, Babylonian, Persian architecture* and *other types of architectures* in these areas. This attracted the *Nomadic Eurasian* to move to these places out of curiosity during the later centuries. In that same period, Greece and the other Europeans developed an interest in India, as did very many other races. Distinctive European races or subrace of the Caucasian race converged to India. The Dravidians' architectural perception with its fundamentals of symmetry and geometric sequence was unique. This incited envy throughout the other parts of the world. It was the attraction to this culture that was instrumental in drawing the Europeans to take over this civilisation by some means or the other. Thus, the conflict of interest and possession embedded with greed started with the Europeans. In the early period the Europeans do not seem to have any real or decent recorded history. They always appear to have been warmongers and destroyers always fighting among themselves. Hence, their convergence to Asia began from the reign of Alexander. The European raid on Asia and other non-European continents has not stopped until now, from then on. It is my biased opinion that intelligence, science, architecture, mathematics and every aspect of their inborn innovativeness, which is embedded in the culture of the Tamil Dravidians migrated to Europe from Asian subcontinent. The priority for the European has been only to make war, and benefit from raiding the wealth, whether it is material wealth or knowledge-based riches. Some of the original Dravidian scripts can be found in the museums of Europe and America even today!

Invasion of Alexander into Dravidian Soil until His Subsequent Death

Chaos and confusion started spreading in the Indian subcontinent soon after the invasion of *Alexander, the Great.* After *Alexander* proved himself to be the master of challenges by taming a powerful horse at a young age, his desire for conquest never stopped. Therefore, he gathered an army from *Macedonia* to satisfy his lust for war. He started conquering one nation after another and finally landed in India via the *Hindu Kush mountain range through the Khyber Pass in 326 BC.* He invited and threatened, with intimidation, the ruling kings to surrender and pay a ransom price to his army. The *Ambi kingdom fell,* but *Purushothaman* the great ruler who was also known as *Porus,* a Dravidian king, wanted to challenge him on the battlefield in *Punjab* near the bank of the Jhelum River. As all Dravidians are great warriors and strategists, the war went on. An elephant cavalry sent from South India also joined with *Porus* to fight against Alexander. Seeing the veracity and ferociousness of the elephants, Alexander lost or almost lost the war as he underestimated the courage and grit of the Dravidians and the majesty of the elephants. Their posture, speed and thundering trumpeting sound caused Alexander's cavalry horses to run amuck in absolute fear and confusion. But the war lasted for little more time. *Porus* was a gentleman and he did not want to rout Alexander completely; this gave Alexander's general a little space to buy time to work out sleazy cunning strategy. As a result, the war turned in favour of Alexander's army. *Porus* is said to have surrendered, at least that is what history records. However, awestruck by the courage and grit of *Porus* and his warriors, Alexander handed the kingdom back to *Porus*. He also assumed even in surrender, that the remnant of *Porus's* army would come back and fight against him again. Alexander was fatally wounded on the battlefield, but he was believed to have survived. *The war in India was the last battle Alexander ever fought and the deadliest he ever faced.* Finally, it is assumed that Alexander was taken care of during his last days by the Dravidian Elamites at Babylon where he breathed his last. Such has always been the gentleness of the Dravidian race. As a result, the Europeans decided not to fight a direct war with the Dravidians. Therefore, they had to create all sorts of underhand methods in the later years to take over the gentle and peaceful Dravidian race. They perplexed and confused them in various ways. And history goes on and on from there.

Result of Alexander Legacy

Alexander had encouraged his generals and soldiers to marry the natives wherever his conquests occurred. Some of the Alexander's generals remained here and ruled some parts of India and other places. Thus, a mixed race was created by the Grecian and Macedonian people. The Greeks were always immersed in mythology. Thus, began the complication and introduction of the different mythologies in the Indian subcontinent and the harmony of the Dravidian race began to get adulterated. Here I am forced to pose a question what were *Alexander's* plans and wisdom for his adventure and war strategy? What was the ulterior motive of his conquest? Was he going to achieve something or establish his own kingdom to bring about order and discipline in the land, which he won over, which was already in harmony and needed no correction? Was he a representative sent on a mission by any other European race to confuse the richness of a people who were peace-loving and lived in harmony with each other? Most of his conquests were in the Asian subcontinents, which had their own riches. May be many of the treasures were moved to Europe through this conquest. The true history and its outcomes will be brought forth to daylight one day.

Those parts which *Alexander* won over in the Indian subcontinent were left with a void in governance. Before the advent of his visit, everything in the Indian subcontinent had been peaceful and harmony had prevailed. Although there were many different tribes, ethnic and linguistic groups following their own culture and their way of life was one of co-existence. They happily mingled with others without any inhibition. They traded between themselves using the barter system. The *war* and *void* thus created by the departure of *Alexander* gave an opportunity for a certain race to use the situation for their own benefit. History speaks of a *Eurasian* race, moving from the central plateau of Asia or the northern part of Siberia to various parts of the world. While some groups left for Europe, one particular group settled down somewhere in Austria and others went on to other parts of Europe. The remaining dispersed to various European countries. The remainder travelled on to Asia. They split up into two groups, again for reasons unknown. One group settled in Persia and the remnants of that race got pushed further down to the south and finally came to the Indian subcontinent. They were accepted by the local Dravidians with their characteristic warmth and were given proper shelter. As they were an alien race, they did not have trade or work skill of their own. But still the Dravidians magnanimously accepted them. The kindness, gentleness, and hospitality provided by the Dravidians were misunderstood by the Aryans as a form of weakness. But they could not match their intelligence and work skill. This possibly occurred between 350 BC and then on. It was thus that the Aryans came and landed in Northern India and later slowly started trickling down to the south. They had only their oral language and gave much importance to certain rituals by compulsion and with their silly traditions to pretend that they were sacred and superficially holier. The Aryans composed their oral language and mixed it with *Persian Avertan, Latin, and the native*

Dravidian Tamil language. This was the birth of the superficial Sanskrit oral language.

Uncanny Aryans

During the period of Alexander or a little before that, due to the advent of the Aryan migration, the philosophy and culture of the local societies changed. There could have been an intermarriage of language and philosophy. Various mythological stories were created to preach the difference between good and bad, something that was already known and in existence within the Dravidian tradition. The Dravidians always lived by the consequences of good and bad. But this infiltration by the Aryans and their uncanny approach in dealing with the situation to convert the sequence into their own benefit caused many problems and wars in the Indian subcontinent. The reason for the collapse of *Dravidian Indus Valley Civilisation* is still a mystery. The Aryan people with their in-built genetic sleazy and slimy nature created confusion among the local society through various methods, thus promoting disharmony among the Dravidians. The Aryans were fairer and better looking than the local Dravidians, who were slightly darker in complexion. This gave them easy passage to the ruling class who gave them some position in governance. They were thus allowed to participate and infiltrate into the local art, culture and literature at a later period. Thus, they took over all these aspects as their own possessions. Even today these cultures continue. Some of the beautiful Aryan ladies were married to the local kings and noble families.

Thus the literature and records were oriented and created to benefit the Aryan race. Hence, history was written according to their whims and fancies. A mixed race thus came into existence first by *European Grecian* descent and then by the *Eurasian (Aryan)* infiltration. They wrote history to suit their own mode with more emphasis on self. As written history was manipulated to suit the Aryans and other European races, an in-depth study is required by scholars.

Veda, Vedic People: Caste System Creation and Vedic Language Evolution

It is generally believed that Sanskrit was not the Aryan's original language because the section that went to Persia adopted Persian as language. The Indo-Europeans (Aryans) transformed their language into Sanskrit. Probably, the more powerful and ancient Dravidian script and expressions could have been used to polish their own Aryan language into Sanskrit and Pali. Tamil, Kurukh, Brahui and Avertan, being oldest languages ever to exist on the Mother Earth contributed more to develop the Aryan language. The Aryans were believed to have brought their four Vedas with them (Rig, Yajur, Sama and Atharva). If so, where did the Vedas originate from? Profoundly speaking, they should have carried them with them when they began their journey at their own starting point, their own place where they came from. If that was true, were the same Vedas not carried to Persia or other parts where the other sections of the Aryan migrated? There is no document to prove this theory.

Obviously, the Indo-Europeans known as the Aryans must have had one common language as they split into groups and that common language would have taken its own form and become sharpened after mixing with highly profound local languages. As the local languages had more meaning and depth, they must have helped the Aryans and Grecians to polish their own language into *Sanskrit* and *Pali*. Simultaneously, the four Vedas could have been epics created out of the local classical teachings with high moral and ethical standards being in practice with the Dravidians, much earlier, in fact prior to many centuries itself. With these riches the Aryans mixed their belief of human relationships which included women and animals etc. Some parts of the Vedas are expressed with a citation of *Ambedkar's* writing. Obviously, the Vedas could not have been thrown from above, only for the Brahmins or otherwise the Vedic people. The terms used like 'Veda' and 'Vedic people', where did they come from? Whose brainchild was this to call these people as Vedic people? The mystery remains with this lingo! These Vedas were professing that those in the high priestly position alone could perform the religious rituals, meaning only the Aryans. This is how the Brahmins (Aryans) took the authority as the medium between the God of worship and the other indigenous people. These Vedas also preach that human beings are created as different classes. The Brahmins (Aryans) were to be considered as the more superior class while the other sections were divided into three or four classes. Such a class system never existed among the Dravidians before the infiltration of Aryans. Although the Dravidians were of different ethnicity, caste and linguistic people, they honoured and respected each other as human beings, equally. More in-depth knowledge and studies are required in this matter. Although these Vedas talk about good and evil, there are more rituals to be executed to attain the goodness. Should any belief be so complicated to reach the Almighty? This is only my logical conclusion.

Ascent of Mauryas with Hellenistic Influences and Origin of Pali

During the period of Alexander's thrust into the Indian subcontinent, the *Nanda dynasty* was already ruling in the North Indian subcontinent from the East in Bengal to Western India between 345 and 321 BC. The war with Alexander disturbed the rhythm of the *Nanda dynasty*. Porus also could have been a part of the *Nanda dynasty*, which could have been a spill-over of the remnant of the *Indus Valley Civilisation. The generals of Alexander who remained to rule parts of Northern India created the Indo-Grecian race, where the Grecian's mythology of different kinds were preached and practiced.* The main general who remained in India was *Seleucus I Nicator,* who ruled regions taken over from the *Nanda dynasty.* In 322 BC, the *Nandas relinquished their power to Chandragupta Maurya. Chandragupta Maurya* is said to belong to the Adithya Tribe, otherwise known as the Adhi Dravidia Tribe. After his ascent to rule the kingdom, he undertook some battles. Unfortunately, he lost his first wife Durdhara. *There was a battle between*

Chandragupta Maurya and the Grecian general Seleucus I Nicator who had served under Alexander. After winning the war, Chandragupta Maurya later married Helen, daughter of Seleucus I Nicator. This enabled Chandragupta Maurya's kingdom to extend far and wide wherever there were pockets of Grecian rule left behind by Alexander. Thus, the large empire was literally given to him on a plate. After marrying Helen, he could easily trade with the Hellenistic states in Europe (Greece and the Roman Empire). This boosted his morale, but he felt empty and fatigued in spirit. As his first wife had leanings towards Jainism, after coming into contact with some Jain guru, Chandragupta Maurya also converted to Jainism and starved himself to death in the later days. This hysteria remained with the family. His son Bindhusara then came to power to rule a large empire, but he also died at the young age of 40 plus, from unknown causes; in the meantime, speculation proposed by the Greek mythology infiltrated into the local in Indian culture and language. This could have caused the advent of a new language called *Pali*, a Greek mixture with some profound Indian language. Kurukh could have given birth to *Pali*. This is a new school of thought. Chandragupta had his capital at *Pataliputra* near the *Middle East of India.*

Bindhusara, the son of Chandragupta was a philanderer. This weakness was well exposed. He had about sixteen wives. From a variety of people without any barrier of caste or creed he had one hundred and sixteen offsprings. Such excesses practiced by Bindhusara saw the end of his life at an early age. Ashoka was one of the offspring of Bindhusara said to be mothered by Subhadarangi as per Ashokavadana.

While mystery remains regarding Ashoka's actual mother, in Ashokavadana, an insertion by the Brahmins was made claiming that Subhadarangi was a daughter of the Brahmin caste, hailing from Telangana. This barrage of siblings, some of them narcotised only with pleasure, gave Ashoka easy passage to the kingdom. As sleaziness is embedded with the Brahminical influence, Subhadarangi as a Brahmin was instrumental in propagating Ashoka's success and also to make use of the Hellenistic influence to their maximum benefit. Thus Ashoka's history was magnified and recorded. Ashoka, as all the other Mauryans had this original Dravidian philosophy, which was good in him, mixed with the sleazy Brahmin influence by his mother along with a warring philosophy embedded with Hellenistic influence. This confusion followed him all through his life. That was the root cause of his act of disowning the world and converting to Buddhism. While Indian philosophy always preaches harmony and brotherhood, the Grecian had a tendency to make war without purpose. This was the state of mind of Ashoka. Under Ashoka, the Mauryan kingdom expanded all over Indian plateau up to Iran border. As there was no resistance due to the void created by Alexander's conquest and also the aid of the Hellenistic states, Ashoka proclaimed himself as a ruler of the entire area with the exception of South India, which was ruled by powerful South Indian kings (Chera, Chola and Pandya).

It appears that Ashoka is said to have been a greatest emperor who ruled a vast area thus granted to him on a plate. Was it a schematic presumption or was the story created to suit someone's convenience as authenticated history? There is a special mention of the ruler Ashoka being great and a very good administrator with foresight. He is said to have erected tanks, an interconnecting irrigation system, and he also planted trees along the roadsides to give shade for people to travel with ease. He also made stone benches for travellers to offload their heavy weights and rest. These are specially mentioned as Ashoka's achievements as per history books. All these factors and much more existed in South India for many years even prior to Ashoka's advent itself. The south Indians had a very good judicial system. Even kings obeyed the law of the land in South India. The Tamil Dravidians were very upright and straightforward from the king to the last subject. These aspects are neither documented nor found in any of the history records. I find most of the history records were either written by the Brahmins/Aryans themselves or by the Europeans who were more connected to the Aryans for unknown reasons.

Ashoka's Kalinga War

I wish to share my knowledge about history of the *Kalinga War*, which Ashoka fought. *Kalinga* is known as Orissa now. It had its own original Dravidian language *Kurukh*. It was ruled by Dravidians and small sections of Kambojas and Sakas (linked to the Iranian tribes), Yavanas (linked to Greece), Paradas and others (South Indian Tamil descent) and Chinas (descent from the Qin dynasty from China living there). The governance of then *Kalinga* or present-day Orissa was of the feudal system. When the Aryan and Mauryan influences eroded into their society, it caused some erosion and complicated their traditions and caste differentiation. It began to inhibit the social mobility and corrode what had survived of the ancient republican tradition. Their warriors who were under the feudal governance were ferocious. Each tribe had mastered their own traditional art of warfare. This made them formidable; they were fighters to their death. Even Ashoka said that he nearly lost the war. Some misfortune or tampering would probably have happened. The war is said to have resulted in Ashoka's victory. Yet, historical documents reveal the *Kalinga War* was not completely won. Ativ Land (Southwest Orissa) still remained intact, although Ashoka had a very big army! The fighting skills, guts, and determination of the people of *Kalinga* gave him distress and war fatigue. Ashoka was the one of the last powerful Mauryan emperors who survived till 240 BC. Thus Maurya kingdom existed only for eighty years with its Hellenistic influences and infiltration. After Ashoka, the empire started to become defragmented. Later, it continued to survive for some more time and withered away. What made the people of *Kalinga* sacrifice their lives in the war until the last man? How was it that Emperor Ashoka was not leading the war in the battlefield? He had to visit the battlefield to listen to the narration from a pathetic lady who lost all her male protectors (father, brother, husband and son). *Is this episode mythical? The drafting of this war portrays a celestial design. Buddhism thus created—was it done to benefit any race? If it had real substance, why did it not take root in the Indian subcontinent? Although Buddhism preaches non-violence and is totally against bloodshed, the states that follow the religion are mostly at war and prone to bloody genocidal acts.*

There is a clear account of Alexander's movement and his war history. But we do not find any clear history of Mauryan warfare, even Ashoka's *Kalinga War.* It is only stated as a drama. The real history of the war is not documented. There is an element of suspicion in this. Historians would have better answers for this. Ashoka embraced Buddhism and allowed it to spread all over the Mauryan Empire. Was Buddhism thus created and does it have its own story? Was it introduced to divert attention or create confusion into the society? After the decline of Buddhism in the Indian subcontinent, Jainism took over in prominence.

Sleazy Entry of Foreign Rulers: Sungas and Kanvas

After Ashoka, the Mauryan Empire started to decline. The last ruler of the Mauryan Empire was *Brihadratha Maurya* who did not rule for a long time due to the Brahminical influences; he was mesmerised in many ways during his rule. He is said to have had illegitimate relationships with many beautiful Aryan/Brahmin women. Thus, he was always under the opium of Brahminical passion. Finally, he met his end by the hand of his own comrade and confidant, Pushyamitra Sunga who was a member of the military personnel. It was he who assassinated Brihadratha Maurya during a military parade. Pushyamitra Sunga was a Brahmin belonging to a certain sect. This is how the foreign race of Aryans (Brahmins) began its rule in a small portion of Middle-Eastern India. The Sunga dynasty lasted almost one hundred years up to 75 BC. As assassination brought power to the Sunga dynasty, assassination also ended its rule. A minister under the Sunga regime, a Brahmin of a different sect, *Vasudeva Kanva*, assassinated the last Sunga ruler Devabhuti and came to power. The Kanva ruler lasted only for 40–45 years (75–30 BC). This is how the sect of different Brahmin rulers took power in a sleazy manner in various pockets of India. At first none of the local people were interested in general administration. Initially, the local Dravidians were not bothered about who was at the helm of governance as they had their own business to attend to. In fact they did not mind whether Rama was in governance or Ravana was in governance. Thus, the Brahmins were allowed to create a general administrative system in which they placed their own people in different administrative positions and created a cobweb of central administration under their jurisdiction. A different sect of Brahmins took over the entire administration under a central rule, which was under a self-governing federal rule under the local Dravidians. Being at the centre of power in administration, they could now cause and create troubles in various parts using strange methods and smother and suppress any section of the local people. The extent of the empire began to decline when ruled by the Sungas and subsequently the Kanvas. Then many offshoots of smaller kingdoms or rulers erupted due to differences with the Brahminical rule, and the local people did not accept being ruled by the Brahmins, an otherwise foreign race from the beginning. The Sungas and Kanvas while in rule established their people in governance and planted them in various fields of authority, as mentioned earlier. The later rulers including the Mughals made use of them for the same administrative purposes. During the course of Brahminical rule, a conflict of interest began to erupt between the Eurasian Brahmins, otherwise known as the Aryans and the Hellenistic Grecians. The Brahmins wanted to root out the Hellenistic influence from that region, and they succeeded. This is how the Brahmins continuously planted themselves in power. The Kanva dynasty fell to the Satavahana dynasty from Andhra Pradesh. They ruled up to 200 AD. But the kingdom was slowly getting fragmented into smaller kingdoms. During this period, a major conflict erupted between Hinduism against Buddhism, again created by the Brahmins. This caused some disturbance even in the Tamil Dravidian land, between 300 and 600 AD. In the same period, the Brahmins also turned against Jainism, which had taken importance during and after Ashoka's reign in North India. The Aryans or Brahmins did not stand any adversity against them; they wanted to be the masters of this beautiful continent by a crookish way. They saw to it that they would eliminate Jainism also. This is how it started to decline and could not spread. Slowly, Aryan Hinduism was proclaimed by the Brahmins and brought into their Vedas. They called themselves the Vedic people. How did they get such an idea to call themselves as Vedic people? Only God knows.

Dravidian Hospitality and Brahmin Misconception

The Dravidians built huge temples according to their own beliefs. Each of the Dravidians was linked to their own so-called gods known as Kula Theyvam, otherwise their ethnical god. Some of them are, namely *Ayyanar,*

Easaki, Mariamman, Kanniamma, Karumariamman, Muniessvaran, Gangaiamma and various others. Each Dravidian carried the name of the place they hailed from, then the ancestral name, followed by their god's name. Hence any Dravidian could be identified by their name itself and the place and sect he belonged to. The big temples were built by Dravidian kings and noblemen. As they consecrated the *Sanctum Sanctorum*, they invited the Brahmins for the services. Initially, the Brahmins were appointed for the cleaning and upkeep of the temples. This work was offered to them because they did not have any trade or work skill at hand. Their race was unfit for any type of hard work. They were rapacious talkers, both men and women. Therefore this job was apt and fit for only them. This is how they started maintaining the *Sanctum Sanctorum* and doing the *Poojas* and other rituals pertaining to temple worship. This is how they brought in their language into worship and stories which went on to mythological episodes. The local people and noblemen then allotted a secular place for them to stay near the temple. It was called *Agraharam* where only the Brahmins stayed. Their rituals were so complicated, that the other races did not want to mingle with them. The Brahmins took advantage of this and proclaimed themselves as untouchable and holier. Thereafter, no one could go near them or use their common passage. The restricted norms went on endlessly. As they were attached to the ruling class, they could formulate any kind of rules and have them enforced, just like in the medieval times. Their consolidation thus slowly crept in, differentiating society since Ashoka's time and continued even during the Jain period. But the Islamic rulers invaded and ruled India from 1200–1600 AD. However, prior to that, many raids had been made by them. During that time, many Brahmins got swept into Islam. This angered the main Brahmin nobles and priests. The animosity which had been built began to brood within the Brahmins against Islam. During the early period, conversion to another religion was done more out of convenience than conviction. Northern India was slowly getting raided by armies from Turkey and thus the Islamic influence began to creep into North India. In South India, there was a steady rule from the early BC days until the disturbance period of 300–600 AD when the three empires of Chera, Chola and Pandya were in constant struggle vying for hegemony to rule over the land, followed by the steady rule by the three Tamil kings. Then the Delhi sultanate attack took place in 1300 AD. After a short period of time, the Nayaks took over power in South India during 1300–1600 AD. Then, it got split into multiple smaller kingdoms. All this confusion was brought about by the Brahmins. The Tamil Dravidians always had managed to provide a steady rule. The Brahmins surgically brought about confusion by bringing in various religious forces from outside. Hence, until today, the Brahmins are hated in Tamil Nadu. Their atrocities which they had committed against the Dravidian people are immense, especially to the Tamilians. They always envied the wealth of the Tamil Dravidians. There is a steady decline in the presence of the Brahmins in Tamil Nadu. Now their migration to Delhi is still causing confusion in Tamil Nadu through central rule. The South Indian Brahmins, especially those from Kerala, who are in high bureaucratic positions, use their position as an opportunity to plot against the Tamilians and Tamil Nadu. For the past six decades they have been ruthlessly taking decisions against the Tamils being advisors to the governing body. This is how Tamil Nadu is supposed to share its natural and industrial wealth to the neighbouring states, while the neighbouring states will not provide the natural course of the river waters to flow through Tamil Nadu but rather waste that resource allowing it to flow into the sea. Most of the Tamilian areas have presently been handed over to various parts of Kerala, Karnataka and Andhra Pradesh. All of these injustices have been caused by the Brahmins against the Tamils. They are also using the intelligence agencies and the army to suppress the aspirations of the Sri Lankan Tamils; these are mainly done by the Brahmins, especially by those from Kerala, who are holding positions as prime minister, principal secretary, and other posts in high places. It is time that a local Tamilian takes over power of these prime positions to bring justice back to the Tamilians and fight for the cause of the Sri Lankan Tamils. When two Keralite fishermen were shot by the Italian marines, they were arrested and harassed by the Indian army and judiciary. Even some of the Americans were arrested for possession of arms and kept behind bars for a long time in a long-drawn legal battle. Although lengthy and prolonged representations have been put forth for the Indian fishermen for their safety, it appears to fall on the deaf ears of the central government because of the Brahminical bureaucracy, intelligence and army. This is a call for a change in the situation and placement of

Tamilians to represent them in high places, which is the utmost need of the hour, before further worsening the situation for the Indian and Sri Lankan Tamils.

Path Laid by Brahmins, Advent of Colonial Rule, Caste and Division

The Brahmins plotted to eliminate Islamic rule by playing into the hands of Europeans. This was the beginning of the advent of the Europeans and the colonial powers. First, the Romans established a commercial protectorate in Malabar. The Roman army was allowed to guard their business establishments at the same time that the Arabs also visited the Malabar Coast for trade. Prior to that, the Syrian soldiers were brought in to protect the Malabar king. They were the first foreign force to arrive in South India. Thus began the taste of India to the Western world soon after the Grecians and Aryans. The Dutch established the *East India Company* for trade during 1600–1820 AD. Then came the Danes, from 1620–1865 AD. They were all for trade and proclamation of the gospel. The Portuguese, with their maritime power, established settlements along the western coast, right along the seaside from 1510–1750 AD. They were mainly instrumental in bringing Catholicism to India, along with trade. The French started infiltration and settlement between 1765 and 1954 AD. They came for trade and colonisation. Then, the British took over the *East India Company* from the Dutch from 1757–1858 AD, and began it as a commercial protectorate. This is how the British army came to India. They landed in West Bengal and slowly made their way down to South India. The Aryans (Brahmins) were instrumental in bringing the colonial powers inside India having made a prior agreement with the colonial powers that they would act as intermediaries between the local people and them. Thus, the British Raj was established in India in the years 1858–1947 AD. The Indians were made slaves to the core by the British, through the Brahmins. The British formulated the *divide and rule policy,* creating conflict within the social fabric and destroyed the unity of the local people. The same method was used by Aryans from early times. Perhaps, this was a part of the tactics of the European or Western race. The Ambassadors used for these purposes were the Brahmins. They were sent out as messengers to manipulate and create caste divisions. Due to this, they started executing the dirty business for the British; they were given high positions in administration, rule, legal matters, revenue and other departments. The Brahmins would go to any extent to please the British or colonial powers. Thus they strengthened their positions in high places of governance. Such phenomena still exist in India. The sleaziness started with the arrival of the Brahmins and has not stopped even today. Thus the sickness caused to the society then, continues to remain in India.

The British were so nasty that they created different townships between them and the local people. There would be a white town, and after a buffer zone, a black town that would consist of the local people. This was the kind of difference shown by the British. Till today there are many bridges that are called *Black Bridges,* the name given by the British to divide the native people. Using the liberty granted by the British to their advantage, the Brahmins intensified their intent to look down upon the Dravidians. The classification of caste system was enforced by the Brahmins, assuming that they were the supernatural race and hence other races were untouchables to them. The Dravidians were then divided into three or four sub-castes, the lowest being totally outcast. This system of division never existed within the Dravidian culture. The caste division was encouraged by the British, which helped the Aryans to literally play masters to all the native Dravidians. The *British Raj* was the worst period in modern India. The Dravidians were treated menially by the Brahmins. The Dravidian ladies were not allowed to wear blouses. They just had to drape a cloth over their upper bodies. They could not use slippers either. Such were atrocities of the Brahmins. The whole scenario was overlooked by the British. The British ruled India directly through the *Viceroy of India* who represented the British monarchy. Was there any respect to Indians? A big, NO. Did we share anything in common? Again, NO! Should we have anything in common with them? NO. Then why do we have COMMONWEALTH, associating with them and following their parliamentary system. A lot of unanswered questions! I would say that the Dravidians were ripped off by the Europeans in many ways. But the wealth lost would always revert back to us in some way or the other. Hence, we always look towards the future with no apprehensions.

Hinduism of Dravidians and Brahmanism of Aryans

The Dravidians had their own pattern of worship; they were really devoted in their worship to their almighty, which was classified as the Six-Fold Religion (*Saivism, Vaishnavaism, Saktham, Gowmaram, Kanapathyam and Sowram*). This did not possess a name called Hinduism; rather it carried sections as either Saivism and Vaishnavaism.

The Brahmins or Aryans did not have any religion or culture but had a different methodology of worship with pretensions to draw the Dravidians into their fold. Hence they created a religion and called it Aryan Hinduism. The Aryans later merged the Dravidian worship of the six-fold religion, and unified it under a common religion, and called it 'Hinduism'. Hence, there was a Dravidian Hinduism quite separate from Aryan Hinduism, which was a fake creation. And although the Aryans (Brahmins) had their own Hinduism, all the temples were built by Dravidians only. Whichever idol (god) was kept inside by the Dravidians was proclaimed by the Aryans to be an avatar of Vishnu or Shiva, which would automatically come under Brahma (the Aryan's god) who would be Brahmins themselves. Whereas the Brahmins themselves are always at war with each other, particularly between the Vaishnavites and Shivites; thus the Aryans were ever confused among themselves and they also confused others. Anyone can identify the various differences in the worship pattern to various gods in *Tamil Nadu, Kerala, Andhra, Karnataka, Orissa, West Bengal and so on.* While the Maharashtra gives importance to Ganapathi, West Bengal gives importance to Durga, Tamil Nadu gives importance to Murugan and Perumal. It only carries the common religious name. We also do not find temple for Brahma. Hence, Hinduism can be classified as a *Congress of Religions,* and their faith is not directed towards one god.

Tamil Excellence Subjugated by Brahmanism

I find in Tamil literature one of the classical secular gifts to mankind. Such a literature has never been written in any other language and anywhere in the world. *Tirukkural* is a two-line verse where all human aspirations are discussed and answered in 1330 couplets and 133 chapters. After the Bible, this is the best circulated reading matter around the world. The other high classical literatures from Tamil are awesome. *They are Tolkappiyam, Thandi Alangaram, Nannul, Chilapathikaram, Manimegalai, Ramayanam and Mahabharatham.* The Dravidian Tamils with their rich heritage never blew their own trumpets like the Aryans or the others. The Mahabharata, claimed to be a so-called Aryan epic, was written by *Vysaya Munivar.* It was translated into Tamil by *Sri Villiputhuraar Azhwar.* The Ramayana, another epic, was written by *Valmiki Munivar,* who was said to originally have been a hunter. *Kambar* translated that into Tamil, and *Tulasi* into Hindi. I have a feeling all these above mentioned writers were of Dravidian race because only the Dravidians, especially the Tamils had advanced expressional powers and ability. I have heard people tell me the Tamil version of the Mahabharata and Ramayana has much better expressions in Tamil than in the original version. It helps me to visualise the richness of the Tamil language. But I emphasise while Hinduism is a congress of religions, it should not be taken as a unified religion for the whole of India. It is a clear promotional factor by Aryans. The Mahabharata and Ramayana are only mythological epics. Let experts ponder over this subject much more.

Reckless and Callous Attitude by the Colonial Powers

I have expressed contempt with various racial discriminations that the Dravidian race had historically undergone for a long period of time under the excuse of some race being superior by colour and complexion. I have empathically stressed the point that the Dravidians were well composed, superior in intelligence, contentment, scientific advancement in all fields, and having linguistically parented all the languages that would arise from this main source. The obnoxious attitudes of the Aryans (Brahmins) and the Europeans (British) have already been discussed. The British and the Aryans usurped the treasures of the Dravidians, especially from the Tamils to claim it as their own, in a most slimy and sleazy methods. And history was written to make these treasures of the Dravidian abilities as their own. They created an artificial imbroglio syndrome in the midst of the Dravidians to achieve their goal. While the so-called European and Aryan race claim to be saints and ascetics and an upright race, beneath their holy garments, they possess the most evil designs within themselves. This deplorable and redundant attitude against the upright, straight and frank race has been very shameful to mankind's history. These kinds of racist attitudes should be eradicated from the modern world.

Varnashrama Dharma: A Vedic Blueprint

As per my analysis, racism started in the world by the Aryans with Varnashrama Dharma in 900 AD. The ancient Aryans lay dormant as far as their political action, from early days until the ninth century AD. Varnam (வர்ணம்) means colour, Dharmam (தர்மம்) means charity, but for Brahmins' charity Shrama Dharmam (சிரம தர்மம்) means self-indulgence. This philosophy was sneaked into the Europeans and Western race, which brought about chaos to the entire African, South American and Asian races, which when unleashed upon them resulted in their slavery. As a result, the slave trade began to flourish within the European race. Until today, the entire world is paying for the brunt of the past mistakes of our human race. I suddenly find the Aryans slowly withdrawing the claim of Aryanship for the last four decades in India. Even when I was a young boy, the Brahmins used to proclaim they were Aryans, thereby claiming a special position. Varnashrama Dharma thus introduced, brought about caste segregation. Brahmins, the fairer coloured race were to be considered the topmost race and the lesser coloured race would be classified into four or five lesser grades as per their skin colour. While this difference in colour and caste never prevailed among the Dravidians. Very many righteous, noble and intellectual Dravidian men were utterly black in colour, but that did not mean they were of a lower caste.

Chaos Creation by Brahmins, Cry for Dravidian Leadership, Unfortunate Language Myth

The Indian National Congress during the time of independence was flooded with Brahmins and they were the main players in authority. They always wanted to dethrone and place the Dravidians in the background, especially the Tamils. Even during the selection of the national language when the voting was done, the House voted on equal terms. *Then President Rajendra Prasad* from a neutral chair opted to take up the position favouring Hindi to be the national language.

While I find Tamil is a wonderful language with life that parented many languages, it is not given the importance it deserves; it is almost 7,000 years old, and Hindi being a mixture of languages had been in existence for only 200 years. This question needs to be answered. I find *Rajaji*, a Brahmin from Tamil Nadu, even tried to introduce Hindi into Tamil Nadu in 1937. Those who had come to survive in Tamil Nadu and do not respect Tamil should leave the state and live somewhere else.

I find a lot of injustice has been done during independence and the formation of India as a country. Many states were not represented properly in the constitution. In my opinion we should not have had the parliamentary system like the British. Rather, we should have chosen a federal system of self-governance for each state. It was the Brahmins at the helm who took the power from British to enslave all the other races under them just as the British had done. This enslavement was endorsed by the British themselves. If a Dravidian had been given the power to rule, India, Pakistan and Bangladesh may not have split into different nations. A Dravidian would have seen that peace and tranquility were maintained in the entire country, including the regions of *Kashmir, Baluchistan, Afghanistan* and right up to Iran. Peace would have prevailed like it did in the good old days of the Indus Valley period, before the advent of the Aryan infiltration. Lanka would have been included, as part of the wider Indian nation. This is my assertive assumption. Nehru, a Kashmiri pundit of the Aryan race (Brahmin), developed only Delhi and fed the Brahmins to the brim. The peace and honeymoon period was thoroughly wasted. The imbalance, inequality that was created by the Brahmins in authority in Delhi induced frustration among all other places except Delhi. This was the root cause for all troubles and future conflicts. Till today the problems addressed are ruthlessly put down under the shadow of Indian rule. Many issues are still brewing in various parts of the country. As proper recognition and share of wealth are not distributed equally, local voices are never heard. I am sure a prudent Dravidian ruler would have set such matters straight had he been given the authority in administration by getting rid of all the Brahmins from the helm of decision making. Thus we could have saved our motherland from all foreign forces that have sneaked in and destroyed the local society thus far.

Marauding Aryans with Manu Sastra

Initially, the Aryans did not have any particular religion. The foreigners who came to India with religion were only the *Syrian Christians, European Christians, Muslims,*

Zoroastrians and *Israelites*. The Aryans thus came, divided themselves initially into two groups, *Sungas* and *Kanvas*, which subsequently split into many groups as per the region of their settlement. They were instrumental in bringing in more foreign powers into India, to make matters worse for the Dravidians. The worst of the infiltration was a race of Huns who were ruthless in their approach. Their main purpose was massacre. All these foreign forces joined together and created a *manu sastra* or code of practice to be strictly followed as per the caste system, which was formed out of *Varnashrama Dharma*. Violation would be met with severe punishment worse even than the present *Sharia Law*. The native Dravidian Indians observed non-violence and were very religious in their beliefs with the practice of either *Buddhism* or *Shaivism* or *Vaishnavism* or *Jainism* or whatever nature worship they practiced, all of which teach non-violence. They tolerated all the sufferings, tortures, and were even murdered, cruelly rendered to them by the foreign forces. The influences of the Sungas and Kanvas got embedded into whichever ruling class succeeded in subjugating the Dravidians constantly, even till today. Now the local voices have began to flare out and representation is slowly emerging to the local people. All these atrocities committed by the foreign forces were endorsed and encouraged by the British, while in rule.

Advaita, Aham Brahmasmi (I am God)

The Brahmins, after subjugating the Dravidians, brought in the Advaita philosophy, which was promoted by Adi Sankara, an Aryan purohit. The Brahmins who did not have any religion of their own brought in the six-fold religion of the Dravidians—which are Shaivism, Vaishnavism, Saktham, Gowmaram, Kanapathya and Sowram—and brought them into one fold under the guise of the Brahman concept, which was to be controlled by the Brahmins. This concept is currently known as the Hindu religion. Thus, the Hindu religion was a creation tailor made to suit and keep the Brahmins at the helm of affairs. Adi Sankara proclaimed Aham Brahmasmi under the Advaita philosophy, which is said to mean 'I am God' or 'I am Brahma'. This is the reason why there are no temples for Brahma, which means under Hinduism, the six-fold religion of the Dravidians should only worship the Brahmins as God. Thus, the Advaita philosophy that advocates the practice of 'Manu Dharma' stringently aims to keep and subjugate the Dravidians and their six-fold religious practice under 'Aham Brahmasmi' so that the Dravidians would always be under control of the Brahmins and worshipping them as God eternally. This practice culminated with support from the British rulers during their period of reign. Only the Brahmins enforced these norms to eternally subjugate the Dravidians.

Misfortune of the Dravidians

As an enlightened Dravidian, I have always wondered at the authenticity and originality of the names given to our country. According to my findings, the original name was Sindh, a word which belongs to the language of the Persians who had migrated to our land. At the same time, Grecian and other influences also prevailed in the land, due to trade. These influences erased the original name of the country and changed it to Indus Valley, a combination of both Persian and Greek influences. This civilisation belongs to the Dravidians and the Tamils, especially the Pandya Dynasty. Various researches are underway to get to the root of the actual history by scholars like Gene D. Matlock. In the same way, the Indukush and other corresponding titles have also migrated from Persia, Arabia and Greece. In later years, these slangs conveniently got changed into the common title of India and Hindus. It was the British and the Europeans through the East India Company who fixed and propagated the names India and Hindu to rule them under one fold with the help of the Aryans.

Aghoris: A Sect of Aryans

It is known that among the early Europeans, there were cannibals too. As the Eurasian Aryan race had come from Europe, it induced a suspicion in my mind that the Aryans could also have been cannibals! I find to my surprise a sect of Brahmins who are called Aghoris who perform witchcraft and who carry skulls and other human body parts hanging around them. These are said to endow them with tantric powers to control nature, cure diseases, etc. This fantasy myth was created by them just to disorient the innocent people living around their area. They normally live near or around cremation centres. They have temples in Varanasi and Kasi. These Sadhus live in these areas on the bank of the river Ganga. It was my opinion that although the Brahmins are strict vegetarians, there may also be some sect very different from that.

Ambedkar's Insight

Book Reference: *Aryans, Jews, Brahmins: Theorising Authority through Myths of Identity* by Dorothy M. Figueira

The Aryans were steeped in the worst kind of debauchery of a social, religious and spiritual nature. The rampant moral decay (Ambedkar, 1979–90: 3.153) of this degraded society manifested itself in their devotion to human sacrifice and genital worship (Ambedkar 1987: 4.294). They indulged in high-stake gambling (Ambedkar, 1987: 3.168; 4.108; 4.295) and were given over to drinking and beef-eating (Ambedkar, 1987: 3.157; 4.111). Even their women indulged in drunken excesses (Ambedkar, 1987: 3.154; 3.169; 4.109; 4.295). The Aryan society was also steeped in sexual immorality (Ambedkar, 1987: 4.229); the Aryans engaged in polyandry, polygamy (Ambedkar, 1987: 4.229), and even incest (Ambedkar, 1987: 3.155; 3.171; 4.109; 4.298). They routinely performed sexual acts in public (Ambedkar, 1987). They shared (Ambedkar, 1987) and rented out their women for sex or as breeding stock (Ambedkar, 1987). Bestiality was prevalent (Ambedkar, 1987). The Aryan society was predicated upon class and social degradation (Ambedkar, 1987: 3.170). Sacrifice, providing a setting for revelry, drunkenness, gambling and sexual promiscuity, showcased the Aryan carnage and debauchery (Ambedkar, 1987: 3.175). When humans were sacrificed, the Aryans indulged in cannibalism. When they sacrificed animals, as in the *asvamedha*, they committed bestiality (Ambedkar, 1987: 3.174).

Ambedkar claimed that this was the reality of the Aryan world and the ideal towards which high-caste reformers aspired.

Ambedkar's Judgement

Ambedkar judged the Aryan religion to be a mass of sacrificial, social, political and sanitary rules possessing no universal value. He deemed that what the Hindus called religion was nothing but an iniquitous code of ordinances (Ambedkar, 1979: 1.75–76) supporting a class ethic that inspired no loyalty to ideals and deprived its adherents of moral freedom and spontaneity. Moreover, he maintained that the Aryan religion was without spiritual content and supported by a canon saturated with evil and wicked thoughts. In the *Rig Veda*, the Aryans did not pray for forgiveness of sins or deliverance from evil. Instead, they praised Indra for killing the pregnant wives of their enemies and otherwise bringing destruction to their foes. As the Aryan religion was never concerned with the righteous life (Ambedkar, 1987: 3.175–6), *it should be destroyed.* It had never ever been a religion, but rather a compendium of laws in dire need of an amendment or even abolition (Ambedkar, 1987:1.76).

Ambedkar also challenged the racial portrayal of the Aryans that depicted them as a fair race with sharp noses as compared with the *Dasa/Dasy* who were believed to be dark-complexioned and flat-nosed. In modern times, the Dasa has been identified with the *shudra* and aboriginal tribe. Ambedkar claimed that the philological evidence of keeping the racial myth alive was as spurious as the Western equation of *varna* with colour. Rather than Muller's reading of *anasa as a-nasa*, without a nose (that is, flat-nosed), Ambedkar sided with Sayana's reading of *an-asa*, signifying devoid of good speech (Ambedkar, 1990: 7.76). He maintained that the Veda had been consistently misread by Brahmin scholars in a racial sense, in order to foster a two-nation theory that benefitted their interests. With the Brahmins as the representatives of the Aryans and the low castes seen as non-Aryans, the Brahmins could foster both their hegemonic power over their brethren as well as kinship with the Europeans. Ambedkar found no evidence that the term *Aryan* was used in the *Rig Veda* in a racial sense. The Dasas were as civilised and powerful as the Aryans (Ambedkar, 1990: 7.105). He did not read any racial distinction between the Aryan and the Dasa, because there are numerous instances in the *Rig Veda* where the *Dasas* become Aryans. Similarly, there is no evidence that the Aryans were a different colour from the *Dasas* (Ambedkar, 1987: 7.85).

Advocate for Aryan Hinduism

Bal Gangadhar Tilak, a stalwart of the Indian National Congress who was a Brahmin by origin, was instrumental in centralising the Aryan Hindutuva across India. He wanted Aryan Hindutuva to be nationalised and that it should become a national religion, while the Dravidian Hindutuva had their own code for the six-fold religion of worshipping their own god. The Aryans or Brahmins wanted to converge the

Dravidian six-fold religion into 'Aham Brahmasmi' by which the Brahmin himself should be worshipped as the *Dravidian's god.*

Mistaken Liberation

Although Gandhi's liberation struggle ended in India's independence from the British, the subsequent irony that is regrettable is that we were sold to Brahmin rules under Nehru. He was a Brahmin of Kashmiri Pandit origin with the name of the Gandhi dynasty, heavily influenced by the Brahmin community. Most of the bureaucrats were orthodox Brahmins who were bent on taking decisions against the local Dravidians and suppressing them with sops. It was a non-Brahmin who brought free primary education to a section of the people, which brightened up the entire section of the Dravidian community in South India, where the literary percentage has gone up very high. Brahmins (Aryans) do not seem to match their intelligence. Even street children seem to shine in their education much easier without any support! Such is the natural intelligence of the local people who had been suppressed for over two thousand years by the Brahmins. The entire section of the northern part of India, including parts of the east and west, has to catch up on this front, a lot more. I am sure the present central leadership, although they follow Hindutuva, would play a much more fair role in the distribution of knowledge power to the downtrodden and lower castes which had been denied or unexposed to knowledge for centuries.

Need of the Hour: Ratification of Injustices

The present Dravidian leadership in India should change the inequality status. Although the previous government called itself to be secular rulers without any impetus towards religion, the rule was secular only for the Brahmins and was used for their sole benefit. *Thank God* it is over. Under the rule of the previous government, the Brahmins were allowed to eat of the fat of the land. All the atrocities and corruptions were instigated only through the Brahmins at the helm. Like the Sungas and Kanvas, they created a cobweb especially the Keralite Brahmins for the employment of their own people in all the key positions such as the railways, army, and Delhi secretariat places, and all over central rule! They have placed themselves even in private companies, which they enter in a sleazy manner and flood it with their own people. Even in world bodies, they have infiltrated on a large scale! Awareness of these aspects should come so that power and position are distributed to all people who are worthy to hold it, in fairness and a lot more dedication. Here, I should mention that the Aryans, for more than two thousand years suppressed the indigenous Dravidians without making any move towards improvement of their knowledge. Due to the fact that they were in power or in administration, they took this opportunity to educate only the Brahmins. All the scholarship, support and aid were given only to the Brahmins. While they claim themselves to be god as Brahma, their epics gave importance only to males as god. There was not much of respect given to the women goddesses. Even *Sita* had to go through a fire walk to prove herself. In the Mahabharata *Draupathi* was disgraced in front of all the men. However, on the other hand, the Dravidians gave great respect to their goddesses, be it for wealth, learning, or power. The Brahmins even did not allow the Dravidians to worship goddess Saraswathi, who is a goddess for learning and the giver of all wisdom. Such were the atrocities committed by the Brahmins, which was overlooked by the British. Hence with the misuse of power, the Brahmins who were in administration mesmerised, subjugated the Dravidians, and servility in its utmost crude form was forced upon the graceful indigenous Dravidians.

Women as Non-entities under Brahmanism

You will find detailed facts about the Brahmin's (Aryan's) attitude towards women under the title *Women in Indo-Aryan Society*.

Aryan-Hinduism is said to be the most oppressive system on record in its suppression of women, from conception to death.

Child Marriage: Girls are to be married even when 5 years old!

Dowry: Vedas prescribe this practice.

Bride-Burning: If the dowry is insufficient. No Property for women.

Mass Wife-Burning (Jauhar): Often 100s are burnt at a time.

Widow-Burning (Sati): Sanctioned by the Vedas and Puranas, and practiced by Krishna's wives; it still continues.

Female Infanticide: The general Vedic attitude towards women is large dowries as prescribed by the Vedas, which meant that a girl was seen as a burden. When a woman gives birth to a daughter, which is shameful, infanticide came about as a convenient way of getting rid of the burden of the girl child.

Source:(http://www.geocities.com/Athens/Agora/4229/in3.htm):

Holy Aryan Texts Sanction all these Customs

Child Marriage: Daughters should be married even at the tender age of 5–6 years. This was the common custom to avoid dowry scandals. But dowry was an essential factor. Vedic law prescribes one-third of the man's age to be age for women to marry a man. Thus, a 5-year-old girl would marry a 15-year-old man, and 20-year-olds would marry 60-year-olds, and 30-year-olds would marry 90-year-olds as per the Aryan's Vedas. This is why the beautiful Brahmin girls whom I have ever known did not marry at all, though they were well-educated, intelligent, good looking, sociable and generously graced with voluptuous looks and salacious expression.

Bride-Burning: The Vedic law bids a bride pay ransom to marry a suitable man of that community. Such was the status of women in the Brahmin or Aryan community. They were considered a burden. Although they reasonably satisfied all norms in human relations, the men and their Vedic priests demanded a ransom to be brought as dowry. The demand would extend to the last moment of the marriage ceremony and if that target of ransom was not met, the bride could even be burnt alive by the family that she was married into in a stage-managed accident. Such tragedies happen even today.

To my surprise, as I had expressed earlier, the laws of the Brahmins and their Vedas were purely oriented to appease the Brahmin men only. That is why a Brahmin priest can perform all the rituals connected to worship and commit any indulgence. There would be no questions asked. The women were treated as tools and slaves for the priest's merriment. I cannot quote all the statements and the laws stated in the Vedas except a few in a nutshell.

1. Wife-Burning
2. Jauhar and Saka or Self-immolation of women
3. Witch-Burning
4. Witch-Burning—Vedic Dark Ages
5. Widow-Burning (Sati)

Many more punishments were enforced on the women as per Vedic law. This list goes on endlessly.

Poor Vedic women being treated as slaves in subjection to their men and by their priest, but the irony was that these norms were superficially enforced on the local Dravidian people as well. While the Aryans (Brahmins) wanted to treat them as slaves and oppress them, they also mercilessly ill-treated them. Such were the atrocities of the Brahmins, unheard of in human history; but sadly endorsed by the European colonial powers, especially the British.

Dravidian Shaivism

Dravidian women enjoyed much greater freedom than their Aryan counterparts.

Repression and Perversions: Incest

Due to the strict restrictions and regulations, one revolting practice set in, something more predominant in Aryan society than in any other in the world: *incest*. Often the girls were unwilling, but were then forced by their brothers/fathers.

References abound even in the Rg Veda, showing that the perversion of brother-sister relationship was introduced by the Aryans:

Pushan is the lover of his sister (Rg Ved VI.55.4) (Apte 11).

Agni is the lover of his own sister (Rg Ved X.3.3) (Apte 11).

The Ashvins are referred to as the sons of Savitar and Ushas who are brother and sister (Apte 11).

The Ashvins married Surya and Savitri who is their sister (RV I.116.19).

Agni is the son of his father and his sister (Rg Ved I.91.7).

Yama wards off his sister Yami, saying marriage between brother and sister is forbidden (R.V.X.10) (Apte 11).

Father-daughter incest occurs in the famous story of Prajapati (later identified with Brahma, in turn incorporated as an incarnation of Vishnu) and his daughter (RV III.31.1–2). However, this was punished. Prajapati is thought to have done something wrong, and he was pierced by Agni as a punishment (Sat. Br. XIII.9) (Apte 63).

It is evident that the strict laws on male-female relations led to the repression of normal practices and the rise of various perversions like brother-sister incest, father-daughter incest, etc. Even to this day, incest of varying degrees (cross-cousin, father-daughter, mother-son, brother-sister, etc.) is extremely common amongst the Indo-Aryans. No other race on earth has ever recorded such a prevalence of this practice. Just as sodomy has its home in Persia, lesbianism in ancient Lesbos, so incest has its home amongst the Indo-Aryans.

Redemption for Women

The findings of the attitudes of the Aryans (Brahmins) towards their own women and the endorsement by the colonial powers, especially the British, sadden me deeply. The revelation of the sufferings of the Aryan or Brahmin ladies under their own men is distressing and disgusting. Although for many decades I had heard of such ill-treatment prevalent in the Aryan community, it is only now that the intensity of those malpractices is being felt by me and my fellow citizens throughout India. This attitude has poisoned the mind of some of the Dravidian men who also indulge in these atrocities, including rape and murder. I am of the school of thought that if a sect of the menfolk cannot accommodate or deal with their women with respect, they should be deemed as animals or savages. Recently in North India, many cases of rape and abuse of women were brought out by the press. When represented by many women groups and other parties, the men in authority in high places judicially justified the actions of the men. These people are of low repute. I am sure this culture would change under Dravidian rule where women would be treated with a lot more respect and honour.

Recklessness of the East India Company and the British

I had also mentioned about the reckless behaviour of the colonial powers, especially the British, endorsing the atrocities by the Aryans and advocating and offering status in prime places. In this way, the British had used historians, scholars and writers and paid the publishing and advertising companies in support of Aryan caste, using taxpayers' money through the *East India Company*. This company was started by the Dutch who also had the same views as the British in suppressing the Dravidians. When they left, the major publishing, media and other industrial houses were left as assets to the Aryans or Brahmins only. Till today most of the national publishing and media establishments are under the Aryans or Brahmins.

Max Müller and Sanskrit

To cite an example of the promotional attitude of the British towards the Brahmins, a German scholar, *Friedrich Max Müller* (1816–1900), whose intention was to advocate Aryanism in Europe and America could not carry out his work there. Hence he chose to work in Britain. He was sent by the British to India to study Sanskrit and promote Aryanism through the East India Company. As I had mentioned earlier, a part of the Aryan race had settled in Austria. *Friedrich Max Müller* could have been the offspring of that race. I also find in certain sections of *Britain, America* and *some European countries,* especially *Scandinavia,* a wide section of Aryan or anti-Semitic people still exist. *Joseph Arthur Comte de Gobineau (1816–1882), a French aristocrat and novelist, wrote about the theory of the Aryans as a master race in his book 'An Essay on the Inequality of the Human Races'.* He enlarged upon the superiority of the white race. He even divided Europe based on skin colour. This could have been the beginning of anti-Semitism in the mid-nineteenth century, which Europe was trying to bring about harmony. Many Asian and African races had amply supported this cause. Greed started setting in among the Europeans. Consequently, Aryanism spread within the European race in many parts of Europe. This philosophy ingrained in *Friedrich Max Müller* from the beginning. *Max Müller, a German-born Philologist and Orientalist lived and studied in Britain.* He was deeply influenced by *Comte de Gobineau*'s theory of the Aryans as a master race. This fuelled his passion to study Sanskrit, for the mastery of which he spent most of his life. His philosophy centred around his own views on Aryanism.

Anti-Semitism

The Eurasians or Aryans migrated more than two thousand years ago into the Indian subcontinent and had been creating confusion and disillusion among the native Dravidians in various ways to take over their possession. They won support and encouragement from the British, Europeans and *Max Müller.* Like *Max Müller,* various other faculties and publishing, promoting and different media houses were used by the *East India Company* for the benefit of the Aryans under the *British Raj*. Though the *Max Müller Bhavan* had been set up in Chennai, India, I really cannot understand why *Max Müller* did not undertake any study on the Dravidians and Tamils. Was he too blind only to see Brahmanism and Sanskrit in the form of Aryanism? On the other hand, *Rev. Robert Caldwell* had done intensive study on the Dravidian language and Dravidinism including the Tamils. His conclusion had been that the Dravidians are Semitic with Semitic language, hence he had been under persecution by the Aryans or Brahmins for many centuries. *Francis Whyte Ellis*, who was a civil servant under the British, had also undertaken immense study on Tamil and other related Dravidian languages and seemed to endorse *Robert Caldwell*'s theory of the uniqueness of the Dravidian language group. *Abbe Dubois*, a French scholar, had undertaken research on the Dravidian origin and its language and he found the Dravidian language to be one of the most ancient languages, contradicting *Max Müller*'s theory completely. The world should play a major role in support of the liberation of Tamils under the Singhalese and stop the carnage and persecution that the poor Tamils had hitherto undergone. Under *Varnashrama Dharma*, slavery and colour segregation were professed to the world by the Brahmins (Aryans). *Racism* was brought in support of *Neo-Nazism* by the Aryans in the form of anti-Semitic attitude with justification. Hence all evil got distributed to the world by the Aryans or the Brahmins.

Injustice to Native Dravidian Languages

I am sad that the Tamil language has not got the deserved recognition under the Indian system, though it is notably more than 7,000 years old, whereas Hindi is only two hundred years old. This is again a misfortune brought about by the Aryans. With due respect to *Rabindranath Tagore*, the national anthem was written in Bengali, which is only 600 years old. Still the centralised effect of the *British Raj* remains with a main section of Indians who can converse and write English fluently as well as any Englishman would do. I find even English is an evolved language from the *Anglo-Saxon language group*, which is only 1,400 years old. During this period, due to colonisation, it has spread its wings far and wide, presently being smothered in all directions by all linguistic groups. With system application and style of communication, it is losing its charm. Its heyday of literary profundity is over. Now it is being butchered in many ways. At this rate, I imagine that this language also would disappear. It is being distorted by the misuse of vocabulary, as in all computing, medical and other applications in short, STEM *(Science, Technology, Engineering and Mathematics)*. The worst part is the digital short form and code communications. Could any language survive this onslaught? So, it is my speculation, if ever we completely lose English to Globlish as recorded by *Guardian Newspapers (2014)*, we may lose English once for all, like *Sanskrit, Pali* and *Latin*.

Aliens' Interaction Invitation

The surviving ancient languages till today have been *Egyptian, Sumerian, Persian, Chinese* and *Tamil.* These languages could have been spoken or used by the aliens in outer space. Hence if you want to communicate with some surviving civilisations out there, it would be prudent to send signals or communications through these languages only. There may be a chance to get a reply from alien civilisations, who are said to trade and traverse within themselves all around our cosmos. Hence it would be sensible to store all science, engineering, mathematics and other important relevant data in old languages like *Egyptian, Sumerian, Hebrew, Prakrit, Persian, Chinese and Tamil.*

Uniqueness of Tamil Dravidian

I find that the Dravidians always possessed natural intelligence. Even today, they are proving themselves to be great and profound in all fields. They participate in all research and exploration, including space. In the field of computing, *Pillai,* who created e-mail, is a Tamil Dravidian and many of the Silicon Valley topnotchers are Dravidians. In recent years, all spell bee competitions in the *United States* are being won by South Indians (Dravidians only). Hence the Dravidian intelligence is an established fact.

Intellectual Property and Intelligence Assets

While the West claims intellectual property rights and other findings of ours as theirs and also have patent rights over them, I must stress that for the last five decades our intelligentsia have been taken over by the *West* by luring youngsters with fancy lifestyles, resulting in our brain drain. While we invest our assets in educating our offspring equipping them for scientific innovations, they become assets for the Western world. While they give their hard work and earn well, pay taxes for the benefit of the *West*, we have become victims here, being sucked out of our assets in a subtle way. We are never compensated for this by the *West*. While they make a great deal in improving their economy, we are left to lag behind. The world body has to give attention to these factors.

If the West did not apply sleaziness to take away our possession through various means, including infiltration of the Aryan race into our society and manipulating through the East India Company to strip out our assets working along with the Dravidian race to share our talents and excellence, the world would have been better organised with more harmony and more riches for all mankind to share.

Civic and Social Norms

I find that the West and the Europeans give much priority to civic order and discipline. Their governance preaches allegiance to their country but does not attach much importance to social norms. This has resulted in the development of the potential of the individual outside the social frame, resulting in a detachment of the individual from society. That is the reason why a lot of social networking platforms are available and highly saleable in these modern days, out of a desperate craving for social affinity. The Asian and other communities give priority to social and family norms. They believe in sharing and caring. While these factors ensure more peace and harmony, they lag behind in monetary enrichment. They also lack civic sense and civic norms, which creates disorder among them. Hence *I would advocate a judicious mixture of family ties and civic sense, one complementing the other, thereby enriching the human race with a blend of both love and care, and a better social order.* On this note, I proceed on to my personal persona.

A SALUTE TO THE PATHFINDERS

As I embarked on my assignment, I was unsure how I would convey my thoughts, but now that I have reached the concluding part, I wonder to what extent I have succeeded in fulfilling my mission.

Now, going back to the later decades of the twentieth century, which was the golden era for all our good friends, I would mention that the best of movies ever produced had come out during this period—whether *classical, biblical, action, adventure, comedy, crime, erotica, fantasy, historical, horror, mystery, paranormal, philosophical, political, realistic, romance, slice of life* or *thriller*. All these inputs gave us a little more insight and adequate preparation for our future. Here I would cite a few lines of a lyric from the popular movie *Sound of Music* was sung by *Julie Andrews*:

> *Perhaps I had a wicked childhood*
> *Perhaps I had a miserable youth*
> *But somewhere in my wicked, miserable past…*
> *So somewhere in my youth or childhood*
> *I must have done something good…*

The song goes on.

I feel the intuition to write this book could be the result of having done something good in the past and with it something bad in my youth or my childhood.

To present a little narration of my past, I had to take a deep breath for some introspection. As a result,

I want to briefly mention about my origin, nativity, ancestry and community that I belong to, and the deep-rooted culture and the way of life I had inherited from my venerable forefathers. This epilogue presents the closing remarks pertaining to our travel, the enlightened inspiration, the personal relationship we had developed with various unknown fellow travellers and people we met, the lessons we learned from other parts of the world, and the opportunities to probe into history and many issues that affect the present world. Regarding these issues, I have expressed my concern for our nation and civilisation with deep regret.

Our ancestry can be traced back to the harsh and horrid land of *Nazareth* in *Tirunelveli District, Tamil Nadu,* where the soil acts as a blotting element, resulting in the rain water getting sucked inside. Where the soil is said to be enriched with titanium, the land is so dry and parched that only Palmyra tree (panai maram) and Babool tree (karuvela maram) can survive. The stub roots beneath (branch roots) are so spread out that they are able to retain the soil from erosion or becoming dust. Everything that comes from the Palmyra tree is useful; from the leaf to the root. The toddy, popularly known as *pathaneer,* if taken fresh from the tree in the mornings, is sweet and healthy with ample calcium and minerals. The beauty lies in sipping it from the leaf of the Palmyra tree, which is offered to you in the form of a cute little boat-shaped bowl. The toddy is brought down from the top of the tree by the Palmyra climbers. The jaggery (karuppatti), which is made from the Palmyra juice is sweet and can be used even by diabetic patients in place of sugar. The *fans* (visiri) made out of the dried Palmyra leaf are such a luxury, gifting free breeze when electricity fails us so miserably, particularly during summer. The fruit from the tree (*panampalam*) is so delicious and rich in vitamins and minerals. You can find the old and the young walking under these trees in the mornings just for the heck of it though they offer no shade! Even the stem of a dead Palmyra tree is used to make furniture and the leaf is wound to make mats and coir for cushions; even the timber is used for roofing material and for other construction purposes. Thus, no part of the tree is wasted, whether it is dead or alive.

Originally we were Palmyra tree climbers. The learning we got from our ancestors regarding ascent and descent of climbing trees is remarkable—while you climb up a Palmyra tree, you always look up; while climbing down, you also have to look up. Needless to stress, we are a race that looks up always and thus our heritage has been always being progressive, towards vision and mission beyond. We never set permanent goalposts, taught by our ancestry. We never bend our back, we are always upright and straight; there is no slyness and sleaziness—that's why I believe the Lord Jesus chose us and segregated us with a purpose. Towards that perspective, I am going to present the concluding chapter.

I was born on 6 July 1951 to a well-refined, organised, orthodox Anglican Christian family exercising all the religious rituals meticulously. Such was the order and discipline of our community. I was baptised in the *Anglican St. John's Church in Nazareth, Tamil Nadu, South India,* under SPG (Society for Propagating the Gospel) tradition. The church has become a cathedral now. My father wanted to name me *Nimrod* after the great skilful enthusiastic hunter, a descendant from

Noah, while my paternal grandmother was adamant to baptise me as *Yeshurun* from the Bible, which means 'the most upright', and I am happy and proud of her decision! Since my birth, I have conformed to orthodox Anglican religious rituals like attending church both morning and evening, saying prayers regularly, memorising Bible verses and prayers, including famous hymns. Such is the background I belong to, and to which I owe all my respect and adoration for my ancestors.

In the religious sphere, the first missionaries to arrive in *Nazareth* were the London missionaries. When the London Missionary Society was formed in the eighteenth century as an interdenominational body for spreading the gospel, it sent out its missionaries to India. They were the first missionaries to arrive in South India and come to *Nazareth* also. They professed Christianity, but they did not plant any church or institution. They proceeded to Nagercoil, the southernmost part of Tamil Nadu, where they planted churches, formulated service order and liturgy. From there they carried on to Malaysia and other countries. Subsequently, Anglican missionaries started to flood in Southern India and Andhra Pradesh where they had a rich harvest of souls; many became Christians by conviction. *St. John's Church in Nazareth* was consecrated as SPG church with highest discipline and order of service in the early twentieth century. Till today, they continue the same order of service worshipping both in the mornings and evenings. CMS (Church Missionary Society) mission also planted many churches in that area.

In the entire area of Tirunelveli and Tuticorin District where revival went on at a great pace, many embraced Christianity. It was a voluntary submission of finding the real truth. The aspirations to find the real truth lingered on with our ancestors from early days. The conversion was not on material basis rather it was the result of the illumination of the inner soul with conviction. The missionaries who had planted the seeds of faith rejoiced over the fruits of their labour.

Along with SPG missionaries, CMS missionaries also joined. They played a great role in the revival and social development. Though they were of European descent, they were completely detached from the colonial power and the East India Company ideology and their political impetus. They were on their own mission to propagate real gospel and to redeem people from bondage from all kinds of social and psychological slavery.

While the colonial power enjoyed the fruit of their occupation, the missionaries enjoyed the fruit of their labour for Christ's sake. The rich harvest of souls culminated in building churches with unique proportions and to great heights, though most of the churches were built with the help of local labourers with a unique sense of engineering skills inbuilt in them. Their architectural expression was simply profound and splendid. Till today, no one really knows the kind of mortar or the binding materials used in these constructions. They say jaggery and egg white were mixed with lime mortar.

The missionaries were instrumental in building many educational and technical institutions which brought revival to the locals spiritually and intellectually. They craved for knowledge and honed their skills. Their language, mathematical and scientific acquisitions were unimaginable. Untill today, these districts have a high percentage of literacy and leading educational institutions. While Anglican missionaries propagated Protestantism in the interior of South India, the Portuguese were mainly instrumental in propagating Catholicism along the coastal area of Southeast and Southwest of India up to Goa. *Saint Francis Xavier* was a pioneer in this field. He travelled far and wide. The missionaries also planted churches with architectural wonders along the coastal area. They instituted educational centres to uplift lower section of the people in and around South India. Their service to the community is awesome. Even now Catholicism is very profound in South India. St. Thomas is said to have been buried in India. And his bones are preserved in *St. Thomas Basilica in Chennai.*

Though initially I grew up around my native place, circumstances brought me to Chennai where environment and situation were totally different. In my young days, I was not studious, mostly distracted to observe nature and surroundings. Linguistically I was mediocre. Landing in Chennai, I had opportunities to meet my friends *Terry, Tony, Vela* and so on. My association with friends changed my perception and fundamentals for better and for worse! But my religious anchor kept my buoyancy with reasonable stability. This new environment taught me everything good and bad—the language, intractability, communication skills, instinct to observe and understand—and this enabled me to make proper judgement of people and circumstances. These skills equipped me with suitable body language that enhanced all the other faculties.

It was a golden era as well—we all spent our boyhood days in Purasawalkam, Chennai, India. The latter part of the twentieth century can be classified as a golden era. The prime period was from 1960 to 1985 where all the good that could evolve in the world happened. The music industry which was normally traditional began to turn chaotic—yet gave a lot of meaning from *Elvis, Beatles to Michael Jackson*. In the sports field, boxing professionalism began to flourish with constraints of the monopoly of power. Legends played a great role with artistry. To sum up, I can only cite *Cassius Clay* turned *Muhammad Ali* was a genius. And so were *Sugar Ray Leonard* and *Héctor Camacho*. In soccer, *Pelé* was awesome, but I would bet any day for *Diego Maradona* for his excellence, and in tennis, who can ever forget the consistency, accuracy and cool posture of *Björn Borg*! Though in women's tennis, she did not get to the helm, I used to be fascinated by *Gabriela Sabatini* who gave the wake-up call to the world for equal status of women's tennis with men. In Formula One race, one can never forget the legend *Ayrton Senna*, and the other legend, the barefoot marathon runner *Abebe Bikila*, not to forget another legend, *Nadia Comaneci* who scored 10 in gymnastics! I am sure with this little narration, nobody can dispute that we travelled in the golden decades of the twentieth century.

The limelight of our time that I could ever spell out was the match of a lifetime of *Bobby Fischer* with *Boris Spassky*. Though *Bobby Fischer* was so great, he had to adopt his sleaziness to win over *Boris Spassky*. I still remember a chair had to be flown specially for him and he would shift direction at odd times. But anyway he won. Finally, it was victory that mattered. This match encouraged us to play chess whenever and wherever we could. *Terry* was given a small chessboard by his father. The coins could be buttoned up to its base. Hence as we walked along the street of Purasawalkam with great pride, we would play the game of chess many a time. We were enamoured by the crowd flocking to see us play in the middle of the road. It was only a distance of a little more than one kilometre. By the time we reached the destination for common tea party among friends, it took almost two hours to cover that area playing chess. One more illuminating game that attracted us was playing with the *Rubik* cube. This gave us excellence in computing and mathematical skills. Such was the fortunate background, which moulded us for a better future. One fine day, we all woke up from our tea party to scatter in our own direction to take a step forward to find each one's future. The decision to dump the tea party along with the amendments that we had formulated within that tea union was the greatest decision of our lives. The folks who remained within the tea party are still hanging around in street corners and howling like foxes.

Quite naturally, all of us returned to seriousness to put life in order. This helped us to establish our families for a better future. As we all are stepping into the twilight years of life, each one is allured to leave something as remnant of each one's career. In this connection, I was discussing with my dear friend *Vela* who told me that nowadays whenever he starts any new venture that is proposed to him, he would term it as *Swan Song* of his career. Since I did not know the meaning of that, *Vela* had to explain to me in detail about *Swan Song*. That it is an ancient Greek metaphorical phrase for final gesture, effort or performance given just before death or retirement. I hope though this is my first *Swan Song* recitation like the poetry goes:

> *The silver Swan, who, living, had no Note,*
> *when Death approached, unlocked her silent throat.*
> *Leaning her breast upon the reedy shore,*
> *thus sang her first and last, and sang no more:*
> *"Farewell, all joys! O Death, come close mine eyes!*
> *More Geese than Swans now live, more Fools than Wise."*

But I sincerely hope that this may not be the last. I like to swing and sing more.

CONCLUSION

Ending this epilogue takes me back to the beginning where I dedicated this book to my father.

A couple of events come to mind as lessons that helped me take my life forward. I was then barely ten and my elder sister just touching a double figure in age, and my younger sister not even five. It was a kite flying season then. Flying a kite is an art practised by many youngsters from those days. One day, I happened to get hold of one of the kites that had been cut off and landing on our little terrace. It was a big one. The people here call it Baana Kaathadi. My interest then was to fly it, hence I discussed it with my sisters. I had gathered pieces of falling threads during that kite-flying season and knotted them together to form a roll. The thread is coated with special kind of gum mixed with various sharp particles. (The process is called Manja.) It is fun flying the kites attached to this thread and thrilling to watch the kites dancing in the skies during the kite-flying contests. The challenge of the contest is to cut as many strings of other kites as possible through ours to clear the path and make ours soar higher! This is like a cockfight in the sky.

The next day was Sunday. In the evening, my sisters and I went up to the terrace. To my strange luck, I could fly the kite. As I let go of the thread, the kite went higher and higher and my sisters were very happy. They felt their brother was flying a rocket. My little sister ran down and fetched our father who came and joined the fun and frolic, and he also flew the kite. After about half an hour, he said, "See the kite, how beautifully it is fly-ing." He made it move from left to right. The kite turned in all direction as it was guided. After some time, my father who had a long thumbnail told us to watch him as he was cutting the thread. We were fascinated and astonished by his action. We watched in eager anticipa-tion. As the kite flew off from us, we cupped our hands behind our neck and said, "Abba!" He smiled back at us and brought the three of us under his fold. "Children, look at the kite, it is going far away! But look at the sky beyond the place where the kite is flying, the stars and the moon." And then he brought us back down to take our books and study. This lingered in my mind for many years. Probably, he sermonised without actually using many words. Never fix your vision on a specific object in submission or addiction; rather, look beyond to infinity.

Many years passed, and as everything gets weathered by time, my father who was once strong and solid was battered with sickness. His body had shrunk drastically. I disliked seeing his worn-out profile. One day as I entered the house, he was sitting on the couch. He looked very haggard. As I crossed him, he rolled a tiny coin in front of me. With a feeble voice, he said, "Son, pick that up, please." I was rather annoyed. But I bent down and picked up the coin. As I stood up to look at the coin, my eyes were focused on the face of the coin. My father said again, "Son, learn to turn the coin and keep this coin with you always." I held the coin in my palm, entered my room, sat down on my cot and kept on turning the coin repeatedly. I began to see the two faces of the coin. Since then, I have never failed to see the other side of anything. These teachings of my dear father had ingrained in me and have guided me in all my endeavours. On the question of turning, I recently came across a video clipping of a father's interaction with his little daughter—Little one was asked to play with her toys while the father was gazing through his favourite magazines. She was bent on distracting her father. Little annoyed, the father tore page with a map on it into pieces and asked her to fix it. The little girl sorted the puzzle in no time. Astonished by her accomplishment, the father politely inquired as to how she could archive that. The little girl replied with joy that the other side had a human face on it and it was easy to fix, then she hugged her father in full contentment ran out to play outside. Dazed by the turn of events, the father cupped his face in contemplation. This has also taught me that in life everything is reciprocal and what goes up will always come down into a deeper hole. All that you do and exercise will revert back to you like a boomerang.

Recently, I happened to watch First Angelus Message by Pope Francis wherein he spoke of the inner wisdom of *God's mercy and forgiveness. God never tires of forgiving us, never! ...the problem is that we get tired, we don't want to, we get tired of asking forgiveness. Let us never get tired. Let us never get tired. He is the loving Father who always forgives, who has that heart of mercy for all of us. And let us also learn to be merciful to everyone.*

As I narrate this, I express with deep sorrow the event of the recent past. In the name of *Democracy*— the leader of the world's most powerful country teamed up with the leader of the allied nations during the last decade of the 20th century and in the first decade of the 21st century. They messed up *Democracy* into **demo-mockery-see** and smothered the international community with dossiers of false reports and poisoned the world politics causing chaos and mayhem. I have termed this pair as B squared. This led the world into one crisis after another. At first, the financial turmoil, the after effect of which is making every human being on this entire planet pay a huge price to rectify the grave mistake of the few defaulting leaders, while some enriched themselves with massive profits, and in the bargain, massacred innocent civilians with genocidal acts. I am sure, as I strongly believe everything in life is reciprocal, what evil one implants will always revert back multiple-fold and cascade down to generations. Even though one changes one's own garment to merge with another sect of a religion, the sins would never be wiped out. In the recent past, I happened to have a glimpse of Peter Marshall's great American prayer "May our Freedom not being seen as the right to do as we please; but as an opportunity to do as to what is absolutely right."

As a result of the previous mess up, a new and dangerous Caliphas has been created and the borders are being extended into the natural boundaries. Time will tell the outcome of this, probably new history will be written. Can we ever condone the past mistakes of the invading nations?

As I continue, one more event that impressed me was the CNN documentary presented by *Errol*

Barnett regarding *Human Family Tree.* It upheld the view that the common gene to which the entire human race belongs and comes from *Sub-Saharan Africa.* According to official findings, skin colours are adaptations to climates. Hence, if we are warring over colour, *it is high time we stop it.*

Oneness and togetherness have been represented by people in all walks of life. In that context, I remember the greatest singers *Michael Jackson* and *Lionel Richie* who, along with stalwarts sang the song, "*We Are the World.*"

> *There comes a time when we need a certain call*
> *When the world must come together as one*
> *There are people dying*
> *And it's time to lend a hand to life*
> *The greatest gift of all …*
> *We are the world, we are the children*
> *We are the ones who make a brighter day*
> *So let's start giving*
> *There's a choice we're making*
> *We're saving our own lives*
> *It's true we'll make a better day*
> *Just you and me.....*

How apt this message is to the present world where animosity and indifference shown by some people have dominated the world from the beginning.

Talking of solidarity, I recall the statement made by the Indo-American astronaut, *Sunita Williams,* on her return to earth after her space exploration. On a visit to her home country India, she made the following statement:

"There is something very big out there for all of us, and we should realise that we are all citizens of the universe."

She delivered this message with both her arms outstretched to make us feel that the world community is one and our limit is the universe. Hence, it is my conclusion that the world is very wide and there is space for all of us. Furthermore, there is a bigger space for all of us to cherish in the universe—the eternal paradise. Hence, in oneness, let us take our journey forward.

On this note, as always, it's my natural tendency to look up for strength and guidance, I quote these words from the Bible from Psalm 121, verses 1 and 2:

> *I will lift up my eyes unto the hills,*
> *from which comes my help.*
> *My help comes from the LORD,*
> *who made heaven and earth.*

And these words have steered the course of my life.

I find that today certain section of people's perceptions of some major religion and faith are totally distorted. Blinded by their personal conviction and allegiance to their god/gods, they denounce the ideologies of others in society and end up in utter confusion like that seen in the construction of the Biblical Tower of Babel. Man's ceaseless effort to reach heaven by his own work is an exercise in futility. If we would only sink our differences and learn to live in love, ours is truly the world, a heaven on earth. As we mature, love grows; love endures. I recall a few lines from the Bible—from the thirteenth chapter of First Corinthians:

When I was a child,
I spoke as a child,
I understood as a child,
I thought as a child; but when I became a man,
I put away childish things.
For now, we see in a mirror, dimly,
but then face to face. Now I know in part,
but then I shall know just as I also am known.
And now abide faith, hope, love, these three;
but the greatest of these is love.

(Reference: New King James Version)

My closing message is a reminder of the importance of oneness and openness along with a vision and mission, to turn the coin to see the other side, to see beyond the present. It is my desire to undertake more travels and pursue on an endless journey. On this note, I sign off. Until we meet again for a journey into the future...